The Most Ungrateful Englishman

Andrew Lee

Published by
Corpus Publishing Limited
PO Box 8, Lydney,
Gloucestershire GL15 6YD

ISBN 1 903333 24 5
Printed and Bound in Finland

10 9 8 7 6 5 4 3 2 1

DEDICATION

This book would not have been possible without the contribution of three people
and it is, with all its flaws, dedicated to them. The first is David Oliver, a valued
friend who has been a tireless supporter of this project. David is an Oxford-educated
classicist whose superior knowledge of Latin helped make the long-winded process
of transcription a little more bearable. He bore my enthusiasm for Adam with
remarkable patience, even being foolish enough to encourage me to expand on the
subject on far too many occasions. He has shown tolerance and patience to a level
beyond that which was strictly wise. He has read and re-read, criticised and
challenged, encouraged and provoked and has been an inspiration throughout. I
could not have asked for a more genuine friend and co-conspirator.

The second is my wife. Gail is not a classicist nor would she profess to be an
historian. In fact it could be said that her interest in history, to say nothing of
mediaeval history, is at best oblique. She is probably thoroughly fed up with Adam
Easton to boot. She has nonetheless encouraged me, often against her better
judgement, and has been both remarkably supportive and eternally tolerant. She has
never (well seldom, anyway) complained of my frequent trips to Rome that have
often sounded more like holidays than study, and has herself endured endless tours
of sites around Europe connected to Adam's story. I am very grateful for the
encouragement and support that you have given me.

Finally there is John Graham, better known as Araucaria and a legend amongst
crossword puzzlers. Away from the intellectual challenge of setting his puzzles, John
is rather less well known for his great knowledge of theology and of the mediaeval
texts that surrounded and influenced Adam's world. Together with his sister, Mary
Holtby, he was extremely helpful in editing the Visitation Office. His knowledge
and helpfulness over matters liturgical were a great help to me during this exercise.
He too has been a valued critic and has, in his own inimitable and gentle fashion,
pulled me up on more than one potential howler before I got too far down the track.

ACKNOWLEDGEMENTS

As someone who has spent most of his life outside the world of academia I can only count myself an amateur historian. I am therefore more than a little indebted to my former tutor at University College, Professor David D'Avray, for his assistance in getting access to the Vatican and University College libraries. He also helped me avoid some major pitfalls in the earlier chapters of this work. I thank him for his tolerance and support in equal measure. I must also acknowledge the important work of Messrs Pantin, Macfarlane and Harvey, who have done much to keep Adam's story alive and relevant for a new generation of historians.

Richard Schwarz has been a great friend throughout this project and proved an invaluable help (and also an extremely patient one). He has helped me find information on Jewish scholarship and, through his friend Rabbi Gluck, provided some fascinating insights into the process of Jewish interpretation of the Torah and Talmud.

In the same vein, John Shember, as erudite a chap as one could hope to meet and a complete outsider to the project, also lent his considerable reserves of advice and support, to say nothing of more than an occasional glass of claret, during the writing stage.

I also thank a friend and erstwhile work colleague, Kjell Nace, whose intimate acquaintance with the Swedish language was extremely useful in deciphering some of the documentation relating to St Brigit.

Life can sometimes throw up pleasant surprises, and as both an outsider and also something of a sceptic, it was really quite refreshing to find the encouragement and support that so many people gave me in so many different ways. Thanks to everyone and apologies to any who I have inadvertently forgotten to mention.

First there were the many archivists who gave me help once the little difficulty of establishing my bona fides had been overcome. The cathedral librarians and record keepers at Westminster Abbey (Richard Mortimer), Worcester (David Morrison), Hereford (Joan Williams), Edinburgh University (Tricia Boyd) and Durham (Richard Higgins) merit a special mention. They could not have been more helpful and, much to my surprise, turned out to be quite interested in Adam as well. Mr Reynolds, the University Librarian at Cambridge, and Gill Cannell at the Parker Library of Corpus Christi were also extremely patient and helpful in letting me get to see some of Adam's book collection at first hand. I must also thank

Lambeth Palace Library for being equally accommodating and most hospitable, particularly on the day I turned up without all the relevant documents to prove who I was. All the Norwich Record Office staff that I met, whether working from the old and cold concrete monolith or their rather fine new accommodation, were always very friendly and helpful.

The same must be said of many of the staff in the Vatican Archive and Library, who remain surprisingly tolerant of those of us who can but struggle with and abuse the Italian language. They found the patience and understanding to construe a meaning from my garbled mess of Italian, French and English not always in that order and often all in the same sentence. Somehow they always found the right manuscripts. In particular I gratefully acknowledge the kindness of Sister Catherine Clarke who helped me find my way around the admissions process and the business of getting an access card.

Then again a special thank-you is due to the kind staff of the English College in Rome, who posted me their only copy of the special edition of the Venerabile, published to celebrate 600 years of the College, so saving me the trouble of having to get it copied. Given the risk involved in trusting it to both the Italian and British post offices, this was something of a gesture of faith!

I'd also like to salute the enthusiastic and helpful (well beyond the call of duty) staff at Westminster Abbey, who helped me identify Simon Langham's tomb and then, not content with simply giving permission to me to take photographs, ruled off the area and then waited with me to ensure I had time and space to myself to take whatever photographs I needed. Theirs must be a thankless task and their friendliness and absolute lack of officiousness were really quite touching.

To the friendly bunch at St Mary's Lutterworth, the Parish Church of John Wyclif, from the current Rector, Mervyn Cousins, to the treasurer Peter Gray and Parish Officer Kath Rhoades many thanks for being so hospitable.

Finally I owe a large debt of gratitude to one man who fundamentally changed my own perception of history. His name is Alan Stacey, he worked for many years at Kings School, Worcester and he was a truly inspirational teacher. There is a lot of clichéd talk these days about this sort of thing but Alan was the genuine article. He was not a crammer of facts, he was a teacher of ideas – whether they happened to be on the curriculum or not. He was the sort of chap who would make you think about things from a different point of view and he discouraged the notion of right and wrong answers to complex questions. I suspect there are far too few of his sort left in the teaching profession.

ADAM'S TRAVELS IN EUROPE AND CENTRAL ITALY, 1368-1397

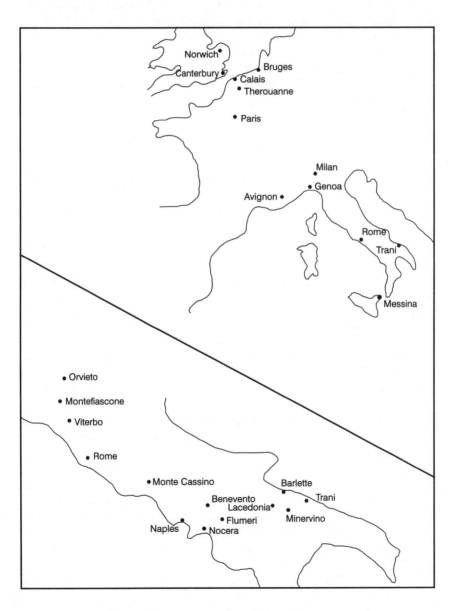

CONTENTS

PROLOGUE

Imagine, for a moment, a history that might have been. Imagine that the Church of England had not been founded to satisfy the sexual hunger of a syphilitic Welsh usurper. Consider how different the popular history of our country would be if the Reformation had happened 150 years earlier, in the time not of Henry VIII but of Edward III. How irrelevant might the Tudor monarchs seem to us now?

What would have been the outcome of a 15th Century dominated not by the Wars of the Roses but by the Wars of Religion? Imagine a papacy alienated and split between three popes, perhaps one English, one French and one Italian.

Sometimes history is as interesting for what did not happen as for what did. At one crucial moment, in the eighth decade of the 14th Century, the course of English history did indeed hover at the start of a chain of events that could have delivered any of those possibilities.

That the history of England, indeed of Europe, took a different course depended not on the great movements of political history, not on great warrior kings or great battles, not even on tumultuous confrontations in parliament or civil riots. This was a transformation played out in one of history's back rooms, run by one of those quieter individuals who are easy to overlook and whose significance is sometimes lost.

The quiet characters from history are often no less interesting and no less significant than the generals, orators and kings. But without those famous battles and speeches to remember them by, we lose sight of them altogether. That critical change of the 1370s was engineered by just such a quiet man. A man from a humble background who, from his inherent love of learning and writing, grew in stature to become one of the great Catholic churchmen of England. He lived at a time of great violence and chaos, witnessing in the course of his lifetime the Black Death, the Hundred Years' War, the Great Schism and the Peasants' Revolt. If he was a quiet character, he certainly was not a passive one, and he influenced the world around him as much as he was influenced by it. In his hour of need, the King of England wrote letters in his defence, on his death bed his blessing was sought from the House of Lancaster, and one of England's finest writers wrote a book in his honour.

The name of our quiet man is Adam Easton.

He has indeed been forgotten. His story and his name have all but vanished from the national consciousness. Adam Easton is an enigma. Even in the village of his birth there is nothing remaining to mark his passing. But it was not always so. John Bale, writing in the 16th Century, considered

Adam not only to have been amongst the greatest scholars of his day, but acknowledged him as one of the more worthy writers of the English language. Just two centuries later, in a history of the English clergy, Bishop Godwin devoted a full page to Adam and left barely a few lines for Thomas, Cardinal Wolsey. History can be a fickle mistress, and historians, given time, can be woefully inconsistent.

The life and death of Adam was filled with contradictions. A devout Benedictine, he chose to flout the rules of his monastic order whilst believing passionately in the religious life. A conservative member of the Church, he wrote an extraordinary defence of the rights of a woman before God and the Church. Deposed and imprisoned by the Pope, he remained astonishingly loyal to him and to his memory. His story is full of the twists and intrigue that characterised the world in which he lived.

He may have been forgotten, but tantalising glimpses of his life and the monastic world in which he thrived remain. The passage of time has drawn a veil over periods of his life, and sometimes we struggle to fit the pieces together. Yet the image on his tomb, one of the finest examples of early Renaissance carving in Rome, gives us a clear idea of what he looked like. That remains a great rarity for the 14th Century, even if the tomb itself is shrouded in mystery and the inscription on it contains two glaring and apparently inexplicable errors.

In this book we will attempt to piece together the jigsaw and provide an account of this elusive Englishman. But first, there are a couple of things that it is useful to understand about the world in which Adam lived.

I. Church and State

We must now travel back in time to the city of Rome on Christmas Eve in the Year of Our Lord 800. In a grand ceremony in old St Peter's the King of the Franks, Charles the Great – Charlemagne – was crowned Emperor by Pope Leo III. More than three hundred years after the collapse of the first Roman Empire, the coronation and the re-establishment of the new "Holy Roman Empire" must have seemed to be a true watershed moment to those who were present. With a new Emperor in place, stability and peace would return to Italy and the destructive power of the Lombards would be crushed. Basking in the glow of this new era's dawn, few who were present could have been aware of the sinister implications lying within the minutiae of the coronation ceremony that they had witnessed.

It was a ceremony the importance of which would echo through Western Europe. The coronation laid the grounds for a philosophical and political controversy that would be at the forefront of European politics until the age of Reformation and the religious wars of the 16th Century, which finally made it irrelevant.

Let us start by looking at the ceremony from the point of view of the Church. The Pope, as God's lieutenant on Earth, had a duty to crown the Emperor. Indeed the Emperor was dependent on the papal coronation for his acceptance as Emperor. Without a papal blessing and approval, the Emperor had no claim as a legitimate authority. During his own coronation service, Louis the Pious, Charlemagne's successor, added further substance to this view when he prostrated himself three times before the Pope. Once crowned, the Emperor was responsible for secular affairs but surrendered authority to the institution of the Church for all matters of a religious nature. An irresponsible Emperor could, in theory, be removed and replaced by the nominee of the Pope. We might describe this system as a pyramid with the Pope at the top, with kings and temporal lords reporting to him on secular matters, and archbishops, bishops and abbots (even in the realm of the King) reporting directly to the Pope on religious affairs.

The view of the secular authority, the Emperor and the various kings of Europe was, not surprisingly, rather different. Secular rulers were not content to accept any principle whereby they might simply be replaced at the whim of a distant churchman, however senior he might be. An alternative theory evolved with not one but two pyramids. The King or Emperor sat at the top of a pyramid NEXT to the Pope, not reporting to him. All the King's subjects, archbishops and bishops included, reported to the King on all matters of political or administrative import. The Pope was then responsible for religious orthodoxy, and it was only in that capacity that the clerics of the realm had any right, in the view of Kings, to consult with the Pope without first seeking the royal opinion.

Of course, both Charlemagne and Louis saw nothing sinister in the circumstances of their coronation. Strong and self-confident rulers, whose authority was unquestioned, they might themselves have been perfectly happy to follow the Church's thinking on the matter. If these early Emperors were a little blinded by the importance of a grand-sounding title, the full significance of what had happened was not lost on some of their more cynical and strategically minded successors. In the same way, initially the Popes were only too grateful to the secular rulers for keeping the Lombards in check and bringing peace to Rome, but once they got used to the idea, there was more time to reflect on the importance of power and status.

A dispute evolved between these two views of the way the world worked. It provoked wars, created rival Emperors and rival Popes, and eventually led to the break-up of the Church itself. From the royal point of view, the power of the Church was hard to dislodge, as its members formed the only educated part of the population, the section from which the King might recruit, say, a chancellor, a tax collector or anyone who would have the ability to draw up written records. Education as much as philosophical principle ensured the religious community's position at the heart of secular government.

Nor was this game of power, pyramids and hierarchies a remote conflict played out in central Italy. It had a very real resonance for the kingdom of England. After all, William the Conqueror attacked England with papal blessing as a crusader against the blaspheming Harold. Henry II's personal struggle with Thomas à Becket was driven by the problem of which rights belonged to the Church and which to the State, and King John in his hour of need took his crown from the Pope's envoy as a vassal of the Holy Father. The rival views of Kings and Popes on the hierarchy of power was the central conflict that engulfed Adam's life.

II. Catholic Church plc

Although the growth of towns, their merchants and guilds had gathered pace, the institutions of 14th Century life still operated on a very small scale. There were no large business structures, no corporations and no substantial government bureaucracies. Merchants rarely operated more than one ship at a time and most of the economy outside the towns was based on providing enough food to eat for the community, rather than having large surpluses to trade.

Today if parents are anxious for the future of their children, they might persuade them to get a good job working for a bank or a solid blue-chip company such as IBM. They hope their offspring will find jobs that offer security and opportunity. They look to companies that have been around for a long time and have track records of success and respectability.

The 14th Century did not offer the luxury of such a choice. If a promising child wanted to make something of himself, there was just one institution that offered stability, respectability and the prospect of advancement: the Church. Unusually for the mediaeval world, it offered the prospect of advancement for the low born as well as the second and third sons of the nobility. To describe the Church in the 14th Century as a meritocracy is going too far, but for the man who found himself in the right place at the right time, opportunity might very well knock. Because it offered such prospects and could support substantial communities of monks and clergy, it is helpful to think of the institution of the Church not just as a mere vehicle for managing religion, but as a multinational property company. Since the time of the Roman Empire, the Church had been accumulating a network of land, wealth and artistic treasures, which at one time made it such an obvious target for Vikings and Vandals, Goths and Visigoths. Yet if the Church appeared vulnerable at times, it remained supremely successful at getting into the minds of its tormenters. As each invader in turn submitted to conversion, so further gifts of land and gold flowed towards the Church. In England, the institution of the Church was relatively undisturbed by the invasion of the Normans, and it kept its land and wealth even if some of the senior personnel changed.

Of course, every layman was expected to pay a tithe (tenth) of his annual income in cash or in kind for the well-being of the parish priest. On top of this, the parish church had its own land. In the past the land might have been worked on behalf of the priest by the local peasants for so many days a month or a day a week. Over time, and certainly by the 13th Century, with tithe payments by then sufficient to provide food for the priest's table, and with no need or desire to store surplus goods, the priest would let out his land in return for cash – perhaps to the same peasants who had formerly worked the land on his behalf.

The humble parish priest was at the bottom of the religious ladder. It was all very well to ensure that he had some land available from which he could make extra income, but how could the Church support a whole administrative community, pay a papal auditor, for instance, or a cardinal, through the same system?

Ask any barrow boy. The principles of business are perfectly simple. He buys his apples and pears from the farmer or the wholesaler for 50 pence a kilo and sells them on the market for 60 pence a kilo. Every ten pence of surplus is his profit, giving the barrow boy the means to buy food for himself, to clothe himself and to put a roof over his head. What the Church realised was that the living provided by the local parish church was considerably in excess of what was needed to comfortably support the life of a humble clerk. In its own way, it too had a "profit" element from each parish church. So the Church appointed its grandees and officials to the livings of several churches. The official would calculate the income from his benefice, adding up the value of rents, the sale of crops and the tithes due. Let us say that this amounted to £66 per annum, as it was in the case of Adam's holding at Somersham.[i] Then for a fixed annual fee of, say, £16 he would employ a clerk to do the work of priest for the community. The £50 profit would help to fund his lifestyle and work, often many miles from the churches from which he made a living.

By accumulating appointments to several churches in this way, a Church official could find himself with a very substantial income. Obviously, the more parishes he was appointed priest to, the greater his wealth. It is hardly surprising that a parish vicarage was often referred to as a "living". A senior cleric might expect to receive the grant of many such "livings", not just parish churches, but also salaried positions in cathedrals and abbeys. In this way he could afford to gather around him his own court. The more learned members might acquire a library; the less reputable ones might give their lives to good living and corpulence...

INTRODUCTION

The Roof Bosses of Somersham Church

I first came across Adam Easton as a name, lost amongst the long list of vicars on the wall of a church in a remote corner of Huntingdonshire. The collection of humble parish priests of St John's Church, Somersham, contains no obvious traces of the great and good. The names of junior clerks and untitled clergy recall a succession of rural clergymen, some better educated than others, ministering to the needs of the local population. There is nothing here to suggest that Adam was one of the most powerful churchmen of his day, or for that matter that Simon, his predecessor as vicar of Somersham (who does not even merit a surname), had reached the same elevated status.

St John's Church was re-roofed in the late 14th Century, and some six centuries later that same wooden roof is still intact. Mounted half way down each of the main crossbeams is a series of wooden bosses. The bosses bear an unusual collection of artisan carvings that have always been considered to be nothing more than a random, possibly pagan, rustic iconography.

Entering the church from the north porch I was struck by two carvings depicting Richard II with his Queen, Anne of Bohemia. This really took me by surprise. What on earth were they doing in a rural church in Huntingdonshire? There was no obvious connection between either the village or the church and the world of royalty. Equally out of place was the sequence of stone carvings, several seeming to be of monks in various poses, that leap from the north and south walls of the church. St John's Church has no particular connection with monastic life. The nearest communities of monks would have been at either Ely to the north east or Sawtry to the north west, each some 15 miles away. Everything about these images seems wrong and out of place. In one respect, however, the roof bosses are helpful. They enable us to date the roof very precisely, for Anne was only Richard's Queen from 1382 to 1394, and we must suppose that this was the period in which the church was re-roofed.

But what of the stone monks and the rustic wooden carvings of the bosses?

Let us return to Adam, an ordinary name in a long line of seemingly undistinguished clergymen. It struck me that there is one obvious way in which both the carved monks and the roof bosses could be linked directly to the church. But it is not because the carvings tell the story of the church. Rather, it seems to me that the roof boss carvings represent a crude depiction of the key events of the life of Adam of Easton. If that is right then the relevance of the depiction of Richard II falls into place. The other carvings too seem to be more than loosely associated with the world of Adam. Some of them use representations of images that can be found on Adam's tomb, whilst others appear as references that reflect very specific events from his life. The carvings are not finely executed, although they are the more interesting for their rustic style. Several of them show traces of paint, and once they would all have been brightly coloured, so that when they were first placed on the oak beams high above the pews, the story they told would have stood out from the dark wood of the beams.

The carvings of stone monks also made sense in the context of Adam's story. Not because the church had any connection with a monastery, but because monasticism had a connection with Adam, and Adam in turn with the church. Adam was a Benedictine monk who entered the community in the city of Norwich and served his order throughout his life. And perhaps Norwich was significant for another reason. It is interesting that one of the outstanding features of the cloisters at Norwich is the collection of fine roof boss carvings. Perhaps this was the inspiration behind Adam's plan for Somersham? If the roof bosses do indeed tell his story, then the relevance of the carved monks and their place in the church suddenly becomes plain.

So many centuries later this suggestion can only be a matter of conjecture, but it is one that has a certain symmetry to it.

Chapter 1

Adam of Easton

*"Listen carefully my son, to the
master's instructions and attend
to them with the ear of your heart"*[i]

Trying Times

It was high summer in Rome, the year was 1378 and the Church was in crisis. In April a new pope had been elected and he took the name Urban VI. By May he had offended his own Church officials in Rome. By June he had insulted the Queen of Naples and her consort. By July the cardinals were worried about their decision.

At the beginning of August a group of cardinals left Rome to escape the summer heat. At the time it seemed innocent enough: part of an established routine whereby the cardinals and other courtiers made an annual pilgrimage to spend the summer in the cool air of the hill towns around Rome. They settled at the town of Anagni, well beyond the reach of the papal troops and the influence of Urban. Here they suddenly announced that they were concerned about certain irregularities in the process of the election of the new Pope. By the end of the month, encouraged by the French King, they sent a proclamation to Rome announcing that they had elected their own, rival French Pope.

With two popes claiming to be the one true representative of God on Earth, undignified and unbrotherly feuding broke out. Each pope railed against the other, calling him an "anti-pope", each called on the various princes, dukes and kings of Europe to show their support for the one true pope. Ever cynical, the secular rulers lined up to back the candidate from whom they stood to gain most. These were dangerous times, when the crime of treason might appear dressed in the clothes of heresy. Lesser mortals did well to keep their heads down and hold their peace. However, not every kingdom had yet decided which particular pope to back, and some were deeply worried about the reputation of the Church. So, early in 1379, two delegations arrived in Rome to interrogate those who had witnessed the events of the preceding months. Their aim: to establish the truth behind the political manoeuvrings that had led to this state of chaos. On the basis of their inquiries they would establish which pope had the best claim to be the "true" pope. The investigations might even serve to make some who had already committed themselves change their minds.

The first of the "investigators" to arrive in Rome was Matthew Clementis, at the head of a delegation from the kingdom of Aragon. In spring 1379 he commenced proceedings, bringing before his inquisition the senior clerics and cardinals who had witnessed the election at first hand. On March 9, an English monk was brought before the Aragonese for questioning. He was not a cardinal, but he had access to the inner sanctum of cardinals in the curia during the election. He would undoubtedly have been in a good position to know what happened. His name was Adam Easton.

In the dark inner sanctum of the Vatican, the Spanish bishop, Alfonso of Jaen, led the interrogation. There was no torture or beating involved, but with so much at stake the pressure on the monk must have been immense. The quiet of the room was broken only by the soft, deliberate speech of the interrogator, the poor light and the sombre clothing of the monks in attendance stifled the soul. The atmosphere was intimidating, the questions unremitting. There was no room for sympathy for those being questioned; on each testimony that was given the future of the Church could depend. Nor could there be any backing away from the testimony after the event, as the series of questions and answers that made up the interrogation were silently recorded by the Aragonese delegates in an affidavit. At the end of the interrogation, the monk was obliged to swear his testimony as true and then sign. The English monk was in a very delicate position. If his testimony contradicted others, his reputation and perhaps even his life might be at stake, particularly if, once the dispute was resolved, it turned out that he had backed the wrong candidate. And the death that a heretic could expect in the 14th Century would be as slow as it would be painful.

Under the circumstances Adam could be forgiven for hedging his bets, but that was not his style. Adam was no shrinking violet. Each question from Alfonso he answered confidently and in detail. The testimony the delegation took from him was not the casual observation of a timid bystander. He had seen at first hand the most controversial events surrounding the election of Urban VI, and Adam was only too eager to tell what he had seen. It was an assertive and very self-assured account. He expressed no doubts and there was no possibility that anyone could misinterpret his belief in which candidate had the greater claim. He took the time to pour scorn on those who elected Urban VI, took favours from him and then changed their minds in favour of a new pope with new favours to offer. The rest of the document was full of detail: where he had been, what he had heard, verbatim quotes, and observations expressed in the precise, legalistic language of an educated and legally trained monk.

Adam held his nerve and was confident in his testimony. Yet despite all those flowing words, the confident assertions and accusations, there was just one astonishing moment of uncertainty, and it occurred right at the start of his statement when he was asked to identify himself. When asked to give his age Adam Easton responded only that he was "etatis xl annorum et ultra", in other words being 40 years and older. Surely he knew how old he was? This was, after all, an affidavit and a monk with Adam's legal training knew not to deal lightly with such a document. What an odd detail to be so imprecise over.

Finding Adam

Mediaeval history can be difficult to piece together. Most of the detailed written accounts that cover every aspect of our lives today simply did not exist back then. This was a world without a census, without newspapers, diaries, and, for the most part, without written history. To make matters worse, the 14th Century was a time of turmoil. War, pestilence and religious controversy permeated everyday existence, disrupting ordinary lives and the smooth running of civil and religious government in equal measure. Inevitably this took its toll on the few records that were made in the period, many of which have since been lost or destroyed.

In times of crisis, large chunks of the written record simply disappeared. Court and manor rolls were written down on parchment in abbreviated Latin. Seldom were duplicates made and if a document was destroyed by fire it was virtually impossible to reconstruct the information. Not surprisingly, many fires were not accidents. At the height of the Peasants' Revolt, a number of Church documents were burnt, destroying the records of villagers, their land holdings and therefore the amount of tax they were due to pay. As the perpetrators well knew, to reconstruct the record would be a mammoth task and in the meantime no-one could assess them for tax.

Finding out about anyone from so long ago can be difficult enough, and in the case of Adam Easton we have very little to go on. There is doubt as to who his parents were, when he was born and even in which village he was brought up. The early part of his life is completely shrouded in the mists of mediaeval history.

However, there are some clues, starting with his name. The monasteries of 14th Century England had taken up the practice of using toponyms (see Appendix II) to name their monks and identify one from the other by reference to the village from which they hailed. Adam's name was written, throughout his life, as "Adam de Estone". That may have been the way his name survived in recorded history, but he would never have been known by the title "de Estone" as a boy in his village. The use of the word "de" in a name gives us a clue that this was a toponym, a name derived from a place and not a surname derived from a trade or ancient family. The fact that Adam was known as Adam de Estone, not simply as Adam Estone, suggests that he came from a village with a name something like Estone. Rather confusingly, the word "Estone" appears with several different spellings, which complicates matters and allows a number of possibilities. It had been suggested that Adam might have been born in a village named Aston or Eston, but there are no likely candidates in East Anglia, and Easton is the most likely.

Accepting that Adam came from a village called Easton is a good start, but then which one? Easton is not an uncommon name in England and in the past, historians have been known to claim that Adam came from as far afield as Norfolk, Hertfordshire or Herefordshire, and there is another village of Easton in Huntingdonshire. It is only because of his long association with the monastery at Norwich (and recent work by Joan Greatrix showing the relatively localised geographical distribution of monks from their monasteries) that we can be more confident that it was in the Norfolk village of Easton that Adam was born. The village had a close connection with the monastery at Norwich, and this, as well as its proximity to the city, makes it the most likely candidate.

Prince or Pauper?

So was Adam from a wealthy family, as tradition has suggested, or from one of the peasant families working the fields around the village of Easton? Let us return to Rome and that difficult moment when Adam started to give his testimony. Why could Adam only stutter out that his age was "etatis xl annorum et ultra"? It seems so odd that Adam should be guilty of such imprecision in a legal document in which he would wish to give a precise and detailed account of everything.

Odd perhaps, unless of course Adam did not actually know his date of birth.

Official church records of births, marriages and deaths rarely pre-date the 16th Century, so the fact that any one person might not know their date of birth is not unusual. The affidavit in Rome is as helpful for what it tells us of Adam's background as for the clues it gives to his age. Parents of peasant stock were usually uneducated and almost certainly illiterate. To them there was little value in knowing the year of their son's birth, and even if they did know the date they would certainly have had no means of recording it. Knowing one year from another had little purpose for people whose lives were guided only by the vagaries of the seasons and the unpredictability of the weather. For a peasant farmer, life and death depended on the timing and quality of the harvest and knowing when to sow the seed for the new season's crops. If Adam did not know his own date of birth, he must have come from a peasant family, and if Adam was from a peasant family, we at least know the name of the village in which they were farming.

The fact that Adam did not know his date of birth should not lead us to dismiss his estimate. He must have had a sense of his age, at least from the time when he started his formal education, and if his choice of words "40 years and more" can be taken to mean that he believed he was between 40 and 50 then this would give a birth date between 1328 and 1338.

We can also find other clues to his age. We do know the date of his graduation from university, 1364, and by working back from this date we can calculate his approximate date of birth. Going to university in the 14th Century was not the brief three- or four-year interlude between the world of schooling and the world of work that it is today. It was an end in itself. Adam could expect to undertake a full 15 years of study for a Bachelor's degree and two more for a Doctorate, on top of which he would have spent at least seven years away from the university, back in Norwich. If we then assume that he was in his late teens on first going to university then that gives a likely date of birth somewhere around 1325 (see Appendix I). Whilst this date is a little bit earlier than Adam's own estimate, we can at least say with some confidence that he was born between the years 1325 and 1330.

The Village of Easton, Norfolk

Just to the west of Norwich, backing onto a particularly ugly stretch of the A47 trunk road, lies the village of Easton. It is a modern village with houses clustered in estates across a patch of raised ground all but swallowed by the expanding city of Norwich. But if we peel back the veneer of semi-detached brick houses, there is an older Easton, an ancient settlement mentioned in both the Danegeld and Domesday records.

There is little left of that village today. Only the church remains, a simple building that sits at the edge of a broad sweep of arable land to the west of the village, in splendid isolation from the modern houses.

Easton Church was built in the 13th Century, and by the standards of the county of Norfolk it was simply decorated inside. Even so, the white-washed walls, plain glass and unadorned interior left to us by the Puritans betray little trace of an older, grander religious iconography carved into its wood and stone. At the dawn of the 14th Century it was still a new building, and the pride of the local community. It may have been plain and simple, but over the years it provided the inspiration for men from the village to take up a career in the church. The village of Easton had well-established connections with the Church, in particular with the Benedictine Priory of Norwich. It was the priors who controlled the parish church in Easton, appointing the rector until the middle of the 14th Century, and occasionally allowing monks to spend time in the local community. The same priors had organised the building of the brand new parish church in Easton.

The local manor of Easton was held by the Bateman family,[iii] wealthy merchants from Norwich with strong connections to the Church. One of their sons, William, had taken the favoured career option for the younger sons of local nobility and entered the Church. By 1344 he had been appointed Bishop of Norwich. He made regular tours of all the church lands, but the local family manor at Easton would have been the area he knew best. These frequent "visitations" allowed him to manage the revenues of the cathedral chapter and priory and to check on the moral rectitude of the clergy, but at the same time William was also looking for recruits to the Church.

For most of the villagers such matters were of little consequence. If the Lord Bishop passed amongst them in his finery, it did not affect them unduly. The Church kept to itself, took from them what it needed and provided comfort to their souls, at a price, in times of need. Their village was a farming community and the fields surrounding it lay in good arable country, so life for the farmer should, in theory, have been comfortable enough. The only problem with farming is that it is a vocation that is completely at the mercy of the climate.

One Thing after Another

The 13th Century had, generally speaking, been a time of plenty, and the lot of the farmer had improved. Land holdings of lord and peasant alike had grown, and as more marginal land was cleared and brought under the plough so the crops had increased and with it the wealth of the farmers. For the first time any farmer whose fields had produced a surplus could sell what he did not need at the local markets that were springing up across the country. The cash raised in the market could be used to buy produce the farmer could not grow, to store wealth for harder times or simply to buy larger strips of land.

The first quarter of the 14th Century saw a rapid reversal of fortunes for the English farmer. Stories of harvest failure, excessive rain, unseasonable storms and widespread famine populate the chronicles of the time.

In 1315 there was a famine so great that across England "meat and eggs began to run out, capons and fowl could hardly be found, animals died of pest, swine could not be fed because of the excessive price of fodder... The summer rains were so heavy that grain could not ripen. It could hardly be gathered and used to bake bread down to the said feast day unless it was first put in vessels to dry... Four pennies worth of coarse bread was not enough to feed a common man for one day. The usual kinds of meat, suitable for eating, were too scarce; horse meat was precious; plump dogs were stolen. And, according to many reports, men and women in many places secretly ate their own children..."[iv] As if that were not bad enough, conditions failed to improve and in the following year the same chronicler reported that "so many men had died that it was especially difficult for the living to bury the dead."[v] Before the year was out "dysentery breeding on the rotten corpses infected entire households."[vi] Farming across England was not a happy profession.

In 1318 an earthquake terrified the population on the feast of Sancti Bricii (November 13). The following year saw a catastrophic outbreak of a plague that affected cattle all over England "as great as any that could be remembered". The only reason why more humans did not die was that they noticed that "the dogs and crows eating the dead bodies of the herds of cattle immediately swelled up and they fell down dead".[vii] The disease lasted in Essex from Easter right throughout the rest of 1319. Just two years later in 1321[viii] there was more famine and widespread mortality across most parts of England. The agrarian economy was not getting a chance to get back on its feet. The severe impact on the rural communities of disease, famine and death over a sustained period is hard to imagine in our world of overstocked supermarkets. In a mere handful of years the population had been decimated and the farmers who worked the land had suffered the loss of their livestock and crops, and with it the ability to feed their own families.

The Peasant's Lot

In the years immediately prior to Adam's birth, the village of Easton did not escape the afflictions that had hit the livelihood of the English peasant farmer. The winters in this part of England are cold, and biting easterly winds blast the raised ground around a village where there is little in the way of shelter. As the population was rocked by disease, crop failure and the deaths of their livestock, so the strips of land that the peasants worked now seemed hopelessly inefficient. After paying tithes to the church and rent to the lord of the manor, what was left would barely support a family. Family members were expected to provide their labour free for the benefit of the lord of the manor in addition to having to look after their own crops. Inevitably the burden of working the lord's fields fell on them at the very time when they needed to be tending to their own. The following example of a cottager living on a Huntingdonshire manor shows just how much the peasant farmer was required to do in return for his cottage and a few meagre strips of land:

...the cottager Baldwin [who] holds a cottage and gives 2d. for Witefe and he owes by week except harvest one [day's] work and in harvest each week 3 [days'] work. So that through no feast will he be quit from a work unless from Christmas up to Pentecost and he should fetch a bundle of charcoal at Christmas and carry [it] to the water or to the lord's manorial courtyard and he shall plough in the year 3 acres and owes 6 hens and 6 eggs and he owes carrying service on his back without a horse and he should at the lord's visit [to the manor] carry a bundle of branches and he shall make a quarter of malt and therefrom he is quit from 3 [days'] work and he shall find thrice in the year a man at brewing and he owes a work at weeding and a work at lifting hay and [provide]a man at reaping and at the great boon with food a man and in the morrow a man without food and at Waterbedripe a man and he should guard the prison through a night and bring prisoners to Ely.[ix]

The humble cottager had to carry out all those different duties before he could look after his own crops, and it must have had a devastating impact on his life. The period of the harvest is brief enough, and after several years of failure the peasants must have been anxious about missing a potential life-or-death opportunity to gather in their crops. The calls that the lord could make on a peasant's time also affected his opportunity to earn money by selling his labour to farmers with larger land holdings. Even if the peasant farmer had agreed to pay a money rent instead of working his obligation days for the lord, his ability to pay depended on having surplus crops to sell at a market. After so many ruined harvests in a row, the option of working the obligation days must have seemed a safer bet than paying rent.

The first half of the 14th Century was particularly hard on the peasant farmer in Norfolk and not just because of the famines and disease that had devastated the land. The balance of the agricultural economy was shifting away from arable crops, the mainstay of the small farmer, to sheep farming and the wool trade. Sheep farmers needed plenty of land to put to grass, but they did not need labour. As the wool merchants accumulated substantial fortunes at the expense of the peasant cultivators, so they expanded their land holdings. Using the power and influence derived from their increasing wealth, the sheep farmers encouraged the grassing over of manorial lands and enclosed common lands for their sheep, thereby depriving the small-scale arable farmers of the opportunity to keep their own livestock. The very livelihood of the peasant cultivator was threatened. Those farmers in Suffolk and Norfolk who continued growing crops had a much harder life than at any time in the past hundred years.

Damnation and the Wages of Sin

The wool merchants of Norfolk were not the only men making a killing. The Church was growing rich on the wages of sin, or more to the point, on the fear of the wages of sin. Preaching in pictures to a largely illiterate audience, the great doors of the cathedral cities across Europe still show in stark terms what happened to those who did not toe the line. Great panoramas of judgement day dominated the entrance to these monolithic buildings, cast in fine stone and stained glass. On the west door of Leon cathedral, demons eat those of the damned who are not consigned to boiling pots of oil. On the south door at Chartres naked fiends prod and push the damned towards their fate. At Amiens, a great toothed whale swallows men whole, whilst demons appear from under ledges, peering around columns and from under the feet of the condemned, beating them with sticks and prodding them with spears. As Christ sits in judgement on the souls of men and women, weighing their lives in the balance, he and his church offer just two choices: salvation or damnation. Eternal damnation.

And you did not have to live in a big cathedral city to get the message. The traditional white-washed interior of the English parish church is a relic of the two Cromwells, Thomas and Oliver. In Adam's time, across East Anglia in particular, the chancel arch of the parish church was used as a vast canvas on which to depict the day of judgement, complete with St Michael weighing and judging the souls of the dead. And as the dead are shown rising from their tombs, so the chancel arch was used to divide them: those on the left taken by St Peter to salvation, those on the right surrounded by flames, serpents, chains and visions of eternal torture. The unfortunates were taken off by gruesome demons to a graphic vision of hell. As the congregation of laymen gazed up towards the choir and took in the strange ceremonies conducted in Latin, this great message in paint glared back at them. Occasionally, Mary would be shown interceding with St Michael and tipping the scales in favour of the poor sinner, but by and large the message was one of death and destruction for those who failed to follow the way of the true Church. Remnants of these paintings still survive in many of the parish churches in the region and give us a real sense of the visual impact with which the Church delivered its message.

Anyone gazing on those images could have no doubt as to what happened to those who lived a less than pure life. The Church could play on its position as honest broker interceding with God on behalf of the wretched earthly sinner awaiting the time of judgement. Sin today and an eternity of horrific pain, suffering and misery would surely await the sinner on that day of days!

Of course, those who wished to atone for their sins, to be judged pure and granted eternal salvation, did not necessarily have to live a pure life. The Church was there to help the wayward sinner back to the path of righteousness, and if the sinner had fallen by the wayside, he could still insure himself against eternal damnation. In fact, the Church could insure the humble sinner not only for sins past, but even for sins yet to be committed. And as with modern insurance premiums, the amount the sinner had to pay would be in proportion to the amount of sin, or the risk the Church was insuring against. The Church would happily intervene on the sinner's behalf on the day of judgement, but only if his or her premiums were up to date.

In a society where religion and religious ritual were important elements of daily life, the Church was a vital institution to the cynical as well as the sincere, and those great famines of the early 14th Century had helped to focus the minds of waverers. You defied God and His Church at your peril. And so to join the Church was to join an institution of the greatest importance to everyone in society, from the most mighty king to the humblest peasant. Those images of death and damnation were there to inspire, they were the recruitment posters for the chosen. To become an official in the service of the Church was as sure a way to be on the path to eternal salvation as one could aspire to – but who might join? Did God "call" the humble peasant or artisan to join His Church, or might the honest man choose the religious life himself from a fear of damnation?

The Church could afford to be choosy over those it allowed to join the club. The prerequisites for admission involved some degree of literacy and a lot of determination. It was not a career for the faint-hearted, and somehow the Church had to ensure that those who did join were committed to propagating the images of the "right path" and the "wrong path". Above all else, they had to believe in the quality of the insurance they were selling.

The Church Finds Adam

Adam grew up as an ordinary village boy in Easton. As a peasant's son he had very little prospect of any sort of formal education. Most of his childhood would have been spent helping in the fields, working the narrow strips of manorial land that had been allocated to his family. Simply helping his family survive from one year to the next was a task that would have absorbed all his youthful energy.

If the boy's future looked bleak in Easton, there were few other options available to the son of a peasant. As Adam looked around him at the wretched life of the cottagers, his eyes would have fallen enviously on the village church. The rector had no need to work the freezing fields, no obligations to meet in labouring for others on the narrow strips of land. He could attend to the souls of his charges whilst they paid him in produce, rents and tithes. Armed with all the food he might need for the harshest winter, the rector could look forward to a comfortable existence and possibly even greater promotion within the Church hierarchy. The Church offered the one possibility of escape from the finely balanced annual fight for survival amidst the fields of Norfolk.

There were others from the village of Easton who had taken advantage of the religious connection to escape the hardship of a farmer's life. These were men who Adam and his family knew – Easton was, after all, a small community, and the opportunity that the Church offered to escape drudgery and uncertainty was there for everyone to see. As Adam was growing up in Easton, one villager, a certain Edmund, established himself as a rector in the village of Coltishall, whilst another, Roger de Easton,[x] was a monk at the priory of Norwich. In 1335 he claimed expenses from the cellarer for entertaining guests in the cloisters.[xi] Perhaps his guests were family and friends from his own village, come to see how well he had done for himself.

And Roger had done well. In 1344 he was appointed to oversee the installation of a new prior, an honour that would only have been granted to a senior monk. The example of Roger, now prominent in the priory of the city of Norwich just six miles down the road, might well have proved inspirational to Adam. Roger may even have groomed Adam as a recruit to the monastery of Norwich, for the church could be quite proactive in seeking out new recruits. Yet for Adam to have been "spotted" as a suitable candidate for monastic life, he must have shown some interest and skill in learning.

How could he have shown any promise as a clerk without acquiring the building blocks of an education? Schools did exist in mediaeval England, but they were few and far between. Mostly they were under the patronage of the bishops[xii] and could be found only in the major cathedral cities, and here the number of pupils taken in was very small. The problem for a village boy was that without even a basic education to start with, being spotted and sent to one of the new schools was a lottery and the odds were stacked against you. The most likely source of help for a young child was the rector of Easton church, Nicholas de Gosford.[xiii] The rector or priest was usually the only educated man that the villagers of rural England would know. The more educated of the rectors and vicars could provide basic instruction to the children in their pastoral care, however informally. Here Adam must have been lucky, as there was no obligation on the priest to offer an education, and many of the clerks who were appointed as vicars and rectors were but poorly educated themselves. Nicholas would have taught little more than the basics of reading and writing, possibly some very simple arithmetic. Perhaps he noticed something exceptional about Adam's ability or his desire to learn, and perhaps he mentioned this to Roger de Easton.

At such a tender age, for all the mediaeval forebodings of hell and damnation, it is hard to know what drove Adam to look to a future in the

Church. Did he have a sense of religious calling, or was this simply an easy way of escaping a hard and unrewarding life in Easton? Perhaps his parents had died and left him orphaned and in the care of the Church, and the monks in Easton took pity on him. In all the written works in Adam's hand that survive we have no clues as to who his parents were or what was their fate. Adam's later life shows little cynicism and a genuine piety that might make a fitting climax to a life in religious service driven by a sense of calling. Unfortunately, his early life, as we shall see, was not always so selflessly motivated. As to the motives of his childhood, we can only guess at them.

A Journey into the Unknown

Adam obviously showed some promise with his studies, because in the early 1340s he left his village with a precious letter of introduction, possibly from Nicholas de Gosford, possibly Roger de Easton, aiming to gain acceptance as a novice monk at one of the nearby priories. This was Adam's key to a new life of opportunity and the possibility of comfort, even of great wealth. As he set out on the six-mile walk down the road to the city of Norwich, he could scarcely have realised how this short journey would change his life. He would, in effect, pass out of one world and enter a new one.

His destination, Norwich, was, in Adam's day, one of the biggest cities in England. A metropolis by mediaeval standards of around 8,000 souls, Norwich lay in the midst of a county filled with a patchwork of small villages and manor farms where it would be rare to find communities of more than 200 or 300 souls. Compared with the mud and thatch cottages of the village farmers, or even the solid timber and stone of the local manor house, the great gothic cathedral at Norwich was an edifice towering over the surrounding countryside. A monolith of a building out of all proportion to any man-made structure Adam had seen before, its spire soaring 315 feet into the sky, Norwich Cathedral was the second tallest building in England. In our towerblock-filled cities it is hard to imagine the impact of the majestic masonry on a mediaeval peasant. The imposing effect of the cathedral was accentuated by its position on top of a hill. Norwich is built on one of the few areas of raised ground in the county of Norfolk, and the houses of its citizens huddled around the crest of a gently sloping hill, filling the gap between the secular castle mound at one end of the city and the religious powerhouse of Norwich cathedral at the other. The buildings that represented the power of the Church and State glared at each other across the hill top. Standing aloof from the smaller dwellings in between them, the two great buildings of the city represented the two sources of mediaeval authority. As Adam would soon discover, the separation was both mental and physical.

The world of the Church was not designed to be welcoming for the outsider. The Benedictine priory next door to the cathedral was surrounded by walls, shutting it away from the secular world outside. On the other side of the hill the great Norman keep of Norwich Castle had a mound and a wooden palisade to keep the treasury in and the townsfolk out.

In between the two lay the city, a busy commercial centre where wool merchants rubbed shoulders with wealthy Church dignitaries. At the front of the priory, in an open square known as the Tomblands, there were regular and thriving markets for produce and fairs for the local horse traders. For a young peasant boy it was a city full of wonders. After wandering through the markets, marvelling at the spices and herbs he had never before seen and the cloth he could scarcely afford, buffeted by the hustle of the markets, intimidated by the wealthy dressed in their fine cloth, the young boy finally arrived outside the priory gates in Norwich, clutching his letter of introduction. Did the City of Norwich seem too imposing and grandiose for the peasant's son from Easton as stood there trying to summon up the courage to knock on the priory door and seek admission?

Perhaps he simply had a different destination in mind. Whatever the reason, he did not try to gain entry at the priory of Norwich, but instead walked down the hill to the bridge at the Bishop's Gate, crossed the River Wensum and climbed up to the small priory of St Leonard's[xiv] on the opposite bank of the river.

The track led him through thick deciduous woods that flowed up the hillside, right to the very gates of the priory. This was no tranquil idyll of quiet thought and contemplation. The woodlands outside St Leonard's were a valuable source of building material and at times resembled a construction site. Large quantities of timber were brought to Norwich to provide roofing materials and support beams for the cloisters of Norwich priory[xv]. Eventually Adam reached the priory gate. St Leonard's stood on a ridge just below the brow of the hill looking back over Norwich. Adam, tired and hungry from his long walk, knocked at the gate, hoping the monks would look on him favourably as a potential novice.

The monks inside ignored him.

This was not what he had expected. Adam can have had very little with him in the way of provisions and would have gone hungry as he waited for something to happen. At first he had no choice but to wait and hope that the monks might have pity on him. Quite what the passers-by made of the young boy camped outside the monastery gate day after day is hard to imagine. He would have had to beg for bread from travellers as they walked past the priory and on down the hill to the Bishop's Gate. How many times must he have thought about giving up and going back home? He would gaze back over the fine views of Norwich, the immense cathedral dominating the skyline with its own grand priory snug in its shadow. As a statement of authority, the buildings that embodied the rule of the Church stood head and shoulders above the buildings of other, worldly, powers. Perhaps Adam was encouraged by this outstanding image of the power of the Church he wanted to serve.

On the other side of the priory wall, the reason for Adam's wait was clear – a test was in progress. The Benedictine monks of St Leonard's were obliged to ignore a prospective monk for five days before they could even consider answering the door to him. Only the most resolute of youngsters could hope to join the Benedictine brotherhood. And so Adam waited. Occasionally, he knocked, hoping for some change of heart by the monks inside, but mostly he waited. He was clearly a determined boy, and the monks must have liked the look of him, for after the regulation five days had elapsed, they opened the gates and welcomed him inside to start his life in the Church. He would join on the lowest rung of the ladder as an uneducated novice monk.

St Leonard's

The priory of St Leonard's was a much smaller affair than at Norwich – it rarely housed more than a dozen monks at a time. In such a small community there would be no more than two or three novices. As Adam walked through the priory gatehouse he would have found just a few small buildings: church, dormitory, cellar, library and kitchen. In larger priories it was common to have cloisters that allowed the monks to walk in silent contemplation between services; St Leonard's had extensive walled grounds where the monks could find peace and solitude. There is nothing left of St Leonard's priory today. It stood at the top of the road that is still named St Leonard's, and despite the 20th Century addition of a gasworks, Norwich Cathedral is still clearly visible from the site of the old priory.

From the moment when he finally gained entry into the priory, Adam lived the life of a novice with the other young boys who had been admitted. An elder brother was charged with looking after their moral and spiritual growth, his main task being to instil regularly into the youngsters how tough the life of a monk was. Indeed, the whole thrust of the initial period of induction was to make everything about the life of the monk seem so onerous that only the most dedicated would persevere. A novice's belongings were removed for safe keeping. They would only be permanently confiscated if he became a fully-fledged monk. For Adam, a peasant farmer's son, the loss would pass unnoticed; he would not have had much with him except for the clothes he was wearing on the day he arrived. In return for parting with all their worldly goods, each novice was given an outfit "of a cost not to exceed one hundred shillings".[xvi] For novices from poor backgrounds such an outfit must have seemed more in keeping with luxurious living than a vow of poverty!

St Leonard's was founded early in the 12th Century by Herbert de Losinga, before the "mother" priory next to the cathedral, and was originally used to house the monks who were to enter the main priory on its completion. Once the main priory was completed Herbert kept St Leonard's going as an outreach priory. Norwich priory and its "daughter houses" adopted the Benedictine Rule, and their monks were known as Black Monks from the colour of the Benedictine cowl or cloak. The Prior of St Leonard's was appointed by the Prior of Norwich, and he had to provide accounts to him at least once a year. Not surprisingly, the role of prior in such a small house was less onerous than the same job in Norwich, and the Prior of St Leonard's was often an elderly Benedictine in semi-retirement. The quiet woodland setting and fine views made it the ideal spot for contemplation in later life.

Seizing the chance to escape the toil in the fields of Norfolk may sound like an obvious path to take, but monastic life was not intended to be a soft option. The choice Adam had made was not an easy one. The Benedictines took the religious life seriously. Adam was expected to give up earthly pleasures for vows of chastity, obedience and poverty and to devote himself to a life focused on worship and contemplation. A tall order for a barely pubescent boy.

The Rule

The Benedictine Rule covered every aspect of a monk's life, and it was intended to reinforce an austere existence. After the novice monks had spent two months at St Leonard's, the prior read out to them the full text of the Rule of Benedict. After the reading, the novices were reminded how harsh the Rule was and what it meant to be a monk. Any novice who looked within himself and felt unable to accept life under the Rule was invited to leave. Unlike much of modern religion, the terms of the Rule were considered to be non-negotiable! The committed novice who affirmed his intention to stay continued to live his life under the guidance of the Rule and after a further six months the process was repeated. The monk who showed himself firm in his purpose was then left once more to live the monastic life for a final four months before the process was repeated a third time. It was as if the Rule was attempting to mimic the three denials of Christ by St Peter. If, after this third time, the novice monk was still willing to follow the ways of the Rule, he was finally, almost reluctantly, received into the wider community of monks. From this point on he would live his entire life under the guidance of the Rule and would not be free to leave the community without the authority of the Church at large.

One year after he had first been admitted through the gates of St Leonard's, Adam was invited to come before the little community and in a

THE MOST UNGRATEFUL ENGLISHMAN

formal service in the priory chapel to swear obedience to God and the monastic life. He was then asked to draw up a formal document by which, in the name of the saints and the holy relics of the priory, he stated his obedience to the Rule and to his chosen life. The fact that the novice drew up the document himself is evidence of the quality of the education provided to the young men during their time as novices.

St Leonard's could not boast any of the actual body parts of the saint, but amongst its collection of relics was a famous jewelled image of Saint Leonard that had become an object of pilgrimage in itself. Leonard was a French monk from the era of King Clovis, and he was an extremely popular saint in Northern Europe. In England, in particular, many churches and priories were dedicated to his name. As a Benedictine, Leonard was a perfect role model, a saint fitting and proper to be the dedicatee of the daughter priory of Norwich. His example and his shrine provided poignancy for the novice monk swearing to follow the Rule of Benedict.

The young Adam took his vow on the shrine of St Leonard. Advancing towards the altar he placed his signed document in front of the jewelled image of the Saint. Facing the congregation of monks he implored: "Receive me Lord as you have promised, and I shall live, do not disappoint me in my hope." The novice then demonstrated his humility by ritually prostrating himself before the feet of each monk in the community and donating all the possessions that he had brought with him to the monastery. From this point on, Adam was considered to be a fully-fledged Benedictine monk and subject for the rest of his life to obedience to his Prior in particular and the Church in general.

A Monk's Life. . .

The Rule that Adam had pledged to follow was not accommodating for those accustomed to a life of ease and leisure. True, a monk could be allowed half a bottle of wine a day, but this dispensation was not willingly granted. St Benedict tells us that even in his time "monks should not drink wine at all, but since the monks of our day cannot be convinced of this, let us agree to drink moderately and not to the point of excess". In the event of any doubt "the superior will determine when local conditions, work or summer heat indicate a need for a greater amount."[xvii] The dietary rules were a little more strict, stipulating that no red meat might ever be eaten (no food may be offered from any animal with four legs). Two dishes of cooked food were to be provided to the monks every day, either vegetarian or poultry or fish. The monks were allowed one pound of bread each per day, but less for younger brothers. The mediaeval mind did not accommodate the idea that the younger brothers might appreciate more food to aid their growth! However, one man's poverty may be another man's riches. For the monks from poorer backgrounds, the monastic life offered certainty and even a touch of luxury. Regular food, warm clothing, a roof over your head and a community of brothers added up to comfort well beyond that afforded by a life as a 14th Century farmer. All in all it made the monk's life something to aspire to.

Monastic life was based around a daily routine of reflection and prayer, a life strictly regimented to allow the minimum time for un-Christian thoughts and idle hands. Each day the brothers were required to gather eight times for the singing of psalms and antiphons, for prayer and readings from the gospels. In keeping with the biblical texts, the monks were exhorted to rise at midnight to ensure that the Lord was praised as instructed in the Book of Psalms (Psalm 119: at midnight I will rise to give thanks unto thee because of thy righteous judgments). In the small hours of the morning the monks would rise to say Matins (sometimes known as Nocturnes) followed by Lauds. In between they might pass time in quiet contemplation. After Lauds they would return once more to bed. Rising with the daylight, they would sit down together, chatting or thinking pure thoughts, before attending Prime, the first service after dawn. During the daylight hours the routine of the monks was divided up into three-hourly parcels. Immediately after Prime the monks would wash and spend time at whatever work the prior should deem necessary. Three hours after Prime they would return to the chapel for the service of Terce, followed by more work. Six hours after Prime came the service of Sext, following which the monks would wash in the lavatorium and then take dinner in the refectory. Meal times were orderly affairs, the monks taking their food in silence whilst one of their brothers read an appropriately uplifting piece from the scriptures. Communication between brothers during meals was usually through a complex system of sign language that allowed food to be passed around without interrupting the reader. To ensure that no brother was perceived to be of higher rank than another, they took it in turns to serve on each other at meal times.

Nine hours after Prime they returned to worship for None, followed by more work. In the early evening Vespers would be followed by supper. The monks would then return to the refectory for a drink together before attending the final service of the day, Compline. Their religious duties for the day now finished, they processed to the dorter (dormitory) and retired to bed.[xviii] Over the course of just one week the monks would have recited every one of the 150 psalms!

Hygiene did not receive the priority it would today. The brothers might be expected to wash each others' feet and once a week shave their heads and face, but baths were considered a luxury – a sign of softness and indulgence and quite unsuited to the monks' calling.

At night the monks would sleep in dormitories of up to 20 depending on the size of the house, supervised by an elder brother of the monastery. They were allowed one pillow and a woollen blanket. For clothing a monk might have nothing more than a tunic and a woollen cowl, with either sandals or shoes for his feet. All forms of personal possessions were forbidden, and the beds of brothers might be inspected routinely lest they had hidden anything for their own use.

During the hours that were set aside for work, the monks were at the mercy of their prior. The Benedictines believed that giving the monks work would allow them to find spiritual improvement through their labours, and it was the prior who would determine the most fitting type of work for each brother. He would be put to work for around six hours every day on anything from administration to hard manual labour. That might include working in the fields – the Rule charges the monks that they must not be shy of working on the harvest if there should be no other labour to assist them. Among the administrative tasks a monk might be asked to do would be working in the scriptorium. In the days before printing, the manual copying of texts was the only way of reproducing written work, and the monasteries put great store by the size of their libraries. Copying was the main means by which a monastic community might improve and expand its library. As the libraries grew, so each monastery could trade copied works with others to increase the range of material available to the monks.

Thus was the routine that a Benedictine monk was expected to follow day in and day out for the rest of his life. The only variation came on feast days, when the Prior of St Leonard's would take the brothers down the hill to Bishop's Bridge and over the Wensum to the mother priory of Norwich, where the monks would join their brethren in services and say a mass[xix]. The festival of St Leonard on November 6 obviously had a particular resonance for the Benedictines of St Leonard's, and the Priory at Norwich accorded the festival a much greater prominence than it had in other English priories, with special antiphons, a type of psalm, recited for the day.

Winter would make the spartan lives of the monks that much more harsh. Such fires as the monks might build to alleviate the biting cold would have little effect on the worst of the Norfolk weather. In 1337 England suffered one of the worst winters of the century. It was so cold that "the frost lasted from 5 Kalends December until 4 Ides February... wheat was very expensive".[xx]

. . .Or Not!

The life of the monk was, in summary, strictly organised into rounds of work, reflection and prayer. This was the theory, and as anyone who has read Chaucer's tales of friars and monks will know, not necessarily the practice! By the second half of the 14th Century, there was a popular perception that monks were failing to stick to their Rule and indulging themselves in feasting and the accumulation of wealth. There is plenty of evidence from the monastery at Norwich to suggest that these suspicions were well founded. The monks found ready excuses to avoid going to services, and by the end of the 13th Century records show that red meat was regularly being eaten in the refectory. The daily ration of bread appears to have doubled to two pounds a day and, on at least one occasion, Norwich Priory records show that 13,000 eggs were bought for just one week.[xxi] For a community of just 300 people this does not sound like a model of abstinence, let alone a life of poverty.

When the Bishop of Norwich, William Bateman, conducted his visitation (a kind of formal inspection) of Norwich Priory in 1347 he complained that the monks would habitually eat meat and go off into the city to dine with friends. It sounded more like a social club than a monastery. There was worse behaviour as well. Bateman hinted that women from the city were regularly staying in the monastery at night, and not just as a guest of one of the community in a fashion that might have been considered seemly.[xxii] Monastic principles were clearly under threat.

Adam's own small monastic house was not exempt. St Leonard's may have contained no more than a handful of monks, but they still fell prey to outside influences. The mother priory of Norwich may have been clearly visible from the hill on which St Leonard's had been built, but it was distant enough for the prior of St Leonard's to forget to make his annual return of cash and goods to the prior and bishop in Norwich. An irritated Bateman ordered "that the prior of St Leonard who for some years was in an acting capacity should complete a full and detailed account of all offerings rendered and all those who have come to visit the aforesaid priory and of the expenses he has received, and that he should render this account in the format and timescale which are customary (ie annually) with the servants and officials of our mother church. The said prior should undertake no work of magnitude or ostentatious expense without the consent of a council of the chapter of prior and elders."[xxiii] There is not a little suspicion from the records of William Bateman's visitation that the prior kept the goodies for himself and his brothers and that it was used for good living. And sometimes the wealth did not reach the brothers. Bateman "issue[d] a binding injunction and order to the prior of St Leonard, the confessors and the recipients of income and money to the effect that they should distribute the stated sums of money on the stated terms to individual monks as preferred. A double penalty will apply if they defer the distribution of the sum on the stated terms and fail to comply with this order within the space of twenty days."[xxiv]

The impact of such laxity on the young Adam must have made its mark. After all, the whole point of the monastic life was to improve the soul through self-denial and poverty. Yet monasteries, even small houses such as St Leonard's, could be very rich.

The apparent contradiction was easy for the Benedictines to explain away: the individual monks were poor, they had no possessions of their own and therefore they had followed the letter of Benedict's Rule. However, the corporate body, the monastery as a whole, could be very rich indeed. The monasteries were reaping the rewards of land rents from their vast holdings, profiting from the work of lay brothers, exploiting the learning of the monks and always expanding their property and wealth via donations and legacies from a guilt-ridden laity. Not surprisingly, the rather cynical way in which the Benedictines could distinguish between the corporate wealth of the monastery and the technical poverty of the monks became a focus for criticism during Adam's life. Adam often appears to be an arch-conservative on Church matters, and he remained a man of principle under circumstances in which many lesser mortals would have faltered. But that is not the whole story. Reading his treatises on religion and given his belief in the traditions of the Church, one cannot help but get the impression that, officially at least, he was uncritical of the lapses creeping into monastic life. He didn't mind bending the rules when it suited, and he maintained a sense of fun and ease in his manner of living for much of his life. He may have been ordained in the Benedictine Order, but he saw no reason to be over-literal in following the Benedictine Rule. Yet although he was no strict disciplinarian, Adam was a pragmatist, and what he did insist on was that the official view of the church was strictly laid down. The image of the Church, the authority with which the Church ruled over its own people, and the religious life was fundamental, the actual practice of the monks in private mattered somewhat less.

Education, Education, Education

By the mid 1340s Adam was clearly showing promise as an outstanding scholar, and the limitations of the small priory of St Leonard's had reached the point where the Prior of Norwich considered he should be transferred to the mother priory across the River Wensum. Whether it was felt that the excesses at St Leonard's were damaging the moral fibre of the young monk is a moot point; the surviving records suggest that the mother priory's indulgences were even greater. Given the future direction of Adam's career, it seems more likely that the small library at St Leonard's was starting to act as a barrier to his studies. Although there are no detailed records from Adam's time at St Leonard's, a century later an inventory of the books taken in 1422 clearly shows up the limitations[xxv]. True, there was both a bible and a copy of the Sentences of Peter Lombard – the essential schoolbook for the aspiring mediaeval cleric – but aside from these there was a meagre collection of barely 50 books. Among them there were one or two tomes that might have helped a promising student in the arts of the day, a grammar book, Aristotle on physics, the Summa of Thomas Aquinas, and a book by Innocent on the Decretals together some selected works of Augustine. It was hardly a well-stocked collection.

Not everything at St Leonard's was done on such a small scale. The buttery and kitchen were somewhat better provisioned than the library. The large kitchen contained two small and four large barrels for beer, with a seventh barrel kept for alegar (a vinegar formed by fermenting surplus beer stocks). It seems the priorities at St Leonard's were possibly not in the area of education!

And yet the prospect of a formal education was one of the great attractions of the Benedictine priories for many young men of Adam's era. There were opportunities in the towns, but not many. The guilds could offer some limited form of education through the apprenticeship system, and in Norwich the Almonry School[xxvi] offered an elementary education to 13 boys. A number of cathedral cities also offered education through small schools run under the patronage of the local bishop. This was all well and good if you lived in a town and your talents were spotted, but the majority of the population lived in the countryside. London, by far the largest city, had a population of barely 60,000 out of a total population for England of around five million.

By becoming a novice monk, a boy from the countryside at least put himself in a place where there was a possibility of education and, if he shined, who knows how far he would be allowed to go. A career in the Church offered a rewarding opportunity to exploit that education. Throughout the mediaeval era the work of administering the secular realm, raising taxes for the King, and keeping royal accounts was nearly always undertaken by monks and bishops. The Church was the only organisation able to offer in quantity the skills needed to record the money to be raised and to account in writing for the amounts that had been paid over.

However, the Church felt that it was not getting the best from the system that it controlled. The Lateran Councils of 1179 and 1215 required every cathedral chapter to provide lectures and studies in the arts and theology. The Benedictines had been particularly worried that a lack of education not only reflected poorly on the monasteries, but prevented monks from fulfilling their full potential and giving the Order a greater influence within the Church. By the 13th Century all novices received an elementary education, whilst monks might be expected, according to their abilities, to undertake what amounted to a general arts course to a standard that we might describe as A Level. A course on theology would be offered at the monastery for those who showed a particular aptitude, with outside lecturers supplementing the skills of local monks. There were no formal tests equivalent to the exams that we have today, but it was expected that a monk would complete between six and ten years of study. At least by insisting on a long period of learning, the monasteries knew that only the more determined, if not necessarily the most skilled, would go on to further education.

Norwich Priory in particular had substantial libraries, and the general range of books available to the monk students was much wider than the meagre fragments kept in the library of St Leonard's. Simon de Bouzoun, the Prior of Norwich, would have wanted to house all his most promising scholars at the mother priory, and as Adam had clearly shown some promise, the Prior wanted him in an environment where his studies could be overseen and nurtured. At Norwich, Adam would be given the chance to study using the extensive collection of books in the library of the cathedral priory and to swap notes with other promising scholars of his own generation.

Transfer to the Mother Priory

On joining Norwich, Adam was entering a very different type of community. St Leonard's was a small priory where the duties and responsibilities of the brothers were shared by the community. A major Benedictine house such as Norwich was run in a more structured way. The priory was a complete and self-sufficient community with its own gardens to grow food, and an alehouse, mill and bakery all within the monastery grounds. In addition there was a granary, an infirmary, a guest house for visitors, and administrative offices to look after the vast estates that the monks held in the countryside around Norwich. Rather like St Leonard's, the whole community was walled in, though in the case of Norwich, this was as much to keep jealous townsfolk from breaking in and doing mischief as it was to prevent monks from getting out and doing the same.

Within the monastery a small army of officials ensured that everything ran smoothly. The cellarer was responsible for organising provisions for the kitchen, the almoner dispensed money for charitable causes, the kitchener prepared and cooked the food for the refectory, the pittancer specialised in providing dishes of either eggs or fish for the monks, and the communar seems to have organised major building projects. A number of the brothers acted as estate managers on behalf of the priory. In addition to their own neatly ordered community, the monks exercised a great influence on the economy of Norwich by providing wool and surplus food from their estates to the markets of the city. All in all the monastery at Norwich was a large and complex community, almost a complete town within a town.

The priory and cathedral that had overwhelmed Adam in his youth rapidly became a part of his routine. In hours of contemplation he would walk around the cloisters in silence with his brother monks, admiring the vaulted ceiling and its outstanding collection of painted roof bosses. Unfortunately, the cloisters were poorly lit, and only the North Cloister received a decent amount of sunlight during the day. Being warmer, this part of the cloisters tended to be the preserve of the older monks, or those working on transcribing manuscripts. Under the dark skies of an East Anglian winter, the cloisters must have been a gloomy and rather cold place for a monk to spend much of the day. And not always were the cloisters a haven of tranquillity and calm reflection. Work on building and decorating the cloisters carried on throughout the 14th Century. At times it must have been like wandering around a building site, and as the monks processed quietly amongst the gothic vaulting, they would have had to dodge the masons as they chiselled marble pillars into shape. Overhead, carpenters and painters added to the decoration to the stone and created the ornate roof-boss carvings.

The nature of the working day was also a little different at Norwich to that experienced at St Leonard's. The great priories of cities such as Norwich tended to have their own workforce to take care of the hard graft of farming and the heavier, burdensome work associated with running the monastery. So when the prior allocated the monks their tasks these would usually feature indoor work, such as the administration of the priory estates, copying manuscripts in the scriptorium or working in the kitchens or the cellars. A successful student such as Adam might spend much of his hours of labour working on copying out illuminated manuscripts. The advantage of being a diligent student is that when the prior was handing out the work for the day, you were more likely to get the softer options.

The Scholar's Life

Adam blossomed at Norwich. His natural ability and the speed of progress of his studies had been remarked upon. The Prior was himself a noted scholar, with a keen interest in collecting books, in particular those from the relatively new genre of historical chronicles. Among his personal collection of works, which he bequeathed to the library at Norwich Priory, were the chronicles of Roger of Wendover, Matthew of Westminster and the Polychronicon of Ranulf Higden.[xxvii] As Adam started to immerse himself in the library at Norwich, perhaps Prior Simon recognised in him the same scholarly interest that had played such a great part in his own career. This must have pleased him, not least because it justified the decision to transfer the young monk to the community of Norwich. As Adam really started to shine as a scholar it became evident that he was amongst the most promising at the priory, and by the mid 1340s he had been marked down for greater advancement. Adam was selected as one of the Norwich monks to go to Oxford University.

The new university was still in its first flush of youth, and the monk scholars of the Benedictine houses had a substantial presence there, with their own college established on the edge of the city. In 1336, Pope Benedict XII instituted a ruling that all monasteries should send one in 20 of their monks to the new universities springing up across Europe, and what had previously been a voluntary code of practice was turned into a formal requirement of the monastic system. Although the numbers going to study at the new college at Oxford increased after 1336, and Norwich in particular sent a regular supply of monk students, it was still a privilege that only the most able scholars could hope to attain. These monk scholars had their studies and living costs funded entirely by their own monastery. Numbers remained low (not always reaching the levels prescribed by Benedict XII) in order to keep the expenses at a manageable level.

When it came to choosing which of the monks who had completed the required period of study should go on to Oxford, the university relied on the local prior and a complex election process. The prior would co-opt eight brothers as fellow electors, including the brother who acted as the young monk's instructor. Then, in a ritual designed to emulate the election of the pope, the electors were locked up until they reached their decision. The fact that Prior Simon de Bouzan and his colleagues chose Adam tells us much of the progress of his education at Norwich and of the esteem in which he was already held by his brother monks.

Based on the dates of his graduation and his likely date of birth, Adam had probably completed no more than six years of education at St Leonard's and Norwich before he was selected. His work must have shown great promise to have been sent to Oxford after the minimum permitted period of education; perhaps the Prior was taking a chance on him.

Adam set off for the Benedictine-run Gloucester College at the University of Oxford, probably for the opening term of 1347. It was a long journey by the standards of the time and it was the first time that Adam had ever left the county of his birth.

Chapter 2

Oxford

"Clothed then with faith and the performance of good works, let us set out on this way..."

Early days at Oxford

The English Benedictines realised that the provision of a local education service based in their priories and cathedral chapters was not sufficient to bring out the best in the best of their monks. In 1277 the general chapter of the Black Monks recommended the founding of a college at Oxford, and Gloucester Abbey offered the land on which to build it. Funds were raised from the Benedictine monasteries across southern England and in 1291 Gloucester College came into existence. Norwich Priory was an enthusiastic supporter of the new college from the beginning and provided substantial financial contributions towards the cost of the building works.

Set back from the street on the western edge of the old city and surrounded by substantial grounds, the college was insulated from the noise and bustle of mediaeval Oxford. A suitable retreat perhaps for monk scholars accustomed to keeping the temptations of the outside world at arm's length. Some of the student accommodation from Adam's day has survived, and from this we can get an idea of how the college might have looked. The surviving mediaeval buildings form a solid block along the side of a quadrangle. The buildings are split into four two-storey houses built in the soft yellow stone of the Cotswolds. Each house was in turn divided into rooms or camerae for the monks of a different monastery, although judging by the size of the houses, there can only have been a handful in residence from each monastery, perhaps half a dozen at the most. From the records of

Worcester College[i] we know that at least 15 Benedictine monasteries kept camerae at Gloucester College. The house of the Norwich monks has not survived, but others have, bearing the coats of arms of the monks from Pershore, Glastonbury, Malmesbury and Canterbury who attended Gloucester College at the same time as Adam. The arms of each monastery are carved into the stone above the entrance to each house, and we can imagine that there must have been a good deal of friendly (and perhaps unbrotherly) rivalry between the monks of the different houses.

Gloucester College, an establishment created by the monastic orders for the monastic orders, inevitably felt the full force of the dissolution of the monasteries under Henry VIII. And yet, against all the odds, it has survived. With a change of name and a large injection of cash in the 18th Century the institution that Adam knew has survived to this day as Worcester College.

Life in the University of Oxford that Adam entered in the mid 1340s would be scarcely recognisable to an undergraduate today. The three-year course that constitutes for most students a brief bridge between school and employment was not the usual option for the 14th Century monk students. Although some came to Gloucester College for an informal education and left without a degree, those that came intending to complete the full course of study were in for a long ride. The student of Arts was required to study for no less than eight years before obtaining his degree. The degree itself consisted of a set course of study, and the range of subjects considered to be part of the "Liberal Arts" would certainly not be recognisable to an Arts student today. The undergraduate could expect to study grammar, rhetoric, logic, arithmetic, geometry, astronomy, natural philosophy, moral philosophy and metaphysics. In fact, to us it sounds much more like a course in the sciences.

As a monk scholar, Adam would also be expected to take a degree in Theology. However, it was not possible to start the Theology course until the student had first passed the full course in the Arts. The Theology degree was supposed to take at least seven years, so when added to the eight years of the Arts degree, the monk student could expect to spend around 15 years of his life studying. A man might expect to be middle-aged by the time he had completed his formal education!

For the next few years Adam worked through the programme of set studies. Modern students facing the problems of grants and loans will be unamused to learn of the generosity of the mediaeval orders towards their monk students. The priory at Norwich was at great pains to provide for their brother students at Oxford. An undergraduate could expect to receive £5 towards the cost of travel between Norwich and Oxford and on top of this, a living allowance of £15 each year.[ii] In the mid 14th Century this represented a very substantial sum, especially compared to the earnings of others. A ploughman might expect to earn 7 shillings a year, a shepherd perhaps 10 shillings, and even a church clerk or vicar of a small church might have to live on as little as £5 a year.[iii] The student's grant was provided from the funds of the Benedictine House that the scholar originated from and it was intentionally generous. The allowance was to ensure the students had sufficient provisions to live on and to help avoid the need for the "slyness that is such a feature of modern times", a sentiment that seems as relevant today as it did when the Benedictines wrote it down. In addition to being provided with funds, the Benedictine students could expect to be housed in the College at their brothers' expense.

Biological Warfare

In 1347 the young Adam was settling into the routine of studying at Oxford. On the other side of Europe, in the Crimea, a Mongol army was laying siege to the Genoese trading post of Kaffa. The Mongols were not making much headway. The Mongol army was an efficient fighting machine, but despite countless successes on the open field of battle, it had never been at its best when confronted by town walls. The Mongols were running out of ideas, and, to make matters worse, a virulent disease was running through their army. The Mongols started to despair of dealing with the mounting piles of corpses and the falling numbers of armed men at their disposal. Necessity proved to be the mother of invention. The crisis caused by the disease gave the Mongols their big idea. Why not catapult the pestilence-ridden carcases of their dead warriors over the walls and into the stubborn town? From a purely military point of view the scheme was an instant success. Simple in concept, brilliant in execution, it remains one of the first recorded instances of the use of biological warfare. In the end the Mongols unwittingly brought down not just the city of Kaffa but the whole of Europe.

The Genoese defenders were rapidly overrun by the same sickness as the Mongols, and in the confined streets of the town the pestilence spread quickly. As those sailors and merchants who were left alive fled from the stricken city, their boats took the Black Death back to every port in which they berthed. And each of those ports had in turn its own fleet of ready-made plague carriers able to transmit the disease with alarming speed.

The population was oblivious to the significance of the rats that infested the dockyards and ships of the continent, and had no hope of understanding the link between the fleas carried by the rats and the pestilence. Instead the disease seemed to appear mysteriously, far from where it was last reported, almost as if it were by the will of divine providence.

The Black Death spread rapidly across the continent of Europe. In Florence, Boccaccio described the symptoms at the start of "The Decameron" noting that "in men and women alike it first betrayed itself by the emergence of certain tumours in the groin or the armpits, some of which grew as large as a common apple, others as an egg, some more, some less, which the common folk called gavoccioli. From the two said parts of the body this deadly gavocciolo soon began to propagate and spread itself in all directions indifferently; after which the form of the malady began to change, black spots or livid making their appearance in many cases on the arm or the thigh or elsewhere, now few and large, now minute and numerous. And as the gavocciolo had been and still was an infallible token of approaching death, such also were these spots on whomsoever they shewed themselves."

Back in England, the year 1348 started ominously. Great rainstorms swept across the country, flooding the land and making it hard to plant seed for the new season's crops. Such grains as germinated rotted in the ground. Matters deteriorated further in June when a ship from Gascony landed at the port of Melcombe Regis (now better known as Weymouth) in Dorset, bringing with it the same disease that the Genoese had brought from Kaffa. Henry Knighton cried that "from this year to the year following there was widespread death across the whole world". The plague spread out from Dorset right across southern England, moving rapidly from village to village, causing widespread disruption and sparing neither lord nor pauper. Knighton reported that "the sorrowful pestilence made its way along the coast via Southampton and then came to Bristol, where almost the whole company of the town perished, as if anticipating sudden death; for few stayed in their beds more than three days, or two days or even half a day, then cruel death snatched them."[iv] By December the disease had reached London, where eventually 18,000 of a population of 60,000 would die of it. Early the following year the Archbishop of Canterbury became one of its high-profile victims. Adam had good cause to be happy that he had left Norwich behind. In England's second city and the surrounding countryside the impact of the plague was at its most devastating. In March 1349 it entered the city of Norwich, arriving from the south west via the town of Sudbury. The plague took hold, and by April 1349 it was prevalent throughout the county of Norfolk. The impact on the rural population was such that it was said that in Norfolk more than 57,000 people, equivalent to the entire population of 14th Century London, had died of the plague by July 1349[v]. It was not until the end of 1349 that the full effects and the rapid spread of the disease started to lessen. Of the 60 brothers that had lived at Norwich Priory before the outbreak, barely half survived to see Christmas Day in 1350.[vi]

Adam was doubly lucky to be at Oxford, for the sector of society most hard hit by the plague was, inevitably, the priests and monks who were accustomed to minister to the needs of the dying. Glancing through the registers of Bishop Bateman's Norwich See, the regular round of new appointments of vicars and church officials gives testament to the increasing death rate. According to the calculations of the papal court, in just one day in Avignon 1,312 died. In nearby Montpelier, of 140 friars, only seven were left alive. So many were dying that it was barely possible to find time to hear every confession and grant absolution. In desperation the Pope was obliged to order that full remission of all sins be granted to those who were alone and dying of the plague.[vii] The scale of the plague that hit Europe in 1348 was out of all proportion to anything that had preceded it. Sometimes the tallies of the dead and descriptions of the disease seem almost clichéd, but the impact they had on the chroniclers of the day is deeply disturbing and the facts as they saw them bear repeating.

If the onslaught of plague caused panic in many sectors of society, to the Benedictine monks and indeed the Church at large, the issue was not purely medical. The wrath of God had manifested itself to mankind. Matteo Villani echoed the beliefs of many when he bemoaned the fact that the pestilence was "a Divine intervention which aimed at nothing less than the destruction of mankind." His fellow Italian, Boccaccio, cried that the plague had been "sent upon us mortals by God in His just wrath by way of retribution for our iniquities."[viii] As some started to think of the plague as a punishment from on high, so others focused their attention on the abuses, wealth and corruption of the Church, and a papacy that seemed focused more on wealth than religion.

Back in Oxford, the impact of the Black Death may have seemed less severe, but only for the student population. The Benedictine colleges had properties outside the town gates where the students could retreat to avoid the worst ravages of the plague-ridden town. As the students enjoyed a rural life of peaceful contemplation and relative ease, the townsfolk of Oxford were left to their world of narrow streets and poor sanitation. As panic took hold and casualties rose ever higher, the people of Oxford had nowhere to run. The town suffered severe loss of life, as the townsfolk living in close proximity to one another provided the perfect opportunity for the plague to spread from family to family. Adam and many of his brother students may have survived the pestilence intact, but this left understandable resentment amongst the townsfolk who suffered such great loss of life from among their own during the time of the plague. By the end of 1349 the worst of the pestilence had passed, and as the impact of the disease subsided, the monk students slowly returned to their Oxford colleges. The atmosphere in the town was strained and the students returning safely were greeted with contempt. A simmering tension was barely held beneath the surface of a fragile community shattered by the intensity and scale of death.

A Confident Scholar

The 14th Century Oxford students represented the intellectual elite of their generation. So what if the privileged life of the scholars and young monks had preserved many of them from death? Privilege was a fact of life that many had become used to in their monasteries, and if the anger of the townsfolk went unnoticed, it was as much a reflection of the perceived status of monk scholars amongst their own kin as any conscious insensitivity. Adam settled back into the routine of Gloucester College and the rigours of his Bachelor of Arts course. The monk students were still supposed to combine the life of a monk with their studies of the arts. Adam would be expected to attend the usual services required of any Benedictine monk and to observe the rules of fasting and eating, as well as exercising moderation when drinking wine. His coursework for the Arts degree would involve a study of standard scholastic texts, several of which he may already have seen at Norwich. Adam adapted ably to the scholar's life and progressed rapidly with his studies. Here was a young monk who was taking Oxford in his stride, and he was certainly gaining in confidence, as an incident in 1352 showed.

Occasionally the monks were required to return to their home priory, usually for important events in the life of the community, such as the coronation of a new bishop in the cathedral or the appointment of a new prior for the monastery. The priory wished to remind the students that they continued to be a part of the community even when they were living outside it. In the early summer of 1352, all the monk students from Norwich priory had been asked to break from their studies and return to their priory. No reason was given, but the priory expected obedience from its students just as it would expect obedience from the brothers living within the priory walls. Obedience to the prior was a fundamental principle of the Rule of Benedict. Adam and at least one of his fellow students, known only as "John", declined to return. In June 1352 William Bateman, Bishop of Norwich, wrote to them, complaining that they had failed to obey the specific instruction of their Prior.[ix] The Bishop accused the monks of showing a "high spirit of rebellion" and they were threatened with excommunication if they failed to return to Norwich within three days. The Bishop saw no reason to give any further explanation, and his threat was of such magnitude that it could not be brushed aside lightly. The Priory of Norwich came under the jurisdiction of the Bishop of Norwich, and one might well imagine that Adam's promising career was about to be cut very short. Excommunication would see him removed from Oxford. He would have been placed under the auspices of the Prior of Norwich, separated from his brother monks at Norwich until he was considered to have made good his fault.

The young Adam was not to be so easily browbeaten by his Bishop. He wrote back to explain why it was illogical to be recalled to Norwich and, by implication, why the Bishop was wrong to have written to him at all. He reminded William Bateman that he had not been recalled to Norwich when Prior Laurence de Leck had been elected in April 1352, and he demanded a reason of the no doubt fuming Bishop as to why he should be recalled now. Clearly the purpose of the Prior's request, which Bateman does not give, was not connected to the election of either the Prior or Bishop. Bishop Bateman may have had good cause to regret that the by-product of the advocacy that the young monks learnt at Oxford was a capacity for insubordination. What brother John thought of Adam's reply is not recorded, but he must have been horrified at the prospect of being damned by association. Adam was unconcerned. He had confidence in his own abilities as an advocate, so much so that he went on to make an even grander gesture.

He appealed his case directly to the Pope.

It is hard not to admire the sheer guts of the man. In an age where deference and fealty were expected, this young scholar from a humble background showed no sign of being overawed by the authority of the Bishop, Lord of a large city, cathedral and Priory, all of which, just a few short years earlier, Adam had found so intimidating. Yet the young scholar put his faith in logic and advocacy and he prepared to argue his case. And he seems to have pulled it off as well! There is no record of the case having been taken up in the papal court, nor any sort of retribution from either Adam's Bishop or his Prior. Adam remained at Oxford and continued with his studies.

The Exotic World of Scholasticism

So our young monk moved seamlessly from his work on the Bachelor of Arts course onto the esoteric world of the Bachelor of Theology studies. The ideology and approach to learning in Adam's time is very difficult to make sense of in the 21st Century. Theology leaned heavily on the philosophy of "Scholasticism" and the great outpourings of scholastic writers of the 12th Century, men such as Thomas Aquinas, Abelard, Anselm and Duns Scotius, who had thrived on professional rivalry, debating the issues of the day. For the first time since the fall of the Roman Empire, there was a substantial intellectual movement at large in Western Europe.

Scholastic study involved an exotic mixture of church dogma and philosophical process, and whilst the scholastic mind did not preclude original thought, it had to operate within the fixed boundaries of knowledge defined by religious orthodoxy. The basic premise for the Scholastics was that at the beginning of time man started out with a perfect vision of God, an understanding of the purpose of creation and access to the total quantity of knowledge. That, however, was but a brief and happy state of affairs before the "Fall". Once man had left Eden behind it was all downhill from then on.

That perfect state could be regained, said the Scholastics, but only by acquiring "perfect" or "total" knowledge. This was the purpose of study. Man could move slowly towards re-acquiring that knowledge as he studied, banking his accumulated learning as he went. The fund of overall knowledge could then be increased by building on the knowledge of those who had gone before.

The goal of acquiring that perfect knowledge was to re-establish a position where man could once again contemplate the divine essence, to look upon God and understand the purpose of His creation. The theme of man seeking a perfect vision of God is a recurrent one in both the scholastic texts and Oxford lessons. Of course, sin would shift man backwards in his drive to regain perfect knowledge, but then divine intervention, signs and miracles could all result in a step forwards as well.

Scholastic methods concentrated on understanding and defining the mystical and spiritual aspects of Christian teaching. There was inevitably less scope for free thinking. The roadmap by which man could regain his perfect knowledge was, of course, the Bible, a book judged to be infallible. However, if the word of the Bible was infallible, the way the word was interpreted was a great focus for scholastic study. That interpretation left plenty of room for manoeuvre and intellectual debate. Yet given the paramount importance of the Bible to the Scholastics and their fondness for interpretation of biblical passages to support (often contrary) arguments, what was surprising was that throughout the period of their intellectual supremacy there was no attempt to challenge the basis on which the Bible had been derived from the original Hebrew. The 4th Century translation of St Jerome, the Vulgate (Latin) Bible, was taken as the standard text that formed the starting point for debate.

Instead, teaching this rather introverted style of theology at Oxford relied heavily on the written interpretations of the scriptures by Peter Lombard and in particular his 13th Century text "The Sentences". Lombard was regarded by the 14th Century as the definitive interpretor of the biblical texts and his arguments formed the bedrock of debates within the university.

The fact that the totality of knowledge was framed within Christian orthodoxy, and the Bible in particular, did not mean discounting the body of classical knowledge. Aristotle, Plato, Cicero and Ovid all had their place in scholastic study. Bernard of Chartres was moved to observe that as they stood on the shoulders of giants (the classical writers who had gone before) it was only natural that modern scholars could see further than their predecessors[x].

Reading through these "Scholastic" treatises today, the subject matter seems alien when viewed from the perspective of the scientific and factually based approach that pervades much of modern learning. Yet some of the religious arguments of the day did address the sort of conundrums that we might still recognise, even when they are dressed in the theological language of the basic texts of 14th Century study. For instance, where we might ponder on the nature of infinity, Peter Lombard in the first book of The Sentences indulges in a discussion on whether God begat himself or not.[xi] It is perfectly possible to discern a similar thought process, a logic that lies behind both ways of stating the question, it is just that the scholastic version is formulated within a different context.

If some Scholastic thinking can be understood in modern terms, other aspects are firmly framed in the language and mindset of the mediaeval world. A glimpse into the more esoteric side of scholastic thinking can be found in the fourth book of The Sentences, where Lombard engages the reader in a debate on the difference between a sacrament and a sign[xii]. This was an important tool in the construction of Scholastic thought, as a divine intervention could speed up the acquisition of perfect knowledge. Therefore it was important to be able to tell whether God was intervening or not.

Lombard tells us that a sacrament is a sacred thing, the visible form of an invisible grace. In other words, it is something that can be seen by a human that has been sent by a divine force. A sign, on the other hand, is something from outside the self that can bear upon the senses in such a way as to cause something to come into the mind. Peter now states the obvious (a rarity indeed) that a sign can be a perfectly natural event, such as a smoking fire. But it can also be a "given sign". In other words, the event has been directed by a higher power. If it is so great a "given sign" that the sign is sanctified or filled with obvious religious virtue and meaning, then it is also a sacrament. Therefore Peter can conclude that all sacraments are necessarily signs, but not all signs are sacraments. Inevitably, debate and intellectual curiosity cannot be focused on the nature of things, on looking for support in facts or in experiment and observation, but on quasi-science and the techniques of argument, rhetoric and logic. The only way that evidence as such is called upon to support an argument is by reference to the Bible, and as we have noted already, the freedom to interpret the word of the Bible meant that the same line in the scriptures could often be used to justify opposite sides of an argument.

The Oxford University of Adam's time was akin to a debating society, with verbal disputations featuring as major events in the curriculum. Without the need for observation, empirical facts or experiment, it was perfectly natural to evolve a system of teaching via debate. It allowed the students to weigh up the merits of intellectual argument and rhetoric by observation, to learn the skills of logical argument from the great masters of the day. The Four Books of the Sentences, a work that Adam had studied already at Norwich and St Leonard's, was the basic text of the Oxford degree in Theology, and the source of many of the texts that would have been debated by the scholars. The course prescribed extensive study of the text, also that of the biblical texts on which Lombard drew for his own writings, and then attendance at debates. In order to gain a degree, the student had to study texts and attend debates for at least four years. In his fifth year he was allowed to oppose or dispute the motion in the religious debates. This did not necessarily mean he would argue against the text or motion, merely that he would put forward an initial view of the motion. In his seventh year he was allowed to respond, in other words to take and analyse the argument put forward by the opposer and, reverting to the motion, assess the quality of the argument of the opposer. Then the student might "incept" or graduate. There was no other assessment process, no written papers and no final exams. The efforts of 15 years of study and learning of ancient texts were determined by the performance and wits of the undergraduate in open debate with his colleagues.

Exile from Oxford

Adam was showing some aptitude for the study of scholastic thought and theology but he was about to receive a double blow to his progress. The first came from Oxford. There had been tension for nearly a century between the old "town" of Oxford and the "newcomer" students who, from the town's perspective, must have seemed to be taking over the place. The way the students had abandoned the town during the plague outbreak to seek sanctuary on Gloucester Abbey lands outside Oxford had not helped. The ill feeling between the two reached a climax in a brawl at a tavern between the innkeeper and a group of students on St Scholastica's day, February 10, 1355.[xiii] The brawl rapidly grew into a larger confrontation, and both students and townsmen called for their supporters to join the battle. The townspeople, led by John de Bedeford and John de Norton,[xiv] rang the "common bell of the town", calling the citizens to arms. At one stage a mob of peasants from the countryside around Oxford descended on the town "with banners unfurled" to help fight the students. The gates of the town were burnt and the houses of scholars ransacked, whilst the scholars themselves and their servants who did not flee were mutilated, imprisoned and, in at least six cases, killed. Although the rioting was supposed to have been spontaneous, the way in which the disturbance had unfolded bore all the hallmarks of careful planning. Nor was it just the scholars who were attacked. Anyone found in religious regalia was either assumed to be a scholar or damned as guilty by association. The fighting continued over several days and scandalised the priories who had sent their monks to the town for an education. This was not the sort of education they had in mind. Much of the property of the colleges in the town had been destroyed, and the surviving scholars and their masters had fled to the monastic estates around Oxford, where they stayed for most of the following year. Adam survived unscathed, but the routine of university life had been badly disrupted.

The second blow came from further afield. Back in Norwich the monks were feeling the full impact of a very different type of assault. Since the beginning of the 14th Century the mendicant friars had been making life increasingly uncomfortable for the established orders of Benedictine monks across the country. As their name implied, the mendicants poured scorn on the wealth that the monasteries acquired whilst acting under their own particular vow of poverty. The main difference between mendicant friars and established monks was that although the monks took a vow of poverty individually, there was nothing to stop the monastery acquiring great wealth corporately. The friars, on the other hand, took the vow of poverty to apply equally on a personal and corporate level.[xv] Although they too stood accused of lax living and accumulating great wealth, the movement proved to be very popular. Already the city of Norwich had seen an establishment of Dominican Friars, Franciscans, Carmelites, and Austin Friars[xvi]. There had even been a fifth house, that of the Order of the Friars Minor, but all the members had died during the plague. The friars represented a real threat to the regular routine of the local Church, as they took a zealous role in preaching their message to the townspeople in Norwich. Preaching was not just a good way of getting your message over, it was a very lucrative money-spinner, as the preacher could usually expect alms from the crowd at the end of his performance. Of course, the more people who were drawn by the power of his preaching, the greater the amount of alms a friar might expect to receive for his order. What was particularly galling for the Prior of Norwich was that the friars had taken to preaching in the cathedral, on the very doorstep of his priory.

The biggest headache that the friars caused to the established church arose from their mobility. Although the friars were based mostly in towns at one particular house or convent, they still might choose to move around the country at will, living on the charity of the people as they went. The parish priests felt the impact of the friars as deeply as the monks. The friars took alms and payment for attending to burials and confessions, as well as preaching, in each activity taking a share of income that had previously been left to the local priest. This unpredictability was uncomfortable for a Church in which everyone had a slot in the hierarchy and you always knew where everyone else was meant to be. The friars could roam around looking for easy money, and only when they found a rich seam to plunder could they be relied on to stay put for a while. This seemed like unfair competition to many humble clerks and rectors tied to whatever living they had been given.

With the establishment of so many bold friars preaching and poaching in the city of Norwich, the Benedictine Prior, Nicholas de Hoo,[xvii] needed help. He called on the monks of his priory currently at Oxford to come back and defend the monastery by preaching in competition with the friars. Adam was particularly talented in this area. As we have seen already, his argumentative, legalistic frame of mind could be daunting for those who were not expecting such powers in one so young. In his new role as a preacher he would have made a formidable opponent and one who was not well disposed towards the friars. Whilst at Oxford, Adam had come under the influence of Richard FitzRalph, Archbishop of Armagh and a virulent opponent of the mendicants. Aside from the friars impinging on the wealth of his fellow clergy, his main objection to them was that, unlike the other orders of monks who fit into the regular hierarchy of the church under the usual authority of bishops and archbishops, the friars answered to no-one other than the Pope. For legalistic minds with a fondness for good order, this was far too anarchistic a way of running religion.

FitzRalph had written and preached against the various orders of friars, and he was particularly concerned that the friars too had found a way around their protestation of living a life of poverty. The trick was a neat one, rather similar to a modern sale and leaseback transaction. The friars gave their wealth to the Pope, who leased it back to their order for their use in doing God's work on Earth. The friars could honestly claim that they owned nothing corporately or individually, but they certainly had material possessions that they could have use of! It must have galled Adam and FitzRalph that the public at large seemed to idolise the friars for the sincerity of their poverty because they could not see the trick that the Friars had pulled. It was even worse for two Benedictines who had to watch as their order was castigated for its own "trick" of owning wealth corporately rather than individually. Whether or not it was motivated by jealously of the skill with which the friars worked their argument, both Adam and FitzRalph would remain opponents of the friars throughout their lives.

Fighting the Friars

Faced with a dangerous situation in Oxford and an absolute need from his prior in Norwich, it was inevitable that Adam should find himself back in Norwich shortly after 1355. By the summer of 1356 Adam was already preaching against the friars. On the Feast of the Assumption, August 15, he was paid a fee by the prior (in flagrant contradiction of the Rule of Benedict, to which he had sworn fealty) of six shillings and eight pence.[xviii] That Adam's contribution to the war of words with the friars was increasingly important after his return to Norwich is clear from the fact that his prior kept him back in the city for so long. He allowed Adam to educate the local monks in the skills of argument and debate. Adam became a regular preacher at the cathedral, drawing on the skills he had learnt from the debates at Oxford. Once the Benedictines had their own star preachers back home, the prior felt confident enough to ban the friars from preaching in the cathedral, and once again the Benedictines drew the crowds and the alms that went with them.

Whilst the exercise had proved Adam's skill at debate and the power of his advocacy, it did not progress his studies. Adam did not return to Oxford before 1363, some eight years after he left, which shows just how much work was needed to counter the power of the friars in Norwich. Such a long break from his regular course of study might, under different circumstances, have jeopardised his chances of gaining a degree. The Benedictines had put a lot of resources into the university colleges of Oxford and they wanted to see students getting some benefit from that investment. There is certainly no doubt that, even though Prior Nicholas needed his services, Adam was being missed at Oxford. Around 1361 Prior Nicholas wrote a response to a letter from the prior of students at Gloucester College in terms that clearly show that, however much Adam was wanted back at Oxford, Norwich needed him too. It is an important letter, as it tells us a lot, not just about what Adam was doing in Norwich but his progress in his studies[xix] (from Pantin's translation):

> "To the venerable fathers and lords, the prior and the whole company of Black Monks studying at Oxford, from your humble servants the prior and convent of Norwich, reverences and honours due to such fathers with all prompt desire to please.
>
> By the tenor of your reverend letters we understand the deplorable infertility of the sons of the mother university studying at Oxford, to such an extent, as you assert, that out of the whole order of Black Monks there are scarcely to be found three bachelors studying theology at the present time; among whom your most gracious goodness considers our brother and your fellow, Adam Estone, to be senior, and

out of the militia of scholastic labour, in the course of his studies to be the nearest to the doctor's reward. Wherefore you have asked us, with sincere affection, to send him back next year and effectually restore him to the maternal bosom of the schools whence we have recalled him for a short time for a certain cause. Indeed reverend fathers and lords, with the greatest desire we would like to accede to your wishes, as we ought, if we were not hindered by the reasons given below.

For of old in our cathedral church, situated as it is in such a populous city and country, it has been the custom to have many sermons of God's word preached to the people at certain times; and this duty used to be undertaken, at the cost of entreaties and gifts, yet with some difficulty by the mendicant friars, who are the enemies of our order, and indeed of all churchmen, loosing their backbiting mouths at everyone. However with unanimous deliberation, considering it a shame and a detriment to us that these preachings in our own church should be undertaken by friars, we have decided altogether to exclude all friars, and so far have imposed that laborious work upon our own brethren. But because the harvest is laborious and great, and our labourers are wearied and few, we have thought it necessary to set up our said brother Adam as a subtle and experienced reeve over these reapers who are thus wearied; lest the sheaves of the word of God, bound up in bundles, be incautiously sown amongst biting, envious men and the mouths of those that speak iniquity. Who also, our said brother (Adam) may baffle the backbiting mouths of those that rise up against us and impose silence upon these sadducees. For certain matters against sound doctrine and the liberty of the church were brought forward by certain friars, whom by true doctrine he has restrained from their erroneous way, and will shortly, God willing, completely triumph over them. For blessed be the Most High, his doctrine enjoys special favour among clergy and people. But if his absence came to be known at present, we fear that they (i.e. the friars) would at once come up like mice out of their holes, and we have no one else to resist them in wisdom or learning, but they would proudly make broad their fringes exceedingly.

Wherefore lest these things or worse happen, it seems to us necessary either to recall Thomas Brinton, or to keep our brother Adam for a short time. We hope indeed soon to exalt them both to the pinnacle of the doctorate, God willing, and with the intervention of your gracious help. May it please your reverend fatherhood and the lordship of your whole venerable company to have us favourably excused in these and other altogether necessary things. For we would shudder greatly, God knows, to offend such a company, or to delude with feigned excuses such a congregated flower of the order. May the wisdom of God the Father enlighten your scholastic acts, to the exaltation of the universal church and the special honour of the whole order.

Amen."

That was quite some commendation. Even allowing for a little latitude and exaggeration from a prior wanting to have his own way, the expertise and esteem in which Adam's preaching skills were held shines through. It was hardly surprising to hear that one as expert in the debating skills of Oxford should be so adept at refuting argument through stand-up preaching, outwitting and out-arguing the poor friars against whom he was sent. However, the comparison with Thomas Brinton, apparently the Prior's second choice for the task, is particularly interesting. Thomas was a fine advocate in his own right who, as Bishop of Rochester, would come to be regarded as one of the finest preachers of his time. If, in 1361, Adam showed more promise and, in the mind of Prior Nicholas at least, he was the outstanding scholar of his priory, then we can assume that his prowess was remarkable even by Oxford standards.

Prior Nicholas also gives us a valuable insight into Adam's progress in his studies. By 1356, when he returned to Norwich, Adam cannot have completed much more than nine or ten years of study out of the normal 15, and he must have finished the Arts course in very quick time. Yet in this letter Adam is noted as one of just three students at the college who were already "bacularii" which suggests he had already been awarded a degree in the Arts. The Arts faculty at Oxford had a great deal of prestige, and uniquely Masters of Arts were allowed to either stand or sit at their discretion[xx] during debates, and they were allowed two desks for their books where other students were obliged to share. Given the usual size of mediaeval manuscripts, this was a decent concession!

Adam, however, had gone still further. From the tone adopted by Prior Nicholas, it appears that, by the time Adam left Oxford in 1355, he was considered very close to the point of getting his degree in Theology. The rules of the university did allow for "graces" by which exceptional students could be accelerated through the process, in particular by being allowed to take part in debates after less than the usual four years of study, on the basis that their knowledge or acumen made them worthy and challenging opposers. Prior Nicholas was hinting in his letter that the skill with which Adam had been fighting his corner for the true doctrine of the Church (at least as perceived by the Benedictines) should count in some way towards the required time-serving in debates at Oxford. To this extent he appears to have been asking indirectly for Adam to be granted a grace to spend less time studying on his return. Given that the process of gaining a Doctorate in Theology depended heavily on debating skills, the Prior's asssertion that

Adam had gained much through his preaching that was relevant to his degree seems entirely reasonable.

Oxford in Need

Whilst the friars were a serious threat to the Benedictines, there were other concerns weighing on the order. They were worried about the fallout from the Oxford riots. The Black Monks had gone to a lot of trouble to establish Gloucester College and build up its reputation as a place of learning, and they wanted to see it used. Yet since 1355 more members of the order had been sent to the safer climes of the City of Cambridge to further their studies. It was important to the credibility of Oxford that as many high-profile students as possible should return to the city.

This was not the only issue at hand. Oxford had a number of problems of its own with the friars. The university complained that people would no longer send their sons to Oxford for fear that they would fall under the influence of the friars[xxi] and join their ranks. The friars were demonised, accused of abducting young boys and scholars alike and brainwashing them until they agreed to follow their rule. They were even attacked for neglecting the education of those scholars in their care at Oxford, preferring instead that their students should work amongst the community, preaching and attending to confession and burial, and thereby earning money for the friars. Several of those scholars who trained under the friars and obtained their degrees were talked of as being so called "Wax Doctors".[xxii] This term of derision stemmed from the fact that they used letters from those of influence to gain "graces", thereby shortening their degree and gaining the honour without a full course of study. The "wax" was the wax seal that the great and the good would attach to the letter granting the graces. And just for good measure, the friars were also being attacked for the usual crimes of preaching at the expense of monks and priests and more unusually, for unorthodox teaching. In 1358 a certain Friar John overstepped the mark to such an extent that he was condemned to read a public recantation and to pay a fine of 100 shillings to the university. He was banned from lecturing in Theology for life. Quite what he said wrong is unfortunately not recorded.

Clearly Adam was now needed to help combat the influence of the friars in Oxford. In the end the pressure that the Oxford brothers put on Prior Nicholas paid off, and Adam returned to Gloucester College in 1363. The Norwich rolls for that year record the cost, paid by the communar, of his travel and of taking all his books back with him in two entries, the first of 113 shillings and four pence and the second for 41 shillings and four pence.[xxiii] When compared to the usual five pounds[xxiv] for a year's travel, it seems that the trip was a major upheaval.

A Scholastic Debate

Adam resumed his studies at Oxford, and the strong hint dropped by Prior Nicholas seems to have had an immediate effect. Shortly after his return he was regularly determining and responding in the religious debates at the college. To be taking such a lead role in these debates, and to be responding in particular, he must have been recognised as a senior student close to being awarded a degree. Some transcripts of the debates in which he took part are still preserved in a folio of manuscripts in Worcester Cathedral Library[xxv]. They are interesting, as they give a real flavour, not just of the process of the debate itself, but also of the workings of the mediaeval mind and the philosophy behind the debates.

One of those debates takes for its main theme the question, "Could Adam in his state of innocence (i.e. before the incident with the apple, the serpent and the Fall of Man) see God as naturally (an immediate vision) as the angels can see God?" (the full text is included in Latin in Appendix III). This was a favourite Scholastic subject and it examined the state of perfection that Man had been trying to regain since the time of The Fall. The subject matter is clearly linked to the texts of Peter Lombard and revolves around a theme taken from The Sentences.[xxvi] The topic shows that Adam was quite prepared to explore some of the more difficult Scholastic subjects, but perhaps he may have chosen the text because it was a pun on his name. It is almost as if he was asking from a personal position, "can I, Adam Easton, see God in my state of innocence as a monk?" This rather playful approach to weighty matters would be a recurring theme throughout his life, and, as we shall see from time to time, Adam was fond of word games and codes.

The theme was disputed with Master Nicholas Radcliffe, whom the transcript called "the respondent". Following normal Oxford rules he was most likely the more senior of the two men, and possibly already a bachelor of theology. Radcliffe was a Benedictine monk from the Abbey of St Albans who would go on to take Easton's side in battles still to come, but for the moment he was not only his opponent, but also his assessor.

Adam demonstrated his skills as an advocate once again. When faced with a tricky question, he hedged his bets. First he gave three arguments in favour of the proposition, from which we must assume that this was his preferred opinion, but at the end of his case he outlined the opposing argument. It is an unusual piece of advocacy in which he sought to impose his views whilst indicating that he was perfectly aware of the opposing arguments to which he attached (clearly) little merit.

It is perhaps difficult for us, from a 21st Century viewpoint, to follow an argument about the facial contemplation of God, never mind understand not only precisely what angels were but how they might have had such a view of God. And Adam had to debate whether that view was different before and after the Fall of Man. It is a subject from the heart of the world of orthodox rhetorical argument and requires creative thought as well as logic. However, the most difficult aspect of this doctrinal argument is that the cases for and against were composed and interpreted solely through logic and rhetoric and unsupported by observation. Certainly the scholastic texts were called up to defend a point of view, but only because they themselves highlighted well-established lines of argument equally based on logic and rhetoric. The creative way in which these forms of argument could be drawn from doctrinal orthodoxy can best be illustrated by following the text of Adam's debate:

His opening salvo seems straightforward enough. Before original sin, he tells us, Adam saw God in just the same way as the angels did. His view of the divine essence (God) was just as natural, and he did not need a medium through which to see God.

The second line of argument is a little harder to grasp, that Adam in his state of innocence was disposed or inclined to see God as if his soul had been separate from himself. Here Adam appears to be arguing that the pure soul, unimpeded by sin, can see God in a direct way irrespective of the frailty of the body of the man to which the soul is attached.

The final argument put forward asserts that Adam, before The Fall, had such a perfect love of God that seeing God must be the natural end consequence of that perfect love. Therefore, because he wanted to see God because he loved God, he could see God just as the angels did.

All clear so far? Adam the monk was now ready to pronounce that he had a clear understanding of the other side of the case. The alternative argument, asserted brother Easton, is that the Adam in Eden was alive (in the condition of life) and that anyone who has not passed outside the condition of life cannot see God in a perfect way. This point of view was supported by a quote from St Augustine in his work De Trinitate, but somehow it lacks conviction. The arguments are so ethereal that it is impossible to allow that one has substantially more merit than the other. All appear equally plausible, but Adam Easton clearly came down in favour of the motion.

Radcliffe started off his Responsario with an admission that this was not an easy question to debate, but he clearly had an ace up his sleeve. He played the card early by asking what exactly is meant by "an immediate vision of the divine essence?" A trap was being sprung. Radcliffe went on to suggest that an immediate vision means the same as looking upon the very face of God. This is something that only God can grant, and He will grant it as and when, and only when, He wishes. Thus if any being has not been specifically granted such a privilege, it cannot be offered to them whatever their state of innocence.

So, in fact, the angels themselves did not have an immediate vision of God. If the angels did not have an immediate vision, then Man in his state of innocence cannot have had one either. Radcliffe was now attacking the wording of the motion rather than Adam's chosen line of argument.

Radcliffe went on to call upon an impressive array of Doctors of the Church whose writings backed up his argument. He quoted extensively from Hugh of St Victor and also from Augustine. He did allow that Adam and the angels may have seen the divine essence or God intuitively. By this Radcliffe meant that the view of God was an image, perhaps as we might see an image of God in a painting or a photograph. But it was not a clear view of the actual face of God.

He then looked at Adam Easton's proposition about the mind being separate from the body and therefore having a greater purity and hence a better view of God. Radcliffe suggested that both the mind and the spirit of Man before the Fall were equally pure. Therefore, Man had two views of God, one from the soul and one from the body, but both were the same, intuitive views of God not actually a full-on facial view.

Finally we are offered an even stranger development of the argument. Radcliffe asserted that the act by which Adam loved God is itself a species or being with its own faculties and senses. So now we have Adam as a person or being and the "Act of Love" as a person or being. By implication this new "being" can no more see the face of God than either Adam himself or his soul. In conclusion, Radcliffe defers his opinion as following the Master of the Sentences and asserts that the opposite of the motion is now proven. In this argument at least, Adam had been defeated.

It is impossible to look at the texts of these debates without wondering how on Earth they were judged. A line of argument in which an action can be interpreted from doctrine without anything of an objective nature underpinning it makes any evaluation of the argument subjective. Yet this was Adam's world, full off surreal argument, orthodoxy and, at times, eccentric justification.

The intellectual challenge may occasionally have bordered on the obscure, but life at Oxford was certainly never dull. Even as he was preparing to incept in 1364, another major riot broke out between the townsfolk of Oxford and the scholars. A four-day battle erupted between the factions[xxvii], but at least on this occasion no one was killed. Once again the atmosphere in the city was tense, and the citizens were forced to pay reparations to the scholars. It must have been a difficult environment against which to be finalising an academic career, the culmination of 17 years' work.

The Doctor's Reward

Back in Gloucester College, there were battles to be fought with words and ideas. Adam may have lost the occasional debate with Radcliffe and the other graduates, but his studies and performance in the debating chamber were considered to be well advanced. He must have had a very busy time preparing for and participating in numerous debates throughout 1363 and 1364. Interestingly, when Adam went on to undertake the Determination or Lecture for his inception or graduation, he took a similar text to that which we looked at above: "whether Adam in his state of innocence had an immediate vision of God". On this occasion he argued strongly against the motion.[xxviii] However, he did not use the same reference points as Radcliffe but had gone on to research his own sources and drew on a far greater range of authority. In a broad-ranging argument he drew on no less than three of the finest church theologians of the mediaeval era, Thomas Aquinas (Doctor Communis), Henry of Ghent (Doctor Solemnis) and Duns Scotius (Doctor Subtilis), showing not just that he had read these masters, but that he understood their line of reasoning. Once again he was showing a strongly independent streak to his character but, if nothing else, he was shrewd enough to learn from his mistakes.

By the time he graduated, Adam had moved ahead of Radcliffe in his studies. When the debate for his inception was held at Vespers, Radcliffe was once again responding,[xxix] and by tradition it was usual for a Bachelor of Theology to respond at the Vespers debate where a Doctor was incepting, so we must assume that Radcliffe had still not received his own doctorate.[xxx]

Adam was undoubtedly the academic star of his generation. Thomas Brinton, the future bishop, was a well-respected fellow monk from Norwich who had remained at Oxford throughout the dispute with the friars. He incepted at the same time as Adam, yet because he had stayed at Oxford in the late 1350s he must have had something like six years more tuition than Adam.

As tradition dictated, the two new doctors from Norwich Priory marked the event with a substantial feast. Norwich Priory sent funds to Oxford to ensure that the incepting monks could expect a somewhat unholy celebration of their new-found status. The sacrist sent 26 shillings and seven pence[xxxi] for both men. The refectorer contributed 40 shillings to Adam[xxxii] and the cellarer 30 shillings.[xxxiii] The priory had been more than generous. A total contribution of some £8 amounted to an annual salary for many men in 1365, when a whole sheep might cost just one shilling, a goose just four pence and a calf seven shillings and six pence. The two learned doctors would indulge the college with a substantial feast, something to remember for years to come. After so many years of study, incepting was not an event to be taken lightly.

Whatever vows the Benedictines may have taken, it must have been quite a party.

Chapter 3

Doctor of the Sacred Pages

Let us get up then at long last, for the Scriptures
rouse us...

Prior of Students

When Adam incepted, or graduated, in 1364, he did so not as a mere Bachelor, but as a Doctor of Theology. He was in his late thirties, so no child prodigy, but the rapid progress and success of his studies suggests that he was a man of unusual skill and learning.

As a Doctor of Theology (sometimes described as a Master of the Sacred Pages), Adam might well have returned to Norwich to instruct his fellow students and preach in the cathedral. A monk of his talents could hope to become prior of one of the daughter houses of Norwich, moving on in time to become either Prior of Norwich itself or even, with a touch of good fortune, Bishop. Strictly speaking, Adam had no option but to return to Norwich. The Benedictine Rule forbade him to be away from his monastery without the express permission of his Prior, and by implication the Bishop to whom the Prior was accountable. However, the powers that be in Norwich were generally sympathetic to his ambitions. His erstwhile adversary William Bateman had been replaced by Thomas Percy as Bishop, and Nicholas de Hoo, who had been so grateful for Adam's help in fighting the friars, remained in charge of the Priory. Happily for Adam, neither demanded that he return to Norwich in the period immediately following his inception.

So when the Black Monks offered him the appointment as their Prior of Students at Gloucester College he was free to accept it. The Prior of Students was, in the first instance, elected by his fellow students at Gloucester College. However, the Abbot of nearby Abingdon was tasked by the Benedictines with keeping an eye on the election and ensuring the nominee was a responsible monk who would meet with the approval of the whole order[i], as most of the Benedictine houses were represented at Oxford. With the backing of his colleagues, and more importantly his order, there would now be little possibility of opposition or a summons back to Norwich. His academic skills were clearly highly regarded at Oxford and as Prior of Students for Gloucester College he would be largely free to pursue his studies.

The appointment as Prior of Students was a neat solution for Adam. On the one hand it saved him from a possible recall to his priory, whilst on the other it gave him a senior position within the church hierarchy. Perhaps Adam recognised that his independent streak might not sit well within the framework of a provincial monastery.

The intellectual life and the challenge of the Oxford debates sat easily with a character like Adam Easton. He had already gone well beyond the usual curriculum of study of the set rota of approved texts. He was prepared to question and challenge the scope of scholastic learning, even if at this stage he wished to stay within its boundaries. As we follow the transcription of the debates in which Adam fought out the finer points of Christian orthodoxy and logic with his fellow academics, it becomes clear just how important it was for scholars to have read the major texts of the scholastic canon when it came to constructing their arguments. To establish creative variations within a strand of argument without straying into heresy also required a detailed knowledge of the principle orthodox theological texts and an acceptance of the infallibility of the Bible. The colleges provided libraries for their students in much the same way as they do today, and the influential texts, such as those of Peter Lombard and his fellows, would have been available in sufficient quantities for all scholars to become familiar with them at first hand.

Starting a Library

At Oxford Adam had already started to stray beyond the boundaries of the standard texts of scholasticism, many written a century or so earlier. He was not content to rely on those texts that happened to be available in the libraries of Oxford. He had a questioning mind and was already starting to push beyond the usual limits of scholastic scholarship. The problem with the state of learning at Oxford was that since the explosive outpourings of the 12th Century, scholastic writing had stagnated. There were fewer new texts coming into circulation, and no great new teachers or brilliant minds appearing with new lines of argument to add to the debates. And Adam was not prepared to work entirely within the traditional or orthodox lines of argument, as he demonstrated time and time again throughout his career. He wanted not just to question and challenge accepted learning, but, as we shall see, to research for himself the areas where he found more questions than answers. Even whilst he was still at Oxford we see a young man who carried many of the trappings of the Renaissance.

Adam used his extended stay at the University to start building up his own private library. It says something for his intellectual curiosity that he wanted to own his own books and be able to study contemporary texts with the same vigour as the more traditional books accepted as orthodoxy by the Church. In an era in which the only way to reproduce a book was to laboriously copy it out by hand, personal ownership of texts was a sign of enhanced status even for a scholar. Although many of the scholars sent to Oxford from Norwich Priory had their own books, Adam's enthusiasm was exceptional. Quite how exceptional is shown by the entries in the Communar Rolls for the cost of taking books back to Oxford. When in 1344 the scholars Etturius de Tunstale, John de Wetele and Walter de Stokton returned to their studies, the cost of transporting their books (together with all their other belongings) amounted to five shillings, six shillings and four shillings and sixpence respectively.[ii] When Adam returned in 1363 the cost of carrying his books alone amounted to 113 shillings and four pence! Sadly, few books remain of what must have been a very substantial library, but four have survived, three in England and one in Avignon. In each of these books Adam is named as the owner, and in each inscription he is described simply as "a monk of Norwich", so they must date from his days at Oxford.

These four surviving books tell us something about his early interests as a scholar and the direction that his life would take in the future. Not only do they give us personal glimpses of the student at work, they are also not unconnected with each other.

"De Pauperie Salvatoris"

Perhaps the most interesting is "De Pauperie Salvatoris", the book by Richard FitzRalph, Archbishop of Armagh, that documented his views on, amongst other things, the status and role of the friars. The book was written in the form of a dialogue between FitzRalph and a companion, John, and discussed the issues surrounding the way of life adopted by the friars. Adam's copy is now part of the manuscript collection held at the Parker Library of Corpus Christi College in Cambridge.[iii]

FitzRalph was greatly preoccupied with the trick by which the friars had managed to keep the use of all their wealth and possessions whilst ownership of them was notionally vested in the Pope. Much of the early part of "De Pauperie Salvatoris" is devoted to a discussion of the difference between "dominion", or ownership, and "use". Adam clearly used the book a great deal for the Archbishop's work is annotated throughout by a furious hand, scribbling sometimes several lines in the margins of the text. This changes dramatically when we get to Book VII, which is titled "De Mendicate Fratrem et eorum privileges". Suddenly Adam is scribbling whole paragraphs in the margins and noting down and underlining points that he might take for his own use. It is oddly satisfying to see Adam as a normal student, using his text books just as a modern student might. Even if books were more precious in the 14th Century and we might look in horror at notations on a beautifully illustrated manuscript, they add interest to the manuscript itself. As books were hand copied, they often contained mistakes and omissions, and so occasionally Adam noted in the margin a word that appeared to be missing from the text[iv] as he tried to make the sentence make sense. To emphasise important paragraphs, he underlined them in ink or noted in the margin a summary of the main point of the paragraph. Even at this early stage in his life it seems that the subjects that interested him were power and authority, whether in terms of rights to property or in terms of the hierarchy of power.

Oddly enough, it is only towards the end of the manuscript, on folio 88, that we find the inscription "I Liber Dni Ade Estone Monachi Norwiciensis" identifying Adam as the owner. The inscription, in bold blue capitals, appears to be in exactly the same hand as the page headings and chapter numbers that appear throughout the book. If the same person who had transcribed the book had inscribed Adam's name in the text, this could indicate that the copy had been made specifically for him, perhaps as a gift from Richard FitzRalph himself. As an elder churchman who had spent several years at Oxford, FitzRalph would have admired Adam's work preaching against the friars in Norwich and may have offered him the book as ammunition in his work. Judging from the way Adam annotated the book, he certainly found it a useful source of ideas.

"Inventarium Iuris Canonici"

The second of Adam's books from his Oxford days, a copy of the "Inventarium Iuris Canonici"[v] by Berenger Stedelli, Bishop of Beziers (in south west France), is also in the Corpus Christi collection. A relatively new text book on canon law at the time Adam was in Oxford, this was not light reading but central to the path that Adam followed in his career. Again Adam covered the margins with points that interested him, summaries of the text and remarks that he might use to argue a case in one of the debates. Every now and again, to emphasise a point, he would draw a hand in the margin pointing to something he considered significant.[vi] It can seem strange to see the playful doodles of a student in a mediaeval manuscript, but it is refreshing to see the way human touches can be timeless and independent of technology and change. It is more than just a human touch, though, it shows a lighter, almost playful, side of Adam's character, even when he is surrounded by serious matters. It is a glimpse of the inner man.

The bold, red inscription on the first folio of the "Inventarium Iuris Canonici" states that it belongs to the church of Norwich and to Adam, a monk of the same place. It is hard not to wonder if Adam had not simply appropriated the book from the priory library and kept it with him for his studies! Certainly that would be one way to start building a library. Perhaps he had arranged for his own copy to be made by the monks in the priory scriptorium and they had kept the reference to Norwich from the original. The world of books was unburdened with copyright law in Adam's time.

The "Collectiones of William of St Amour"

The third book surviving from Adam's library is the vast "Collectiones of William of St Amour".[vii] It is a surprising book to find in Adam's collection for the simple reason that it had been condemned and its author excommunicated. The Collectiones represented a summary of William's beliefs, completed in 1266 during the time when he had been under sentence of excommunication by Pope Alexander IV. Although views on William and his supporters had changed with each successive pope for the previous half century, any work that had on several occasions been condemned as heretical could be a dangerous book to own.

This did not worry Adam, who had the first folio inscribed with his name just as he had with the "Inventarium Iuris Canonici", suggesting that Adam had acquired it from Norwich Priory for his own use – with or without the Prior's knowledge. For the Collectiones to be one of the first books that Adam acquired for his own collection shows that he must have had a taste for controversy. Certainly he was not worried about courting official criticism, as we have seen in his confrontation with Bishop Bateman. It may be that, unlike the work of the Bishop of Beziers, Norwich Priory was only too happy to pass the Collectiones on to its monk scholar.

William of St Amour was one of the first Doctors of the Church to speak out against the friars. The fact that Adam owned both the Collectiones and "De Pauperie Salvatoris" suggests that during his time at Oxford he saw the friars as the greatest single threat to the established Catholic Church and religious order. Not surprising in a man who had spent seven years of his life resisting the influence of the friars and preaching against them, Adam was anxious to gather the widest possible range of arguments to use against the friars and their special privileges. The Collectiones is a work that was clearly influential on Adam, but unlike "De Pauperie Salvatoris", it was a century old when Adam acquired it. With both books in his collection, Adam could draw on the threads that linked the arguments of Richard FitzRalph and William of St Amour, giving him a broad base for his own personal fight against the friars.

For William, the friars represented disorder because they made their living from begging. They therefore had no firm income, no regular routine and could not be subject to an ordered way of living in the way that monks could. As the income from begging fluctuated, they might suddenly appear in an area in large numbers, and this was bad for regulation. This anarchic way of life did not, for William, sit comfortably with the order necessary for a virtuous life. For a man who represented religious order, hierarchy and the power structures of the established Church, it is not surprising that Adam should find comfort in the writings of William of St Amour.

What is perhaps much more surprising about William is that John Wyclif also regarded him as a great writer and an influence. Wyclif, a secular scholar who was naturally critical of religious authority, was an outspoken critic of the friars, albeit from a very different theological position from Adam. Given the collision path that Easton and Wyclif started down whilst they were at Oxford, it is tantalising to speculate whether Wyclif might have borrowed Adam's copy of William of St Amour to further his own studies.

"Medical Treatises of Bernadus de Gordonio"[viii]

This was perhaps the most unlikely book of the four to be found in Adam's collection although there can be little doubt as to its ownership. The first folio proudly bears a similar inscription to the others: "Liber ecclesie norwycen' per magistrum ade de estone monachum dicti loci". Bernadus was a professor of Montpellier who wrote extensively on medical subjects, and he too was a modern writer in Adam's time, having died around 1318. As we have seen, it was perfectly usual for general science to be included in the core curriculum of the Arts degree that Adam had to obtain before studying theology.

Yet it was one thing to have to study science using the books available to borrow from his priory and from Gloucester College. It was quite another for Adam to go to the great trouble and expense of having a personal copy made up as part of his collection. The book must still have been in his possession in 1376 (it probably remained in Avignon after Adam left the city in that year), so it was clearly a subject he found fascinating and a text that he valued. It certainly shows us a very much broader scope to Adam's interests as a scholar than the theology treatises that, however controversial, are exactly what we might expect to make up the reading matter of a monk scholar.

Four Glimpses into a Scholar's Soul

So what do Adam's surviving books tell us about Brother Easton, Doctor of Theology? William of St Amour was a controversial writer, but the fact that Adam not only owned the book, but clearly used and developed William's ideas, was remarkable. Owning books that had been considered heresy not 50 years earlier was risky if it was not foolhardy.

"De Pauperie Salvatoris" and "Inventarium Iuris Canonici" marked Adam out as unusual for a young student because he was prepared to make use of contemporary works, not just established classics. One book, "De Pauperie Salvatoris" was written at much the same time as Adam was studying at Oxford, and the other was hardly a classic given that Berenger Stedelli had written it as recently as 1300 and the author himself had only died in 1323. Other students may have hacked their way through Peter Lombard and waited for newer texts to receive the stamp of approval and orthodoxy. Not Adam. Here was a forward thinking student whose spirit of enquiry was unusual for his time.

The final book, the medical tract by Gordino, was even more exotic. Not only did it dwell extensively on sexual health, a highly unusual topic for the mediaeval world, let alone for a monk, it was also off the beaten track for a Doctor of Theology. Its presence in his collection shows that Adam did not restrict his studies to the narrow world of theology and doctrine and was interested in the more general sciences and philosophy of his age.

He was no scholastic purist. In a time when the dynamic flourishes of new scholastic thought were becoming a jaded, distant memory, Adam belonged to a new era. With an intellectual vigour that meant that he was prepared to look at new works himself and make up his own mind, this new Doctor had moved beyond the scholastic world. Adam's academic curiosity belonged to the Renaissance, and not to a world that was still content to debate the finer points of whether angels were able to see the face of God. Unfortunately he was nearly a full century ahead of his time.

Lost in Translation

Whatever the official demands of the new role, it is unlikely that looking after the students of his college was ever very high on Adam's own agenda. His role as Prior of the Students placed Adam in a perfect position to further his own intellectual curiosity and his studies took precedence. Adam was starting to be recognised as a linguist and had already developed considerable skills in ancient Greek and Latin. Nor was he satisfied with reading works in translation. In a world without spell checkers, word processors and instant translation, it was perfectly natural to fear that errors by the translator might make a significant difference to the way in which the work was interpreted. In the world of scholastic debate the Bible was considered the major factual source of argument, and the words of the Bible were read literally. Against this background, an error in translation could become very important. Adam realised that an inaccurate translation could fundamentally affect the arguments being used in the disputes in Oxford, and indeed in the wider Church beyond. Adam's approach to study was characterised by a combination of an obsessive attention to detail and an enquiring nature. He used his time at university to learn Greek in some depth so that he could study the Greek masters with the same directness of understanding that he could apply to those doctrines and texts of the Church that had, like Peter Lombard's, been first written in Latin.

He was also starting to look again at the Book of Kings and wondering if the translation from Hebrew into Latin had been rendered accurately. He already had some basic Hebrew knowledge, but Oxford did not have a vibrant Jewish community amongst its scholars to help expand his knowledge and put his theory to the test. As far as the Bible was concerned, scholars relied upon, and by and large accepted without question, the translation of St Jerome. Adam realised that if he revisited the Hebrew original, there was plenty of scope to revise the Bible through retranslation, without challenging the fundamental infallibility of the text. This was a principle that other scholastic doctors had accepted, but none had done anything about. The road that Adam now started along would be one of great significance to scholars of his generation.

Things Fall Apart

For all his intellectual ambitions, the new doctor could not avoid giving at least a cursory nod to the tasks expected of a Prior of Students for Gloucester College, the real reasons the Benedictines had given him the job in the first place. It was primarily an administrative role in which he was expected to attend to his flock and ensure that they kept up with their studies and maintained the reputation of their order. The Benedictines worried that, away from the monastic houses in which their students had been educated, the monks would enjoy freedoms that their calling should have denied them. The Prior of Students was meant to be a senior figure, but also one who had studied at the college and knew its habits and rules. In an ideal world, he would be an esteemed scholar notable for the diligence with which he exercised his rule over the other monk scholars.[ix] Adam was nearly 40 years old by the time he was appointed Prior, and as a more mature graduate of the system, the Benedictines would have expected the college to be in safe hands. Unfortunately, the monks often felt a stronger loyalty to the monastery that had sent them to Oxford than to Gloucester College. The system of the camerae only encouraged this sense of loyalty and made it difficult for the Prior of Students to exercise any kind of discipline and order over the students.

Adam had been a successful scholar but as an administrator he was still learning, and perhaps at this stage of his life he found this side of his job rather dull. All the available evidence suggests that Adam was not a very successful Prior of Students. The students evidently found Adam a convivial host, but that was not meant to be the point. It did not help matters that a number of the monk students under his care were not the most diligent of scholars. One in particular, a certain John Loccombe, had something of a track record for avoiding his studies and enjoying the pleasures of hunting and fishing instead.[x] He had already been summoned back to his "home" priory of Glastonbury to account for his behaviour, and Adam was clearly not having much success in helping him mend his ways. On September 20, 1366, some two years into Adam's tenure, the president of the Black Monks, the Abbot of St Albans, was obliged to write to the Abbot of Glastonbury "who should examine I. Loccombe our dear brother and fellow monk of our order from your monastery who is charged with incontinence [sexual excesses in this context] again at Oxford University, as we are told by brother Adam Easton, monk of Norwich and prior of students at the said university".[xi] If it is refreshing to note that after a mere 650 years of undergraduates studying in Oxford, some facets of student life have barely changed, not everyone was happy with Adam's regime at Gloucester College.

The letter from the Abbot of St Albans stuck to the facts and contained no hint of a criticism of Adam. All the same, the Abbot of Glastonbury must have been perplexed. What on Earth was he supposed to do from a distance? Surely it was up to the man on the spot, the Prior of Students, to handle the matter? Could he not control his students? Needless to say, the Abbot was far too polite to say any of this! Whatever Adam's excuses, his apparent failure to control the students suggests that too much of his attention was taken up by his own studies.

Even when he was able, on occasion, to put his advanced learning to good use for the benefit of his order, matters did not always run smoothly. Adam had earned his reputation as an able advocate, and now he was starting to get involved in administration of the law and excelling at it. But as ever with Adam, this was mainly on his own terms. In 1367 Prior Nicholas at Norwich wrote (the addressee is unknown but was most likely the president of the Benedictine order in England) to recommend Adam's skills in just such an area "on which subject and the reason why we have been so long in writing back to you, we offer in our defence to your paternal reverence our dear comrade Adam of Easton, who was responsible for proposing the present [legal] matters. If it pleases you to place faith in him, in regard to the material we have sent previously and other matters that we have set out orally to your reverence, and if there is anything more you wish us to do, we will arrange for it to be done to the extent that we are able".[xii] Adam had managed to hold up an important piece of legal administration, presumably in order to concentrate on some of his own studies. It is notable that no excuses are offered for the delay. If he was clearly not the most efficient of the Benedictine lawyers, at least his work was held in high enough regard for him to be drafting legal codes on behalf of his entire brotherhood. Indeed, the tone of the letter suggests that it was felt better to wait a little longer for Adam to do the job than have someone take it over and mess it up.

A Star Scholar in Search of a Role

It is hard to escape the conclusion that the Benedictines were wondering if they really had put the right man in the right job. No one could doubt Adam's academic excellence, but as a Prior of Students he had hardly been an unqualified success. On his own account, Adam had started a major academic challenge of his own whilst at Oxford, considering and reviewing St Jerome's translation of the Old Testament. But that was not what he was paid to do. Ultimately the translation would be the cornerstone of his great work in support of the Church. At Oxford in 1367, though, all that could be said for Adam was that he did not appear to be terribly good, or perhaps to be fair, not terribly interested in, the job he had been employed to do. It says something for the Benedictine order that his next move was not banishment back to his priory in Norwich. If he had been less than successful, at least the brotherhood recognised his talents for what they were and realised they could be put to better use.

Adam still managed to use his remaining time in Oxford to good effect, enhancing his reputation as a Doctor of Theology and demonstrating his skills in the debates of the college. Adam was already recognised in England as a talented intellectual, but thanks to the Benedictine network, he was now coming to the attention of a much wider audience. Up until 1367 Adam could consider himself, by the standards of the time, to be reasonably well travelled. In an age when the majority of the population hardly roamed beyond the boundaries of the parish they were born into, he had left the village of his birth for good. He had travelled to the Priory of Norwich and then to the City of Oxford and had commuted between the two great cities more than once. If this was more than most could aspire to, Adam had still never crossed the sea or travelled to the limits of the realm of his king and sovereign, Edward III.

Even so, word of his abilities and his work started to spread across foreign fields.

Chapter 4

The Diplomacy of Cardinal Langham

Seeking his workman in a multitude of people, the Lord calls out to him and lifts his voice again, "Is there anyone here who yearns for life and desires to see good days?"

The Archbishop in disgrace

By August 1368 Simon Langham had been Archbishop of Canterbury for barely two years, but already matters were starting to get out of hand. Simon, a Benedictine monk from the Abbey of Westminster, had enjoyed a successful career both within the Church and as a court official. He may have chosen to follow a religious calling, but he was a pragmatist. In an age where the only formal education available came from the Church, the Crown relied on senior churchmen to fill the important posts of the royal administration. It was not a coincidence that for much of the mediaeval period the Chancellor of England was a serving bishop. Many churchmen found little problem in serving God and their monarch in equal measure, and Simon was no exception. When he was promoted to the Bishopric of Ely, then one of the richest in England, he showed his gratitude with his loyal support of his sovereign. Further promotions followed as he became first the royal Treasurer and later Chancellor of England. However, having a king as self-assured and belligerent as Edward III to deal with did not make his role especially easy or particularly comfortable. In 1365, Edward, knowing that he could rely on the support of his Chancellor, asked him to push through the Act of Praemunire. Simon now had to think carefully about his loyalties, because Edward's Praemunire presented a real conundrum for a churchman. It was a new legal device first enacted in 1353. Praemunire was, in theory, a general Act to prevent the introduction of foreign authority into England that might challenge that of the King. In practice it was aimed at one foreign authority in particular, the Pope.

The Plantagenet kings had good reason to have a chip on their shoulder about papal influence and the right of the supreme pontiff to interfere in the affairs of their kingdom. The reason dated back to the rule of King John. John got himself into a fix by alienating the Pope and the Barons at the same time. Pope Innocent III responded by placing England under an interdict;the Barons by threatening open revolt. Needing support to secure finances for his treasury to fund the dispute with the Barons, John had been forced to appeal to the Pope to have the interdict removed. Spotting an opportunity, Pandulf, the papal legate to England, engineered a humiliating repositioning of the relationship between King and Pope. King John was obliged to relinquish his kingdom to Pope Innocent who then, via his legate, passed it back to the King. John, by this action, had explicitly acknowledged that the kingdom of England was gifted to the Plantagenets by the Pope. The move served to reinforce the papal position of authority over secular rulers that had been such a bone of contention since the advent of the Holy Roman Empire. By passing the Statute of Praemunire, Edward started the process of reversing the humiliation of John. The Act put him in a position to challenge the Pope's right to collect revenues from the Church in England. For a warrior king who was always looking for hard cash to finance the next conflict, this was a pragmatic move first and foremost. However, he could also prevent the Pope from instructing his prelates and clergy, and they in turn could neither seek guidance from the Pope, nor remit Church taxes to him without incurring the wrath of their sovereign. More importantly, from a philosophical point of view, Praemunire reinforced the royal perception of the correct hierarchy over matters secular and religious. Simon Langham had little to be happy about. Passing the Act of Praemunire put the Bishop of Ely in a difficult position. In theory at least he owed as great an allegiance to the Pope as to the King, and he knew that Praemunire tacitly reduced papal power in the realm of England (albeit restoring it to the status quo that existed before John's reign). In the end, whatever doubts he might have had, Simon had attended to his King's demands. Later in the same year, as the consequence of the Act of Praemunire, the English refused to pay the papal tribute or tax. Simon was promoted to the Archbishopric of Canterbury in recognition of his services to the crown.

Edward III had every reason to be pleased with the outcome. He had reinforced his view that clergy and secular subjects alike reported to the monarch in all things, and had placed his own man in charge of the English church at Canterbury. From the royal perspective, the only area in which the clergy could seek guidance from an authority other than the King was in matters spiritual and theological. Issues such as the appointment of clerics and collection of Church revenues were strictly in the remit of the crown. By passing the Act of Praemunire, Edward expressed his interpretation of the relationship between English clerics and the pope in very plain terms.

The popes, of course, saw the world in a very different light, and that was not about to change on the whim of a mere king. The assertion of superiority made through the cunning of Pope Innocent III had been followed in 1302 by the bull "Unam Sanctam", issued in the name of Pope Boniface VIII. Boniface declared that everyone, whether king or bishop, poor or rich, was under the authority of the Church and its supreme head on Earth, the pope. He suffered heavily for his ideals. Imprisoned by agents of King Philip of France, a humiliation that made a mockery of his stated position, he died soon afterwards. Yet the power of his words proved a little more enduring. He had reinforced by public proclamation the position of a church in conflict with the secular rulers of Europe and had died a martyr's death in that cause.

Edward III did not really intend to deny the Pope access to his clergy or to refuse his right to authority over spiritual or clerical matters, for he showed very little personal interest in the finer points of doctrine. However, he did want to make a point and to impress upon his subjects that where the Pope enacted his will in England, he only did so with royal permission. Simon Langham's promotion to Archbishop of Canterbury was a fitting climax to a career of royal service, and after a couple of years of further loyal service to his King, and without any sign of retribution from Rome, the matter seemed to have been settled.

Pope Urban V, an astute and cunning man, had other ideas. He had not played his last card. On September 22, 1368 he offered Simon promotion to the rank of Cardinal, a rare honour that had been offered to no more than 11 Englishmen in the entire history of the Church. Without thinking twice, Simon accepted the honour and the undoubted riches that came with it. As a cardinal, the Archbishop would be expected to travel to the papal court that had just recently returned to Rome. It was an ill-considered move on the part of a man who should have known better. Edward was furious. He had not appointed Simon as Archbishop of Canterbury so he could go swanning off to Rome. He expected his former Chancellor to control the Church in England and keep it in line. It was supposed to be a hands-on job. It was certainly not a task that could be carried out satisfactorily from Southern Europe under the guidance of the Pope, the one person whose influence in England Edward had sought to curb. He pointed out that, under the very Statute of Praemunire that Simon had himself promulgated not three years earlier, he had no right to accept the Cardinal's hat without royal permission. He most certainly had no right to travel to a foreign court in a foreign land and take up an official position there. Instead of seeing the promotion as a reward for his faithful Archbishop, Edward turned nasty. The King confiscated Simon's positions and revenues, leaving him without any means of financial support. In a fit of pique, Simon resigned as Archbishop of Canterbury in November 1367. This only made his position weaker, as he had now effectively cut himself off from the income of the Archbishopric. From now on he would be dependent on the goodwill of the monastery at Canterbury and the attitude of his sovereign.

As the reality of his position sank in, Simon realised he had made a serious mistake. Yet he was still determined to fulfil his destiny, and, in attempt to make peace with his sovereign, he applied to leave through the proper channels (at least as defined by Edward). He formally requested Edward's permission to travel to the papal court, but the King, true to form, refused Simon permission to travel out of England at all. Edward had a point to make. The ex-Archbishop remained in Kent, with none of his old religious positions intact to support him financially, and unable to take up his new office. Reduced to living the life of a humble monk, albeit in the manor house of Otford[i] (a manor owned by the monks of Canterbury) Simon was now in a very difficult position.

A Job in Rome

As Simon sulked angrily in Kent, Adam Easton was making his first journey back to England from Rome. It was May 1368. The English monk had travelled to the Eternal City during 1367,[ii] having finally given up his role at Gloucester College to further his career at the papal court. This was not a surprising change of direction. Adam had not exactly covered himself in glory as Prior of Students, and the trials and tribulations of keeping tabs on the young monks in Oxford had not appealed to his sense of purpose. Adam's replacement as Prior of Students was John Welles, a man who would become a loyal and close supporter of his cause in years to come.

For Adam, the appeal of Oxford must have faded after a couple of years when set against the glamour of a career at the papal court and a decent salary to go with it. As it happened, the reigning pope, Urban V, was also a Benedictine monk and on the look-out for talented monks from his own order to serve in his court. The Benedictine mafia was already hard at work, scouring the monasteries and universities to recruit administrators to meet that need. In 1364[iii] Nicholas de Hoo, the very Prior of Norwich who had written so enthusiastically to Oxford University about Adam's skills, had visited Urban's court in Avignon to pursue a suit on behalf of the Norwich monks. It seems likely that he was just as enthusiastic about his protégé to the courtiers of Urban V as he had been to the scholars at Oxford. However, as Adam had recently been appointed as Prior of Students, he was not available. Instead, shortly after Nicholas's visit, the Pope brought Thomas Brinton, the Benedictine monk who had studied with Adam at Norwich and Oxford, to his court. By November 1366 Thomas was working in Avignon as proctor for the English Benedictines, and he was being paid rather handsomely for his services, at a rate of at least two florins per day.[iv]

As Adam's outstanding skills as a theologian and scholar had been brought to Urban's attention, he was actively persuaded to follow in Brinton's footsteps. It was not a difficult decision, particularly as his role as Prior of Students was not really working out. When Thomas Brinton returned to England during the course of 1367, the purpose of Adam's first trip away from his homeland was to replace him in some kind of semi-official role at the curia on behalf of the English Benedictines. In the event his stay at the curia proved to be rather short-lived. By 1367 Urban had moved to Rome, and as the salary Adam had inherited from Thomas Brinton was paid for by various clerics in Avignon, it is not at all certain that Adam was able to draw funds to support his posting. In any case, Urban had picked out the former prior for his standing as an academic and more importantly his undoubted skills in advocacy. The Pope had a rather delicate mission and he needed a reliable person to act for him. Adam was to be sent back to England bearing a bull from the Pope that attacked "those wicked men fighting against the interest of the Roman church and its subjects"[v]. Urban suspected that papal taxes were not being collected for the Pope but instead were being siphoned off by the King and his officials. Worse still, there was more than a suspicion that the King was supporting the bands of English mercenaries who were then laying waste to large tracts of central Italy. These bands were a menace, roaming through the papal states owing allegiance to the highest payer and often betraying their own comrades in the interests of a better offer. Was it not possible, Urban pondered, that the King was using the taxes due to the Church to pay the very armies that were causing him so much distress? This was a difficult enough issue for the Pope to deal with at the best of times, without the Statute of Praemunire to add to the trouble.

Adam had been presented with a poisoned chalice. The official line to be taken in disputes of this nature was to employ tact and diplomacy. It would never do to attack the person of the King per se, but the point could be made that he was being badly advised. However, since the passing of the Act of Praemunire, to question the King's judgement, no matter how delicately, was fraught with danger. For an English agent of a foreign power to question the King's judgement was tantamount to an act of treason. This was not the first time that Edward III had dealt with an interfering pope. In the full flush of youthful vigour in the 1350s, Edward became embroiled in a dispute with his then Bishop of Ely, Thomas De L'isle. De L'isle had been charged with having burnt down five cottages and having a man murdered at the manor of Colne in Huntingdonshire, which happened to border the Bishop's own property. Unfortunately for Bishop Thomas, the manor belonged to Blanche de Wake, a cousin of Edward, and she appealed to the King for help. Bishop Thomas had a rather arrogant manner, and he managed to incur Edward's wrath from the start. As the proceedings in court started to go against him, the Bishop appealed his case to Pope Innocent VI. This only made matters worse, and Edward concluded that a foreign power was being encouraged to interfere with English affairs. Fearing for his life, Bishop Thomas fled to Avignon. Pope Innocent had intervened reluctantly to help the unfortunate bishop, and, as he got dragged in deeper, he was forced to excommunicate those who had taken Blanche's part in the dispute. Edward was enraged at the effrontery of the Pope for daring to interfere with English affairs. When the papal messengers arrived in England to announce the excommunications, the King imprisoned them and warned Innocent what would happen if any further missives were sent. Several of the unfortunate messengers were later put to death.

Now in the same role as papal messenger, Adam had been given an extremely dangerous mission, but he does not seem to have fully appreciated the risks involved. Urban no doubt counted on Adam's track record as an advocate, and reckoned that his bold stance in favour of logic and law in the face of secular authority would make him the perfect candidate for the job. Yet the timing could not have been worse. Adam returned from Rome and walked straight into the dispute between Archbishop Langham and his king.

Simon and Adam Strike a Deal

As Simon waited, stranded in Otford waiting for permission to leave the country, Adam arrived in Kent with his Papal Bull. The former archbishop must have met Adam either at Otford or whilst visiting his monks at Canterbury. Simon warned him that his mission was foolhardy, and that he should forget about the Bull. It is interesting to note that although the papal archives in Rome clearly show that Adam left Rome with Urban's Bull, there is no evidence from the court rolls of Edward III that he ever delivered it to the King. This would have suited Simon's purpose rather well. The last thing he needed was for a major conflict to erupt between the King and Pope, and Adam's Bull was certain to trigger one. If he was to have any hope of getting royal permission to leave England he needed Church and State to be on friendly terms.

And Simon had good reason to want to draw on Adam's experience and skills. After all, both men shared a common background and may have known about each other already. They were both Benedictines who shared the common goal of wanting to build their careers in the Church overseas. The Archbishop had not stayed at Oxford as a scholar but Langham too had become embroiled in Oxford politics when he had removed John Wyclif from the headship of Canterbury Hall. Wyclif had shown an early inclination to prefer and advance the education of secular scholars over monks, who were then a major force in the University. Wyclif had no intention of accepting the ruling of the Church and was already trying to get secular support for his reinstatement. Adam was an Oxford insider: he had come across Wyclif and, although at this stage in his life there had been no dispute between them, he could pass on a lot of useful information. Adam's inside knowledge would be invaluable for handling the dispute that was brewing.

Simon had other uses in mind for Adam. However long it took him to get away from England, when Simon eventually got to the papal court he would need a man like Adam to help him with the administration and organisation of his staff. Adam, with his recent experience of being prior to the monk students of Gloucester College, would (in principle at least) have the right skills for the job. More importantly, Simon needed a scholar to help him with the legal matters and diplomacy that featured so large in the work of the Cardinal.

By the 14th Century, the pope used the cardinals in much the same way as kings used princes and dukes, to make up a body of advisers and followers who could be useful to him. A prelate might be made a cardinal for his skill in Church law, his administrative prowess or his financial astuteness as much for his religious virtue. The cardinals were courtiers to the Church, providing advice and support to the ruling pope and helping in the running of the Church. A cardinal in the great papal court of Avignon was expected to maintain a substantial court of his own, and it was not uncommon to have some 50 souls in attendance on a cardinal.

Adam was the sort of person with whom Simon could work. The former Prior may not always have been the most diligent administrator, but he was an achiever. He was accomplished at realising plans that he considered to be important, even if that was at the expense of other people's priorities. He was also not afraid of challenging authority when it was merited, and he had a track record as a supreme advocate well used to speaking his mind. The two men were very well matched.

Simon had never been terribly popular outside the rarefied world of the royal court, and now to this was added the disadvantage of being in the King's bad books. Success always breeds petty envy and jealousy, and although he was very determined and usually succeeded in getting things done, Simon's style of man management left a lot to be desired. It was said that at every promotion he left behind subordinates who were grateful to be free of him. Even after he left England, his high-handed manner meant that resentment lived on among his former colleagues. For example, he contributed funds from his personal fortune towards the rebuilding work at Westminster Abbey, then took a close personal interest to the dismay of others. He wrote to the Prior regularly, berating him for the lack of progress with the project, hardly paying any attention to the explanations offered him. With every letter he asked for detailed reports of what would be done, and, more to the point, when it would be done, an attention to detail that others found annoying. Whilst future generations admiring the Abbey at Westminster might have cause to thank Simon for his focused mind and dogged determination to see the building work completed, the rulers of the Abbey at the time disliked his attitude and his persistent interference.

Simon's lack of friends amongst the English community of Benedictines meant he had an urgent need for someone who could help him build a court from scratch at Avignon. Adam fitted the bill. He accepted the job as Simon's "Socius" and in return Simon, as England's most senior churchman, would use his elevated status to excuse Adam's failure to deliver Urban's Bull once they reached the papal court. For the moment, though, Simon was stuck in Canterbury, unable to leave England and yet unwelcome in it.

"Socius"

By 1368 Adam was around 40 years old and had spent nearly half of his life in Oxford. The rewards of travelling abroad once more and working at the highest level in the Church, in the court of a cardinal, presented a significant opportunity. Better still, because he had been invited by the most senior English prelate of the Church, he would have no need to get permission from either his Prior in Norwich or the Chapter of English Benedictines.

What is less clear is the nature of the job he had agreed to do. Our understanding of the term "socius" has faded somewhat over the centuries. Even contemporary documents can be unhelpful. A glossary of the titles and roles for those who served in a cardinal's court, together with the place in the court hierarchy of each position, was laid down formally in a text written in Avignon known as "La Maison Cardinalice".[vi] There is no mention of a socius anywhere in the text. Nonetheless, it was clearly a title that meant something very specific to the clerical world of the middle ages, as the word was used elsewhere in contemporary texts. For instance, Robert de Bury was described as being the socius of Thomas Pykis, the precentor of Ely.[vii] The precentor was by no means the most senior cleric of the priory, akin to Simon's new role as head of a cardinal's court, and there is no obvious parallel between the structure of an abbey and that of a cardinal's court either. So the term appears to have been used generically, Robert being some sort of aide to Thomas Pykis.

Adam's title was not the result of a manuscript error or a poor transcription either, as he is described as Langham's socius in three different documents spanning the ten years[viii] of his service with Simon Langham. Judging by the role that Adam played alongside Simon, it seems that he was more than just a secretary, perhaps a sort of general fixer, an amalgam of head of the household, legal advisor and canon law expert on hand for the thornier issues that a cardinal's life might throw up. The modern equivalent perhaps of a personal assistant to either a company's chief executive or a minister in the government. One thing is clear: it was a good job. Unfortunately, until Simon could get permission to leave England, the post was meaningless, and, by the end of 1368, Adam had no more means of financial support than Simon.

The Long Journey to Rome

By February 1369 Edward decided that Simon had been kept in England long enough to make his point. The cardinal elect was granted permission to leave the country, and together with his new socius set out for Rome before the King had a chance to change his mind. Travel was a dangerous business in the mediaeval era, and the two Benedictines must have considered the long journey to Rome with some trepidation. Even finding the best Channel crossing proved difficult. The most obvious route was barred to them as the area around Calais was a war zone. Bruges was a much safer destination, still a seaport in the 14th Century, it was a merchant city that was generally friendly to the English. A large English merchant community had been established in the city for more than a century, it even had its own church, the Blessed Virgin and St Thomas the Martyr.[ix] From Bruges the journey would be difficult. The two monks would have to cross the kingdom of France, a daunting prospect for two Englishmen as France was still officially at war with England. Although, as churchmen, they could be considered neutral, there was no certainty as to how the French king would react.

Nor could they be sure of their destination. Just as they set off on the long overland journey they received word that the papal court had moved from the Eternal City to the town of Viterbo just to the north of Rome.

The Pope as a Prince

Much of the region around Rome in modern day Lazio, Umbria and Marche was at least nominally under the control of the pope. Although we tend to think of the pope in a purely religious role based in a postage stamp state in the centre of Rome, throughout the mediaeval period the pope was an important secular prince as well as being head of the Roman Church. Rome, the capital of the Papal States, was the official seat of papal power. But the city had long since proved tough to govern. Violent mobs and powerful baronial families had frequently forced the popes to abandon the city to set up court in the nearby cities of Viterbo, Orvieto and Montefiascone. From here they could escape the ravages of disease and political unrest in Rome and govern the state at arm's length from the Roman mob. In 1305, Clement V had made a far more dramatic move when he transferred the seat of papal power to Avignon in Southern France. The next pope, John XXII, saw this as a permanent move. A walled city on the bank of the fast-flowing Rhone, Avignon offered a warm climate without the extremes of heat of an Italian summer. Away from the attentions of the rioting mobs and the baronial families, the popes found the smaller French city a more congenial place to live. The centre of the town filled up with the cardinals, their households and entourages, whilst tradesmen moved on Avignon to service the growing court. Avignon became a by-word for wealth and comfortable living. Overnight, the pope had been turned into an absentee landholder governing central Italy through a series of ambassadors or legates. The Romans may have proved ungovernable when the pope was in residence, but they disliked the absence of their ruler even more. Public order in the Papal States gradually deteriorated. From 1305 onwards there was a state of near anarchy, with brigands and private armies rampaging around the countryside. Tax collection became virtually impossible, and, to cap it all, in 1367 there was a violent uprising in Perugia.

Urban V was desperate to restore order, and decided that the only way to respond was to restore direct government and move the papal court back to Italy. It was never likely to be an easy task. The Pope moved his court from the port town of Corneto to Viterbo, to Rome, then back to Viterbo before finally moving on to Montefiascone, each time hoping to establish a permanent presence in a secure part of the Papal States.

Paris, Rome and Montefiascone

Whilst Urban was trying to establish some kind of permanent authority in Rome, Adam and Simon made their way through Flanders and on to the court of the French King, Charles V. Any worries they might have had about dealing with the French proved to be unfounded. Charles received the Englishmen in Paris with due honour and offered money towards their expenses.[x] Perhaps he found their presence welcome, these two churchmen who had so recently been at odds with his great adversary, the English King. Taking their leave of Charles after a few days in Paris, they set out once again for Italy. Since the 9th Century there was an established pilgrims route from Canterbury to Rome, the Via Francigena and this the two men now took once they had left Paris behind. The road took them from the Ile de France out through the Duchy of Burgundy to Besancon, Lausanne and up to the St Bernard Pass. At least the delay in setting off from England meant that by the time they reached the winding tracks that take the pilgrim over 8,000 feet above sea level, the winter snows had melted and the pass was easier to negotiate. From here they followed the tracks back down into the Aosta valley, passing onto the Lombard plain by the ancient city of Pavia and crossing the Duchy of Milan before finally meandering through the Tuscan hills and the volcanic landscape that protects the approaches to Rome. Journeying via the fortified cities of Lucca, San Gimignano and Siena the two churchmen finally arrived in Viterbo in early May 1369. There, just a few hours' ride to the north of Rome, they were met by a fellow Englishman, Alexander de Neville[xi] (Bishop of Durham), with an entourage made up of English clerks and clergy based in Rome. Neville brought them news that the papal court had moved on once more but he invited the two travellers to join him and head back to Rome before seeking out the papal court. After a journey that had taken some two months to complete, the two monks entered the city at the head of a grand procession of papal courtiers and no less than 17 cardinals. The group wound through the streets with great solemnity towards the greatest of all the pilgrimage sites, St Peter's itself. Simon had not visited Rome before, and so they spent a few days taking stock of the ancient, if rather decrepit, grandeur of the city.

Rome had fallen on hard times when the popes left for Avignon, and much of the city had slowly corroded into a state of ruin and decay. Alongside the ancient relics of the early Christian saints and the remnants of imperial Rome enclosed within the loop of the Tiber, the city that the Englishmen found had sheep grazing in the Circus Maximus whilst nearby the Coliseum was being dismantled stone by stone to provide building materials for local houses. When Brigit of Sweden spoke of Rome as a city whose "days are numbered... now the gates of Rome are deserted for those who guarded them have been led astray by avarice. The walls have been razed because they pay no heed when the souls of men perish"[xii] she was talking literally as well as figuratively about the state of the city. With Urban's return to Italy, a great effort was being made to restore the city and its buildings to their former glory. As the English party toured the great pilgrim churches and admired the classical remains of Rome, they were enjoying a city that was still in the early stages of its renovation.

Eventually rumours reached Rome that the papal court had finally settled at Montefiascone, just to the north of Rome. The two English monks took their leave and made their way back along the road to Viterbo, past the ancient volcano of Mount Cimino, and on to Montefiascone beyond. Rising 1,500 feet out of the fertile volcanic soils of Lazio, the town of Montefiascone casts a striking image of grandeur onto the plain below. From far on the horizon the hazy outlines of the papal palace and cathedral merge in the summer heat into a surreal giant dominating the land around them.

Montefiascone is neither the largest nor grandest of the hill towns in the vicinity of Rome, but sitting as it does on top of a steep-sided hill, it enjoys an excellent defensive position. The long, steep road winds its way up from the plain following the line of the high ground to approach the city from the east. Montefiascone exists on three separate planes each higher than the last so that the traveller must move from one to the next as if he were ascending through Dante's spheres of paradise. The lower plane is surrounded by an outer wall that follows the contours around the acropolis on which the town is built. The walls enclose a haphazard collection of lopsided piazzas and houses crammed together in irregular patterns. The heart of this outer city is crushed between the citadel at the top of the hill from where the streets appear to run straight down the side of the hill, like water run off after a storm.

As the traveller ascends to the Piazza Vittorio Emanuele he is confronted by a new set of walls and the next plane. Here in the inner city the narrow streets and apartments of the papal courtiers cling to the sides of the volcanic peak. Finally a narrow track of hairpin bends takes the weary pilgrim to the third plane, the summit of the city and, fittingly, the lodgings of the pope. Not so much a palace but a large fortress, the Rocca dei Papi straddles the summit with a walled courtyard, pleasure gardens and practical essentials, such as a well.

From this papal castle on top of the city the importance of the site becomes obvious. In uncertain times, with mercenary bands ranging across central Italy, strong walls and a clear view over the surrounding countryside were worth their weight in gold. The citadel gave the Pope a stunning (and strategically important) view out over Lake Bolsena to the north and out towards Mount Cimino to the south. Yet the most important aspect to the layout of Montefiascone was that in dangerous and unpredictable times, the Pope could defend himself against not just outsiders, but also against the citizens of Montefiascone themselves should they prove restless and rebellious subjects.

Just 100 kilometres north of Rome, Montefiascone was close enough for Urban to exert an influence on his erstwhile capital but far enough away to be safe from its fractious nobles and riotous populace.

A New Cardinal is blessed

Conditions in the town and particularly in the inner sanctum of the papal city were, to say the least, cramped. Huddled below the citadel, the papal courtiers, cardinals, clerks, advocates and nuncios were crammed into a community that is still quite small today. The heavily fortified papal palace dominated the skyline. The building was strictly functional, built of large stone blocks rising from the volcanic rock of the hill. The lower windows were narrow and designed with defence in mind. Only in the upper quarters, where Urban had his apartments, was there a little more concession to luxury, with timbered roofs and brick walls that were at one time plastered. Here Simon Langham was received by Urban, and next door in the grand domed cathedral of Montefiascone, on May 24, 1369 he was formally admitted to the Curia as the Cardinal of Canterbury.[xiii]

Montefiascone presented a quiet alternative to Roman life, and with three sets of city walls as protection Urban felt secure enough to establish the papal mint in the city. Yet even though he would stay here for nearly two years, the court never really had any sense of permanence or stability. Urban made return visits to Rome, but rarely stayed in the Eternal City for more than a few days at a time, and in April he had been forced to leave by a rioting mob. From the moment that the two Englishmen arrived in Montefiascone, the town was rife with rumours of Urban's departure, not just from Montefiascone but possibly that he would leave Italy altogether. It was a very disturbing situation, with the political landscape of central Italy spinning beyond Urban's control. Adam and Simon must have wondered what they had let themselves in for.

Not that the disturbed situation did not offer possibilities. With the Pope's court wallowing in a crisis of indecision, and the cities of the Papal States showing little inclination to obey their lord and master the Pope, the Holy Roman Emperor saw an opportunity. From the days of Charlemagne, Holy Roman Emperors had been intricately involved in Italian politics. Most of the governing class of the city states of central and northern Italy split into two parties, one pro Emperor (Ghibellines) and one pro Pope (Guelphs). The unrest of the 1370s offered the Emperor, Charles IV of Luxembourg, a perfect excuse to extend his influence over the Italian peninsula once more. The Emperor's agents started lobbying the cardinals to see if they might be sympathetic.

Other monarchs with a position of influence in Italy saw an opportunity to advance their own causes, selecting members of the papal court who they thought were most likely to be sympathetic to their interests. Being in the right place at the right time could be a very rewarding occupation for a Cardinal. By January 1370 William Daventry was able to write to Simon from Venice with some good news. Queen Joanna I of Naples, Fernando I, King of Portugal, and John V Palaeologus, Emperor of Constantinople, would offer large sums of money to the Cardinal of Canterbury if he would be prepared to work for their cause.[xiv] William's letter gives a glimpse of the unsettling court intrigue and the unstable politics that dominated Italy throughout the summer and autumn of 1369. Tempting as, no doubt, these offers were, in the end Simon chose not to take their money and to stay loyal to the one king he was trying to represent at the papal court: Edward III. He did not relish the prospect of another dispute with Edward, even from the relatively safe distance of Montefiascone.

In the meantime, Urban V was prevaricating. He had to face up to the reality that since his arrival in Italy he had proved totally unable to control the city of Rome either directly or even from the safety of Montefiascone. If the Pope could not maintain his authority over the Eternal City, then what was the point of staying in Italy at all? The Pope was a Frenchman, and the Italians always doubted the sincerity of the move he had made to bring the papal court back to Italy. They had mixed feelings about the return of the papal presence to Italy. On the one hand they welcomed the papacy to the throne of St Peter, the place they felt it belonged, but on the other hand they resented the close attentions of the papal tax collectors. The same mixed emotions greeted the rumours that were starting to circulate around the court in Montefiascone, rumours that said that Urban was preparing to return to Avignon.

A Certain John Wyclif

If Adam and Simon had hoped that they could distract themselves from the uncertainties of life in the papal court with the comforts of the Italian climate, and banish all thoughts of England under a pile of theological treatises, they were sadly mistaken. The first issue to cross their desks was that of John Wyclif. When we last came across Wyclif, Simon had just removed him from the headship of Canterbury Hall College in Oxford. In the period since the two Benedictines had left England, Wyclif had turned the tables and had all the monk scholars expelled from the college. It appeared that John Wyclif was minded to mount a direct challenge to the authority of the English Benedictines. He replaced the monks in Canterbury Hall with secular scholars, who dutifully showed their gratitude by electing Wyclif as warden of the college.[xv] As the college had originally been established, like Gloucester College, for the benefit of Benedictine monk scholars, this was a step too far for Simon and Adam. They were naturally drawn to the cause of their brother monks, and lobbied the Pope and the cardinals at the curia with the message that Wyclif was dangerous and needed to be curtailed. A long-running dispute then ensued, with both sides appealing to the papal court. The monastic orders had been investing in education to equip their monks with the expertise to take leading roles in the administration of Church and State alike. They were not about to meekly cave in and agree to give up their college to Wyclif. Adam lobbied hard against Wyclif, and eventually won the day. On May 27, 1370 Thomas Southam, another English Benedictine monk working at the curia, was authorised by the papal court to issue a bull instructing that the secular interlopers be removed from the college. The document was approved by Cardinal Simon and witnessed by Adam Easton, who was described as "venerable" and "a professor of the sacred pages".[xvi] It is not entirely clear what Adam had done to enhance his reputation to such an extent that he should now be considered a professor, but from this point on he was often to be referred to by this title.

Brigit of Sweden

If sorting out Wyclif offered the cardinal and his socius a digression, it could not ultimately distract them from the main talking point at the papal court, the move back to Avignon. By June 1370 the rumours of departure appeared to be vindicated when Urban V announced that, reluctantly, he had decided that the papal court would return to Avignon. The news brought the Swedish mystic Brigit rushing to Montefiascone. The daughter of a Swedish nobleman, Brigit was renowned for her saintly living, obsessive purity and her exemplification of Christian marriage. Above all, she was famed for her powers of prophesy and the divine revelations that she claimed to have received directly from the Virgin Mary.

Brigit was 67 when she came to Urban's court and she had two purposes in mind. The first was largely practical, to get papal blessing for the founding of a new order of nuns at the Swedish monastery of Vadstena. Brigit had, controversially, written her own set of rules to govern the life of her nuns and had claimed that the rules were dictated to her by the Virgin Mary herself. Ideally she wanted Urban to bless her rules as a model for other nunneries around Europe.

Her second purpose was to deliver a sinister message. The place of the pope was, in Brigit's mind at least, clearly at St Peter's in Rome, and it was vital that the initiative started by Urban should be allowed to come to its natural conclusion. Nothing less than a permanent return from the

Babylonian exile at Avignon was good enough for Brigit. Of course Urban might have been tempted to laugh it off as the ravings of a mad woman, but Brigit was not finished. She had been granted a formal audience by Urban in the reception rooms on the upper floor of his fortified palace. Here she stunned the papal court by pronouncing that she had received a premonition from the Virgin Mary that Urban would die if he abandoned Italy for France.[xvii] The dramatic prophesy shocked the town, and left Urban discomforted but just as determined to return to Avignon. Brigit stayed in the papal court for three months and had at least two further audiences with Pope Urban during the period, each time hoping to change his mind.

Brigit's stay in the town left a deep impression on Adam. She was a charismatic woman of striking appearance, and the strict regime with which she ruled her life left a gaunt and haunting impression behind. Brigit had poor Latin, which made communication with the papal entourage difficult, but she travelled with a translator and intermediary, Alfonso of Jaen, a Spanish bishop (whom Adam would meet again[xviii] in very different circumstances). Alfonso seems to have befriended Adam during their time together in Montefiascone. In such a small town, full of narrow alleys and low houses in stone terraces, with the papal courtiers, lawyers and advocates all crammed within the walls of the inner city, it was impossible not to get to know the members of the court and their visitors over even a relatively short period of time. Brigit's dramatic visit to Montefiascone was bound to have an impact on the papal court, but Adam in particular never forgot his encounter with her, nor the force of her prophesy.

Brigit was undoubtedly strong-willed, and for a mediaeval woman unusually outspoken. On August 5 she finally got one of the things she had come for when Urban granted her by papal bull the right to found her convent at Vadstena. Perhaps he was prepared to go that far just to be rid of her. It must have been deeply disturbing for the Pope to cope with an elderly and eccentric woman wandering round the town prophesying his own imminent death. He might have been alarmed by her, he might have wanted to be rid of her, but it was not enough to persuade him to allow Brigit's nuns to have the right to follow a separate rule[xix] – whether or not he believed her claim that the Virgin Mary herself had dictated it in a dream. Nor was Urban open to persuasion on the subject of the return to France, for all Brigit's powerful presence and doom-laden prophesies. Once it was clear that his mind was made up she returned to Rome and shortly afterwards Urban made his own preparations to leave.

By the end of August 1370 the uncertainty surrounding the location of Urban's court had suddenly come to an end. At the end of months of intrigue and rumour, at least Simon and Adam now knew they would eventually be leaving for Avignon, the great city on the Rhone made rich by the papacy.

They were in for a shock.

In the event the two Benedictines would be leaving Montefiascone much sooner than they might have guessed, and for a different destination.

A Papal Peace Mission

Urban V may have been unwilling to stake his papacy on staying in Rome, but he was not without holy ideals of his own. He had long cherished the idea of a crusade to recapture the Holy Land, but the support of England and France was essential to make the project viable, and that support was unlikely unless the two kingdoms could be reconciled with each other. In 1369 the uneasy truce between the two sides appeared to have broken when Charles V resumed hostilities, and in August 1370 the Bishop of Limoges changed allegiance from England to France, taking his city with him. Urban feared that the war was about to flair up irreversibly, and he decided to send an embassy to the two kings in an attempt to agree a more lasting peace and to get agreement on a crusade. In the interests of being seen to be even handed, he chose one French cardinal, John de Dormans, the Cardinal of the Four Crowns, and Simon Langham, the only English cardinal at the curia, to head the delegation.

Simon decided to take Adam with him so as to have available his skills in advocacy during the negotiations and his abilities in the drafting of legal documents. They were joined by another Englishman, Roger de Freton, a papal auditor. The party left Montefiascone with instructions to head for northern France and start negotiations as soon as they arrived.

As they began their journey, a shocking event took place in France that confirmed the Pope's forebodings. On the September 19 the Black Prince sacked Limoges and massacred its civilians, an atrocity that shocked the courts of Western Europe. A response from the French King now looked certain and a major war between England and France inevitable.

A Prophesy Comes True

Oblivious to the gathering storm clouds in western France, on September 5 Urban's court reached the port of Corneto on the Tuscan coast. Here they embarked for Avignon in a fleet of galleys thoughtfully, if rather tactlessly (from the point of view of the Italians), provided by the French King, Charles V. The journey proved to be quiet and uneventful, and before long the dark ravings of the Swedish prophetess had been forgotten. By September 24, still unaware of the butchery at Limoges, Urban V was reinstated in the papal palace of the city he had longed to return to. Life for the papal court returned to normal and all thoughts of Italy faded amongst the comforts, pleasures and good living of Avignon. For the cardinals, many of whom were French, this was figuratively and literally a true homecoming. The troublesome Romans with their mobs and riots, the perennial family conflict between the Orsini and Colunna, all seemed a very long way off. Urban was not a young man, but he had been in good health and after Rome the relatively mild climate of Avignon, seemed to suit him. Freed from the cares of ruling over Italy at close quarters, and reminded once again of the luxuries of Avignon, he seemed delighted with the move back.

Suddenly in the middle of November the Pope fell gravely ill. In vain he vowed meekly to anyone who would listen that he would return to Rome if only God willed that he might recover.[xx] On December 19 he died.

It was less than three months since Urban had left Italy, and Brigit's prophesy had come true in spectacular fashion. Although the mediaeval world put great store by prophesies and soothsayers, and signs were seen and interpreted with regularity, more often than not they were wrong. There was an art to making ambiguous predictions, or adjusting them to fit after the facts of an event had become more clear. Admittedly with so many prophets and sayings at hand, it was inevitable that some would prove to be right, but it was a rarity for a prophesy such as Brigit's, which was so direct and unambiguous, to be borne out by immediate events. Adam was clearly impressed at her determination to persuade Urban to stay in Italy, but coincidence or not, the accuracy of her prediction was truly shocking. It could only point to some form of unimpeachable provenance for the virtues and powers of the Swedish mystic.

The death of Urban left the papal negotiating team in limbo. Heading for northern France, they could have little prospect of making progress with the peace process until the new pope had been appointed. Whilst neither Simon nor John were likely candidates for the papacy, both wanted to exercise their influence over the outcome and take their part in the conclave to elect a new pope. The party hurried back to Avignon, where the two cardinals arrived in good time to enjoy some influence over the selection of yet another Frenchman, Pierre Roger de Beaufort. Cardinal Beaufort was chosen by the curia on December 30, 1370 and took the name Gregory XI. His official coronation was held on January 5, 1371 and he quickly moved to reassure Simon and John that he wished them to carry on with the good work that Urban had given them. On January 11 Gregory wrote to the Archbishop of Canterbury[xxi] to announce that the mission would continue, and all help should be given to his legates in this matter. The cardinals were still in Avignon on March 7,[xxii] when they also wrote to the Archbishop of

Canterbury to seek his support. No-one was in a great hurry to leave, and there was still a real concern about the level of commitment they could expect from the warring parties. Eventually the negotiating team headed north for Flanders in the middle of March, but without Adam. As head of Simon's household he stayed behind in Avignon to look after the ceremonial duties associated with Gregory's coronation. More importantly, he had to attend to the task of collecting the coronation gift that Gregory announced for each of his cardinals. This was a very substantial sum, perhaps in recognition of the faith the cardinals had put in him, perhaps in recognition that he would need their support in the future. Adam accepted the sum of 3,000 florins on behalf of Cardinal Simon and a further, though smaller, gift for himself. Having collected the cash on March 26, 1371 in Avignon[xxiii] and after making suitable banking arrangements, Adam headed off to rejoin the diplomatic mission.

An Impossible Task

Cardinals Simon and John were not making a lot of progress. On April 26 Gregory wrote once more to Archbishop William Whittlesey in the hope that he might use his influence with Edward to get him to meet with his delegation.[xxiv] Whittlesey wrote back, making all the right noises, but his ability to influence Edward was, in reality, somewhat limited. Throughout April and into May the negotiating team were obliged to loiter in the territory of Louis, Count of Flanders, hoping to gain a reception in either Paris or Calais.

The mission was always going to face an uphill struggle. By 1371 Edward III had lost most of the gains of his early reign, and the only English-controlled territory remaining on the French mainland was the strip of land around Calais and the old Plantagenet lands of Aquitaine and Anjou. Inevitably he wanted to get back as much land as possible before signing a peace treaty, and he was in no mood to agree terms now. By the time Adam joined the delegation in May 1371 it had just arrived in Paris. Here Charles V received them, but without the warmth and affection with which he had greeted Adam and Simon in 1369. The French had been successful in the war against Edward and saw an opportunity to drive the English off the continent altogether, so Charles was in no mood for peace either. On May 6 the cardinals wrote once again to Archbishop Whittlesey, asking for assistance in making their mission successful. The letter was countersigned by the Bishop of Paris, Aimeri de Maignac, to emphasise the cross-border appeal the Church was making to bring the warring parties to the negotiating table. Adam, who was described as "circumspectus viris magiis" and "doctore in sacra theologia," witnessed the document.[xxv] The signatories also reminded Whittlesey that the Pope's instruction was that they should receive as much help with their expenses and accommodation from the English Church as they might need. In principle at least, the Church was a multinational organisation in which expenses of officials away from headquarters could be paid for in any country across Europe adhering to the Roman Church. At the time it seems that Whittlesey let discretion get the better part of valour and he declined to reply to the papal delegation, hoping to get some direction in the matter from his King. If his register is to be believed, he didn't write back until October 26, by which time the cardinals had already received greetings from the King. At least by delaying in this way until the King made the first move there was less danger of the Archbishop incurring the royal anger.

The tactics employed by Gregory's delegation would have been very similar to those used in modern diplomacy. An initial meeting would be attempted with both sides to try to establish what they actually wanted and what they might be prepared to trade off. The legates would then retire for a few weeks to digest the difficulty of the task and try to identify the common ground and work on the areas of likely compromise. They would then attempt to bring the parties back to the negotiating table and put to them a proposal for compromise.

As soon as they had finished their audience with Charles, the party moved on from Paris towards Calais to have their initial meeting with Edward to find out what might persuade him to negotiate. To their surprise Edward refused them permission to enter English territory. They were met outside Calais by Sir Arnold Sauvage and Sir Hugh Segrave, who refused them safe conduct throughout the month of May and into the early summer. Eventually Edward stopped stalling and allowed Simon and the English members of the delegation (though it appears neither John nor any of the French) into England.

Adam had some useful skills to offer the world of diplomacy. Ziegelbauer, the historian of the Benedictines, noted that he was a steganographer (or code maker/breaker)[xxvi] of some considerable renown. With his love of classical texts and breadth of linguistic ability, he was well placed to understand the code maker's art. There are glimpses of Adam's interest in codes and encryption throughout his life, and here in the shadowy diplomatic world he had an opportunity to develop and refine his techniques. At least working on codes would have relieved the boredom of sitting around waiting for an audience with the two kings and their representatives.

Simon and Adam were based in Canterbury throughout October and November, where they were entertained by Archbishop Whittlesey. Almost inevitably the Wyclif controversy at Oxford raised its ugly head once more.

They received a letter from the monks at Oxford reporting that, even though the Pope had given judgement in their favour, Wyclif and his followers were simply ignoring it.[xxvii] Any possibility of the Church moving to suppress the troubles that he brought on their college was stalled by events. The two Black Monks had barely been informed of the Wyclif problem when the King announced that he would receive them. In November, having put off the party for as long as he felt prudent, a meeting was fixed between the legation, Edward and Charles for March 1, 1372.[xxviii] This arrangement gave both sides further time to grab as much territory as they could in the intervening period, but for the Church it still represented progress. By November 1371 Simon and Adam were heading back to Calais. At last the two men had made an impact on proceedings, and as they journeyed back they must have felt a sense of relief that the mission was starting to bear fruit. For Adam, the return to France proved to be a watershed. As he boarded the boat and set sail for Calais, Adam looked back at the English coastline for the last time in his life. He was just 45 years old.

After nearly a year of false starts, being ignored, stalled and generally being given the run-around, at last it seemed as if there was progress to report. Simon wrote to Pope Gregory in Avignon to tell him of the planned meeting. The delegations duly assembled at Calais to meet Simon and John on March 1. Gregory wanted to leave nothing to chance. An anxious Pope wrote to all the parties, including both the cardinals in his own delegation, urging them to make sure they attended on the set day. Reinforcements started to arrive as the serious business of the negotiations got under way. A small army of clerks would be needed to help draft up the documentation of any peace treaty. Roger de Freton was joined by William de Barton, who was given a safe conduct to Calais on March 3[xxix] and Adam had at least one clerk working for him. This was probably Richard de Croxton[xxx] (described as a clerk of Ely), who was a signatory to the letter that the cardinals sent from Paris to the Archbishop of Canterbury and was working with the papal party throughout this period.[xxxi] We do know that the praecentor of Ely, following Gregory's instruction, paid out 40 pence towards the expenses of an unnamed clerk's work at Michaelmas 1372,[xxxii] although this may have been a back payment dating to the work that Richard had done with Adam and the papal entourage during 1371.

At last everything was in place to ensure a serious attempt could be made to bring the war to an end. The two kings had run out of excuses and of steam, and if the parties were to meet as planned, there was finally a chance that a deal could be done.

Gregory the Unhelpful

As the delegates gathered outside Calais ready to start bargaining, two new papal envoys arrived. At first no-one knew why they were there. Perhaps they had just come to monitor events and report back. Yet the two men were senior prelates: William, Bishop of Carpentras, and William, Viscount of Turenne. These were not the humble clerks the pope might have sent along for such a routine task. It soon became apparent that the two Williams had the normal papers of introduction from the Pope, and Gregory had decided to add them to the negotiating team.

Everyone was stunned.

Had Simon and John been sacked, or were the two Williams trying to con their way into the negotiations, motivated by the possibility of personal gain? In the end it turned out to be more oversight than deliberate slight. The Pope had simply not thought to inform Simon and John in advance that two new negotiators had been sent to strengthen the team. The cardinals had little choice but to accept the newcomers as part of the mission, and then wonder what on Earth to do with them. It is hard to see what Gregory hoped to gain from a move that unsettled his own team as much as the other delegations. If the cardinals were puzzled, the two warring monarchs must have been delighted. Having finally got to the point at which they could not, with good reason, delay joining the talks any longer, the whole process had been thrown into a state of confusion. If Edward and Charles needed any excuse for prevarication the Pope had handed it to them on a plate. The new delegates had to meet with all the parties before they could add anything to the discussion, and yet it seems that neither man brought anything with them in the way of new ideas. To make matters even worse, the two Williams had brought a request from the Pope for the English Church to levy a papal subsidy. Gregory was trying to force a peace with one hand whilst begging for cash with the other.

If that wasn't complicated enough, the English were still at war with Flanders, and the area around Calais where the peace talks were being held was right on the edge of the war zone. The papal delegation based around the small cathedral city of Theroanne were in constant danger of being caught up in the fighting. Peace between England and Count Louis of Flanders had not really been on Gregory's agenda, mainly as the Count could offer no substantial help with the planned crusade. Yet without the Count of Flanders on board, the talks between England and France were always in danger of being disrupted by the proximity of a live conflict. A peace was eventually negotiated between King Edward and Count Louis, which at least secured a stable background against which the talks could be reconvened. Yet that treaty had barely been concluded when a French army captured the city of La Rochelle. Edward responded by raising an army and waiting for favourable winds to embark them for La Rochelle. The peace process had broken down.

Simon Gives Up

By April the papal delegation were still in the Calais area, at Freton in the diocese of Theroanne, wondering how best to proceed.[xxxiii] In the circumstances the best that they could do was try for a new meeting date and hope that nothing too destructive would happen before then. Reluctantly, the parties agreed to reconvene in Bruges in January 1373, but it was an agreement reached without enthusiasm or conviction. At least in choosing the month of January the cardinals could rely on the fact that the rival armies would be in camp for winter. Simon and John would have some time to try to make the negotiations come to something before the spring campaigning season got under way. This time they also had the support of the Count of Flanders, who, having made his peace with Edward, seems to have made a genuine effort to broker some sort of settlement. Despite the goodwill of the Count and the cardinals, the peace talks broke up after a few weeks.[xxxiv] Once again the English and French kings showed their preference for sorting things out on the battlefield.

By May 1373 Simon could see that he was getting nowhere, and that neither side was really interested in the peace talks. He asked permission to abandon the mission and the Pope reluctantly agreed, commending him for the hard work he had put in, but clearly disappointed that he had given up on the task.[xxxv]

The first half of 1373 must have been a tedious time for Adam. The peace talks might have been interesting if they had started to get going, but moving around the countryside outside Calais with little opportunity for study or even scholarly contemplation must have been tedious. His skills, as a scholar, a jurist or even a negotiator, had barely been called upon. He must have set off back to the papal court at Avignon with a feeling of relief. Neither Adam not his boss had yet managed to have the time to enjoy the life of the papal courtier to the full. When they returned to Avignon, in their different ways, that is precisely what they did.

Chapter 5

Avignon

We shall through patience share in the sufferings of Christ that we may deserve to share in his kingdom.

Babylon!

To just about every Christian in Europe, with the obvious exception of the French King, the move of the papacy to France seemed to be a kind of Babylonian exile. And if it was a Babylonian exile then the city of Avignon represented Babylon itself.

Babylon was doing rather well. The great city that Adam and Simon returned to in 1373 was one of the wealthiest in Europe. Throughout the 14th Century Avignon had gone through a building boom financed by the money that the Church had brought to the city. And at its heart, symbolically and literally, was the new papal palace. It was a building designed to impress and express authority. Towering, sheer cliffs of walls dominate the skyline right across the flood plains of the river Rhone even today. Started in 1316 under Boniface VIII and taking nearly 60 years to build, the palace had only been completed three years before Adam and Simon arrived back in Avignon. It was certainly impressive, but it was only part of a grand design that featured the renovation of the Romanesque cathedral, the rebuilding of much of the city centre and the encircling of all this by new defensive walls. Much of the city that Adam knew can still be seen today, in particular the old centre from the palace to the market squares, and to the north west the famous 12th Century bridge pointing helplessly towards the town of Villeneuve on the opposite bank. All have been preserved by the city's slide towards irrelevance following the departure of the popes.

Yet at its height in the 14th Century, Avignon was one of the great cities of Europe. Under the control of the popes the city flourished as the wealth of the Church poured into the papal treasury. The pope had such a vast hoard of money to manage that a false floor was created in the Palais du Papes just to conceal the treasury. The wealth of Avignon enabled successive popes to create an environment of great luxury and hold ever grander courts. The vast wealth of the Church, the pope and the cardinals ensured that the capital city of the popes became a magnet for a growing army of artisans, small traders and assorted hangers-on, all extracting a decent living supplying the court. Before the arrival of the Black Death, Avignon had a population of between 50,000 and 60,000 (about the same size as London). The great wealth of the papacy in Avignon led to the creation of ever more cardinals to help administer and control it. In the 13th Century barely a handful of cardinals were created during the reign of each pope, the 15 created by Innocent IV being exceptional. In the 70 years that followed 15 was the minimum, and John XXII actually appointed 28 new cardinals. As the number of cardinals grew, they in turn brought their own courts with servants, legal experts and associates looking for positions in the Church.

The city by the Rhone had plenty to recommend it. It enjoys a pleasant Mediterranean climate, cooled by the fast-flowing river of blue-green glacial waters gushing from the Alps down to the Mediterranean coast. Without the extremes of oppressive heat so characteristic of high summer in Rome, and supplied with an abundance of food and good wine from a fertile countryside, the city seemed to be a paradise on Earth.

The French kings in particular found the new home of the papacy much to their taste, not least because of the amount of influence they could exert over their new neighbour. Throughout the Avignon years all the popes were to be French. As the numbers of cardinals grew so the number of French cardinals became a much higher proportion of the papal court than had previously been the case. In fact there were so many French cardinals that a separate faction within the Papal court evolved around those who came from the Poitiers region.

The Machinery behind the Money

The papal administration in Avignon was every bit as vast and impressive as the papal palace and it grew with the size of the court. A sophisticated machine designed to hoover up the wealth of Christendom and channel it into the papal treasury, during the course of the 14th Century it evolved into a complex structure split into two main departments: the Apostolic Chancery, headed by the vice chancellor, and the Apostolic Chamber, headed by a treasurer and chamberlain.

The Chancery attended to petitions from across the Catholic Christian world, covering everything from hopefuls seeking benefices to individuals wanting to have their own private confessor, to carry a portable altar, or asking for indulgence at the hour of their death. To hear petitions, many on relatively small matters, from across the whole of Europe, required a massive administrative effort. To meet that need the structure of the Chancery had a Byzantine complexity that featured small armies of clerks and clerics with different, yet often overlapping, roles to play. With so many involved in the administration it was difficult for an outsider to know where to start. To help the uninitiated find their way through the maze of bureaucracy, an array of lawyers or proctors established themselves at the papal court. These men hired out their services to distant petitioners, offering to help ensure that their petition passed smoothly through the administrative hierarchy and that it was eventually looked upon favourably. Remarkably, the system seems to have worked, and there are few records of complaints of petitions being lost in the system or of not being responded to.

The Apostolic Chamber was responsible for raising taxes levied on Church property. The chamber also raised revenues on benefices whose incumbents owed their appointment to the Pope (this could amount to as much as one third of the total income of the benefice) as well as taking all the income from vacant benefices (the "fructus interclares") where the provision to the benefice was in the gift of the pope.

In addition there was a third chamber, the Camera of the College of Cardinals. This was run by a treasurer or "Cardinal Camerarius", appointed jointly by the Pope and the sacred college of cardinals. During the time in which the curia had been based in Avignon, in fact ever since 1289, it had become the habit of the pope to distribute half of the income of the Church between those cardinals resident at the curia.[i] The main role of the Camera of the College of Cardinals was to manage that half of the Church's income due to the cardinals, and to ensure that it was divided fairly amongst those cardinals who qualified for a share.

The three chambers required substantial manpower to run them effectively. With every document having to be written out by hand, and multiple copies needed, the administration of the church was a labour-intensive business. If a cardinal and his courtiers found themselves in Avignon then they could expect to take part in the running of the papal administration. The legally trained courtiers frequently acted as auditors, notaries or proctors to the Apostolic Chancery either in a private or official capacity.

Of course the cardinals had the added incentive to be in Avignon to ensure that they got their fair cut of Church revenues from the Camerae.

A House Fit for a Cardinal

This was exactly the sort of work at which Adam and Simon might expect to spend their time after their return to the city during the summer of 1373. One of the first things that Adam learned on his arrival was that Thomas Brinton, his old colleague from Norwich and Oxford days, had visited Avignon that very February to receive papal blessing as the newly appointed Bishop of Rochester. It must have been a disappointment to discover that he had just missed his former colleague, and although they remained in touch until Brinton's death, the two would not see each other again.

There was little time to dwell on the matter, as there was work to be done. The cardinal and his socius started by searching the town to find a suite of buildings large enough and impressive enough to hold a cardinal's court. By the mid 14th Century there were a number of substantial buildings in Avignon that were used by various cardinals for this purpose. Simon set up house in one of these, the Livree de Auxerre (also known as Ancienne Livree de Viviers), a mansion house just behind the Palais des Papes on the Rue de Four, where the street joins the Place des Trois Pilats. Nothing is left of the house today, but all of the Avignon "livrees" were grand affairs. Often set back from the street behind high walls, the buildings enclosed verdant courtyards where the lords of the Church could relax and enjoy the fruits of their labours. Whatever else they might be, the livrees needed to be substantial. A cardinal might keep as large a court as a secular nobleman would, and studies of the court of Simon Langham[ii] show that he had somewhat in excess of 50 courtiers living in the mansion house. It was a fluid community, for while some would be permanent members of his household staff, others were simply "familiars" who would benefit from the Cardinal's sponsorship for either posts in the curia or perhaps for a living from which they could earn money.

After nearly three years in northern France, Simon had other good reasons for wanting to settle down in Avignon and establish his court. There were disadvantages of being on the road with a legation, other than the frustrations of dealing with intransigent kings such as Edward and Charles. The biggest and most obvious of these was financial. Remember that the cardinals in Avignon were given half of the income of the church to share amongst themselves. The cardinals, through the Cardinal Camerarius and his chamber, were accustomed to drawing their share of this income every year. These were large sums, as the curia could extract subsidies and taxes from across Christendom, as well as selling various forms of indulgencies, collecting the revenues of empty benefices and various fees for arranging appointments to benefices.

However, not every cardinal would get their share. Any cardinal not at the curia, whether on official papal business or not, would not be entitled to a share in the income. The intention was to encourage cardinals to serve the pope at the papal court rather than staying in their country of origin and perhaps being unduly influenced by their secular ruler. Although Simon had travelled to the papal court in 1368 and for the past three years had served Gregory faithfully as he tried to negotiate peace between England and France, he had nonetheless been absent from the court since 1370. He had missed out on the opportunity to accumulate a substantial amount of money. On his return to Avignon in 1373, he started to receive his share.

A Single European Currency

In addition to his annual share of the Church's income, Simon had other means by which he could accumulate substantial riches. As a senior churchman he could use his influence to obtain the rights to benefices and positions in the Church hierarchy back in England. In his time as cardinal he was appointed Vicar of Wearmouth (which he then exchanged to become Vicar of Somersham), Dean of Lincoln, and prebend of Wistow.[iii] Obviously he could not attend to the daily duties involved in any of these positions, so he hired a clerk to do the work for him for a nominal sum. Simon could then harvest the income from each post and pocket the difference. To collect money from these "livings", he had representatives or "proctors" in England. For example, in 1373, whilst Simon and Adam were still away on legation in Flanders, Thomas Southam drew up a deed[iv] "selling" the right to collect the earnings and profits for Simon of "omnia beneficia sua in Anglia" to William Palmer, canon of Derbeye. Out of the money collected, William was asked to send 1,360 marks to Simon, and pay over 30 marks to the poor and 30 marks for repairs and maintenance across the various benefices.

Once the money had been gathered, in came the vexed question of how to get hard cash from England to Avignon, for a cardinal who might be in England, Avignon or anywhere between the two. Mediaeval finance may have lacked many of the advantages of modern systems and electronic transactions, but it was nonetheless extremely sophisticated. Among Simon's papers are a number of financial documents that illustrate the complexity. One of these, a financial instrument drawn up for Simon in 1375, is pretty close to what we would today call a bill of exchange, even a sort of cheque. Simon's Flemish banker, Francis de Kyto, received 8,000 gold florins that had been collected by William Palmer from Simon's English livings. He agreed to pay over money up to the same value to Simon "on demand".[v] From the document supporting this transaction it is clear that Francis and his partners had offices with cash deposits in Avignon, London and Bruges (and the document also mentions that he had another office in Ghent). Bruges was an important transit point, a major port and one of the prime entry points to Europe from England. As such it was perfectly placed to handle transactions between England and the Continent, and as Francis also had branches in London and Avignon, his firm was well equipped to handle cash transactions between England and the capital city of the Church. The transactions that he undertook for Simon were not so very far removed from that conducted by a modern bank.

Financial transactions were helped by a system in which the money in day-to-day use was based on precious metal. Fixed units of currency, starting with the florin (the name was derived from the town of Florence) used exactly the same amount of precious metal in each coin. Although the names of the currencies varied across Europe and the florins, francs, marks and pounds of Adam's time were, until very recently, still in use across Europe, the coinage itself was based on a standard unit of measure in each country. 14th Century Europe had a monetary system that was both consistent and very close in concept to the modern single currency unit of the Eurozone. There were variations in the value of the florin or its equivalents, a result of the degree to which various rulers debased their coinage, substituting amounts of cheaper, base metals for pure gold, or simply 'clipping' it (shaving off pieces of each coin). For example, the treasury account for Gregory's coronation gift that Adam collected on Simon's behalf (see above) tells us that it was calculated on the basis of 4 francs being equal to 5 florins.[vi] Initially the franc (and indeed the pound) was a gold coin of the same weight and value as the florin and we should have expected that 5 francs would equal 5 florins. Only the debasement of the franc caused the variation in the exchange rate.[vii]

All the Avignon cardinals had such great wealth at their disposal that it paid to spread the risk. After all, banking families had been known to be destroyed by kings and nobles defaulting on their debts. Simon was extremely wealthy and Adam needed to be heavily involved in the management of his financial affairs, dealing with his various accounts and his bankers. Simon used several bankers to handle his affairs. As well as de Kyto, the Florentine family of Strozze worked on Simon's behalf. With offices in London and Avignon, they also wrote bills to transfer money for the cardinal, in one transaction alone in 1372 they received 20,000 florins from England[viii] and transferred it to the cardinal in Avignon. This was a vast sum of money when compared say, with the loan of just £32,000 that Henry V received from the City of London in 1415 for the campaign that led to Agincourt. In fact, by 1376 Simon was even in the slightly embarrassing position of being able to lend 6,000 florins to the Pope himself when Gregory needed help to finance his return to Italy.

Princes of the Church

Wealth on this scale gave Simon the wherewithal to maintain his growing court at Avignon. As the sole English cardinal at the curia, he acted as a conduit through which English clergy seeking to advance their careers might make themselves known at the papal court and perhaps, with Simon's favour, be appointed to a salaried role. Some, like Adam, would have received a salary from Langham for his position as socius. Others, such as Thomas Southam, a contemporary of Adam's from Oxford, were salaried members of Simon's staff but lived elsewhere. Whilst still others, such as Robert de Susted, stayed at the Livree but financed themselves by gaining the income of benefices back in England with Langham's support, the Rectory of Willingham in Susted's case.

Ensconced in the Livree de Auxerre, just a short walk from the papal court, Simon Lnagham's court offered riches and easy living. Simon and Adam, both Benedictines serving the Church, enjoyed the lifestyle of princes of the Church in Avignon, a city famed for its excesses. Their calling as Black Monks did not get in the way of the opulent lifestyle of the cardinals and their courtiers. It was certainly not an existence of abstinence.

The problems of excess had become so embarrassing that twice in the 14th Century the Pope had tried to curb the excesses of the cardinals by trying to limit the amount they ate! In 1316 John XXII laid down strictures that there could be no more than two meat dishes served at a meal. It wasn't that tough a regime, however, as he went on to suggest that a single dish could comprise two kinds of animal or bird if it were boiled and three if it were roasted. Unless of course it was to be game or wildfowl in which case other dishes might be added. A fish dish might contain many different types and preparations of fish, but only counted as one dish as long as they were all served together.[ix] Given that this was supposed to be an attempt to rein back on the existing behaviour of the cardinals, they must have been tucking into mountains of food beforehand. Nor did John's regulation have much impact, for we find Innocent VI trying to implement a similar bull in 1357. The fact that Innocent found it necessary to add a prohibition on the cardinals feasting with each other suggests that Avignon was turning into a gourmands' dining club by the middle of the 14th Century.

When it came to drinking wine, John proffered no restriction or regulation, but recommended the common practice of withdrawing from the table to take wine and spices. Innocent added that familiars when dining with another cardinal should not drink wine at a set table. Worthy sentiments indeed but there is little evidence to suggest that much heed was paid to them.

The households of the cardinals, full of servants, lawyers and familiars, had grown as bloated as the cardinals' stomachs. Innocent decided to try to regulate the size of each cardinal's household as well as legislating on their meals. He suggested that no household should be in excess of 25 souls, and in passing reminded his cardinals of John's exhortation of no more than two meat dishes per meal. Given that Simon Langham, just 20 years later, had close to double the number of courtiers recommended by Innocent, it seems safe to assume that these rules too were largely ignored.

It was impossible to escape the overwhelming impression that Avignon was a debauched society in which cardinals and their courts indulged themselves in one long bout of feasting and drinking. Not perhaps that most perfect model that the court of God's representative on Earth might wish to promote.

Others Have Noticed, Too

The Avignon years were kind to the cardinals, and the Church at large was also making a good living. Anything and everything was up for sale, from relics to the rights to benefices, and that was before taking account of the tithes and clerical taxes that the Church could pull in. The officials of the Church were growing fat on the proceeds. And with riches came corruption, spiritual neglect and an emphasis on human comforts. It was not just the Church that was conspicuously wealthy. The tradesmen and suppliers of Avignon grew rich attending to the whims of the cardinals. The obvious wealth and comfort of the papal court, and the venality of the citizens of Avignon who attended on it, drew criticism from around Europe, and, as the 14th Century wore on, that criticism became ever more vocal. Petrarch had several benefices from which he derived the comfortable living that gave him the luxury of having enough free time to be able to write. That did not prevent the old hypocrite from complaining vociferously about the wealth of the cardinals and the papal court at Avignon. He attacked the system by which the Church had turned itself into a financial institution at the expense of the cure of souls. Chaucer was no innocent either, drawing his livelihood from sinecures awarded to him by the King rather than the Church but the principle was much the same. However, by drawing attention to some of the Church's more infamous behaviour he assured himself of popularity at court and in the country at large. In "The Pardoner's Tale" our hero, the Pardoner, a minor cleric, has a bag of pig bones for sale, which he is passing off to the faithful as the bones of a saint. In "The Shipman's Tale" Chaucer returned to the popular theme of immorality amongst the clergy by having a monk provide sexual comfort to a merchant's wife during her husband's long voyages overseas.

Others raised complaining voices from the very capital of the Church itself. Whilst sharing the comfortable life of Avignon, Dante felt moved to write to the Italian cardinals urging them to "lament over Rome as widowed and deserted... you in truth who are centurions of the first rank of the church militant in neglecting to guide the chariot of the crucified along the well known course have swerved from the way.... you whose duty it was to give light to the flock following you through the forest of this pilgrimage, have brought it with you to the precipice.. you who sell doves in the temple where in bartering for those things that are priceless, you have made them venal to your dishonour".[x]

Yet perhaps the least tainted of the criticism came from within the Church hierarchy itself. Thomas Brinton, Adam's old friend from Norwich and Oxford and now the Bishop of Rochester, was moved angrily to denounce the Roman curia that neither "refuse or spurn gold... Nothing is so closed that it cannot be opened with gold, nothing too hidden that with the influence of coins it can be made public. With gold bishoprics are bought and souls are lost".[xi] Brigit of Sweden, the angry prophetess who had so impressed Adam at Montefiascone, had plenty to say on the venality of the church administration. Her motivation for begging Urban to stay in Rome was driven by her disgust of the venal ways the church had fallen into whilst in Avignon. But if Brigit thought the Church was better off in Rome, Boccaccio had plenty more to say about that. In "The Decameron" he has a Jewish merchant visit Rome where he discovers that the Pope and his cardinals "without distinction of rank they were all sunk in the most disgraceful lewdness, sinning not only in the way of nature but after the manner of the men of Sodom, without any restraint of remorse or shame, in such sort that, when any great favour was to be procured, the influence of the courtesans and boys was of no small moment." Moreover he found them "one and all gluttonous, wine-bibbers, drunkards, and next after lewdness, most addicted to the shameless service of the belly, like brute beasts".[xii]

Nor were these simply cries of complaint from the educated, literary classes of mediaeval Europe. The commoners could not fail to notice either. After all, as they looked up at the stained glass windows and the paintings of Judgement Day what did they see? Overfed clerics wandering around with bags of gold? Salvation for a wealthy and indolent Church whose members were more focused on their own comfort than the spiritual needs of their flock? Where were the gaunt bodies of the fasting, kindly and godly men? Where were the martyrs to the cause of Christ and the model lives of ascetics setting a Christian example? Certainly not in Avignon, and in none too many of the local churches of Christian Europe for that matter. When critics of the Church and reformers of John Wyclif's ilk took aim at a target for their missives, they did not have to look far for ammunition.

Adam Makes Himself Busy

This was the state of the institution at which Adam now found himself at the heart. He was certainly no saint, but he was a pragmatist and for the most part stood aloof from the vices and corruption in evidence all around him. An astute and well-educated monk, he quickly settled into the courtly life of Avignon and started making himself useful in the various Church courts. As he began to find his own way around the capital city of the papacy, he might also have taken the opportunity to pay his respects to one of his early patrons, and his sometime adversary, William Bateman. The old Bishop of Norwich had died in Avignon in 1355 and was buried in the cathedral next door to the Palais des Papes.

At Avignon Adam started to gain recognition beyond his role as socius at the court of Cardinal Simon. In September 1375 the Pope allowed him the right to have his own confessor, a privilege that suggests he was starting to live his life with a measure of independence from his cardinal patron, and Simon appears to have encouraged his protégé to take advantage of the opportunities that came his way.

Aside from paid employment with his current patron, Simon, Adam acted as an unofficial representative of the English Black Monks to the curia. He had maintained his connections with the senior ranks of the Black Monks since his Oxford days and his very first mission to Rome in 1367. The English Benedictines had already found Adam a useful advocate during the difficulties caused by Wyclif over Canterbury Hall in Oxford. With his salary now being paid from Simon's household, Adam could offer the English Benedictines a man at the heart of papal power without the inconvenience of having to pay for someone to represent them. It was a valuable connection for Adam, and he remained a powerful champion of the Benedictine cause throughout his life. Later he would have good cause to be glad of this connection.

A man with Adam's education was always likely to be involved in matters aside from the routine administration of the papal courts. There was other work to do. Adam was asked to use his theological expertise to help with liturgical matters. He and two other masters were asked to look into the possibility of instituting a festival for the transfixion of the Virgin Mary[xiii]. This was no easy assignment. The concept of the Transfixion was that Mary's suffering as mother of Christ was seen to be aligned to Christ's suffering for the good of mankind. In effect this made Mary a co-sufferer for the good of mankind, but the subject matter was fraught with theological difficulty. The basic essence of Christianity was that there was just one God. As soon as theology had to grapple with two individuals who were perceived to have suffered for the salvation of mankind, the explanations became tricky and potentially open to accusations of heresy. As in later years, the curia selected Adam for some of the more difficult theological tasks in recognition of his reputation for great learning. On this occasion, the text was never finished and no copies of it have survived. Not surprisingly the festival was never blessed by Gregory, and his successor Urban VI showed little appetite for the project. Nonetheless, the Transfixion is a good example of the type of work that Adam performed for the curia and is an indication of the regard in which his talents as a theologian were held.

Life in Avignon was not always a pleasant routine of stately Church functions and exercises in intellectual curiosity punctuated by luxurious banquets. In 1374 the whole region around Avignon was ravaged by a major plague epidemic. The pestilence swept through southern France barely a year after Adam and Simon returned. Although both men survived, the outbreak was severe, a large number of citizens perished, and law and order broke down completely. In the confusion and near-anarchy that followed, Simon wrote back to Westminster that "there is now pressing danger in the Roman Court from the epidemic, it does not seem to us wise that money should be sent to us at present; and so we are writing to William Palmer, our proctor, that the money due to us be deposited in your church at Westminster to be kept there by you till we send for it. And we earnestly ask you to be so good as to arrange quickly this matter with the said William that our wishes in the matter may be carried out... Written in haste at Avignon on the 15th April 1374".[xiv]

A Scholar in Hebrew

Once calm returned, the atmosphere in Avignon was entirely in keeping with the scholarly life that Adam had become used to in Oxford. After a long period spent on the roads of northern France and Flanders away from his books and the opportunity for quiet reflection and thought, Adam was grateful for the chance to return to the life of a scholar. The area around Simon's court in the Livree de Auxerre was a quiet part of the city of Avignon. It is near the northern stretch of the city wall, which follows the line of the river Rhone, and the buildings benefit from a cool afternoon breeze from the river. Today the streets are still quiet at any time of day, and feel a world away from the commercial heart of Avignon just a couple of hundred yards up the road. The Palais des Papes, which towers over the whole city, is clearly visible from the end of the Rue de Four but manages to seem distant and remote. The streets around the Livree were mostly residential, and the atmosphere must have been comforting for two men whose formative years had been spent as Benedictine monks. Indeed, the quiet atmosphere of contemplation may have inspired Adam to think once more about furthering his education.

Already a leading scholar well versed in Greek, Latin and Scholastic learning, the central role of the biblical texts had excited his curiosity. How had the precise words in the Bible, which after all were originally in Hebrew, come to be represented in the Latin Vulgate Bible of his day?

The Vulgate Bible relied upon a standard Latin translation from the Hebrew that was little altered since the time of St Jerome, who had authored a translation at the end of the 4th Century. Adam had already gained a limited working knowledge and understanding of Hebrew during his time at Oxford, when he had taken his first steps with this project by re-examining the Book of Kings, but by a happy coincidence Avignon possessed one of the largest communities of Jews in Christian Europe.

The attitude of the papacy to the Jews was strangely at odds with that which might be expected from a state run by the head of a rival religion. The Jews in Avignon were respected as scholars and they were welcome as citizens, although it is true that they were only permitted to live in two areas of the city, they were closely watched, and did not enjoy all the privileges of their gentile fellows. Even so, it seems odd that the Pope felt able to reach an accommodation with the Jews when the leaders of nearly every secular state across Christendom had thrown them out.

Adam made the most of the opportunity and set about making himself busy learning and perfecting his knowledge of Hebrew and debating with the Jewish scholars of Avignon the usage and translation of the Hebrew words in the Old Testament. The two areas of Avignon where the Jews had been allowed to settle were the Quai de la Ligne, around a street known today as Rue de la Vieille Juiverie, and towards the centre of the city in the area around the Rue Jacob. Both were in easy walking distance of the Livree de Auxerre, and we can imagine Adam making a habit of a morning walk through the Jewish Quarter to meet and debate with the scholars before taking the short walk to the Palais des Papes to attend to the formal business of the day at the curia.

In a relatively tolerant atmosphere, there was little stigma attached to Adam and his free association with the Jewish community of Avignon. Over the next three years Adam came to be recognised as one of the leading experts in Hebrew of his generation. Moreover, Adam seems to have genuinely empathised with the Jews and enjoyed their company, and in later years he would write in support of them. It is interesting that exactly at the same time as Adam was fraternising with the Jewish community at Avignon, Thomas Brinton was preaching the virtues of Jewish attitudes from the pulpit of Rochester Cathedral. Brinton noted that the Jews were far more true to their faith in observing holy festivals and far more concerned with giving alms to the poor than the Christian communities.[xv] The fact that both men were unusual in their attitude towards the Jewish faith and community (to say nothing of the role each played in condemning Wyclif) suggests they remained in close touch during this period.

A Revolutionary Approach

Peter Lombard, St Augustine and Thomas Aquinas were the authoritative authors of their day, and all relied heavily on referencing their arguments back to the scriptures. The Bible was the one document that the Scholastics viewed as beyond reproach, the focal point of learning and the one source of facts and truth. As the arguments over the interpretation of the Bible became more intense, it seemed to Adam to be more important to find out if the correct words had been used in the first place. The Scholastic approach had created methods for working with some of the more difficult elements of Bible study. It was all very well drawing up rules to explain away the apparent contradictions in the Bible and to interpret some of the more esoteric bits, but what if the words in Latin were simply wrong? Was there not a danger of incorporating unreliable and corrupt rhetoric and incorrect understanding into standard learning of the day? Adam reasoned that it was essential to know that the Bible had been accurately rendered into Latin.

Brother Easton discovered that even the great authorities of the Scholastic era, the finest of original thinkers, had not sought out the original text of the Bible but had themselves relied on the translations of others. What if those translations were inaccurate? Surely the entire foundation of their logic and argument was in danger of crumbling? The desire to provide an accurate basis for Scholastic study drove Adam to his task.

As he developed his knowledge and understanding, both of the Hebrew language and of the Old Testament texts, he acquired Hebrew books for his personal library, including a copy of David Kimhi's "Sepher Hashorashim",[xvi] a sort of Hebrew dictionary. Adam had a big project in mind, one that had occupied his thoughts since his first days in Oxford, where the opportunities were limited and his lack of linguistic knowledge probably restricted his progress. The project he referred to was nothing less than a complete re-casting of the Old Testament from Hebrew into Latin. Later in life he described how he had planned and worked at the task for more than 20 years,[xvii] testimony if any were needed to the determination with which he was capable of seeing a project through to completion.

The process of playing with religious texts was fraught with danger, and it is easy to forget that the very act of translating the Bible into English in the 14th Century would have been tantamount to heresy. Providing the text of religion uninterpreted to the common and uneducated man was considered to be dangerous. Not only did it remove the monopoly of the religious scholars to interpret the scripture, but it could, in the view of the Church, lead to all kinds of misunderstandings and false conclusions on the part of the uneducated and unguided. It was far better, in the eyes of the Church, to preserve the sacred texts in the language of the responsible and educated, so the scholarly study of Church matters was carried out in Latin, the lingua franca of Catholic religion. As late as 1536, the magnificent William Tyndale perished at the stake for producing his English Bible. Adam needed to take care that the process he undertook could not be challenged as heretical in itself.

The exercise that he now undertook would prove to be highly topical. As kings and popes found themselves in constant conflict over the degree of authority each exercised over the other, so each in turn had their supporters among the scholars of the day, pouring over the Bible for texts that supported their own world view. The understanding of the text of the scriptures was starting to have far-reaching political consequences.

The Talmud and the Torah

To understand the significance of Adam's reworking of the Old Testament, we need to take a quick look at how the books of the Old Testament came down to us in the first place. The books of what Christians call the Old Testament are Hebrew in origin and split into two sections. The first five books, which the Jews believe were passed directly from God to Moses, are known as the Torah. The remaining books of the Old Testament are considered by tradition to be more or less contemporary accounts of what happened to the Jewish people after the time of Moses.

The Torah scrolls were written in Hebrew and in Jewish tradition may never be changed precisely because they contain the word of God. However, Hebrew is not a simple language to comprehend, and the Torah is not only written without punctuation but also with a musical notation to indicate the way in which it was to be chanted. This complicates considerably the process both of translation and interpretation.

The second set of Jewish writings constitutes the Talmud, which although they are not the word of God per se, are considered to be important in understanding the word of God. The Talmud gives guidance on how to read the Torah and get the true meaning behind the combinations of words and intonations. Even so, there is much room for interpretation, and Jewish words can have many meanings according to the way they are used.

To illustrate the point, consider just how diverse the meanings of an English word can be, given differences of pronunciation and usage. The word "close" might mean nearby, or the action of shutting, or perhaps a small street. To understand which meaning to ascribe to the word, we need to hear either the intonation or have a clear understanding of the context in which the word is written.

The great complexity of translating the Hebrew of the Torah, without punctuation and having to understand an obscure musical notation as well as the myriad different meanings that can be ascribed to specific words and roots, was a daunting exercise. When compared with the work of Wyclif and Tyndale who followed him, the task that Adam undertook was on a much higher intellectual plain. The Bible that Wyclif and his followers produced was revolutionary only because it was in English, not because of the nature and content of the material. His starting point was the accepted Bible of Catholic orthodoxy, the translation of St Jerome. If his source material turned out to be inaccurate or open to interpretation, it was of no concern to Wyclif. Many of the early reformers or Protestants failed to see the irony that in their enthusiasm for translating the Bible, they were relying entirely on the original interpretation of a 4th Century Catholic saint.

Unlike Wyclif, Tyndale worked from the original Hebrew, and to that extent produced something of far greater intellectual merit. Unfortunately he did not have the opportunity to seek out and debate the meanings with Jewish scholars, nor was he recognised as an exceptional scholar of Hebrew himself. This left him with a much more one-dimensional, literalistic view of the Torah with all the pitfalls that entails.

True Meaning

Adam was not interested in a mere translation, nor was it his intention to produce his work in English. He wanted nothing less than a complete reworking of the text based on an understanding of the original Hebrew, and he wanted to ensure that the full complexity of meaning was conveyed into the Latin edition.

Such a vast undertaking took up the majority of his time during the years that he spent in Avignon, and as far as we can tell he completed it whilst he was still living in the city. To achieve his purpose he needed to debate the semantics of the Hebrew, to understand precisely what each potentially ambiguous word might mean, to interpret the areas where the meanings had perhaps been left deliberately vague. Whilst he presumably used his copy of the "Sepher Hashorashim"[xviii] as a basic reference work to help create his new Bible, for Adam it was no more than a tool. Translation was only a small part of the exercise.

He tells us that "et ad studium ebrayce veritatis in predictis libris continuo me diverti ubi, textum Ieronimi tenes ab una parte, et textum ebraycum ab alia, cum quator doctoribus seu expositoribus hebreorum fere duobis annis"xix (and to study the true Hebrew text, for two years I worked with St Jerome's text in one hand, the Hebrew text in the other and four doctors of Hebrew with whom to dispute the text). The intense debate and study would produce a version of the Bible that could provide a definitive text and form the basis of all future scholarly work in Latin. Undoubtedly there was much debate between Adam and the scholars, but there is more to Adam's statement than that. Adam was fond of allegory, of word puzzles and games. When Adam said he was debating the scriptures with four Jewish doctors he was almost certainly making a reference to the four levels of interpretation of the Hebrew script. By making this allegorical assertion he drew attention not only to the way in which he was using his knowledge of basic Hebrew, but also to the suggestion that he had in his work something that St Jerome did not.

The Hebrew words in the Bible can be construed in four different ways, if you like on four different levels. The first (pshat), is nothing more than a straightforward reading, what the word says is what the word means. The second level (remez) is that of allusion. The words have a clear meaning to the uninitiated but it is not a literal one. The third level (drash) is harder to comprehend, it cannot be grasped from a literal reading or by allusion; it is perhaps more akin to allegory. If you know the allegory through tradition or through extensive reading of allegory in that tradition, then you can work out the meaning, but without that knowledge the meaning will be lost to you. The fourth and final level (sod) is a mystical area that cannot be grasped without a deeper knowledge of Hebrew learning and philosophy. It was at this level perhaps that Adam leaned most heavily on his Jewish friends for help.

His drive for a better understanding often took him into the Jewish Quarter to engage with the leading Hebrew scholars of the day and to seek their input on the interpretation of the Old Testament, although sadly he did not leave behind a record of the names of the doctors with whom he liked to dispute the text.

It is the study of meaning, the debate, the use of both the Torah and the Talmud that defined Adam's translation. His methods, his spirit of enquiry and his search for truth set him apart from any other translator of the Bible since St Jerome.

Sadly no copy of Adam's Old Testament has survived, and it is very hard to say how much influence it had in international learning. It was completed by 1376, so it would have been current for 150 years by the time of the Reformation. Throughout the 15th Century religious reform movements across Europe started working with vernacular texts, making the process of scholarly research in Latin increasingly outmoded. In a sense it meant that an understanding of the importance of Adam's achievement was lost in the process.

However at the start of the 16th Century the English scholar Robert Wakefield had a copy, probably in Easton's own hand, and he appreciated its significance. Wakefield reported in his book "Syntama De Hebreorum Codicum Incorruptione" that it was a complete and true translation of all of the Old Testament (with the exception of the Book of Psalms). To that extent the Easton Bible was in use at least in the era immediately before the Reformation and it had ended up in the hands of just the sort of scholar for whom it was intended.

A Stirring of Renaissance Scholarship

Adam had kept his own personal library from his Oxford days because, as we have seen, he was not content just to read the set texts of orthodox Catholicism. He wanted to reach beyond the scope of established learning to embrace new ideas and thought. Refusing to follow blindly the whims of accepted authority from his earliest days at Oxford, he had shown that he was prepared to take on authority not just where it appeared to be wrong, but also where it appeared to be irrational. William Bateman had good cause to remember that side of Adam's character. The idea of challenging the accepted texts, the authority inherent in St Jerome's translation, was hardly taken up by Adam in the spirit of rebellion against accepted authority. Nor was it an exercise to prove to the world that Adam's scholarship was superior to that of others. What it did demonstrate was a spirit of enquiry that was truly revolutionary. To undertake a work of this scale to illustrate the errors that had crept into Christian orthodoxy had little to do with the traditional approach of Scholastic learning. The intellectual need for a reinterpretation of the Hebrew texts underpinning the Bible may have been driven by the debates of Scholasticism, but the spirit of enquiry that saw it to completion reveals the essence of the Renaissance.

Adam's Old Testament rewrite was a feat that remained unique in the mediaeval era. His mindset when approaching the tasks connects with the intellectual approach of science and measurement, of analysis and understanding. It broke the bounds of rote learning and received wisdom in which he had been educated. He had educated himself in Hebrew for the sole purpose of being able to complete the task that he had set himself. The dedication and motivation with which Adam was driven to complete the task is in some ways more important than the text which he eventually completed. It shows the curious, scientific mind at work. To undertake the Old Testament translation was not just remarkable for its own sake, it set a precedent for generations to come. The very fact that Adam had challenged

109

the authority that sat within the St Jerome translation was to be an inspiration for others who followed him. In the latter part of the 16th Century the Protestant compilers of the Geneva Bible also believed it was essential to revert to the Hebrew script before translating first into Latin and then into the vernacular. They too saw the importance of having an accurate wording for the Biblical text, because they invoked a literal interpretation of the Bible stories and morals. Whether or not Adam's own translation was used by those later scholars, it is ironic that he, the arch Catholic of his day, should have provided the intellectual model that would inspire the theologians of the Protestant Reformation.

For the next 400 years Adam was recognised as the leading Hebrew scholar of his time. His learning was praised across Europe by a diverse collection of biographers of the Church from the Englishman Godwin[xx], the Venetian Palazzi[xxi], Frenchman Auberius,[xxii] and Roman Cardella[xxiii] as well as the admittedly biased German biographer of the Benedictine order, Magnoald Ziegelbauer[xxiv]. It is also a salutary lesson to us all that a man so universally well regarded for his intellectual achievements could be abandoned by history within the space of a couple of centuries and become so completely forgotten and ignored.

Church v State

The retranslation of the Old Testament was only a first step in a grand design. The world in which Adam grew up was dominated by the regular clashes between secular princes and the pope and his prelates. The central thrust of the argument always came back to the old chestnut of who stood below God as the supreme authority on Earth. Both sides were capable of making extravagant claims for their own position. Sometimes they pulled out quotations from the scriptures that seemed to support their point of view. Yet nearly six centuries after Charlemagne's coronation, there was still no definitive work that summarised and catalogued the Church's position and the intellectual arguments that legitimised it. Adam believed that with his new translation of the Bible he had the material and detail at his disposal to review and revise the entire canon of philosophical and religious arguments about the supremacy of Church and State. Supported by Simon Langham in his endeavours, this is the road that he set off along.

The impetus was provided once again by the activities of their great adversary John Wyclif. Wyclif too had flourished at Oxford and he was growing in confidence. He had moved on from opposing the friars in general and the Benedictines in Oxford, to challenging the absolute power of the Church at large. As he developed his argument he saw an opportunity to link his challenge to the power of the Church to the eternal need by an embattled monarch for new sources of funds. The work of Wyclif and his followers started to gain attention in England precisely because they seemed to offer the King an argument for getting his hands on the wealth of the Church. Amongst other things, Edward was still looking for ways to finance the latest phase of his war against the French. No longer the dynamic leader of his youth, the King was declining fast. An old man of 62, he relied increasingly on the support of John of Gaunt, Duke of Lancaster, to help govern the kingdom, and Gaunt was attracted to some of Wyclif's ideas. Through his influence Wyclif had visited Bruges in 1374 with a delegation from England, intent on resolving some of the issues around the papal subsidy. Gregory had been angling for the subsidy since 1373, when he had used Simon and Adam's negotiations as a context in which to raise the issue. The main aim of the Wyclif delegation was to find ways of avoiding payment altogether. By the time that Wyclif had reached Bruges, Adam and Simon had returned to Avignon and took no further part in negotiations on the Pope's behalf. Neither man seems to have been anxious to reacquaint themselves with the good doctor who had caused them so much irritation in the past. But Wyclif did have his admirers. He had shown some promise during the negotiations and Gaunt started to consider how he could use the philosophy that Wyclif promulgated to the advantage of the crown. As Gaunt took over the day-to-day running of the English government, so Wyclif gained influence. He was granted the living of Lutterworth, a wealthy rectory in Leicestershire, which gave him financial security.

As Wyclif committed more of his philosophy to paper and gained political influence at court in England, so the Benedictines realised that, at least in England, there was now a serious threat to their established position in the Church as well as to their wealth.

The Church Under Fire

As we have seen, the papal adventure in Avignon had successfully focused the diverse critics of the Church on the corruption and venality that flourished under the Provencal sun. By the start of the 14th Century intellectuals had begun to criticise the Church and its practices and to take up the cause of secular monarchs in their dispute with the Church for power and supremacy. The more the Pope looked like a secular prince, and not a very grand one in terms of territory, the less justification there seemed to be for his supremacy, religious or temporal. As the century progressed the arguments against papal power grew more daring and sophisticated.

Dante was one of the first to sound a note of protest, albeit in a somewhat restrained manner, with his work "De Monarchia", completed around 1310. He accepted that there were two spheres of influence in which pope and emperor might each reign supreme, and by definition both should stick to their specialism, spiritual and temporal affairs respectively. However, in stating that the Emperor received his authority directly from God rather than from the pope, Dante was taking his argument both to its logical conclusion and simultaneously downgrading the position of pope as seen through the eyes of the papal world view. Less forgiving popes would have accused him of heresy.

The baton was then taken up by Marsilius of Padua, whose "Defensor Pacis" was completed in 1325. In his world view, power sprang pretty much from the people, who might select both their emperor and their clergy. This was not socialism by another name. The "people" in Marsilius's view were represented by their elected monarch, the Holy Roman Emperor, a man whose election was conducted by a handful of wealthy princes and powerful electors. The Church fared somewhat worse in Marsilius's hands. Marsilius conceived of a Church in which all priests were equal, and refused to recognise that there could be any legitimate hierarchical authority within the Church. In his view the roles of bishop, prior, archbishop and even pope were equally lacking in legitimacy. Naturally, the Pope responded by condemning his ideas as heresy.

But Marsilius was not alone. William of Ockham was writing at much the same time and in a very similar spirit. Born in England around 1280 and educated at Oxford, he produced a series of increasingly strident pamphlets attacking the structure of the Church. William was clearly influenced by these Italian writers and he asserted the traditional imperial view that the Church had no role in secular business, and that in particular the Pope had no authority over the business of the Emperor. When his writings exposed him to the wrath of the Church, he fled to the court of Louis of Bavaria. Here he was protected and he continued to pronounce his views to anyone who would listen. Although William of Ockham died whilst Adam was at Oxford, the young Benedictine scholar would have been exposed to his ideology from early in his career.

John Wyclif was simply taking up the fight from where others had left off. By the time he sat down to pen his own ideas, he could draw on a rich heritage of anti-papal writing.

Disaster!

If ever the Church needed to defend its position and both justify and assert its moral authority in writing, the moment had arrived. Adam warmed to the task, but he had barely had time to gather his thoughts when catastrophe struck. On the July 19, 1376 Simon was relaxing at the Livree de Auxerre in Avignon. He had listened to the reading of the scriptures, enjoyed a good evening meal, and was having a digestive nap when he suffered a massive heart attack. The cardinal was paralysed.[xxv] Just three days later, on July 22, 1376 Simon Langham breathed his last.

It is perhaps hard for us to imagine today just what a profound impact the death of a wealthy patron could have on his dependants in the mediaeval world. Adam looked to Simon for his only reliable source of income. His work for the Benedictines had been unpaid to date, and whilst he had attended the curia with Simon and had become known to the cardinals and their courtiers, he was not entitled to any share in the wealth of the papal court, as he had no official position within it. Patronage was the most effective method for advancement in a very unequal world, and it was inevitable that the death of a patron represented not just a period of great upheaval for his dependants, but potentially the end of their careers. Although Simon was probably no more than 60 when he died, that was considered a good age for the time in which he lived. Adam's career in Avignon had depended on the long life of his patron, but this time his luck had run thin.

The blow of Simon's death was softened a little by a legacy of 200 florins. The bequest was the largest in the cardinal's will, aside from the money left to the two cardinal executors, showing just how important Adam was to Simon, and also demonstrating his seniority in the household. This was a lot of money and would give him a regular income whilst he decided how best to organise his future.

Adam was nominated as executor of the will alongside the cardinals Agrifolio and Pampelona. Administering the will of a senior cardinal of Simon's status was no small task. Not only was there a large fortune to divide and share, there would be many laying claim to a right to a part of it. The fact that Adam had been nominated as an executor by his former patron would keep him at the papal court for a few months longer. More importantly it would give him an opportunity to work with (and prove his usefulness to) the cardinal executors. Adam would need friends in the curia over the months ahead, and the chance to befriend two such senior cardinals was a definite bonus. They might yet help him re-establish himself at court in the months that followed the death of Simon.

Simon left other personal bequests to Adam, aside from the cash, and these show us the lighter side of life at the Avignon court. Adam inherited a golden drinking cup decorated with wooden images from which it is said that Adam liked to drink heavily, or at least regularly.[xxvi] I like to think of the Cardinal and his socius relaxing together in the courtyard of the Livree after a day of working amongst the curiales. I can picture them sitting side by side, sharing the anecdotes of the day as dusk turned to night, staving off the heat of a warm Avignonese summer evening, each with their favourite cup and sharing a flagon or two (and certainly more than the half litre prescribed by the Rule of Benedict) of Chateauneuf du Pape.

The whole idea of inheriting goods personally was naturally at odds with the Benedictine Rule regarding personal ownership, but then the insistence on moderation was not a matter that Adam felt needed to be taken too literally. He was also given a four-poster bed decorated in several colours. A kind gesture but again hardly in keeping with the sleeping arrangements prescribed by the Rule of Benedict!

For all the gifts that Adam had inherited and the fact that Simon had been a generous benefactor, this was an uncomfortable time. Even as the estate was being realised and divided up amongst the heirs, Adam must have pondered the precarious position in which he had been left. He had no obvious source of income beyond his legacy from Simon and no justification for being in Avignon at all without the blessing of his cardinal benefactor. Adam would need to find alternative lodgings to the Livree de Auxerre once the estate had been distributed. The money in Simon's bequest was vital to his ability to remain in Avignon with the curia. At least with a substantial sum of cash he would be able to rent accommodation in the city if he needed to. The glamour of the papal court and the possibility of being able to move amongst the highest officials in his chosen world had infected Adam. The soft, scholarly life at the Avignon court was a far cry from the riotous centre of Oxford where six of his fellow scholars had been murdered by the mob. The warmth of the Provencal summer was a world away from the windswept streets of Norwich, the dark cloisters and the long walk up the hill to the priory of St Leonard's. The light, the warmth and the comfort of the South of France were beguiling.

Adam had set his heart on staying with the court in Avignon.

Chapter 6

Battle is Joined!

Let us ask the Lord with the Prophet
"Who will dwell in your tent Lord,
who will find rest upon your holy mountain?"

John Wyclif Challenges the Church

As Adam contemplated his life in Avignon and thought about what to do with himself following the death of his friend, events started to overtake him. Back in England the rise in influence of John Wyclif and his increasingly acidic rhetoric was turning into a major threat to the Benedictines. Wyclif was amassing powerful friends, and his attacks strayed into areas that threatened both the power and the finances of the Church.

Adam and John Wyclif knew a lot about each other, even though they were not formally acquainted. The two men were, on the face of it, quite evenly matched. Both were men of letters who had proved their value to their masters: Adam to the Church, Wyclif to the Crown. Both had doctorates from Oxford and commanded respect at the university amongst students and fellows alike. Both had taken upon themselves, in very different ways, the role of challenging accepted orthodoxies and developing a questioning attitude to the authority that ruled their lives. They even had a shared interest in the work of William of St Amour and a mutual distrust of the friars. Their paths had crossed before, but over trivial matters. Now representing two opposing world views, they would clash decisively not on the battlefield but in the discreet world of intellectual debate and backroom politics. The outcome had the potential to be just as deadly as any battle.

From the very first, Adam had been as obsessive in his opposition to Wyclif as Simon Langham, without either of them ever giving Wyclif much of a fair hearing. Why then did John Wyclif appear to be so dangerous to the Benedictines? What was it that Wyclif was saying that caused such anxiety and made Adam so determined to suppress his ideas?

On the face of it, much of what Wyclif had to say about the Church sounded remarkably similar to the arguments used by Richard FitzRalph in his tirades against the friars. FitzRalph had attacked the friars for their wealth and the unnatural justifications they came up with to hang onto it, yet the old Archbishop had been exactly the sort of wealthy clergyman that Wyclif had in turn set his sights on. Adam had agreed with FitzRalph that the friars were dangerous because they pretended to be poor. They also posed a threat because they were perceived to be outside the hierarchy of regulation and administration of the Church. Initially the friars were answerable only to the Pope and this, to advocates of the Church hierarchy, seemed to be dangerous (despite the fact that by the middle of the 14th Century the friars were increasingly drawn into the Church hierarchy and subject to Church administration). Wyclif shared many of these views on the friars, and he had seen the arguments against them played out at Oxford. What he did not share was a desire to uphold the hierarchy and order of the Church, which brought in its wake corruption and an infinite capacity to tax ordinary people. Had not the orders of Benedictine monks in the past been just as corrupt in their practices, as devious with their rhetoric, as the friars had been in his time? Wyclif saw an opportunity to take the same set of principles used to attack the friars and turn them back on first the Benedictine monks and then on the entire Church hierarchy.

Unlike many of his colleagues, Adam and his close contacts had watched Wyclif attentively and had seen the danger developing. When Wyclif tried to remove the monks from Canterbury College and turn it over to the secular scholars, Adam had noted the warning. When, despite papal support to return the college to the monks, Wyclif had managed to defer the decision by drumming up secular support at court and in Oxford, Adam had seen the germ of a populist appeal to reject clerical authority.

Wyclif started his offensive by writing pamphlets about the power of the Church and the issues of hierarchy within the Church. The tract De Daemonio Meridiano was a tirade against the English clergy for lax living and wealth. He wrote a "Determination against William Vyrinham" in which he questioned the legitimacy of the religious authority when in conflict with the secular one. Each time a tract went unanswered his ideas grew bolder and, from Adam's perspective, more dangerous. When Wyclif attracted the support of John of Gaunt and started to argue against papal taxes, the very foundation on which the mediaeval Church was built was under threat.

In 1376 Wyclif produced the most brazen and adventurous critique on the Church and State in the "little book" De Civili Dominio. It contained

EDWARD III.

VRBANVS . VI . PAPA . NEAPOLITANVS .

DRAMATIS PERSONAE
Above: Pope Urban VI, King Edward III, King Richard II.
Below: Cardinal Simon Langham (left) and John Wyclif.

THE WAGES OF SIN

Top left: The final trump, Amiens Cathedral, Picardy, France.
Top right: The damned are fed to a whale, Amiens Cathedral.
Above left: The Devil torments the damned, Chesterton Church, Cambridge.
Above right: Devils chain their victims, Bamberg Cathedral, Germany.
Below left: The dead arise for judgement, Lutterworth Church, Leicestershire.
Below right: The saved at prayer, Broughton Church, Huntingdonshire.

ADAM'S EARLY LIFE

Above left: Easton Church.

Above right: Panel from the Despencer screen, Norwich.

Left: The Bishop's Bridge leading to St Leonards.

Below left: Norwich castle.

Below right: Norwich Cathedral and cloister.

OXFORD

Gloucester College, now Worcester College, as
Adam might have remembered it.
Top: Mediaeval cottage, one per monastery.
Above left: The monastic arms show which
monastery's students would be in occupation.
Above right: The cottages seen from the back.
Right: A closer view of one of the cottages.

tenetur sup alijs responde ꝗ quid
atatis de offi. dcl. lici bz̄. e. Can
balicus. e. ca iurre ꝝ. e. ℂ Si
no statuto opice nonpt aittoiu
naue post lapsū tīmini teneatur

**WORLD OF
BOOKS**

Above: Adam's
doodles highlight a
point.
Right: The first folio
of *De Pauperie
Salvatoris*, a gift to
Adam from Richard,
Archbishop of
Armagh.

Both reproduced by
kind permission of the
Master and Fellows of
Corpus Christi
College,
Cambridge ©)

MONASTIC LIFE
Above left: Monks' refectory, Maubronn, Germany.
Above right: The tonsorium, where heads were shaved.
Left: Light streams in to the North Cloister, Norwich.
Bottom left: Monks' dormitory, Eberbach, Germany.
Bottom right: Niche for reading the scriptures in the refectory.

MONTEFIASCONE
Top: The Rocca dei Papi.
Above left: The room inside
the Rocca where Urban V
received guests.
Above right: View of Lake
Bolsena from the Papal
Gardens.
Right: The gate in the outer
town wall.

LIFE IN FRANCE
Above left: Le Palais des Papes, Avignon.
Top right: From the site of Simon Langham's house looking back to the papal palace.
Right: Rue Trois Pilats.
Below left: The ruins of the cathedral at Therouanne.
Below right: The castle at Villeneuve Avignon.

an argument summing up the royal view of the hierarchy on Earth under God, where all bishops and other religious dignitaries owed allegiance to the King and the King only, excepting the principle that the Pope might still be responsible for religious doctrinal matters. The main thrust of Wyclif's argument contained two major strands.

First he turned to the doctrine of grace and lordship. Although couched in the rather particular language of Scholastic learning, the doctrine of grace was a straightforward enough concept. Taking the omnipotence of God as a starting point, it assumed that those in defiance of God's will were damned by their actions and so could not legitimately hold property. God would only grant to each man according to his due, the good would be blessed and the sinner could expect to be deprived. A sinner who owned goods or land was therefore, by this definition, a thief. Only the good and godly could own goods and land. As ownership of property in mediaeval society was tantamount to holding power, by implication only the godly could legitimately hold power. Those who err therefore can neither hold property nor assume power. Wyclif now turned the doctrine of grace on its head and used it to attack the Church from a very different angle.

Christ lived a life of poverty and humility. It therefore followed, argued Wyclif, that those who aspire to follow Christ should do the same. Established monks (as opposed to friars) who refuted wealth individually, but held great estates corporately, were therefore by this argument acting against God's implied will. As a result, as sinners they had no right to hold property, and because they did so they were guilty of theft. The property should therefore be taken away from them. The good doctor had them between a rock and a hard place. By the very fact that the monasteries held property, the monks had sinned. By the very fact that the monks had sinned, their property should and must be taken away from them. The Benedictines had good reason to be worried.

The second strand to his argument addressed the issue of how God's will should be enforced on Earth. If clerics were sinners and thieves, then who had the job of relieving them of their possessions? Not surprisingly, Wyclif stated that the power to enforce God's will lay with the royal, secular power in charge of that region in which God's will needed to be enforced. This in itself was not terribly controversial. God had put kings on earth specifically to do the enforcing, presumably in normal circumstances, at the behest of the Church in religious matters, and on their own account in secular ones. The question Wyclif asks is, "what happens when the religious power, the Church, is in error in entirety?" The royal secular power must be used for the common good, and if the Church had breached its own covenant with God by abusing its position, who would do something about it? For Wyclif and his political masters, the convenient answer of De Civili Dominio is that the royal secular power will administer God's justice on His behalf without reference to the Church or even to the leader of the Church, the Pope himself. This may not have been original thought, but it was dynamite. Taken to its logical conclusion, Wyclif was offering a justification for refusing to pay papal taxes (something he had dealt with when he joined the delegation to Bruges), for confiscating Church goods and having the right to overrule papal decisions on appointments to benefices. In the fight between the royal view of hierarchy and the papal view, Wyclif had just attempted to provide a theological justification for his secular masters. This was powerful ammunition for the English King.

Monarchs had taken this type of view before, although they usually reinforced their position with armies of mercenaries rather than clever words from intellectuals. The Hohenstaufen emperors in Germany had often been prepared to use physical force to back up their own particular view of royal enforcement of God's will over an erring pope. Only recently the Pope had been openly defied by Edward III, whose Statute of Praemunire rescinded, to all intents and purposes, his right to lead the Church in England. There had been even earlier attempts by generations of intellectuals, such as Marsilius of Padua, to express similar views and excite controversy. They had been condemned, because if their arguments were not forcefully rebutted before they gained popular support, then other like-minded spirits would be encouraged to take up the challenge. An assertive Church could rely on the fact that even the most powerful of monarchs feared death and what lay beyond the graves. As a result, given time, secular rulers, even the "Gloria Mundi" himself, the Hohenstaufen emperor Frederick II, had become reconciled with the papacy and the controversial writers condemned as heretics. Good order seemed to return naturally.

Yet to ignore Wyclif at the time when his attacks were hitting home would have been a mistake. Wyclif was no fool, he was an intellectual, a doctor of the Church and he was also a cancer attacking the body of Mother Church. He had already made himself useful to the royal court in England and was under the protection of John of Gaunt, a man who by 1376 was effectively ruling England, as the health of his aging and increasingly senile father, Edward III, declined. The combination of a writer asserting a philosophy that challenged papal power and a strong secular power looking for a means to challenge the Church over issues of taxes and lordship was an explosive cocktail. One would undoubtedly prove extremely useful to the other, and Adam feared the strength of their alliance. However, the real danger to the established Church was that if the ideas that Wyclif was promulgating remained unchallenged, they might gain popular support and take on a life of their own. Adam could not afford to underestimate his opponent.

At the very moment when England, one of the most powerful Christian kingdoms in Europe, was under threat from heresy and schism, the attention of the Church was focused on Italy. Ironically Pope Gregory and his entourage were far more concerned with their own relatively minor secular powers than their pre-eminent religious ones. The Pope's mind was not on events in England. His greatest concern was over the possibility of losing control of his wealthy Italian lands, cities such as Perugia and Florence that he ruled over as a Prince and had recently revolted against his authority. The idea that Wyclif's writing might spawn a major heretical movement, potentially his own "Reformation", was a possibility that only Adam (and Simon before him) seemed to have grasped. Whilst there were those in the English Church who could also see the danger, there was no-one other than Adam to give those fears voice in the Papal Court. So until Adam raised the alarm and attacked Wyclif directly, the Church at large had quite overlooked the threat. The battle with Wyclif would be a long one that took over the next five years of his life and left Adam exhausted from the effort. And right to the end, the outcome remained uncertain.

Administering the Will

All this was a long way off as the heat finally started to wane in the autumn skies over Avignon and the year 1376 drew to a close. Adam was wondering what to do next. He was never the sort of character to hang around feeling sorry for himself, and the world of the Church offered any number of opportunities.

Having reached his 50th year (not a bad age for the time in which he lived) a lesser man would have thought of retiring to his monastery to live out his days. A monk of his experience could expect a senior position at Norwich Priory in recognition of his age and prominence within the Church. This was never going to be enough for Adam, a member of the papal curia, an intellectual and a man who was evidently at the height of his powers. The academic possibilities for a theologian amongst the libraries at the heart of the papal court of Avignon far outstripped the meagre offerings available in England. And in any case he had grown fond of the court life. Up until Simon died, Adam had determined to stay with the papal court and make a career there. Now, however, he faced a difficult problem. The legacy from Simon was generous but not sufficient to sustain the standard of living that was needed to keep pace with the court life of Avignon. If he was to stay at court he would have to establish a more substantial source of income, and a reliable one.

There was another more serious obstacle aside from the practical problem of money. Whilst Simon was alive, Adam had implicit authority to be in Avignon simply because Simon had invited him to join his court. As the senior prelate of the English Church, Simon had every right to maintain his court in Avignon, and Adam, as his socius, held a formal position at that court. This in turn gave him the right to stay away from his monastery in Norwich. That permission had died with Simon, and by rights Adam should have set off for the priory of Norwich as soon as he had completed winding up Simon's affairs. Adam needed a new reason to be at the papal court, and that meant either being granted a formal position and a salary in one of the papal chambers, or petitioning the Pope to give him a benefice, permitting him to stay at court as what was known as a "beneficed religious". This was the system that Cardinal Langham had exploited to get rich. If Adam could just get an appointment to a ripe benefice, he could take the income of the vicarage for himself and then pay a salaried clerk to do the day-to-day work of the vicar. The difference would provide Adam with a decent "living", which would cover the expense of staying on in Avignon.

The income of a vicarage came from several sources. First there were the tithes due from the whole village, then the land rents from those who worked the land belonging to the Church, plus the income from the sale of produce grown on the vicarage lands and given to the incumbent. All of which meant that the vicarage could provide a satisfactory income for a courtier like Adam without the inconvenience to the Pope of having to dip into the papal coffers to pay his salary. Adam could afford to work at the papal court for free, representing the English Benedictines and helping the Pope with the administration in the Apostolic Chambers.

Yet even if he could sort out his money problems, Adam still had to find somewhere to live once Simon's affairs had been finalised and the Livree passed on to a new cardinal. He still had friends amongst the English community at court, men such as Thomas Southam and Edmund Bromfield. Both men were Benedictines and had been at Oxford during the time when Adam was Prior of Students. Bromfield had been made a proctor to the Papal Court in 1375, whilst Southam had been enticed to Avignon via Montefiascone in the court of Simon Langham. Unlike Adam he had not stayed at the Livree but had lodgings near Notre Dame de Miraculis[i] (the present day Porte de La Roche). Whilst it was on the other side of town from the Livree de Auxerre, at least it gave Adam the comforting thought that there was someone in Avignon who might help him with practical matters once the legal business of the will was wrapped up.

Meanwhile Adam had to win the support of Pope Gregory and those who might influence him in supporting a petition for a benefice. It was not a hopeless cause, but he would need help, and most of the other Englishmen with positions at the papal court held relatively junior posts. Without Gregory's backing Adam had little chance of securing his own place at court.

The timing was not good either, as Gregory's mind wandered to matters Italian. In the middle of 1376 Florence rose in open revolt against the Pope, and many of the communes within the Papal States followed suit. Gregory knew that his secular authority in Italy was on the verge of collapse. Faced with disaster, the only way of rescuing the situation was to return in person and try to impose his authority. This would mean attempting to bring the curia back from its Babylonian exile in Avignon once more and risking the wrath of the Roman mobs in the process; but there were few alternatives. Even as Adam was lobbying him for a position at the curia, Gregory was preparing to follow in the footsteps of Urban V. All of a sudden an empty retirement in Norwich must have seemed a very real possibility.

The Cardinals Lend a Hand

Adam's best hope of securing his future lay with his fellow executors, two of whom were cardinals of some standing at Gregory's court. Now he went out of his way to demonstrate that he was worthy of a decent sized benefice. Adam used every opportunity to demonstrate his legal knowledge and skill as an administrator. The two cardinal executors found Adam Easton to be a hard-working and intelligent colleague and they appreciated his help. Over the next few months Adam laid the foundations of a good relationship with both men, and they were to become friends and allies in the curia over the next couple of years. By 1378 Cardinal Agrifolio was prepared to acknowledge that he knew Adam well, they often spoke and occasionally ate together[ii]. Moreover Agrifolio clearly valued his opinion. As a French cleric who held benefices in England, he particularly esteemed Adam's understanding of the English King's view of the world in general, and of foreign clerics, from the Pope downwards, in particular. As for the other cardinal executor, Peter de Monteruc, the Cardinal of Pamplona, Adam stayed in touch with him by letter at least until November 1379.[iii] The fact that both cardinals kept up their association with Adam over the years says much about the respect that he commanded at the highest level in the Church hierarchy.

More importantly, the two cardinals demonstrated their support where Adam needed it most. On September 3, less than three months after the death of Simon Langham, Adam was granted the right to the fruits of the vicarage of Somersham,[iv] one of the richest pickings in Simon's portfolio. There was an interesting curiosity in the petition by which Adam was granted the right to Somersham. He was described as "religiosa zelo", an unusual term, and here it is used about Adam for the first and only time. Perhaps the words hint at the vigour with which he engaged in his study of theology. Possibly others found that enthusiasm a little wearing!

Somersham was worth around £60 per annum,[v] and although Adam would have to pay a clerk to say mass in the parish church, he could still rely on a net annual income of around £50 from the money due to the benefice. On top of the legacy of 200 florins from Simon, it gave him a good deal of financial independence. He now needed to organise his own proctor in England to collect the money from the villagers of Somersham and transfer it to Avignon. In the short term he probably asked Simon's proctor, William Palmer, to carry out the role for him. William knew his way around the parish, from whom the main payments were due and how best to deal with the more truculent of the parishioners. He would also have known and dealt with the bankers Francis de Kyto and Michael Strozzi, through whom he had sent Simon's money across the Channel.

Finally he had established a new direction for his future career in the Church. Now that his petition for a benefice had been favourably received by the Pope, Adam had won the authority to stay on at the curia. He received a formal written confirmation of his permission to stay at the court as a monk of independent means (this unfortunately has not survived in the papal archive). This relieved him of his responsibility to return to the priory of Norwich and secured his future as a member of the papal court.

He was only just in time. At the end of September 1376, two weeks after approving Adam's appointment to Somersham, Gregory and several of his cardinals left Avignon. They made their way to the coast and boarded a Genoese fleet at Marseilles on the first leg of an emotional return journey to Italy. When the fleet called in at Genoa and later Corneto, Gregory sent envoys on ahead to test the political temperature before proceeding. It was, after all, a dangerous venture, given that so many of the towns in the Papal States had taken arms against the Pope and his regent in Italy. By January 14, 1377 the Pope had reached Ostia, the port at the head of the Tiber just a short distance from Rome itself. From here on January 17 the papal party sailed on up the Tiber to Rome, making a formal and splendid entry into the city. But beneath the gloss lay the real reason for the Pope's over-borne return. He sailed up the Tiber because he dared not make the ten-kilometre trip from Ostia to Rome overland, as the region was overrun with bands of armed men and brigands.

A Delegation from England

Back in Avignon, Adam remembered the events of 1371 all too vividly. For all Urban V's good intentions, his Italian venture had turned into a peripatetic papacy as he drifted aimlessly between Rome, Viterbo and Montefiascone before finally giving up and returning to Avignon. A repeat performance under Gregory did not appeal. Adam saw no reason to hurry on to Rome until it became clear that Gregory really was established in Italy and of a mind to stay there. He had only just secured his status at the court in Avignon, and having been provided with the means to enjoy a modest living, he was in no hurry to leave. If he did, it would be a major upheaval. He would have to find new bankers, as de Kyto did not have an office in Rome, and then with new bankers in place he might well need a new proctor to replace William Palmer. Adam wasn't the only member of the papal court to show some reticence to leave. Many of the members of the court, in particular the French cardinals, had no great desire to take their chances in the chaos of Italy before they needed to. At least five of them stayed on in Avignon, waiting to see if Gregory's move to Italy looked as if it would become permanent.

For the moment Adam still had legitimate business in Avignon, attending to the resolution of Simon's affairs. The old cardinal had bequeathed a major part of his possessions to his former Abbey of Westminster, and on October 11 the Prior of Westminster, Richard Merton, arrived in Avignon to collect the inheritance. Merton brought with him John Bokenhall, a fellow monk from Westminster, to help with the work of organising the transport of the money and goods bequeathed to their Abbey.[vi] They were anxious to find out how matters were progressing, and had hurried down to Avignon, taking just 14 days to travel from Bruges. The Westminster monks wanted to secure the estate that had been left to the Abbey before anyone else laid claim to it or challenged the validity of the will. The Abbot too was worried about Gregory's move to Rome. If Simon's executors followed him in the immediate future then the realisation of the bequests in the will would be delayed and the Abbey authorities worried that they might never secure anything that Simon had left them. Merton need not have worried. Neither the cardinal executors nor Adam showed the slightest inclination to leave France for the time being Agrifolio was French in any case and not much inclined to abandon Avignon at all, whilst the Cardinal of Pamplona was still waiting to see which way the wind was blowing. For each man the will of Simon Langham was the ideal excuse not to move to Rome just yet. Richard was pleased to find a fellow Englishman and Benedictine at the heart of the administration of the will. He consulted Adam[vii] on the best way to approach the cardinals' to claim the legacy and sounded him out on just what the Abbey might reasonably expect in total.

After several years in Avignon, Adam had acquired the status of an insider at the papal court. His knowledge of life at the curia and the courtly etiquette of Avignon was valued by outsiders, even senior members of the Church back in England. Now that he also knew both cardinal executors personally he could oil the wheels and reassure the Prior that the Abbey's legacy would be properly protected. Adam set to work, and within a few days things were moving fast. He brought about the necessary introductions, and an interview was arranged with the Cardinal of Pamplona to agree the details of the legacy. This helped Merton to make arrangements for the transport and insurance (via certain merchants in Lucca) of the goods for the journey back to Westminster.

The business was concluded so smoothly that Merton and John Bokenhull now considered travelling on to Rome. For sincere men who had taken their monastic vows, a pilgrimage would be the highlight of their spiritual life, and the Abbey's interest in Simon's will had given the two Westminster men the perfect excuse to be in Avignon, the ideal starting point for such a venture. Following the fall of the crusading kingdoms, it was increasingly hazardous to visit the Holy Land on pilgrimage. However, Rome, and St Peters in particular, offered a safer destination and one which the determined pilgrim would have every chance of reaching. Rome had a magical appeal to the 14th Century mind, and Adam could regale the monks with tales of the great Christian Pilgrimage Churches, the classical wonders of Roman architecture and the magnificent spiritual and cultural wealth of the city. The fact that the Pope was back in residence only added to the appeal.

John wrote back to the Abbey hinting that they would make their pilgrimage. If no complaint came back by return, they could assume that they had the implicit agreement of their chapter to make their journey. When, after a few weeks, no such complaint had been received, the two men started to make their plans to depart. But shortly after Christmas 1376 Richard Merton died suddenly. Poor John Bokenhall completed the sad job of arranging the burial of his erstwhile travelling companion and found he no longer had much appetite for the journey to Rome. He arranged to return home to Westminster with the Abbey's legacy.[viii]

As the unfortunate Bokenhall departed laden with Simon's treasure, Adam's work for his former master was finally drawing to a close. After six months of completing lists, hearing claims and realising Simon's assets for cash, the main points of the will were finalised and most of Simon's possessions were on their way to new homes.

A Plea for Information

Free at last from a small mountain of legal work and established as a beneficed monk attached to the Avignon court, Adam could devote his full attention to his big project. Thomas Brinton, Adam's companion from his student days at Oxford, had written to tip him off that John Wyclif was once again causing trouble. Encouraged by support from the highest circles at court Wyclif was writing tracts against the Church in general and the

Benedictines in particular. Brinton hinted that Adam might like to look into this and use his influence to help restrain Wyclif before matters got out of hand. On November 18, 1376 Adam wrote to Nicholas Littlington at Westminster, to let him know that the Abbey's legacy would soon be heading home to England. Then he went on to offer himself "to you and your church as I prepare to act for your benefit. I humbly and warmly appeal to your reverence that I should have your students make a copy of the words of one master John Wyclif which he was reported to have uttered in Oxford against our order. I have received a written report that he mounted a strong attack on our order, but I cannot obtain a copy of his words. Because you are a father and leading master of the order, I ask that you arrange that I can obtain a copy of his words and also of his comments against the Church, together with the little book (libelli) which he has published with chapters concerning the power of the monarchy. I will happily refund the expenses of the scribes and those working on the project. I plead again that for this task I will fully recompense your reverence in other ways and make sure that you receive full gratitude from your superiors".[ix]

Wyclif's publication of De Civili Domini had opened up the discussion on the powers and authority of monarchy relative to that of the Church. As soon as Adam had received and read the copies of Wyclif's work sent to him by the monks from Westminster he knew he would have to act. The cut and thrust of intellectual debate had been the focus of Adam's life. From sermons against the friars to debates on the finer points of Scholastic ideology, this was the sort of thing at which Adam had excelled. Now he could place his skills at the service of the Church, and he must have been both genuinely excited at the prospect of the mental battle ahead as well as supremely confident in his ability to win. Adam was not a malevolent man and I cannot help but wonder if he did not separate the consequences that would surely follow for Wyclif (assuming Adam was successful) from the pleasure of the intellectual challenge.

It was a cause that Adam knew to be critical for the Church, and an argument that he believed he could win. The tone of Adam's letter to the Abbot of Westminster (see above) is somewhat understated, but even at this early stage in the process, before he had even seen Wyclif's work, it is easy to feel the anticipation, the sheer exhilaration and excitement with which Adam greeted the prospect of an intellectual joust with the man he regarded as his principal opponent.

Eminence Grise

Adam knew that winning the debate with his opponent would, in isolation, never be enough, and he approached the battle with two objectives in mind.

The first and most immediate was to work towards the task of getting Wyclif's ideas condemned and suppressed. This would require a formal edict from Pope Gregory in Rome and a willingness to enforce it from the bishops back in England. If the bishops could be persuaded to act tough, it would make life difficult for Wyclif's secular supporters, who would run the risk of being condemned as heretics.

The second was to create a written justification that showed not just that Wyclif was wrong but why he was wrong. In Avignon, Adam began to sketch out the treatise that he had started to plan with Simon Langham, a text that would resolve once and for all the disputes over the roles of the secular and clerical powers across Europe by justifying each in turn by reference to God's word, as expressed through the Bible. He would draw on the authority of his newly retranslated Old Testament to assert his final position. This treatise would in time become the Defensorium Potestatis Ecclesiastice (Defence of Ecclesiastical Power).

Armed with the texts provided by the monk students of Westminster, it did not take long for Adam to bring the case for condemnation. Not surprisingly, once the formal process got under way he chose to remain anonymous. At this stage of his life Adam might well have contemplated a return to England in the future, and there was no benefit in attracting the personal enmity of John of Gaunt. His name did not appear on any of the bulls delivering condemnation, not even as a named witness as he had been on the earlier papal bull issued to resolve the dispute with Wyclif over Canterbury Hall. Adam worked fast. Given that he wrote to England to get a copy of Wyclif's book in November 1376, and that as he worked on the case he was in Avignon and Gregory was in Rome, the fact that he completed the work by May 1377 was remarkable. The critical bull damning Wyclif appeared at the end of May, condemning 18 specific statements drawn from writings attributed to Wyclif. The main creed of De Civilio Dominio was effectively damned by the Church. The Bull was despatched to the Bishop of London and the Archbishop of Canterbury[x] with orders that the bishops should enforce it and call Wyclif to account. Copies were sent to the University of Oxford and to the King so that there should be no question that Wyclif had not heard of his condemnation.

The fact that the Bull was published in Rome while Adam was still in Avignon may be part of the reason for the absence of his name from the various copies that were made. As Adam worked away, controlling the attacks on his adversary from under a cloak of anonymity, the central role he played in the destruction of Wyclif has become obscure. But for those inclined to look, there are plenty of clues that point to his role as mastermind.

Most significantly, whoever prepared the intellectual groundwork for the

Bull must have been intimately acquainted with the writings of Wyclif in order to be able to identify the core elements of his philosophy. There is no evidence to suggest that Wyclif's works were freely available outside England, and certainly no other member of the papal court, either in Avignon or Rome, was known to have had access to them. If Wyclif's works had been available in Avignon, Adam would not have had to write to England to get hold of his own copies, he would have borrowed them from a colleague's library. What is clear is that Adam was the only person at the papal court equipped to mount so detailed attack on Wyclif and his "dicta".

If we compare the similarities between his own writings and the details from the Bull of condemnation shown in the Archbishop's Register[xi] Adam's involvement becomes ever more obvious. Woven into the fabric of the Defensorium Ecclesiastice Potestate,[xii] Adam lists the main offending sayings (dicta) of Wyclif, and it can be no coincidence that the phrases Adam attacks here are identical to those contained within the papal Bull. It is interesting to note that, when in response to Gregory's Bull, Wyclif wrote complaining that he had been misquoted, the complaint concerned one of the dicta that Adam included in the Defensorium Ecclesiastice Potestate. This was not a coincidence. Adam was writing his attacks on Wyclif for posterity as well as ensuring the man would cease to be an effective critic in his own lifetime.

Then we come to motive. If Adam had not exactly a grudge against Wyclif, he certainly had a consistent record of opposition to the man that had been motivated by a need to protect Benedictine self interest and not much more. Wyclif had been an irritant at Canterbury Hall, and the control over the monopoly of education was crucial to the Church's grip on taxation, administration and dominion in the secular and religious world. He had amassed dangerous friends and gained influence, and it had been at the expense of the powers in England that Adam represented, the monks and the Church. By 1376 Adam knew that Wyclif's attack, if unchecked, would challenge the hegemony of the Church in education, as well as in the bigger issues of authority and taxation. Adam could see the wider implications for the Church hierarchy if Wyclif was allowed to carry on writing his polemics unchecked. Of all the people that Wyclif had come up against, Adam was the one with a clear motive for destroying him.

There is some evidence that Adam put his pen to paper more than once to express his views. The 16th Century writer John Bale listed Adam's written works in the Index Britanniae Scriptorum, amongst which are two works whose titles are unambiguous "De forma procedendi contra hereticos" and "Opus vite contra hereticos". Although unfortunately neither has survived into our times, the "hereticos" of the title is definitive. From what we know of Adam's career it is absolutely clear that the only heretical movement that he ever showed any interest in was that of Wyclif and his followers. Where he attacked other theologians it was because he saw in their teaching the seeds of Wyclif's arguments. Wyclif was the major controversial theologian of Adam's time, the one Adam was most familiar with and the only one that he had attacked repeatedly. If Adam wrote "against heretics" then he was writing attacks on Wyclif.

Finally we come to what undoubtedly is the most intriguing piece of evidence. It only came to light in the mid 1980s when restoration work was being carried out on a mediaeval wall painting in John Wyclif's own church of Lutterworth in Leicestershire. The painting and the interpretation of it is discussed in detail at Appendix V, but of particular interest is the addition to it of two churchmen, one is a cardinal and one a bishop. Quite clearly these two figures were not part of the original painting. They are represented on a different scale to the main painting and in part are out of context with it. They stare up at three skeletons representing death, and it has been suggested that these were added on Wyclif's own instructions. Their position in the painting appears deliberate. It is as if Wyclif is directly accusing his persecutors and warning them of the judgement they must face at the moment of death. The identity of the two men is not difficult to guess. Here at last perhaps we come as close as we can get to seeing Wyclif's signature on the accusation against Adam Easton and his fellow Benedictine Thomas Brinton.

Slowly, Slowly . . .

Back in England, Wyclif may have had powerful friends but he was far from secure in his own position. For the moment John Wyclif's freedom depended on John of Gaunt being prepared to face down the bishops and the authorities at Oxford. Gaunt had provided patronage to Wyclif and seems to have been content to look after him in much the same way as Simon Langham had looked after Adam. Gregory's Bull arrived in 1377, but would it be enforced, indeed who would dare to enforce it?

Gaunt was a very powerful friend. He took the role of protector of England as the kingdom transferred in name at least from his father to his young cousin, the boy king Richard II. Yet Gaunt's own position was constantly under attack from jealous nobles and he needed to re-establish his power and test the limits of his authority. Wyclif could not be sure if John of Gaunt would be powerful enough to protect him from the bishops, and then again, would John be inclined to risk the wrath of the Pope? Gaunt had plenty of enemies at court who might use papal approbation as an excuse to destroy him under the pretext of following the will of the Holy Father. For Wyclif the other big unknown was whether or not the London mob would side with him when the dispute entered the public domain.

Initially the fates sided with John Wyclif. He was the man of the moment, his ideas proved popular in England and he rode his good fortune well. In October 1377, after the coronation of the new King, he was invited to address parliament, where he appears to have won the support of Richard. Shortly after the coronation he was invited to get involved in discussions concerning the payment of taxes to Rome and whether England should refuse to pay. He outlined legal positions that might be taken to evade the payments and his secular masters were duly grateful.

With Gregory's Bull in circulation the Church authorities in England eventually felt obliged to act, but they did so reluctantly and with half an eye on Gaunt and his supporters. The bishops were worried that Wyclif's message had enough populist appeal to whip up support in London. It was all very well for the Pope to make pronouncements from Rome, but he would not have to deal with the unruly mob that might arrive and cause trouble. Their fears on both counts proved to be well founded. When in 1378 Wyclif was at last summoned to attend a hearing in front of the Bishop of London, Gaunt came with him, lending considerable weight to Wyclif's defence. Half way through the hearing the London mob broke into the meeting, shouting support for Wyclif and disrupting proceedings. The process had to be abandoned for the day.

In Oxford, matters proceeded rather more smoothly at first. On receiving the papal Bull condemning Wyclif, the Chancellor acted decisively and placed him under house arrest. Then he had second thoughts. A few days later, he quite inexplicably released his captive and allowed him to go about his business. The Church authorities appeared inept at best and downright cowardly at worst. It had been an inauspicious start to Adam's campaign.

Back in Avignon, Adam watched events unfold from a safe distance, pulling strings in the background, cajoling and using the power of papal authority as necessary. He was not naive. He knew that the condemnation of Wyclif would not be straightforward and that the secular authorities would put the bishops under pressure. He played the long game, using papal authority and his growing network of friends and associates among the Benedictines to bring his victim to book. He maintained a steady assault on both Wyclif and his followers for the next 20 years, always anonymously, but ever present in the background.

It was always going to be a long, drawn-out process, the more so as the secular political power in England was going through uncertain times and final victory could only be assured when the King and his circle were brought on side. Nonetheless, the persecution of the unfortunate Wyclif and then, following his death, that of his followers and friends, was persistent and steady. In 1388 Thomas Southam, Adam's colleague from the days in

Avignon with Simon Langham's court, held an inquisition of Wyclif's followers in London.[xiii] Five years later King Richard, now very much involved on Adam's side, wrote condemning Wyclif's followers and urging support for the Church in their suppression. In 1395 Pope Boniface IX sent more Bulls to England and wrote to Richard, encouraging him in his vigilance and persistence in the suppression of Wyclif's ideas and those of his followers.

Adam fought on relentlessly, on occasion frustrated by the inaction in England, sometimes quietly pleased. Yet as the 1370s drew to a close the Church slowly but surely shut down Wyclif's freedom of expression and blocked his influence at Oxford.

Black Dog

Adam's role in directing the campaign may have become obscured by the passage of time, but John Wyclif had no doubt as to who his persecutor was. However much Adam kept in the background, Wyclif knew that just as the Benedictines had felt the wrath of his tongue most often, it was always the Black Monks who fought back and tried to restrain him. He had deliberately targeted the wealth of their monasteries and it had hit home, it had hurt them. And of all the Benedictines who had been troubled by Wyclif's ideas, Simon Langham and Adam Easton had been the most persistent and public of his opponents. With Simon dead, Wyclif was sure that Adam was behind the attacks.

Initially, Wyclif tried to fight his corner. He issued a tract in the form of a letter to the Pope, explaining his views and published in response to his summons by the bishops to appear before them in London in 1378.[xiv] It was not so much a personal letter to the Pope, as a statement of Wyclif's position and clarification, as if any were needed, that he had no intention of going to Rome to answer for his views. If nothing else, he understood that he would be much safer if he stayed amongst his friends and supporters in England. He stated boldly that he was quite prepared to have his views investigated and that he stood by them, but rather less courageously that he had no intention of travelling into the den of his accusers to defend them!

He attacked Adam more directly in a sermon given in Oxford. Presumably not wanting to name his persecutor for fear of further retribution, he gave the Benedictine monk an alias: "Tolstanus". The name looks like a deliberate mixing up of Tolle and Estone, which in crude Latin would mean Easton the destroyer or perhaps even Easton the thief. He decried the actions of this "black dog" (a derisory allusion to the black Benedictine cowl) and his "stammering whelps".[xv] Wyclif accused Tolstanus of lying to the Pope about what he had said, and of deliberately misquoting him, a favourite whinge from the man who had made a similar complaint in his "Determination on William Vyrinham". It was an issue about which he was clearly sensitive. When the precise interpretation of a phrase could be the difference between heresy and orthodoxy, we should have some sympathy for Wyclif's protestations.

Wyclif illustrated the nature of his complaint about the condemned dicta laid out in Gregory's Bull by focusing on the phrase "in gratia gratificante finaliter" which had been rendered in Gregory's Bull as "in gratia gratifice et fideliter", a misquote that can also be found in the Defensorium, where Adam refers to "in gracia gratificante" (finaliter or fideliter has vanished from the text in this version).[xvi] Oddly enough it was not the substance of the misquoted statement that Wyclif was defending. In context, one version did not actually differ materially from the other, nor was one more or less heretical than the other.

What was important to Wyclif was that this was an example of how his work had been maliciously misrepresented to show the man and his academic prowess in an unflattering light. He took the point further by taking an analogy from the Bible. He compared the words reported in Matthew's gospel "possum destruere templum dei et post triduum aedificare illud" with John's gospel "Solvite templum hoc et in tribus diebus excitabo illud" (if you destroy the temple in three days I will rebuild it). In Matthew the words are given as a report of a false witness against Christ who is deliberately citing Christ as having made an impossible claim, i.e. that he could destroy the temple and quite literally rebuild it in three days. The very similar words when they appear in John's account are given a completely different context, for John states that Christ did indeed use those words, but as an analogy for his death and resurrection three days later.

This is a subtle argument in which Wyclif shows off his debating prowess. He suggests that not one but two villainies had been perpetrated against him. Firstly that Adam had deliberately used different words that changed the meaning of what Wyclif had said in the same way that Matthew claims that Christ had been deliberately misrepresented by the false witness. The second villainy was that by misquoting him he had taken the words out of context to give them a different meaning. John uses very similar words to Matthew, but because the statement in his gospel is an analogy, it has a specific meaning. Taken out of context, however, it would seem like a silly and impossible boast. In the same way, Wyclif claimed, Adam had used different words in a context designed to be unflattering and heretical.

For all the clever arguments, Wyclif's defence was weak and concentrated more on the semantics of Adam's attack than a justification of his own position. Complaining about the Benedictines being "that sect who introduced the art of lying to Oxford"[xvii] was simply name-calling, not the stuff of calculated intellectual debate. Wyclif's defence of his ideas, which were at once cynical and opportunist, lacked the weight of conviction, the real self belief that shines through Adam's own work. For that matter, it lacked the fervour of the reformers who would write without reserve on similar subjects during the 16th Century Reformation. There is a very real sense, reading the full texts of Wyclif's sermon and his letter to Urban VI, that these are the words of a man who knows he has lost the battle. One forms an impression of a man who feels uncertain of the validity of his own argument.

The Net Closes In

Despite the evident support that Wyclif enjoyed in England, it was never likely that the English bishops would continue to disobey a direct papal instruction from Rome. Adam also had supporters in England, particularly amongst his fellow Benedictines, and they now joined forces to move against Wyclif and his followers. Nicholas Radcliffe, the Oxford Doctor who had debated with Adam during the period of his graduation, willingly joined the fight on the side of his former protégé. He wrote attacks on Wyclif's views in a series of treatises written with the Carmelite Peter Stokes, and later he would join the Blackfriars Council and take an active part in suppressing Wyclif's followers. Friars and monks may have had their differences in the 1350s, but they formed a united front when faced with the writings of Wyclif. With a highly vocal and articulate assault gathering pace, to say nothing of a direct instruction from the Pope, the bishops had little choice but to stamp down hard on the emerging heresy. Wyclif was not so much condemned as forbidden to preach and expound upon his written works.

The level of popular support that Wyclif had mustered probably saved his life and prevented a more dogged persecution in England, where the secular power was going through a period of decline. By the time De Civili Dominio was published, Edward III was senile and in the following year he died, being succeeded by the child king Richard II. John of Gaunt struggled to establish his own position as regent for both Edward and Richard during the transition. The crown was in no state to take on the theological fight with the papacy, even if the idea of not paying papal taxes had a distinct appeal.

Adam's attack on Wyclif had been a coup de grace using charges against his works that amounted to heresy. He now brought to bear the full power of papal authority to crush a man who had called that authority into question. It was an attempt to destroy not just the man, but his philosophy. Alone amongst the English intellectual elite, Adam understood the dangers of Wyclif's attacks on the Church and saw where it might lead. By clamping down hard before the ideas had gained a great popularity, Adam manoeuvred the Church into a position of strength and justified its view of its relationship with the state.

Death of a Good Idea

In the end Wyclif's fate was not to be decided in Rome any more than it was in Oxford or London. In May 1381 the tranquillity of life in the Home Counties of England spontaneously combusted. In Essex and Kent the rural population rioted against the imposition of a new Poll Tax, tax collectors were set upon everywhere, some were killed and some chased out of town. In a matter of days, in a once peaceful part of the English countryside tax collectors were on the run and peasant armies were converging on London. Astonished and surprised, the authorities in England were forced to open their eyes to a hitherto unsuspected problem.

Wyclif had presented some radical ideas about the Church being too rich and he had promoted poverty and independence of mind in the clergy. He had discussed the idea of religious texts being presented in the vernacular. After all, why should the common people not read the scriptures themselves and make up their own minds? Why did they need monks and priests to interpret for them? The idea of radical, poor priests going round the country, preaching did not seem to be much of an issue if it meant that the State kept the income from churches and fewer taxes were paid to Rome.

The Peasants' Revolt changed all that. By the high summer of 1381 the need for control and order was highlighted for everyone to see. Radical preachers appeared amongst the mobs, men such as the notorious John Ball preached to the peasant army and whipped up enthusiasm for the revolt and retribution. The authorities had good reason to be nervous. Ball mixed religious egalitarianism with something that sounded remarkably like a socialist agenda in his famous couplet: "Whan Adam dalf and Eve span; Wo was thane a gentilman?"[xviii] a sinister message to the ruling classes well ahead of its time. Thomas Brinton, Adam's former colleague from the monastery at Norwich and now Bishop of Rochester, had seen the revolt from close quarters. Rochester was in the heartland of the Kentish Revolt and the castle, next door to Brinton's cathedral, had been overwhelmed in hours and fallen to the peasant army. According to at least one account,[xix] the Bishop had himself been confronted at Blackheath by Watt Tyler, leader of the Kentish peasants, who explained the rebels' demands to him.

When Bishop Thomas gazed down from his pulpit in 1382 he saw before him a social order that had very nearly been swept away. In March he preached against the revolt and reminded wrongdoers of the penance they should undertake, but interestingly, he railed against itinerant friars, whose absolution, he claimed, was ineffective. In the 1350s Thomas and Adam had attacked the friars for the impact they had on the income of the established Church. No longer. Now if they were to be attacked at all, it was for their itinerant nature, but that complaint could apply to any cleric not under the direct control of a bishop or prior. It was the lack of control over the distribution of the clergy that was at the heart of the matter. Already the Church was identifying the need for an established order and a sense of control. Itineracy was an ill that needed to be addressed urgently. By June Thomas was damning openly and freely all the ideas of Wyclif as heresy[xx]. By February 1383 the uprising again featured at the end of a series of sermons in which Thomas drew the attention of the State to a direct link between the two evils that had so recently afflicted the country.

On May 19, 1382 the Archbishop of Canterbury called a council in London to consider the suppression of Wyclif and his writing. At two o'clock in the afternoon there was an earthquake that was felt the length and breadth of England.[xxi] In 14th Century terms this was an omen. Within a week there had been a second earthquake![xxii] In June 1382 the Archbishop of Canterbury wrote to the Chancellor of Oxford[xxiii] forbidding Wyclif and his followers from preaching, and ordering that condemnation of their ideas be made public in churches throughout Oxford. Wyclif was effectively silenced. In the same month Richard II weighed in by issuing letters patent fully supporting the actions of his archbishop.

For the King, or more importantly his council, 1381 was a turning point. After peasants, reeves and even some lesser nobility had attacked and murdered tax collectors, the secular authority had to come to terms with a serious political reality. It was true that the administrators of the Poll Tax were churchmen, not least the Archbishop of Canterbury, Simon Sudbury. That was inevitable. As the main source of men who could write and count, of course most of the tax collectors would be churchmen, clerks and assorted lower ranks in holy orders. But the Poll Tax was not for the benefit of the Church, it was a tax to raise yet more funds for the King and his council. When the abbeys of Bury St Edmunds and St Albans were attacked, many charters and deeds were destroyed, mostly records of land holdings and rights.[xxiv] The peasants were attempting to destroy the only records that could be used to assess the amount of taxation they should pay. Attacks on the standing of the Church could be tolerated, and on occasion even encouraged, but when the King could not raise funds for his own reasons, that was altogether a different matter. The Peasants' Revolt killed off official enthusiasm for Wyclif's ideology amongst the secular authorities in England. The need for control and order in the Church as in the countryside villages and towns had been clearly demonstrated.

As attitudes hardened, a number of churchmen, notably the less than entirely holy Henry Despenser, Bishop of Norwich, came to the forefront of the process of crushing the rebellion. Suddenly bishops were allies of the State and the Church Military, if not militant, became a valuable resource for crushing troublemakers. And if the uprising were to be quashed with the active participation of religious authority, then who could argue about the righteousness of the State's position?

There were other considerations. Faced with social upheaval on this scale, the authorities found comfort in the political and hierarchical status quo. It was clear that a Church that was both wealthy and hierarchical knew where its members were, and more importantly knew what they were saying and to whom they were saying it. In such an organised structure, firebrand preachers could be identified and curtailed. More to the point, such a Church could provide the administrators to collect the King's taxes, those who kept the records of who lived where and what tax they should pay, records that were stored safely, locked up in the abbeys and churches of England. Taxes paid to Rome might be a burden, but for the moment it seemed to be a price worth paying. The Church and the State needed each other, and any novel ideas that discussed the redistribution of power, however conservatively framed, were bound to be condemned.

In his final battle with Wyclif, Adam had triumphed. The conservative forces within the church that identified with Adam, and his views would enjoy a further century of weak royal power as Lancastrians and Yorkists conspired to keep the English nation in a permanent state of war with itself. The real possibility of a reform movement within the English Church was put on hold. The Lollard followers of Wyclif were condemned with the full support of the English secular authorities. Yet attention had also been drawn to the ease with which a coincidence of royal need and populist rhetoric could be turned against the established Church. For several years in the mid 1370s it had been a close run thing.

Chapter 7

The Defence of Ecclesiastical Power

We have asked the Lord who it is that shall dwell in His tabernacle, we have heard the conditions for dwelling there; and if we fulfil the duties of tenants, we shall be heirs of the kingdom of heaven

Rome

Adam did not allow the Church's condemnation of Wyclif to distract him from the second part of the project, the creation of a definitive text to delineate the boundaries of papal and secular power. He would provide the philosophical bedrock for the absolute and undeniable right of the Church to assert power and authority over matters secular as well as religious. The Church must be seen as the final arbiter of right and wrong, good and evil. It would not just state the position, it would prove it by referencing back to the scriptures. It would place the righteousness of religious authority formally on the record. In order to continue with his magnum opus, Adam needed to stay at the heart of the papal court. He needed access to the great scholars and lawyers of the curia and, above all else, to the texts in the libraries of the cardinals. The papal library in Avignon was a major repository of mediaeval learning and contained no fewer than 2,000 manuscripts, including more than 100 texts in Hebrew.[i] The libraries, however, had a natural tendency to follow the movements of their owners, and after Gregory's return to Rome in January 1377 more and more of the papal courtiers were moving to the city of St Peter. The gradual migration of the cardinals from Avignon to Rome was disruptive to Adam's writing.

136

The longer Gregory stayed in Rome, the more permanent the move seemed to be, and none of the leading prelates of the day wanted to be isolated from the Pope and the favours and revenues available at his court.

For a few months Adam hesitated, hoping to get some sense of whether Gregory would stay in Rome or return to Avignon. Finally he took the plunge. His book, his very raison d'etre, needed more research, and that meant he had to be at the papal court. And so a year after the death of Simon, he set off for Rome.

By November 1377, when Adam was granted the right to have a portable altar, he was almost certainly in the Eternal City.[ii] The right to use a portable altar was something of a status symbol in the mediaeval Church. Travel itself was a rare privilege, and it was travel that gave rise to the need for a portable altar. Those who could justify such a privilege (granted exclusively in the name of the Pope) were inevitably from the higher echelons of society, wealthy merchants, senior clerics and diplomats. The fact that Adam saw fit to petition for the right to use a portable altar suggests that he was travelling, and not in a position to take mass at a regular place of worship. In Avignon he had developed a regular pattern to his life, and, as a Benedictine, that included a regular place of worship. In the city of Rome, Adam was still a stranger. His previous visit had been a brief tourist trek through the pilgrimage churches some eight years earlier, and he had never had the chance to get to know his way around. He was unsettled. He would have to find regular lodgings and a regular place of worship. For a Benedictine accustomed to a routine of prayer and mass this was no small matter, as religious devotion was supposed to account for much of his daily life.

Throughout 1377, first in Avignon and later in Rome, Adam dedicated himself to working on his book. Through this one work he would demonstrate to the theologians and intellectuals of the day why Wyclif was wrong. He called the book "Defensorium Ecclesiastice Potestate" the defence of ecclesiastical power, and it was to be a massive work. It is clear from the prologue that originally the work was intended to comprise no fewer than six volumes. However, the only surviving copies include just one book, so it seems doubtful that Adam ever wrote more than that first volume. Even so the one book that has survived is still a substantial work, with no fewer than 726 handwritten pages.

Judges and Kings

Adam had long been fascinated by the origins of kingship and more specifically how the Bible as the definitive text for matters of Scholastic knowledge covered the origins of kingship. From his first days at Oxford he had studied the four Books of Kings, and this made him curious. It was the way the Books of Kings had been translated into Latin that made him want to go back and re-examine St Jerome's translation. This had led him to his first major project, the retranslation of the Bible from Hebrew into Latin.

How the Bible deals with the way Israel was governed was peculiarly relevant to the ideas of kingship expressed in the mediaeval world. After all, the Book of Judges dealt with chosen men who ruled over Israel as intermediaries between God and his chosen people, holding a status that seems at first sight to have something in common with the role of Pope as understood by the mediaeval papacy. The evolution from a system of Judges "called" or chosen by God, to the Kings called for and chosen by the people of Israel, set Kings and Popes side by side in a Biblical context.

The comparison was not at all flattering, for the Kings may have had the strength of David or the wisdom of Solomon, but they turned out to be flawed individuals who could not stand up to the scrutiny of God. Kings were provided to Israel to please the people, but in the face of the will of God and against the true desire of God. Kings, God clearly understood, were flawed beings, creations of mankind who could not be relied upon, a point made frequently in the first Book of Kings. The Judges of Israel, on the other hand, were God's own chosen intermediaries and generally were seen to come up with the goods and lead Israel back to the path of righteousness.

This ground formed the central plank of Adam's discussion of Kings and Popes and the mediaeval hierarchy. Yet if the people of Israel had turned their back on God by choosing to be ruled by Kings instead of Judges, then no criticism of the mediaeval Jewish people was ever implied by Adam, partly perhaps because he saw the same flaw in mediaeval society. Here too the people had turned from the Popes, the Judges of society, to Kings. It was entirely logical then that he should attach neither judgement nor stigma to the Jews among whom he lived and worked. Not for the first time we see in Adam an unusual lack of prejudice at a time when, outside Avignon, Jewish people were enduring a wave of persecution.

Greek Revival

The grand work that Adam set out to write belonged to a long tradition of esoteric religious treatises dating back 300 years. From Abelard to Peter Lombard and St Thomas Aquinas the pronouncement on the nature of religion and the philosophy of Scholasticism had been written out in narrative text. Adam knew the subject of his own work was bound to be a heavy read, perhaps he had bad memories of working through the other tracts as part of his studies at Norwich and Oxford. So he tried a novel approach, breaking up the narrative into a debate. He presented his material in the form of a conversation between a bishop (Episcopus) and a king

(Rex), to voice the arguments from the two contrary points of view. The idea of using a device by which representatives argue their point of view rather than preparing a long uninterrupted treatise was not original. It was a technique much used by ancient Greek writers, found in Plato in particular. However popular it had been as a device amongst the classical Greek writers, as with many of the classical traditions it had virtually vanished from European writing during the Dark Ages. If Adam was comfortable enough with the dialogue style to use it so extensively in the Defensorium, he must have been intimate with the Greek classics from his days at Gloucester College. This strong hint that he may have been skilled in Greek is hardly surprising given his aptitude in both Latin and Hebrew. Adam was reputed to have been a leading Greek scholar of his time, but today we have little evidence of that reputation apart from the style of the Defensorium. What is clear is that he was one of the earlier scholars to reintroduce the conversational style of written debates to the mainstream of European literature.

Other writers prior to Adam had tried to reintroduce similar techniques to add interest and colour to what might otherwise have been rather hard-going treatises. Richard FitzRalph made use of a dialogue style of writing in "De Pauperie Salvatoris", which was written as a conversation between a certain "John" and "Richard", and this may well have influenced Adam in his approach. However, the characters in FitzRalph's book were simply used to break up the text, without representing points of view or even being developed as characters or even caricatures. We are left with two people having a chat about the moral issues of the day.

In the same rather two-dimensional way Anselm used the technique in his Proslogion, in which two real characters, the author and his monk colleague Boso, debate the finer points of philosophical and religious orthodoxy. However, we learn little about either personality from the debate, nor do they represent anything more than relatively mild agreement. The sense of debate is therefore rather lost.

Adam took the original Greek tradition and enlarged it. The dialogues are used to represent and develop the consistent points of view of each character. The choice of a bishop and a king enables Adam to use the characters as obvious totems for the world view of two groups of people. The characters do not need to be greatly developed, as we find we can predict pretty much what each will say. Yet the ideas and the core of the problems debated at the heart of the Defensorium are brought out by Adam's style. A clear picture is developed of the entrenched position of Church and State through the two characters, Adam employing a style that would find favour for centuries to come. Galileo was still using the same principles to good effect three centuries later when he published "Dialogue on the Two Chief World Systems". It was a technique that suited a writer who wanted to express a view that he might need to claim later was not necessarily his own, but merely a representation of some other person's view (or at least a view that could be regarded as commonplace).

In that respect, Galileo and Adam had something in common.

Magister Adam

Over the centuries since Adam's death there has been considerable debate over who wrote the Defensorium. Although several copies have survived none of them are signed and there is no author named within its pages. In the script we are told that the name of the author is hidden amongst the capital letters at the start of the prologue (cuius nomen continentur in litteris capitalibus parcium huius libri prologi inchoante[iii]). Once again we see some evidence of Adam's love of codes and word games. However, in the Vatican copy, the scribe has helpfully noted in the margins that the author referred to is "Magister Adam", but unhelpfully did not copy the capitals in the same fashion as Adam wrote them. As Adam's original text does not seem to have survived, in modern times no-one has been able to show how the code worked. For once the author was nearly too smart for his own good, as it was only early in the last century that the scholar William Pantin identified it definitively as the work of Adam Easton.[iv]

Adam lived a century before the printing press arrived in Europe, and the only way of reproducing a book was to laboriously copy it out by hand. At least three copies of the Defensorium survive today, and the best preserved is that held in the Vatican Library in Rome (other copies are in Madrid and Seville). The Vatican version was copied out by a Neapolitan monk called Nardellus, who signed his name on the last folio along with the dates when he copied the book. The book is written in two columns to a page and in a small, tightly formed hand. Following the writing of Nardellus is itself a challenge. His copy of the Defensorium is written in the high Gothic script of his day where the letters "m" "n" and "i" can often run together into one indeterminable line, and he used the standard Latin shorthand. Whilst there were abbreviations that were in common usage, nearly every copyist had their own particular quirks, their own forms of abbreviation of words and their own variations on the symbols for abbreviation, and it can take a long while to get used to reading such handwriting.

Nardellus was not as bad as some. His handwriting may not be always easy to read, but at least it was meticulous and neat. It is easy to forget in a world of computers and spell-checking software that not so many years ago works of literature were drafted by hand and that it was a laborious task.

The Defensorium

Adam crafted the debates between Rex and Episcopus across 68 chapters, covering the various issues relating to the hierarchy of the Church and State and the relationship of each with the other. Surprisingly, given the bile with which Protestant and Catholic wrote against each other during the years of the 16th Century, the debate compiled by Adam two centuries earlier was written in a tone of great civility. Rex is clearly a master diplomat and holds his temper when, at various points in the narrative, he is faced with the severest of provocations. He is told repeatedly that the views that he holds, along with those of the doctors whose works he calls upon in support, are false and erroneous. The good monarch accepts with deference the correction offered to him by Episcopus, as if he acknowledges that he is debating with a superior authority. If only real-life kings took such trouble to wait even-temperedly whilst the error of their ways is explained to them.

Of course the bias that we might expect from Adam's specific point of view is there for all to see. There was never any doubt as to who was right and who was wrong, and even after the lengthiest of debates, each chapter closes with Episcopus summing up the true position and explaining the error of Rex's ways, often by reference to the Scriptures in the process. The most frustrating aspect of the Defensorium is that we never really get to see glimpses of Adam's lost retranslation of the Old Testament. Quotes from the Old Testament are surprisingly infrequent; the New Testament is used far more often to support the arguments that Adam wanted to settle. Where we do find the odd quotation, from Deuteronomy or Isaiah, it is too close to the Vulgate version to believe that these were the key passages where Adam had construed a significantly different meaning to that of Jerome.

If his own work was under-represented, he made up for it with that of others. Woven into the text are the works of the great writers of his age, and some of the more dangerous ones (at least from the Church's point of view). We find heretical writers such as Marsilius of Padua and William of Ockham rubbing shoulders with, and being put to rights by, John of Legnano, Richard FitzRalph and Gratian (author of the Decretum). Each writer has his views debated before being put in their rightful context in Easton's view of the universe. Yet whether they are considered right or wrong, all are treated with respect, and this is most notable in the part of the book dealing with John Wyclif. He may be called to account by Adam for being erroneous or holding false views, but he was not to be insulted. When he appears on folio 302 he is the "ingenious lord John", on folio 283 he is not just given his rightful title as "professor of the sacred pages" but he is recalled as a man of great science and learning. Perhaps Adam felt that he could afford a degree of managnimity towards his adversary and here, on the page at least, the debate is portrayed as a civilised discussion between equals.

The tone is always stately, and there is no hint of urgency or of the panic and fear that the Benedictines undoubtedly felt under the withering attacks of Wyclif. Most of the last 50 folios of the Defensorium are devoted to attacking the arguments and propositions of Wyclif and his followers. It is here that we can find verbatim references to the "dicta" of Wyclif that had been condemned in Gregory's Bull, as long and involved arguments are developed around the debate over property, lordship and the complex question of whether king or pope rule over each other. Easton makes clear that temporal lords or kings rule only with permission, not as a matter of God's will (or divine right as later monarchs would express it), and therefore it must follow that a bad or misguided temporal lord can be, indeed must be, replaced by the supreme religious lord, the pope. The conclusion firmly rebuts the propositions Wyclif put forward in De Civilio Dominio and reasserts the orthodox view of the role of the Church.[v]

Easton then takes the argument beyond some of the more esoteric questions on dominion and possession that had obsessed Wyclif and FitzRalph before him and looks at the wealth of the papacy, a common complaint in his day.[vi] Here Adam asserts that there is no harm per se in the Church accumulating wealth, because the Church itself as a body of innocence would necessarily make its resources a force for innocence. The gold in the Church's coffers would be effectively cleansed through ownership by the Church. The greater share of the wealth on earth that ended up with the Church, the greater the spread of good works and virtue across the surface of the earth. It was a mirror to the modern argument that wealth and power corrupt!

Cardinals in Trouble

The defence of the authority and power of the Church was the tour de force of his work but Adam also addressed himself to some specifics as well as the general theme. He allowed himself free reign throughout the Defensorium to defend the official position of the Church across a range of contemporary issues. During the period of the Avignon residence it was not just the wealth and prestige of the Pope that had drawn comment. That of his acolytes had attracted even fiercer criticism.

In the Avignon years the cardinals had taken half of the Church's total income each year, behaving very much in the fashion of secular princes. They acquired grand courts of their own. Their conspicuous wealth and worldly bearing had become a frequent target of popular outrage. Several commentators, not least Petrarch, had written scathing tracts against these "satellites" who "instead of soberness, licentious banquets; instead of pious pilgrimages, preternatural and foul sloth; instead of the bare feet of the apostles, the snowy coursers of brigands fly past us, the horses decked in gold and fed on gold, soon to be shod with gold, if the Lord does not check this slavish luxury. In short, we seem to be among the kings of the Persians or Parthians, before whom we must fall down and worship, and who cannot be approached except presents be offered. O ye unkempt and emaciated old men, is it for this you labored?"[vii]

To a cleric of Adam's standing, intimately involved in the administration of the Church, the cardinals had received unjust treatment and a bad press caused by a lack of understanding of the important role they played in the papal administration. So in chapter 11 of the Defensorium Adam came rushing to their defence. Rex started out by summarising what was clearly a contemporary complaint. Whilst with due deference he insisted that he had the greatest of respect for the rank of cardinal, he could see no justification for creating this high rank within the Church. There was no evidence to recommend such a position in the writing of the scriptures or in the teaching of Christ and the early Church. Surely it followed that the rank of cardinal was an aberration and it should (by implication at least) be abolished. Bishops, archbishops and the like were a different matter, after all they could trace their pedigree back to St Peter.

Not surprisingly, Episcopus was ready with the answer. Not everything that was essential to the good of the Church was sourced from the scriptures, some things had grown through the guidance of the Holy Spirit. The apostles after all were rather like cardinals in the court of Christ: when they dispersed after the death of Christ they took their jurisdiction from Peter. He was not alone in his work however, and he maintained in turn his own following. Those who remained with Peter were like cardinals administering his Church.[viii] Episcopus also noted that if not exactly in the scriptures, then some justification for cardinals can at least be found as far back as Saint Augustine in his "Confessions".

This was certainly a topical note to include in the Defensorium and on that Adam had strong personal views. However it is also hard to avoid the conclusion that by arguing vigorously in favour of cardinals Adam was dropping the Pope a pretty heavy hint about where he would like his own future in the church to be heading!

Out of Step with the Times?

It is difficult to assess the full impact of the Defensorium Ecclesiastice Potestatis. In an age when most of the population were illiterate, books were necessarily aimed at the intellectual elite of society, and although it was written in Latin, most people in Adam's day could read Latin if they could read at all. Aside from the three copies of the book still in existence today[ix] there was at least one other copy in Norwich in the 16th Century, probably a part of Adam's gift to the Priory library. We know that John Whethamstede had a copy made for the Abbey of St Albans and John Bale mentions that Robert Talbot had a copy (Dialogum Regis et Episcopi) in his own collection that he acquired whilst he held the title of Prebend of Norwich between 1547 and 1558.[x] Assuming that this last was not Adam's own copy and that it has not survived, at least six full versions of the text must have existed. It would be remarkable if the five copies of the text we know of represent the total number of copies made, particularly given the opportunity for loss and damage over a period of six centuries.

To understand the significance of the number of copies that might have been made of Adam's work, we must remember that before the arrival of the printing press the only method of reproduction was by copying out the work by hand. For a book on the scale of the Defensorium (even if we focus on the one book that Adam completed rather than the six volumes that were clearly intended) this would be a substantial task that would have taken several months to finish. It is not a process that anyone would go through for a book considered to be unimportant or out of date. When John Whethamstede[xi] had his copy made (some 50 years after Adam wrote the Defensorium) he paid out 40 shillings, quite a substantial sum, to have it copied professionally. Books for the educated elite would be found, for the most part, in monasteries. Common practice and obedience to the Monastic Rules meant of necessity that books tended to be passed around rather than held as personal possessions. One book would be quite sufficient for a whole monastery.

Some historians have suggested that the events that followed the publication of the Defensorium made it obsolete and irrelevant, pointing to the lack of surviving copies as evidence. This is a view distorted with hindsight that does not take account of the way written material was disseminated in the 14th and 15th Centuries.

It is perhaps more helpful to look at the Defensorium as the articulation of Church power at the pinnacle of that power, a book that is the end product of 500 years of political thought evolving from the coronation of Charlemagne to the Schism. Adam's book represents the most complete and carefully worked case for the role of the Pope as the "primus inter pares", the Church as the ultimate arbiter of worldly and religious disputes. It is a work that sums up the accumulation of power and authority at the point before collapse. Yet even after the Schism the influence of the Defensorium can be seen at work. That it was not a treatise of transitory importance is evidenced by the fact that the Vatican copy of the Defensorium was copied some 50 years after Adam wrote it, so it was not a work that had been forgotten almost as soon as it was published. And as the Prebend of Norwich had a copy in his library during the Counter Reformation of

Queen Mary in the 1550s it seems that to those who supported the Catholic view, the Defensorium remained a highly regarded book, influential and authoritative. In the end, to attain the influence that the work claimed for it, the papacy would have had to exercise the power and authority that Adam attributed to it by right. As we shall see, the popes of the later 14th Century failed to provide that sort of inspirational leadership for the Church. This left Adam lacking a model for the Defensorium in contrast to the way that Cesare Borgia provided one so emphatically for Machiavelli's Prince. Without one Adam's work inevitably rings hollow.

The Rescue of the Catholic Orthodoxy

The key to Adam's influence on English history is often overlooked, and we must now return to it. The Reformation may in the estimation of some have made his work less relevant, but too few historians have satisfactorily addressed themselves to the question (let alone answered it) "why did the Reformation not happen 150 years earlier than it did?" In many ways it could have, indeed perhaps it should have. Wyclif had the same principled objection to the Church that Luther developed a century and a half later. His views were similar to those that underpinned the English Reformation of Cranmer and his sovereign. In terms of an attitude to the papacy, Edward III had much in common with Henry VIII. When Edward III passed the Statute of Praemunire there was potential for a split, with a powerful king interested in forcing his will over the tenets of religion and the embodiment of religious power. Had Wyclif written and publicised his views 20 years earlier, events may have taken a very different turn. Had Edward lived longer and with a sound mind into the era of the Great Schism, that might have made the difference. The five years that followed 1377 were a defining moment of English history, every bit as much as the early Reformation years of the 1540s. Here Adam made his mark in his own particular and rather quiet way and in the process stopped a movement in full flow and changed the course of English history in the process.

The fact is that apart from Adam and his repeated attacks on Wyclif, including the intellectual assault represented by the Defensorium, there was little else to stop the confluence of the secular opportunism of John of Gaunt and the religious opportunism of Wyclif. Adam's action preserved the status quo as the Church in Rome entered a period of weakness and decline in its own authority. Rent asunder in the schism following the ill-judged profligacy of the Avignon years, with not one but two (and occasionally three) popes simultaneously claiming to be the true Pope, the Church was fatally damaged. Somehow it managed to struggle on with the same institutions, corruption and wealth as before. It is tempting to ask how the Church survived intact into the early 16th Century. Perhaps it is no coincidence that when the idea of Reformation finally did emerge in England, it was the very next time that a powerful monarch with a European agenda sat on the throne.

If for no other reason, for its crucial final part in the sustained attack on Wyclif the Defensorium deserves to be seen as a significant tract and Adam as a major influence on English history. Isolated from the land of his birth and unclear as to the impact of his actions, Adam must have been frustrated at his inability to exercise direct control over the assault on Wyclif. Slowly he acclimatised himself to a new life in Rome, waiting for news that could take several weeks to get from England to Rome. As he worked on the Defensorium, mapping out his texts and arguments, he wrote at a furious pace determined to bring his work to a conclusion. With the various papal courtiers drifting back to Rome and the machinery of the papal chancery finally starting to get under way in the Vatican, it must have been clear that substantial change was coming. Adam wanted to present his new work as the definitive defence for a newly established papacy returned from Babylonian exile in Avignon. The book would be the launch pad for a new era of papal authority, and the sooner Adam could complete it after the return to Rome, the more authority it would carry in that context.

Even so, it was a substantial volume and in an era of handwritten manuscripts, the very process of writing a book was time consuming. In his own words in the endnote to the copy of the Defensorium preserved in the Vatican, the monk Nardellus de Napoli, who undertook the job of copying the treatise from start to finish, explains what a laborious task it was. He tells us that he did not finish until January 1432, by which time he had been working on it for a year. Nardellus tells us that he started in the reign of Pope Martin V (died February 20, 1431) and finished in the reign of Pope Eugene IV.[xii] If it took Nardellus from well before February 1431 to January 1432 to copy the work, it must have taken Adam at least three years to write it, bearing in mind that the author had to go through the process of drawing an outline of the arguments and researching the texts of the masters and doctors of his day before he even got down to the creative process itself. Even if Adam had started writing and researching at the time he wrote to the Abbott of Westminster in November 1376, it is highly unlikely he would have finished before the Christmas of 1379. The very fact that the dedication in the prologue is to Urban VI not to Gregory XI hints that Adam had not completed his magnum opus until well after the end of 1377.

At any event, by the time the book was to be completed, the world would be a very changed place. Adam was still busy at work on the text of the Defensorium when on March 27, 1378 Gregory XI died in Rome.

Chapter 8

Rent Asunder

He who boasts should make his boast in the Lord

Electing a Pope

For the first time in more than a century the Pope had died in the Holy See and the Roman people would have the chance to experience a papal election. The whole city was alive with fervent expectation. After the Avignon years, during which all the popes chosen had been French, everyone felt that the election of an Italian pope was a real possibility. An Italian pope was more likely to secure the papal presence in Rome and turn the tentative move that Gregory made in 1377 into a permanent return. The same populace which not a year before had been very unsure about the papal presence, and even less sure about the close scrutiny of papal tax collectors, suddenly turned into fanatical supporters of an Italian pope and most importantly, one who would remain in Rome.

The French cardinals were rather less comfortable with the situation they found themselves in. Choosing a new pope had become quite a formalised process. By a tradition that dated from a proclamation of Nicholas II, the new pope was to be chosen by a meeting or conclave of those cardinals who were at the court of the previous pope when he died. The cardinals had to be shut away together to make their decision, and they were not permitted to emerge until a successor had been agreed upon. Nicholas's proclamation had specified that the election should be free from the pressure of secular lords and also the populace of Rome, and if this were not possible, then the election should take place elsewhere.

The French would have much preferred the latter option. The peaceful transition of papal authority that had been so carefully stage managed in

147

Avignon was in imminent danger of being replaced by an election where the whims of the Roman mob might influence the outcome. The cardinals could of course leave the city and hold the election in one of the safer towns in the Roman hinterland. Viterbo, Orvieto or even Montefiascone had each been popular places of refuge for the papal court in the past. If they tried to leave en masse, however, they would risk the wrath of the Romans, who might not feel disposed to let them leave the city alive if they suspected the cardinals' true purpose. On balance it was decided that the safest bet was to stay put and manage the process as well as possible. How the outcome under those circumstances could be said to be beyond the influence of the mob was almost beyond credibility, at least to the French way of looking at things.

Adam was much happier with the situation. His decision to move to Rome had been vindicated and he found himself at the centre of the papal court as one of the most important elections of the century was about to take place. He would be in an excellent position to witness the events surrounding the election as they unfolded in front of him. Although only the cardinals would choose the new pope, as an official of the papal court Adam's work in the apostolic chanceries brought him into regular contact with the cardinals, several of whom he now knew quite well. As an official representative of the Benedictine order he might expect to be asked his opinion on the suitability of the candidates. Before the official conclave started, cardinals and officials moved in and out of their meetings trying to assess the level of support for various candidates. Before long Adam had been told about the various possibilities being considered by the cardinals. He spoke regularly with Cardinal Agrifolio, and sometimes took meals with him, as he did with Cardinal Orsini,[i] and he was still on good terms with the Cardinal of Pamplona.

As he moved from meeting to meeting Adam mingled with the crowds in Rome, listening to their near-nationalist expressions of a desire to bring the papacy back to Rome. A triumphant return would be topped by the election of an Italian pope. All the commentators in Rome at the time of the election later testified to the high emotions running through the crowds. Adam reported the views he had heard on the street to the cardinals as he swapped notes with them on the progress of negotiations. The hopes that the Romans carried in their hearts and on their sleeves were contrasted with the fears of the French cardinals for their safety. The cardinals were trying to reach an agreement on suitable candidates before the formal process of the conclave began. By doing so they could minimise the time needed for the conclave itself and thereby reduce the risk that the mood of the mob might turn ugly before a decision had been made.

They had a tough task ahead of them. Even if the cardinals were minded to choose an Italian pope, there were few suitable candidates among their number. The aged Cardinal Tebaldeschi certainly had credibility, but he was really too old to be a suitable. No one wanted to have to go through the election process again any sooner than was strictly necessary. Cardinal Orsini, a Roman by birth, whilst not being as elderly as Tebaldeschi, had baggage all of his own, for choosing an Orsini would inevitably alienate the powerful, rival Colunna family. If the papacy was to be re-established in Rome, it could not afford a major outbreak of factional fighting between the two rival families that had dominated Roman life for much of the past 500 years. Of the remaining candidates, the Cardinal of Florence was too young to be credible and Simon Brossani, Cardinal of Milan, made it clear that he had no interest in being nominated.

All of which left the college of cardinals deeply divided on what to do next. Aside from the four Italian cardinals, there was one Spanish cardinal and 11 French in Rome at the time of the conclave. The cardinals tended to form factions along national lines, voting en bloc for their preferred candidate, and in 1377 this left no one party in a majority because of a split in the French ranks. The dominance of the French was a legacy from the long years in Avignon, where the close proximity of the French King had helped instil some considerable bias in the process of selecting cardinals. However, the French faction was itself divided between those of the "Limoges" cardinals and the rest. The Limoges or "Limousin" faction came into being in the mid 14th Century when a policy of nepotism resulted in an unusually large number of prelates from the French city being created cardinals. They remained influential even after the return to Rome, and Adam's friend Cardinal Agrifolio was the leading light of their faction. Faced with jealousy and suspicion from the other cardinals, the Limoges faction tended to vote together and formed its own grouping within the college of cardinals. So wary were these Limousins of the antipathy felt by the rest towards the nepotism that had supported their advancement that they were as apt to vote against the French as they were against the Italians.

The four Italian cardinals had a greater influence over the outcome of the conclave than they might have expected because six of the cardinals, all from either the Limoges or French faction, had still not moved from Avignon to Rome and so they took no part in the conclave to elect the new pope. Even so the three different parties each wanted to propose their own candidate, and it quickly became clear that any candidate from one party would be blocked by the other two. The only solution likely to get unanimous agreement was to find a candidate from outside the college of cardinals. So it was that the critical deal between the cardinals happened not in the official discussions during the conclave, but, as Adam reported later,[ii] in the three days leading up to it, when the different factions concluded their negotiations on a compromise candidate. This three-day period was of critical importance to the events that followed.

Once agreement was reached on who was to be chosen as pope, the cardinals still had to put on a show for the populace, going through a formal conclave with due ceremony and emerging having elected the new pontiff. The crowds outside the Vatican naturally assumed that the debate over who should be pope would start with the conclave, and that was when they took an active interest in proceedings. The pope was not just head of the Church, he was also the princely ruler of Rome in a secular capacity, and he taxed the citizens in the same way as a king would, ran the administration, raised armies and fought wars. It mattered to the Roman people who would be their ruler as much as an Englishman might care about who would be his sovereign.

Right Place, Right Time

Adam was in a good position to know the inner workings of the papal court, and he had also been in Rome long enough by April 1377 to know his way around the sacred city. Rome was the capital city of the Catholic Church. The city was full of great churches dating from the earliest time of Christianity, churches that inspired pilgrimages, some because of the bones of the holy men and women they contained, and others who drew the faithful because of the sheer beauty of the decoration and grandeur of their architecture. Dressed in his Benedictine cloak, Adam could lose himself in the midst of the mass of humanity that thronged the streets of Rome, just one more foreign monk amongst the hundreds and thousands that flocked to the holy city. They might be on pilgrimage themselves or simply be attached to one of the many monasteries in Rome. Either way, no one would notice a Black Monk in a Roman crowd. Unlike some of his colleagues Adam did care to know what the Roman citizens thought of the choices being made on their behalf, and that's why he had his ear so firmly to the common ground.

The conclave to elect the new pope opened on April 7, barely a week after Gregory's death, with a view to choosing a successor with the minimum of disruption. The careful groundwork undertaken by the cardinals ensured that the most significant conclave in the history of the papacy was also destined to be the shortest. As soon as the cardinals entered the conclave, crowds of Romans converged on the Vatican, anxious to hear of the outcome. It was said that the captains of the guard sealed the gates of the city so that none of the cardinals could sneak out until the business of the day had been properly attended to. Adam, mingling among the crowds outside, noticed that many knights were distributed amongst the throng[iii] to keep order. The crowds outside the Vatican shouted "Romano lo volemo, o almanco Italiano" (we want a Roman or at least an Italian)." The state and spirit of the crowd became a matter of serious debate later, but Adam was adamant that most of the crowd milling around the buildings of the Vatican were familiars and courtiers of the very cardinals who were locked inside the conclave. Moreover, the mood was jovial, with the foreign courtiers mocking the Romans and their shouts of "we want a Roman pope". The crowds were chattering amongst themselves and generally in a festive mood. Several commentators suggested, quite plausibly, that they were drunk on wine.

In the conclave, the business was straightforward and the atmosphere was relaxed. Of course, the difficult part of the negotiations had already been resolved in the three days leading up to April 7. Once the factions had agreed to disagree on electing one of the existing cardinals they had cast around the ranks of the senior churchmen looking for an alternative. The Italians had proposed Bartholomew Prignano, the Archbishop of Bari, a known reformer and an austere cleric. Best of all he was an Italian, albeit from Naples rather than Rome. In the end a sincere pontiff, albeit a man of low birth and crude manners whom the French were sure they would be able to manipulate, seemed to be the perfect compromise. The cardinals quickly reached a unanimous decision to elect Prignano, and with that prepared themselves for the formal business of the conclave. All they needed to do now was to sit tight and go through the motions of pretending to debate intensely over whom to choose.

However, there was just one slight problem that still had to be addressed. Prignano was known to be a prickly character, and it was by no means certain that the Archbishop would accept the papal tiara. The cardinals needed to secure his agreement, and with it the succession, before the crowds became too unruly and with that in mind they sent a message to summon the Archbishop to appear before the conclave. Unfortunately the activity of the papal messengers started rumours circulating amongst the crowds that the cardinals had reached a decision. Cardinal Orsini watched in horror as the swelling crowds converged on the Vatican and he feared disorder.

Farce

All the careful stage management and preparation was in danger of unravelling. Orsini, a Roman from one of the leading families of the city, was acutely alert to the danger and acted instinctively. He reassured the mob, telling them that they should go immediately to St Peter's, thinking that they would understand from this that a decision had been made. At St

Peter's they should await the formal announcement of the cardinals' decision. It was a bold move that relied heavily on Prignano accepting their offer, but unfortunately the mob either misheard or misunderstood. Spotting the Cardinal of St Peter's, the ancient and frail Cardinal Tebaldeschi, at a window near to Orsini, they assumed that Orsini was telling them that it was Tebaldeschi who had been chosen. Tebaldeschi was an Italian based in Rome, exactly the sort of choice the Romans had hoped for, and they were elated. After 80 years of waiting for a permanent papal return from Avignon they were in no mind to be put off. The crowd rushed into the Vatican to claim Tebaldeschi for themselves, filling the corridors and antechambers. In a moment of panic the cardinals presented them with the unfortunate old man and decked him with the papal regalia. The crowd, fuelled in some cases with alcoholic enthusiasm, seized Tebaldeschi and, lifting him above their heads, carried the poor cardinal in triumph to St Peter's. He did his best to protest and explain their misunderstanding, but he was powerless to influence a crowd that was not listening. Tebaldeschi panicked and started shouting and abusing the mob around him. The Cardinal of St Peter's, in genuine fear for his life, looked more like a madman than the new head of the Church, but he was a Roman madman so that was all right! The wily Agrifolio, seeing the events unfolding outside, thought it better not to interrupt, the life of his colleague seeming somehow less important than his own. On a more practical note, the distraction of the crowd gave Prignano the opportunity to pass into the conclave more or less unobserved. He confirmed to the agitated cardinals that he would accept their offer, but only after insisting that they confirm to him that he was their unanimous choice and that they considered the election to be free and fair. By now several of the French cardinals were so worried by the actions of the mob that they were in no mood to argue over technicalities. Prignano got to hear what he wanted. Before nightfall several of the French left the city, whilst others took refuge in the Castello St Angelo, where a Breton garrison that had been in the pay of Gregory XI was in residence.

Later that evening Adam found himself in the company of a papal courtier, Egidius de Velinse. Both men were well aware that Prignano was the chosen man and that Tebaldeschi had only been used as a decoy. Egidius told Adam that he feared that the cardinals would lose their resolution in the face of the drunken crowds of Romans. The Englishman replied with a great deal more confidence than the situation justified "either the lords (cardinals) are men or they are women. If women, they will change their minds like women. If men, their voices will be bound firmly and unchanging for ever."[iv] However, even Adam could not have been that confident, for he added, "I am very concerned that neither faction will permit the ascendancy of the other and that the decision will undoubtedly go to a third conclave". Perhaps they would just leave the unfortunate Tebaldeschi as the new pope. In fact were it not for his advanced age and frailty, the Roman cardinal might well have made a very decent compromise candidate.

Adam's first instinct was proved right. The following morning good order and common sense prevailed and the mix-up with Tebaldeschi was resolved. Orsini explained to the crowds that Prignano was ready to accept the papal throne as the unanimous choice of the cardinals, and everyone dutifully traipsed off to St Peter's once again. Later that day Adam was present in the cathedral to witness Orsini perform the coronation of Bartholomew Prignano. He took the name Pope Urban VI.

An Italian Pope

For all the chaos of the preceding days, the result was really rather pleasing. All the factions of cardinals within the conclave had saved face and a credible candidate had been elected. The Romans had been presented with an Italian pope, albeit not a true Roman, and the conclave had been more or less unanimous in appointing him. Even the six cardinals who had remained in Avignon wrote to confirm that they approved of his nomination and offered their submission to him as the true Pope. An outbreak of self congratulation overcame the cardinals. The day after the election Cardinal Agrifolio told Adam that not since the time of St Peter had a pope been so piously elected and that the Holy Spirit had been amongst them when they made the decision to choose him.[v] He asked Adam how the news of Urban's election would be received in England, by the King and his allies in particular. Agrifolio held a number of benefices in England, and he was rather more concerned with the prospects for hanging on to them than he was with the weightier matters of international diplomacy. Adam may have been on good terms with Agrifolio but, as we have seen before, he was a man inclined to speak his mind. He told the cardinal that the news would undoubtedly be welcome in England, and had it not been for the interference of a number of French popes and cardinals in support of the French king's cause, peace between England and France might have been acheived a long time ago. There can be little doubt that Adam still had in the back of his mind the fate of his own diplomatic mission in the 1370s, and he seems to have taken that failure rather personally. His retort was quite unfair and unreasonably patriotic. At the time the English King had had as much interest in prolonging the war as the French, and had been just as keen to manoeuvre events so as to avoid any possibility of peace. In 1378 the English welcomed the coronation of a Pope who was not French and was determined not to be based in France, but this demonstrated their own self interest and had nothing to do with promulgating a lasting peace with France. And at this stage neither the English nor the French knew quite what to expect from Urban VI.

Adam had managed to keep himself extremely well informed throughout the process of electing the new pope. He knew his way around the papal court and he was adept at getting an insider's view on how things were progressing. He even prized out of Bertrand Atgerius, the Cardinal of the Friars Minor, the observation that before entering the conclave he had sent word to Urban saying that he would voice support for him as Pope.[vi] After the election Adam used his position as an insider at court to circulate amongst those cardinals he knew well, gauging their reaction to the new Pontiff, whilst at the same time looking for supporters to secure his own advancement. The election was a major talking point in the subsequent weeks, not least because it had so nearly gone horribly wrong. As a senior intellectual based within the papal court Adam was a person whose opinions were worth courting. He wrote to the Cardinal of Pamplona, dined with Iacobo de Orsini and met up with Pedro de Luna, taking every opportunity to discuss the election and the possibilities that the new papacy might provide. He even stayed at Agrifolio's house on the night of the election so that he might be formally presented to Urban the morning after his coronation ceremony had taken place. If Urban was going to be a popular Pope with a power base in Rome, Adam wanted to be sure that he took an early opportunity to be favourably received into his good grace.

By the end of April everything was going well for the new regime. Across the city of Rome there was just one topic of conversation; an Italian Pope had been elected in the Holy City and there was no more talk of running back to Avignon. Things had gone much better than anyone could have dared to hope, and in the papal court there was general relief. As the news spread across Italy and then to Catholic Europe, it became clear that Urban had a high approval rating. Inevitably, any decision that removed the papacy from Avignon would have been greeted with pleasure by the English and therefore by definition would be considered as less than optimal by the French. Yet with all the cardinals submitting to the new Pope, even the French King had few options but to accept the decision.

Urban came to the papacy with a reputation as an austere cleric, a man who was renowned for wearing a hair shirt and for having strident views on the onset of decadence in the court of the Church, and as such he was surely the right man for the times. He was a reformer, and his cardinals could only expect that once he had been enthroned he would want to change things. Urban had the opportunity to set about reform in a dignified fashion, cleansing some of the abuses of the Church and seeking to bring together the various factions of cardinals to act as a unified court. He had the goodwill both of the cardinals and the Roman populace, and if his reforms were to be far reaching, few would have any grounds for objecting. He might even elect a few Italian cardinals to balance out the French majority in the papal court, without the interference of the French King. He might approach one or two of the wealthier cardinals discretely and pressure them into curbing their ostentatious style of living for the good of the Church. He might also consider a goodwill visit to Avignon to meet those cardinals who had not been in Rome at the time of his election and satisfy them as to his integrity and his intentions. This would certainly help to appease the French King.

Urban VI – His Own Man

The new pope did none of these things. The cardinals had chosen a man with a reputation as a reformer and reform was what they would get. In their enthusiasm at finding a compromise candidate they rather neglected to look at Prignano's record as a diplomat and a tactician. Urban got straight into his stride by attacking simony, berating the practice of Church officials having more than one benefice, a system that had enabled so many of them to live in luxury. It was a fair point, and certainly the practice had attracted much criticism from the Church's critics of the day. Urban, however, was determined to make the point in his own special way. The new Pope promised that if his cardinals took advantage of the system, he would strip them of their ill-gotten gains with the same rigour as he would a junior clerk. To make matters worse, he aired his views in public and to the great embarrassment of the cardinals.

Mutterings and rumours started. Some of the cardinals began to wonder to themselves if they might perhaps have been ill advised in their choice of Pope. Adam had little to fear from the purity being demanded of the papal courtiers by the new Pope. As luck would have it, and certainly not for want of trying, he still had just the one benefice in Somersham to provide his living and that made him one of the few to comply with Urban's views on simony. Adam probably admired the sincerity with which Urban went about his business, just allowing himself to smile inwardly at the man's lack of tact. It was also obvious that the treatise that Adam was working to conclude would be of particular interest to such an assertive Pope. Urban VI would have more cause than most to value a written defence of his authority. Perhaps this might be the moment for Adam to gain promotion to a more significant position within the papal court?

Urban made it clear that he would have no further dealings with the idea of a papal court based in Avignon, in such close proximity to French territory. He would not even agree to a visit, never mind a commitment to keeping the papal court in the city for at least part of each year. The French and Limousin cardinals were particularly unhappy that Urban had refused to go to Avignon, either to accept the fealty of those cardinals who had stayed behind or to make a gesture towards the French King. Not everyone was prepared to agree that the place of the papacy properly belonged in Rome.

Ignoring the reaction to his crude methods and manners, Urban spent the first weeks of his papacy securing his position amongst his natural allies in Rome. The citizens at least were happy, they had their Italian Pope, and he had announced his firm intention to keep the papacy in their city. When the Breton mercenaries in the Castello St Angelo refused to raise Urban's colours, the Pope immediately besieged the castle and, with populist support, forced its surrender. Joanna, Queen of Naples, the kingdom on the southern border of the Papal States, had also good reason to applaud the election of Urban VI. He heralded from the capital of her own kingdom, and now it seemed as if Urban's election would give a new opportunity for peace between two states, healing a long history of fractious relations.

Encouraged by the popularity that his Italian papacy inspired, Urban started to consider how he might consolidate his power. Rumours started to circulate that the Pope was preparing to promote some 20 Italian prelates to the cardinalate, a move that would produce a pro Italian/anti French majority at a stroke. The French and Limousin cardinals started to fear that the pace of change was not much to their liking, and declared that they would retire from Rome in May because of the extreme heat. This in itself was hardly exceptional. In times past it had been common practice for popes and cardinals alike to take advantage of the cooler air of the hill towns around Rome. They offered a more comfortable lifestyle and a pleasanter climate than the sweltering, disease-ridden banks of the Tiber. The cardinals travelled up to the town of Anagni, continuing all the while to protest their loyalty to the new Pope, who remained steadfastly in his new capital. But as soon as they had reached their destination they began to consider their options.

Urban was not minded to move. He was an Italian, a Neapolitan used to the heat of summer, and he was enjoying the popular acclaim of his new papacy and a groundswell of support from right across the Italian peninsula. In June he briefly visited Tivoli as the guest of Otto of Brunswick, the fourth husband of Joanna, Queen of Naples, and a man with whom he had quarrelled before becoming Pope. Urban was a man who bore grudges, and he never forgot when he had been crossed. At lunch the unfortunate Otto, who was bringing drink to the papal entourage, was left on his knees bearing a wine ewer for the Pontiff to drink from. The Pope left him kneeling for many minutes whilst he pointedly pretended not to notice him. Eventually some of the embarrassed cardinals tried to save face, saying, "Holy father it is time for you to drink". Urban managed to ignore every hint offered.[vii] On such apparently trivial matter, kingdoms could rise and fall. Joanna took the insult personally. Urban haughtily refused any sort of apology, he could see no fault in his actions, and Joanna shunned the Pope from this moment on. Urban had lost his first major ally.

Schism

Meanwhile, the cardinals at Anagni were starting to make noises about possible problems with the legitimacy of the election. At first they did this discreetly, looking on the matter as one of technicalities and something for intellectual debate rather then outright concern. For the time being they continued to acknowledge Urban as the rightful Pope. Adam noted with scorn in his own account of the events of 1378 that even as these same cardinals absented themselves from the curia and questioned the legitimacy of the election of Urban, they were petitioning Urban for favours and benefices[viii] for themselves, their friends and relatives. There are plenty of petitions benefiting those Anagni cardinals in the papal archives which support Adam's assertion. Back in Rome, Urban was progressing his plans to increase the number of cardinals by promoting Italians and their supporters, but having allowed the rumours to get out he then failed to get the new cardinals in place quickly. This was typical of Urban. Having caused offence by announcing his intentions in advance, he failed to act, leaving him with new enemies but without getting the advantages that would have accrued to him by actually following through.

By the end of July rumours reached the French King, Charles V, that the French and Limousin cardinals were cooped up in Anagni and he saw an opportunity to turn events to his advantage, starting to negotiate with them directly. On August 2, 1378 the cardinals in Anagni delivered the coup de grace, declaring in unnecessarily arrogant terms that the election of Urban VI was to be considered null and void. They justified their declaration by stating that the election had been unduly influenced by the behaviour of the Roman mob. As a result of the influence of the mob, the Anagni cardinals declared, they had chosen the Italian Prignano against their better judgement. Under the rules for papal elections laid down in Nicholas II's proclamation, this was a perfectly legitimate objection. That is, if it were true.

This first declaration left the Church in crisis; the manoeuvrings of Charles V of France ensured it would be rent asunder. Realising that the cardinals were about to reject Urban VI, he wrote to them at Anagni urging them to select a new Pope, at the same time suggesting that they might like to find one with more Francophile tendencies. There was one obvious candidate, Robert of Geneva, the son of the Count of Savoy and a distant relative of Charles himself. The unfortunate fact that he had only recently personally sanctioned the massacre of some 4,000 men, women and children at Cesena, a town that had actually been his ally, was hardly sufficient to stand in the way of his excellent French credentials. Nor could the fact that the small minority of cardinals in Anagni had no right to enter a conclave without at least a token gesture towards summoning their colleagues to join them, be allowed to stand in the way. The French cardinals at Anagni, barely able to contain their delight at the prospect of making a swift return to the pleasures of Avignon, duly obliged their King by electing his preferred candidate. Robert took the title Clement VII on September 20, moving rapidly to return his followers to Avignon, and by doing so instigated the Great Schism of the Catholic Church. The Church now had two Popes, each claiming absolute legitimacy and ruling from the two traditional seats of the papacy, Clement in Avignon and Urban in Rome.

With two Popes to choose between, the theory of an absolute papal authority that Adam sought to assert and promote in the Defensorium was a hopeless cause. Barely five years before the Pope was imperiously directing attempts to broker peace between warring kings. Now he was fighting for their support. The secular princes in Europe could line up behind a Pope of their choosing and change sides if their chosen Prince of the Church did not do things just as they liked. Adam, sternly principled, lined up behind Urban who, irrespective of his rather undiplomatic manner, was, in Adam's view, quite properly elected and therefore not in a position where his legitimacy could be challenged. An English monk in Rome might well make his stand on matters of principle. The secular rulers of Europe, on the other hand, had fewer scruples, and other priorities. They chose between the two rivals on rather more pragmatic grounds. Charles V of France supported Clement VII because he was pro-French, a distant relative and frankly his choice anyway. The Emperor backed Urban VI for no better reason than the fact that he was opposed to Charles V. The Scandinavian countries, Hungary and the pro-imperial cities of Italy followed the lead of the Emperor. Only the two Spanish kingdoms of Castile and Aragon struggled to decide on either candidate and, initially at least, remained neutral.

The English Decide

As the momentous developments unfolded in Italy, the English Parliament assembled at Gloucester in 1378 intending to declare its support for the new Pope on behalf of the 10-year-old King Richard. There is some doubt as to whether the English knew about the election of Robert of Geneva and the formal beginning of the Schism at the start of the parliament. In one account of the parliament the King ordered both sides of the dispute to be heard before the Archbishop of Canterbury and that he would then advise parliament on which deserved the backing of England.[ix] As that particular account, the Eulogium Historiarum, may well have been prepared by John Trevor, a known associate of Adam Easton, there is more than a faint possibility of bias, but the idea that both sides were present and presented their case is also supported by Thomas Walsingham's Historia Anglicana.

If parliament had sought advice from Rome, they would have looked to men like John Trevor and Adam Easton, senior prelates who had witnessed most of the events at first hand. They certainly would have had the benefit of Adam's views on how the election had been conducted and the fact that most of the cardinals had concluded that it was a valid process. If an envoy from Rome was present at the parliament, it would have been someone from his circle.

The account of the sermon given by the Archbishop of Canterbury, Simon Sudbury, in his register follows a line of argument remarkably similar in form to those given by Adam Easton when he gave his own testimony on the election. There is good reason to suppose that the English decision was influenced by Adam's circle, if not by the Black Monk himself.

There were of course other sound political reasons for backing Urban, starting with the confiscation of the many rich benefices held in England by cardinals that had supported Clement. Agrifolio would be particularly unfortunate in this respect, for in his testimony to the King of Aragon's delegation, he noted that the value of his property in England amounted to 3,000 florins per annum.[x] This was why he had been so anxious to ask Adam how the English King would regard the election of Pope Urban. With a French "anti-pope" elected and installed in Avignon the English now had all the excuses they needed to do a bit of wealth reallocation. The King would take advantage of the situation and look after the "vacancies" until some suitable anti-French cleric could be found to take over. There was no realistic possibility that Agrifolio would get to keep his rich benefices in England. When Adam had answered Agrifolio so confidently in April 1378 the issues before them were very different. Several French cardinals would pay very dearly for their selection of a rival French pope.

The bigger picture of European politics also demanded that the English support Urban. Just to spite the growing ambitions of the French Charles V would be a good enough reason for most English kings, but as the Scottish King had quite predictably lined up with Charles V and the French in backing Clement, it was inevitable that the English would remain firm in their loyalty to Urban. And that was exactly the conclusion of the parliament of Gloucester.

An Independent Investigation

If the reaction of the English, French and Scots had been predictable, several of the secular rulers of Europe were as concerned about the damage to the reputation of the Church as others were excited by the opportunity it offered. The Church was part of a stable infrastructure that helped maintain the authority of those who held the reigns of power over those who did not. Some rulers understood that the loss of credibility of the Church was an issue that they should take seriously. Concern about the events that had led to the calamity grew to the degree that in the spring of 1379 deputations arrived from the Kings of Aragon and Castile to launch an inquiry in Rome. Both kingdoms had taken a principled stand on the Schism and had yet to declare their allegiance. The inquiry was a genuine attempt to ascertain which Pope had the more legitimate claim; before that states committed themselves to one side or the other. All the cardinals and other members of the court who had been present during the events of 1378 had good reason to make their case as strongly as possible. Several volumes of depositions taken from the leading members of the papal court at the time are still preserved in the Vatican archives and give us vivid glimpses of the justifications that the two sides used to support their case. Depositions or affidavits were given by all the leading members of the court irrespective of their view of the election, and both sides seemed to have been convinced that the inquiry was worth treating seriously. Aside from some of the cardinals who had taken part in the election Adam was the only member of the curia asked to give two depositions, the first in March 1379 and a second in November the same year.

The interest in Adam's view, a result of the very precise and legalistic interpretation he offered of the pro-Urban position, was understandable. Adam's own standing at the papal court as an administrator, advocate and proctor for the Benedictines was enhanced by his reputation as a scholar. The work that he had already completed on the Bible, his fight against Wyclif's heresy and his as yet unpublished work in defence of the Church all added to his status. Even if Clement's supporters disagreed with his account, Adam would put the arguments to them that would have to be countered if their cause was to have any credibility.

The delegation from Castile, however, had another interest in Adam's views. He was the only Englishman who had intimate knowledge of the events that took place in the summer of 1378; he had been close to the members of the curia during the election (the two other Englishmen who gave testimony, William Andrews and Robert Stratton, offer much less detail in their statements). As the Wyclif affair and even the parliament of Gloucester had shown, he was in a position to influence the English Church and perhaps even the English secular authority. And the English secular authority was starting to take a close interest in the affairs of Castile. John of Gaunt, Duke of Lancaster and uncle of King Richard II, had a claim on the throne of Castile through his wife, Constance, the only daughter of the last King, Pedro III. As the boy king Richard established himself on the English throne, so John turned his thoughts to Castile. Richard encouraged his uncle. Adding another throne to the family collection would enhance the prestige of the dynasty with the added benefit of removing a very powerful ruler from his own doorstep. The Castilians wanted an insight into the English view for good reason, although in the end it was not until 1386 that Gaunt led the English invasion of the Spanish peninsula to claim his inheritance.

The first delegation to arrive in Rome in early 1379 was a team sent by the King of Aragon, led by Matthew Clementis, and they also had a personal interest in Adam's view. Adam was one of the first to be asked to testify. On March 9, 1379 he was brought before the inquiry only to find himself confronted by an old acquaintance, Alfonso of Jaen. Alfonso had travelled with Brigit of Sweden to Montefiascone, where they had met Adam in the company of Simon Langham. In years to come Adam and Alfonso would work together to champion the cause of Brigit's canonisation, but for now they faced each other in a very different environment. This was not a place for reminiscences of times past. In the dark interior of the Vatican Palace Alfonso questioned Adam on every aspect of the election. Adam faced unremitting questions demanding full and unambiguous responses, a slow and deliberate process that would leave no room for wavering. The monks scribbled away in the dark room, recording every word of Adam's testimony. Words that might be used against him in the future if he found himself in the wrong hands. Adam was in a position of great danger. If he backed the wrong candidate, his fate might be unpleasant.

Adam set out his stall in unambiguous terms. The testimony that Adam gave to the Spanish dismissed the view of Clement's supporters, and he gave hard evidence to support his assertions. Most importantly, Adam reminded his inquisitors that the decision to elect Urban had been taken before the conclave began, and therefore before the mob had assembled. In his view it was therefore preposterous to suggest the mob had influenced the decision. He asked the question that if Urban was not the legitimate Pope, then why had the rebel cardinals petitioned him so ardently for favours? Adam did not leave any doubt that the real reason the cardinals abandoned Urban was not out of any conviction that he had been wrongly elected, but because they found him "strict and stern towards their morals and customs."[xi] He also noted that the crowds in Rome, far from being intimidating, had mostly been made up of familiars and courtiers of the very cardinals who had claimed to be intimidated.[xii] If the crowds had been boisterous, it was with good humour, not malice, and many of them were merry with drink and in no mood to threaten anyone.

In later depositions Agrifolio and the Cardinal of Florence did try to dispute some of the facts of Adam's testimony, but without much conviction. The Cardinal of Florence came up with the most creative embellishment of the facts. He admitted that he had indeed shown Adam a letter to the Emperor, stating that the election of Urban had been perfectly above board. He claimed, however, that afterwards he had slipped a note to the Emperor in with the letter, telling the Emperor to ignore the letter, as events had been rather different to those he had written down![xiii] Agrifolio tried to find elements within Adam's own testimony that he could dispute and thereby cast doubt over the validity of what Adam had said. He did not dispute that he knew Adam, or that they were on good terms, and all he could take issue with was Adam's claim that he had stayed at his house the night before they went to meet the new Pope, a fact he emphatically denied.[xiv] Whether it was true or not, it was hardly a fact that had any bearing on the legitimacy of Urban's election; it could only be used to question Adam's own integrity. Compared to the other testimonies of the key players, Adam's account seems to have been called into question far less, and this gives us some comfort that it is a reliable source of detail for the events that led up to the Schism.

In the end the inquiry brought nothing but discomfort for the Church. Searching for the truth might have been an honourable intention, but the spectacle of cardinal after cardinal accusing each other of, at best, having a poor memory, at worst of lying about events, was particularly unedifying. Nor did the inquiry really pronounce absolutely the legitimacy of either Pope. It rolled on ponderously, rather in the manner of modern public inquiries, shifting between Rome and Avignon and still asking questions in 1386.[xv] The reputation of the Church as a whole suffered greatly as a result. In the end both Castile (in 1380) and Aragon (in 1387) sided with Clement.

New Cardinals for Old

In the short term Urban had a practical problem to deal with. He had an urgent need to create new cardinals to fill his court with replacements for those who had now defected to join Clement VII in Avignon. The six cardinals who had stayed behind in Avignon found that their lack of haste had been rewarded with the return of the papal court, albeit with a new master. They defected without further thought. Urban needed loyal cardinals, and he looked to the lands that had supported him as a source of new recruits. His original intention of filling the College of Cardinals with Italians and their allies was no longer folly, it was an absolute necessity. England was an obvious possibility, but his first choice, the patrician bishop of London, William de Courtney, politely turned him down. Simon Langham had been the last Englishman to accept the cardinal's hat, but then Edward III had been the sort of overbearing monarch who might make foreign travel seem attractive. By 1379, with the young King Richard II on the throne, the possibility of influence and advancement made staying in England a rather more appealing option for Courtney and his family. His rejection of a cardinal's appointment may not have been a direct snub to Urban's offer, but more a matter of having a very good reason to remain in England.

Urban finally appointed 24 new cardinals to his court in September 1378[xvi] and, not surprisingly, there were few Frenchmen on the list. The majority came from Imperial Germany and Italy, the main areas of support for Urban's papacy.

In the meantime Adam was bringing his work on the Defensorium to a conclusion. Some historians have suggested that the work must have been completed before the Schism because Adam fails to mention it. Yet there are a number of good reasons why the absence of any mention of the Schism does not necessarily indicate the date by which the book was complete. If Adam did not finish the work until 1380 or perhaps 1381, it is unrealistic to imagine that he would have rewritten the entire book at a point when he must have been well over half way through, just to take account of the fallout from the political crises all around him.

It is also important to remember that what we know with hindsight as the Great Schism was unlikely to have been quite so obvious a split from the viewpoint of the summer of 1378. To Adam and the other courtiers who stayed in Rome, it must initially have looked like a temporary hiccup, with the various secular rulers playing their usual games. Schisms had happened before, many times, and anti-Popes were nothing new either. The history of the papacy in the years before Avignon had been plagued with this sort of dispute, which on the whole tended to get settled quite quickly. A rapprochement and a deal to settle the dispute would surely follow, either Urban or Clement would get the papacy and the other a suitably large pay-off and a strong position the next time there was a papal election. It just needed someone to broker the settlement. It was only as the new year of 1379 gradually wore on that it became apparent that the two sides were moving further apart and no-one was willing to broker a deal.

This Time it's for Real

Neither Pope was seriously looking for help in making peace. Urban was based in Rome surrounded by his Italian cardinals and he refused to treat with Clement, who in turn had brought all of the French and Limousin cardinals back to Avignon. Adam was preoccupied with the inquiry into the Schism during 1379, giving his written testimonies and swapping notes with his friends and other courtiers to see what everyone else was saying about the papal election. Apart from the inquiry into the election, Adam spent most of the period from 1378 to 1381 working in the libraries of the classic texts of the Christian Church stored in Rome, researching and writing. I would suggest that the Defensorium was probably not finished until 1381 (it is dedicated to Urban which, if nothing else, demonstrates that he had not finished it until after Urban's election in April 1378) and that would at least explain why Adam's life in Rome appears to be so uneventful.

From the start Adam had little time for Pope Clement. He had a genuine belief in the legitimacy of Urban's election that events, as well as his testimony, would bear witness to over the next five years. His disgust at the venality and self-serving way in which the French attempted to carve out their own interest seems genuine. Nor had Clement's reputation been enhanced by the massacre at Cesena, albeit that much of the dirty work was carried out by English mercenaries. Of course Adam had enjoyed life in Avignon, there is no reason to suppose that he shared Petrarch's disapproval of either the city or the lifestyle of the senior churchmen. If Adam was being cynical, he may have preferred to back Urban for no other reason than he had exhausted the value of the libraries of Avignon already and had yet to make the most of those in Rome. Yet Adam does not come across as a cynical person. He was always more interested in the intellectual side of Church life and hardly noticed the deep-seated corruption all around him even when he benefited from it. To an extent he was quite prepared to enjoy the privileges of life within the Church hierarchy, but at the same time had some sympathy with those who sought to curb the excesses of the cardinals. He even appeared to admire Urban's reforming zeal, if not his way of going about things.

Adam certainly had the opportunity to get to know Pope Urban in the first couple of years of his papacy. Their paths had not crossed before and Adam would have been anxious to befriend the new head of the Church, to make himself useful and to ensure his presence and ability were noted. His future career would depend on it. He was first introduced to Urban VI by Cardinal Agrifolio in the week immediately after his election. Then, as time wore on and many of the scholars, prelates and cardinals left for the court of Pope Clement in Avignon, there were few left in Rome who had served the papal court as long as Adam or who had as great a familiarity with its processes. Urban was also unfamiliar with the methods of the papal court as, unusually, he had not served as a cardinal, and although he had worked in one of the papal chanceries in Rome, in the main the papal court had been based in Avignon.

By the time he presented the completed volumes of the Defensorium to Urban, Adam was someone Urban had come to know and trust. Urban VI had taken the events of the Schism as a personal betrayal. At times his latent insecurity bordered on paranoia. Meanwhile Adam, an able administrator, a skilled theologian had above all remained unswervingly loyal to the new Pope through the most trying of times. The gift of his life's work was a significant gesture to Urban not just because it was written as a faithful treatise on the power of the Church, in the Pope's eyes it was a badly needed gesture of solidarity.

Chapter 9

Cardinal of England

We must run and do now what will profit us forever

Cardinal Adam

As the members of the papal court basked in the warmth of an Italian spring, news reached Rome of one of the coldest English winters in living memory. The fields were so deeply frosted that they could not be ploughed, and by early February the ice floes built up so heavily on the River Medway that Rochester bridge was crushed under their weight,[i] and it took until 1388[ii] to rebuild it. Under the blue skies and warm sun of his adopted home, Adam had every reason to be pleased with his lot in life, and it was about to get much better. His loyalty and service to the Roman Pope had not gone unnoticed. By 1381 Urban was in the middle of a full-blown crisis over the falling number of cardinals he maintained at his court. The lack of tact and diplomacy that became a defining characteristic of his papacy did not help. Johannes de Croso and Guido de Malosicco started the rot when they left Rome in December 1378 and did not return. They were followed by a steady flow of cardinal defectors crossing the Alps to join a delighted Clement in Avignon.

As if that was not bad enough, death was proving nearly as destructive to the ranks of Urban's cardinals as the pontiff's bad grace and ill manners. It was not a great surprise when the frail Cardinal Tebaldeschi died in September 1378, but by December 1381 he had been joined by Johannes Ocko de Wlasim, Guilelmus Sanseverinus, Elziarus de Sabrano, Agapitus de Colunna, Ludovicus de Altavilla, Thomas de Prignano and Stephanus de Colunna,[iii] all of whom had only been promoted in 1378. The very best that could be said in a superstitious age was that Urban's choice of cardinals was plagued by bad luck. In December 1381 Urban held a consistory to promote a further batch of six cardinals to keep the numbers up to a credible level. By now England was one of the few powerful kingdoms of Christendom that still supported Urban's papacy, and it was the only one without representation within the cardinalate. Urban was anxious to find a suitable English candidate to cement that loyalty. Adam was the only obvious choice: highly regarded, a member of the papal court and a man with experience of delicate diplomatic situations. The other candidates under consideration were all Italians, including three men whose lives would become intertwined with his own over the next few years, Petrus Tomacellus (the future Boniface IX), Ludovicus Donati, the Cardinal of Venice, and Bartholomew de Cucurno, the Cardinal of Genoa.[iv]

On December 21, 1381 Adam of Easton, monk of Norwich, was officially instituted as a cardinal of the Catholic Church, the 26th cardinal that Urban had created since his coronation just three years earlier. He was only the 12th Englishman in history to have been made a cardinal. The formal investiture took place in the great, old gothic cathedral of St Peter's in Rome, the mother church of the Catholic faith. An honour, Adam could reflect, that had been denied to Cardinal Langham by the circumstances of the time.

Not bad for the peasant's son from the village of Easton. The news from England must have brought home to him quite how far he had travelled and how far removed he was now from the station in life to which he had been born. Norfolk had been ripped apart by the Peasants' Uprising earlier in 1381, the rebels had forced their way into Norwich and taken over the castle whilst others plundered the countryside. As the authorities slowly restored order, revenge was swift and merciless. Henry Despenser the warrior Bishop of Norwich, a military man first and foremost, regarded his bishopric as a good source of income to pursue his natural bent for military action. Masterminding the retaking of Norwich and the savage repression of the local peasants sat more comfortably on his shoulders than administering the rites of the Catholic Church. Even as Adam was preparing for his elevation to the status of cardinal, peasants from the Norfolk countryside, from his own village and those tied to his own Benedictine monastery of Norwich were being hunted down and killed.

Meanwhile Adam wandered through the fine libraries of Rome studying the ancient texts of Christianity, wearing the fine robes that were customary for princes of the Church and taking a break from his busy schedule once in a while to drink Italian wine from the finely sculpted cup bequeathed him by Simon Langham. The peasant's life he had been born to in Easton must have seemed incomprehensible to him now. Yet you cannot help but wonder what he felt for the people he had once lived amongst as they suffered cruelly at the hands of Despenser. Did he remember the names of the villagers he had grown up amongst and wonder on their fate? Did men from families that he knew die at the hands of the avenging bishop? He did not record his views on the uprising, and if he had any sympathy for the peasants' cause it would not have been safe for him to say what he felt. Despite his views on Wyclif and the authority of the Church hierarchy, the sufferings of the farmers of Norfolk must have tugged at his heart. Perhaps it was fortunate that so far away in Rome there was very little he could do.

A Cardinal's Life

Adam was lucky to escape the privations of rural life in England and had made the most of his opportunity. As a cardinal he had risen as high in the Church as most could aspire to, and if the rather puritanical style of Urban's papacy meant that there would be no generous cash hand-outs for a new cardinal there were still plenty of opportunities to exploit. So what might Adam expect from his new role as a cardinal? Activities for those cardinals who stayed at the papal court tended to be split into one of three roles, political, administrative or theological, usually depending on the individual's background and expertise. Simon Langham, a career politician and sometime Chancellor of England, was always cut out for a political role and hence was despatched on his diplomatic mission to bring about peace between England and France. When the papacy was based at Avignon, the Limousin cardinals were known as administrators, and Agrifolio in particular excelled in this field. Adam on the other hand was a theologian first and foremost; although he might play his part in the chancery courts of Rome that would never be his strongest suit. As a noted scholar the work he might expect to do at the court would include giving opinions on religious orthodoxy and the legal issues surrounding appointments, writing in defence of the positions taken by the Church on the issues of the day and considering the texts of religious observance. He had already been asked to prepare an order of service for the Transfixion before becoming a cardinal.

Rome was an ideal place for a theologian cardinal to be based. The great minds of the day tended to graduate to the leading courts, and even after the Schism, that meant that Rome was an intellectual powerhouse for those debating religious issues. Then there were the libraries and the sacred texts of Christianity. The presence in Rome of so many leading figures and, more importantly, their libraries and scripts, made the city the perfect place for a theologian to ply his trade. Rome may have lacked the tranquil, scholarly atmosphere of Avignon, but it certainly had the necessary equipment.

Simony or Nepotism?

Adam looked forward to settling down and enjoying the role of cardinal scholar and theologian. He might once have hoped to form a court in much the way that Simon had done in Avignon and attract like-minded intellectuals from around Europe. He was not to be so lucky. With a reforming Pope raging against the practice of cardinals building up a portfolio of benefices, any possibility of seeking to enhance his own income would be at best impolitic. With the income from his benefice of Somersham he could support his own work in Rome, but it was not enough to support a substantial court. However, not all was lost, for Urban turned out to be rather less scrupulous than everyone had suspected. He had railed against the cardinals for their easy living and wealth, but then chose to do nothing about it. Not for the first time he managed to offend his more loyal supporters, but without taking the action that would at least have forced neutral observers to acknowledge that he was doing something to reform the Church. Urban had a nephew for whom he had high hopes, and if he was prepared to upbraid his cardinals for their poor morals, he overlooked the same faults in Francisco, whose behaviour was considerably worse. The young man was made a cardinal, an office for which he had no obvious qualifications, and if Urban the great reformer and the scourge of corruption had no qualms about being accused of nepotism, the cardinals took note nonetheless.

Urban's campaign against corruption was not the only factor limiting the ambitions of Cardinal Adam. The political troubles that the Pope had brought upon the Church kept the papal court in a permanent state of flux. Rome was already full of rumours that the papal court was moving to Naples as Urban tried to secure a political legacy for his nephew. The news conjured up images of the unfortunate Urban V and his papacy that had wandered aimlessly among the hill towns of Lazio, hoping vainly to find a permanent home. In such troubled times, even if Adam had the income, which he did not in 1381, this was no time to appoint courtiers, to establish a grand residence in Rome or to contemplate the revenues available for staying at the court. Throughout the early years of his time as a cardinal we see no references to members of his court, or to familiars looking for his patronage. The absence of these names is truly noteworthy. It tells us much about the state of the court under Urban and the lot of the cardinals who trailed around Italy in the wake of his political machinations.

Urban had started his papacy with powerful supporters, and even after the Schism he could draw upon an impressive list of allies. He now set to work alienating most of them, and he started with those who were geographically closest. He had already fallen out with Otto, husband of Queen Joanna of Naples, whom he publicly humiliated at Tivoli in April 1378. Joanna had broken off ties with Urban as a result. Otto and Joanna had their own dynastic ambitions and wanted to arrange the marriage of the Marquis of Montferrat (a relative of the Byzantine Emperor) to Maria, the daughter of Frederick III of Sicily. Perhaps in a moment of weakness, possibly in the spirit of compromise, they asked the Pope to bless the marriage. Urban not only refused to bless the marriage, he put forward his nephew as a husband for Maria. Whilst this might be politically interesting for the papacy, uniting the Papal States and Sicily under one ruler and leaving the Kingdom of Naples sandwiched between the two, it was never going to be agreeable to Joanna. Once again Urban demonstrated his ability to be both tactless and foolhardy. A suitably insulting rejection was sent back to Queen Joanna and the outraged Queen changed her allegiance to Pope Clement without further ado.

Urban reacted with a predictable bout of rage and pronounced her excommunicate on April 29, 1380. In a gesture of supreme arrogance (which nonetheless fell neatly in line with the views that Adam put forward in the Defensorium) Urban offered the throne of Naples to Louis of Hungary, who had supported him throughout the difficult times of the Schism. In the same way as Wyclif might have suggested that a bad religious regime could be overthrown by the secular power, so Adam had argued that it was the duty of the religious authority to replace a corrupted secular ruler. Adam may have outlined the principle involved, but he surely would not have recommended going about it in the ham-fisted fashion with which Urban was accustomed to conduct diplomacy. The will of God was all very well, but a bit of popular support down on Earth was a helpful resource to draw on. Unfortunately, this was not the sort of pragmatism that Urban was inclined to adopt.

By the end of the year the Kingdom of Castile had seen more than enough of Urban VI and threw in its lot with Clement and the Avignon papacy.

The Crown of Naples for Sale

Louis of Hungary was astute enough to decline Urban's kind offer of someone else's throne. However, he was not prepared to pass up such a good opportunity altogether or risk offending the Pope, so he proposed that his nephew, Charles of Durazzo, be offered the kingdom. Charles was more enthusiastic, and his reputation as a successful soldier made him an ideal candidate for Urban's war against Joanna. Urban readily agreed to Louis' proposal and gave Charles every encouragement. The young man who would be king spent the rest of the year raising troops in Hungary and in November 1380 he led his army across the Alps and arrived in northern Italy.

Urban invited him to Rome, where he was welcomed and made a senator of the city. The Pope arranged for the coronation service to be held at St Peter's, as it could not be held on Neapolitan territory. The coronation was designed to encapsulate the views of hierarchy on Earth endorsed by the Church and spelt out by Adam in the Defensorium. The purpose was to show clearly to all that the Kingdom of Naples was in the Pope's gift and had been bestowed on Charles at his specific instruction. On June 1, 1381 Adam was present[v] with other cardinals from the papal court as Charles III was duly crowned as the new King of Naples (and Sicily and Jerusalem as well). Adam was asked to sign documents affirming Charles's coronation and giving title of the kingdom to him.

Urban VI had engineered a minor diplomatic triumph, a mirror image of the Pope crowning the first Holy Roman Emperor in Rome all those centuries ago. The Church was stating its case in unambiguous terms; kings were appointed by popes and not the other way round. In a slightly less dignified adjunct to the proceedings Urban managed to extract from Charles a promise of a couple of castles at Capua and Nocera and a pension of 7,000 florins a year for the worthless Francisco in exchange for putting Charles on the throne. Charles had yet to get the full measure of his holy sponsor and he readily agreed.

The new king now had the unenviable task of fighting to secure his kingdom. In practical terms that meant getting rid of Otto and Joanna. More by luck than judgement, for once Urban was to be successful on the diplomatic front. Many of the cardinals he created in 1378 had been Neapolitan, whilst most of the troops loyal to Otto and Joanna were foreign mercenaries, either French or German. The populace of southern Italy rose in support of Charles, forcing Otto and Joanna to retreat into the city of Naples.

Wealth and Work

1382 would be a bad year for Queen Joanna, but back in Rome life for the English cardinal was starting to improve. He was slowly building his status within the papal court and starting to muster his financial resources. On February 4, 1382 Nicholas Luke of the Lombard banking house of Guinigii, based in London, had a writ notarised in Adam's favour in the sum of £150.[vi] As Simon Langham had done, Adam used a banking house to organise the transfer of money collected from his benefice in England to the papal court in Rome. International banking tended to be dominated by different groups in the different states of Europe. When Simon had wanted to transfer money from London to Avignon, the Burgundian bankers of Bruges and Ghent were perfectly placed to handle the transaction. However, for moving money between London and Rome, it was the Lombards from the area around Milan and the Florentines that tended to dominate the world of banking. At the time the money was sent over, Somersham was his only benefice and worth 95 marks per annum (about £66). As the amount paid over to him represented two or three years of revenue, the harvest and profits must have been particularly good in 1381! The impact of the Peasants' Revolt the previous summer had clearly not adversely affected the incomes of the village of Somersham.

Adam had been cautious in his ambition while Urban raged against the wealth of his cardinals. When it became clear that Urban was spending more and more of his time helping along the career of Francisco, he took the opportunity to ask for a little more. Adam was not greedy, he petitioned for just one new benefice, the deaconry of York. He was taking a risk asking for anything at all, but it was a risk worth taking. Urban did not object, and even went as far as to ratify an appointment that the English King Richard claimed was, nominally at least, in his gift. Adam was granted the benefice by royal assent on October 28, 1382.[vii] With a new source of wealth to draw on Adam could at last anticipate a more settled life at the papal court, if not an existence quite as comfortable as that which he had enjoyed in Avignon. Better still, Richard granted royal letters patent acknowledging Adam to have duties that by custom were overseas and agreeing to him being represented in England by two proctors, John Waltham a canon of York, and Thomas Daweney.[viii] This was a great help to Adam. With the King's blessing he could now assign English representatives to collect money for him and remit it to Rome. For the moment at least the young King could not do enough for the new cardinal.

Meanwhile, Adam's workload at the papal court was building up and the new cardinal was finding that his services were in demand. The Benedictines were quick to call in their marker on their protégé, and as Adam owed much of his success to support from his Benedictine brothers, he was not slow to make himself useful to them. He procured a Bull, probably in 1383, to provide new privileges for the General Chapter of the Benedictines in England. Unfortunately, the benefit proved to be short-lived as John, the monk charged with bringing it back to England, was robbed by his travelling companion as they crossed the province of Zeeland in the Low Countries.[ix] The importance of keeping a written document safe in a world without photocopies and faxes is easy to forget. Often there would only be one copy of a deed or Bull, and if it was lost there was no proof of the title or privileges that it had contained. The only consolation for the Benedictines was the mental image of the bitter disappointment of the robber when he finally realised there was no monetary value in what he had taken. At least with Adam working at the centre of papal power the

Benedictines could ask for a new Bull to be drawn up without too much difficulty.[x]

Another Brush with the Old Enemy

The Cardinal's reputation as a scholar and a theologian brought him further important experiences during the course of the year. One of these was renewing an acquaintance with the old enemy from the land of his birth. Nicholas of Hereford was a follower and confidante of John Wyclif who had been investigated by the Church authorities in England. Wyclif and his friends had received less protection from royalty in the aftermath of the Peasants' Revolt and the new-found fervour for a Church based on order and control. Nicholas had been heavily involved in the preparation of a Bible written in the English language, something Wyclif felt strongly about. The ordinary man should be entitled to read the word of God himself, not to have to work it out by gazing at elaborate stained glass windows and stone carvings. Nicholas of Hereford, possibly feeling that the political situation in England had rather coloured the views of the local clergy, decided to appeal his case to Rome, and he arrived in the eternal city during 1382.

The official position of the Church remained unchanged. The biblical text was complex and confusing, far too confusing for the uneducated mind. It was therefore necessary for the Church to interpret the lessons of the Bible so they could be clearly understood. The idea of preparing an English Bible was necessarily abhorrent to the established Church. Who knew how the uneducated might interpret what was written?

Nicholas missed the point. He failed to follow the logic used by his detractors and came to Rome only to protest that his English Bible was in fact a true translation and contained nothing but the word of God. The newly appointed English Cardinal was the ideal person to help Urban to frame a damning judgement on Nicholas of Hereford. Not only was he a fellow Englishman, he was intimately acquainted with Wyclif and his followers and, after all, he had himself translated the Bible. Of course Easton's work was staged within the confines of Church orthodoxy being an acceptable retranslation from Hebrew into Latin. His motive was to ensure that scholars and learned men were working with an accurate text, not taking St Jerome at face value. As such it had offered an enhancement to learning within the Church without threatening to provide information to those whose lack of learning would surely lead to misunderstandings.

To Adam, the work that Nicholas had undertaken was deeply flawed in more than one respect, and he must have sneered at what he would have seen as poor scholarship. Nicholas had merely undertaken an English translation of the vernacular, and he had failed to perceive the likelihood of incorporating the errors of St Jerome in the English version. So what sort of scholarship was that? And then of course Adam as a Church scholar could have no truck with the very idea of providing such a poorly constructed text for the common man to misinterpret.

The unfortunate Nicholas seems to have spent most of his time rehearsing the wrong arguments. He persisted in insisting that the English language Bible was a good and honest translation, whilst the Church establishment stuck to their view that the very act of producing a vernacular Bible was a crime. Inevitably Urban found against him and Nicholas was imprisoned in Rome for heresy.

Other Work for a Busy Cardinal

Later in the same year Adam was asked to investigate another important matter of doctrine. Urban had been lobbied by the Swedish clergy to consider the canonisation of Brigit, the Swedish mystic whom Adam had met at Montefiascone. Whatever Urban may have felt personally of the case for considering her elevation to the congregation of Saints of the Church, the Pope was starting to realise that he needed to hang on to the few powerful friends he had left. The Swedish King had continued to voice his support for Rome during the Schism, and that made Brigit's case compelling. Urban appointed a commission of three cardinals to look into her case, Adam plus Johannes de Amelia, Cardinal of Corfu, and Lucas de Gentilibus, the Cardinal Bishop of Nocerinus.[xi] The point of the commission was to examine Brigit's life to consider if it might stand up to the closest scrutiny and form a worthy model of Catholic virtue. This was no simple matter of looking into the womanly virtue of Brigit and the example of her life, for unusually for a woman of her times, Brigit had written extensively and had been in the public eye. Her work included a monastic rule and a series of prophesies, and for their author to be considered worthy of canonisation, these would now have to be examined for orthodoxy. As this would include her exhortations to Pope Urban V not to take the court back to Avignon, it was a task that required sensitive and diplomatic handling. Adam was selected not just because he had met Brigit at Montefiascone but because he also knew her daughter Catherine, who had stayed in Rome to lobby the Pope for her mother's canonisation (Catherine and Adam were both in Rome during the election in 1378, and also in 1379, when she too gave an affidavit to the inquiry into the Schism).

The commission would be time-consuming but it did not prevent Adam from being asked to take on another major theological exercise. He was invited to look into the merits of the creation of a service for the Visitation of the Virgin Mary, and to write an order of service that he deemed a fit celebration. The Visitation, the visit of Mary to her cousin Elizabeth to discuss her impregnation by the Holy Spirit, was a simple enough story and uncontroversial in itself, but it contained difficult material in the background. To write the office satisfactorily it would be impossible to avoid the subject of the impregnation of the Virgin Mary by the Holy Spirit, in itself one of the most awkward theological issues the Church had to present to the faithful. Not least it combined the issues of sex and faith, issues that have never sat comfortably together for Christian Churches through the ages. It is easy to understand how the idea of God impregnating a woman required some sensitive handling. The ideal service of celebration required a delicate mixture of discretion as to the detail of the event, with an appropriate element of adulation for the miracle of divine intervention.

The writing of new services, rites and masses were relatively infrequent during the mediaeval era, and to be asked to work on the creation of one was a rare enough honour. Adam had already been asked to draft a service for the Transfixion, although Urban had decided not to progress that idea. The fact that he was now being asked to create a service for the Visitation suggests that not only did Urban admire his work, but is testament to Adam's general reputation as one of the finest theologians of his time.

Trouble in Suffolk

If Adam enjoyed the challenge that the flow of scholarly tasks brought, there was also rather less palatable work to be done to solve a political problem brewing in England. Richard II, or at least the council working on his behalf, were getting involved in a complex and bitter dispute with Urban VI over the appointment of an Abbot to the Abbey of Bury St Edmunds. In 1379 Abbot Brinkley died and the monks of Bury elected John Tymworth as the new Abbot with full approval of the king.[xii] The Abbot sent a delegation to Rome to seek confirmation of the appointment, but was told by the King not to go himself as the route would be dangerous and he would need to pass through territory controlled by supporters of Clement.

Urban had also heard of the death of Abbot Brinkley. He had for some time been looking for a position to give to an Englishman and Proctor at the papal court, Edmund Bromfield. On hearing of the Abbot's death, Urban immediately awarded the abbey to Bromfield, claiming it was within his gift. When Tymworth's delegation arrived Urban greeted them civilly but pointed out that for at least a century it had been required custom for a new Abbot to make a personal appearance in Rome to be accepted into his Abbacy. Urban allowed Bromfield to depart with his blessing as Abbot, and shortly after he was formally instituted as such. Bromfield appears to have picked up Urban's diplomatic skills during his sojourn at the Roman court, for within a few days of his arrival at Bury he had alienated most of the monks. Those monks who had originally supported Tymworth's election started to make life awkward for the new Abbot, repudiating his authority. Fearing reprisal, two of the monks fled to the monastery of St Albans where they were granted protection by Abbot Thomas.[xiii] To receive the monks was irregular to say the least, but Abbot Thomas knew a thing or two about English politics. Within a matter of weeks the King was taking action. He felt affronted, not least as his candidate for the election had been ignored and arguably had never been given a fair hearing. Richard ordered Bromfield's arrest and the unfortunate cleric was brought to London and interrogated. Richard demanded to know by what right he took his role as Abbot at an abbey where the abbacy was in the King's opinion, in his gift. The unfortunate Bromfield was promptly shut away in the Tower of London, and it was only thanks to the intervention of the Prior of Cambridge that he was eventually moved to the more pleasant confinement of Nottingham Castle, where he was kept for a further three years.

In the meantime, the Peasants' Uprising of 1381 was gaining momentum, and a rag tag army of some 50,000 souls rampaged across East Anglia from Cambridge to Newmarket and on to Bury. For reasons that are no longer clear, the peasants protested at the treatment of Bromfield, and at the height of the insurgency a defenceless King Richard was forced to promise the release of the former Abbot. Inevitably, as soon as order had been restored to the countryside and the uprising brutally suppressed, the offer was rescinded. The unfortunate Bromfield had hardly asked the peasants to take up his cause, but he now stood in danger of losing his life as well as his abbey.

This was the minefield that Adam entered into. His diplomatic skills needed to be at their best, he had to tread carefully to find a solution without offending either his sovereign or the Pope in whose court he served. Adam knew Bromfield, they had been at the papal court together for at least three years, and this must have made matters even more difficult for him. However, he could not afford to appear partial. Adam suggested to Urban that there should be a new election and all the monks should be free to vote for which candidate they preferred. The Pope was far from convinced, and was certainly inclined to dispute Richard's right to nominate the Abbot of Bury in the first place. The argument over Bury had all the potential to turn into an argument over papal versus royal supremacy. And at Bury the argument was complicated by the fact that the English King remained one of Urban's dwindling band of royal supporters.

In the end, and not without a considerable struggle, Adam got his way, and in the summer of 1384 a new election was held, and both Pope and King agreed to abide by the result. John Tymworth was unanimously elected and Urban was as good as his word, offering his blessing through the papal legate to England, William Courtney. King and Pope considered that honour was satisfied, and as a result Adam managed to persuade the King to release Bromfield from his imprisonment at Nottingham.

Urban must have been reasonably impressed with Adam's performance, because by May 1383 he had passed him another difficult dispute of the same nature. A row had blown up between Peter Komar and Francis of Podnawicz, both of whom claimed to have been properly elected Abbot of Milo in Bohemia.[xiv] Initially Urban appointed a commission of three cardinals, but as the dispute dragged on another two joined them. Possibly because of his recent experience with the delicate negotiations at Bury, Adam took the lead role in assessing the merits of each case despite being one of the more junior cardinals on the team. Milo, in the diocese of Prague and in the heartland of the Holy Roman Empire, was another sensitive dispute not least because the Emperor had also remained a loyal supporter of Urban. Urban not only gave Adam wide powers to run the case, he was also allowed to give Peter 300 florins a year towards his expenses. Quite what Francis made of this was not recorded, though it could hardly have boded well. Yet perhaps to his surprise, at the end of a lengthy investigation Adam awarded him the monastery, so he had little to complain about.

Urban's First Crusade

Political life in Urban's papacy never ran smoothly. To the mind of his Holiness, an anti-Pope was every bit as much an infidel as a Saracen. Accepting this as a starting point, it seemed only reasonable that the Pope should call upon the faithful to take military action against the unbelievers and the monarchs who supported them. As the French King and his Flemish allies had backed the anti-Pope Clement it seemed only reasonable that if the English wished to bring down the enemies of the true Pope, they should be given the same blessings and indulgences that they would have received if they had fought to liberate Jerusalem.

The Bishop of Norwich, Sir Henry Despenser, sought to capitalise on the situation and approached Urban with the idea of a military sortie into Flanders. The Pope was only too easily persuaded to grant the adventure the status of a crusade. Adam, the English cardinal with strong connections to Norwich, must have been the conduit for Despenser to gain a papal blessing for his plan. It is not possible to be certain quite how far Adam was involved in the squalid politics of Despenser's crusade, but whatever his feelings about Despenser's role in crushing the Norfolk peasantry, he could hardly have ignored the Bishop of his home town. Henry Despenser duly received a Papal Bull blessing his crusade and was granted the use of a standard form of indulgence offering the following terms:

> By the authority apostolical to me in this behalf committed, we absolve thee A.B from all thy sins confessed with thy mouth, and being contrite with thy heart, and whereof thou wouldst be confessed if they came into thy memory; and we grant unto thee plenary remission of sins, and we promise unto thee the recompense of the just, and an increase of everlasting salvation. And as many privileges as are granted to them that go to fight for the Holy Land, we grant unto thee; and we impart to thee a share in the suffrages of the prayers and good works of the universal synod of the church, and of the holy catholic church.[xv]

The battling bishop was authorised to offer this generous dispensation to any who provided funds or offered their arms in his service. Needless to say, the man who had wrought such destruction and suffering on the peasantry of Norfolk following the revolt of 1381 was not greatly interested in the purely religious aspects of his crusade. The advantage of leading a crusade lay in the opportunity to raise funds from the faithful and the gullible who believed that by pouring money into his coffers their sins would be forgiven and time in purgatory reduced. With all the formalities attended to, his adventure quickly revealed itself as a military exercise that might bring considerable financial gain, provide some additions to the English possessions in France and the possibility of hostages to take back to England for ransom. And if the anti-Pope and his cohorts of supporters got a bashing in the process, then so much the better for everyone involved.

It was a rather grubby affair and proved to be thankfully short-lived. The Bishop arrived in Calais on May 17, and having unsuccessfully attacked Gravelines and Ypres retreated back to England at Michaelmas 1383.[xvi] Whatever part Adam had in helping to get a blessing for the crusade and organising the papal Bulls necessary to approve it, it was a role he would want to forget.

A Southern Jaunt for the Summer

Back in Italy, by the summer of 1383 Urban was also on the move. The situation in southern Italy had been worrying the new Pope for some time, but the constant defections to Avignon and the consequent high turnover of clerks and cardinals had been too much of a distraction. By the end of 1382, with some sort of order re-established in the papal administration,

Urban could focus his attention on securing the borders of the Papal States. He still hoped to secure status and an inheritance for his nephew, Francisco.

Events in Naples had not been running quite as Urban had scripted them. The Pope had excommunicated Joanna, insulted her husband and performed a coronation service for the man he intended should replace her. Thus far all had gone well.

Joanna realised that her situation was getting desperate, and as Charles and his army descended on her kingdom she begged her kinsman Louis of Anjou to come to her aid. Louis sensed that here was a good opportunity for his family to extend their influence into Italy and readily agreed. Soon he was heading for Naples with his own army, only a few days behind Charles. The idea of an army full of supporters of Clement passing through central Italy filled the Pope with foreboding. He was minded to take action immediately, and he too set off for Naples, but he had no intention of travelling alone. Having been so badly let down in Anagni, Urban was not prepared to let his watchful eye drift from his cardinals. Wherever the Pope went, the cardinals went with him too. The cardinals did not share Urban's view of the world and were insulted by his rather condescendingly paternal attitude towards them. They lobbied him hard, looking for as many good reasons as possible for Urban to stay in Rome and let events in Naples unfold. Adam, who had not travelled south of Rome before, offered no objection; after all, this would undoubtedly be a short trip and everyone would soon be back in Rome. He could see little reason to court Urban's wrath over such a trivial matter and in any case the trip came at a good moment for the English Cardinal. The affairs of Bury St Edmunds were still at an impasse and none of Adam's other projects had got very far off the ground. The expedition sounded like a pleasant break from the routine of the business of the papal court.

His colleagues were less trusting, and at the time when Urban was ready to leave for Naples five of the cardinals flatly refused to travel with him. Urban dealt with the situation in his own unique way. He deprived them all of their cardinals' hats, creating at a single stroke five new defectors to anti-Pope Clement's camp.

Chapter 10

Neapolitan Tragedy

I will teach you the fear of the Lord.
Run while you have the light of life,
that the darkness of death may not overtake you

Autumn in Naples

At the height of the Roman summer, Urban led his remaining cardinals out of Rome to the pleasant hill town of Tivoli, which they reached on July 13, 1383. Tivoli provided a pleasant distraction from the heat of the Roman plain, with her olive groves and fruit trees set into step terraces that splashed the low hills with patches of green. Warming gusts of air caressed the blue skies and mingled among the dark shadows cast by the cypress trees. Tivoli was a lush and fruitful Garden of Eden in vivid contrast to the heat and stench of Rome. However, Urban was in a hurry and the stay in Tivoli was destined to be brief. Soon the party was heading south, following the line of the Apennine foothills on the 150-mile journey to Naples. As Urban had insisted on all the cardinals coming with him, each with their own courtiers and the necessary baggage train to support them, progress was painfully slow. The inland route was less direct and harder going than the road along the coastal plain, but safer. Later that year, in December, 16 English clergy who took the coastal road were seized by Spanish pirates and taken back to Spain as prisoners[i] held for ransom.

The entourage reached Valmontone on August 19. It did not reach Ferentino, just 50 miles south east of Rome, until mid September, by which time it was barely a third of the way to Naples. Travelling slowly down the centre of Italy, they all made their way to the town of Frosinone. Slowly the landscape around them changed, becoming less verdant with sparse woodland and occasional olive groves giving way to rocky outcrops and dusty fields where the herds of cows gradually gave way to buffalo. The party finally arrived at Monte Cassino, where they took the winding mountain track to the famous abbey, which they reached on October 3.[ii] If Urban's progress from Rome had been erratic and slow, it had nonetheless presented Adam with the chance to visit the most important Benedictine monastery of all. Monte Cassino, founded by Benedict himself, was the house from whence the Benedictines had spread across the known world. For a monk of Adam's calling, the chance to visit a shrine of such great importance was a major bonus. Urban's motives were somewhat more practical. The party stayed at the abbey just long enough to attend mass and refresh themselves heartily at the abbot's expense.

As Adam looked down from the heights of Monte Cassino, gazing across the glassy expanse of the Bay of Naples and inland towards Vesuvius, he could not begin to imagine the events that the fates had in store for him. Following the Apennine foothills, the road bathed in cool mountain air each morning, the journey was hardly troublesome. Adam could reflect upon the fortunate circumstances in which he had been able to prove his value to the Pope, staying loyal when more faint-hearted souls had started to defect. And even Naples can look attractive from such a distance and from such a height.

All he had to do now was stand by Urban and before long he might find himself well placed to be his successor. The trip was turning out to be full of potential for the English Cardinal.

Urban Sticks his Foot in it

By the time the papal courtiers moved down from the heights of Monte Cassino and onto the plains, word had reached King Charles of the imminent arrival of His Holiness Urban VI. It was an unwelcome development. Charles had always imagined that Urban would leave him to get on with the job of securing his new kingdom, it was a military matter and he was a military man. The King was immediately suspicious of Urban's intentions.

Charles might be the new King of Naples, but he was the outsider, and Urban, Neapolitan by birth, was the local boy made good. He realised that he owed his kingdom to Urban's generosity, but he knew enough about the man to be wary of him. He feared the loyalty that the Neapolitans might feel towards their kinsman and wanted to keep Urban at arm's length if at all possible. He hurried to make plans to meet the Pope outside his capital.

Urban picked up the pace and, dragging his reluctant cardinals along with him, he headed for Capua, one of the towns that Charles Durazzo had promised to donate to Francisco. Capua shut its gates on the Pope and his nephew, and after a few hours of waiting it became clear that the citizens were not about to hand their town over to Francisco. Rebuffed and suspecting a lack of integrity on Charles's part, Urban moved on towards Naples with his cardinals and Charles hurried to meet him with his army. The two parties met just outside the town of Aversa on October 30, 1383. Charles received the papal entourage with due ceremony, and, on the surface, relations between the two parties remained cordial. The King, however, rapidly concluded that Urban was going to be his usual obstreperous self. Charles might still be inclined to accept the Pope as his overlord in principle, but he had an army with him and Urban didn't. For his part Urban managed to argue with the King from the start and took every opportunity to make himself disagreeable. Charles's patience had limits and before the day was out he had imprisoned Urban in the castle of Aversa. The cardinals spent the whole of the next day negotiating with Charles, and Adam, the senior diplomat in the party, once more found Urban trying his negotiating skills to the limit. Charles reluctantly agreed to release the Pope the following day.

For much of the previous 300 years Popes had routinely intervened in the affairs of Naples and Sicily. Often they had been unpopular, regularly weaving an intricate political web around the various dynastic claimants to the Neapolitan throne, playing one off against the other when it suited the ambitions of the papacy. However, Urban had managed to fall out with both rival claimants to the throne at the same time and that was a unique achievement. Charles had to be careful, though. He needed Urban's blessing and authority in his campaign against Louis of Anjou, and Urban could take some comfort from the fact that a Naples that was ruled by Charles would for the moment at least, be a new royal supporter of his cause rather than one with allegiance to Clement.

Not without some difficulty Charles and Urban were reconciled to the pragmatic need for each other's support. The papal courtiers processed into the city of Naples in the company of Charles and his own entourage. Naples made a poor comparison with Rome. The autumn months were much hotter and it had been a particularly dry summer. The city lacked the splendour, the fine gilded churches and the easy life that the Mother City of the faithful provided. Adam has not left behind any thoughts or recollections on the place, or indeed any of the other towns that Urban stopped at on the journey, which probably tells us plenty about the trip.

Urban's Second Crusade

Louis of Anjou had made rather more rapid progress than Urban. Aware that passing close to Rome or Naples would be risky with the Pope and his allies in control of the area west of the Apennines, Louis took his army down the east coast of Italy and rapidly took control of Puglia and Calabria. His initial campaigns, whilst not greeted enthusiastically, met a modicum of support from the local population.

Meanwhile, Urban kept his cardinals in Naples for the New Year and there they were joined by King Charles at the wedding of Francisco, Urban's worthless nephew.[iii] Here at last the Pope could complete the formalities of securing Francisco's inheritance and with it his family's powerbase in the Kingdom of Naples. Charles was reluctant to antagonise the citizens of Capua and they in their turn had made it clear that Francisco was unwelcome. Instead the King agreed to hand over the castle of Nocera near to Salerno, and confirmed the previously agreed pension of 7,000 florins per annum. Both sides agreed that this would be paid until such time as Charles should be in a position to deliver the Dukedom of Taranto, which had fallen rather inconveniently under Louis of Anjou's control. The formalities of the deal between Charles and Francisco would be finalised only once the troublesome Louis had been dealt with.

On New Year's Day 1384 Urban fulfilled his part of the bargain, proclaiming Charles to be the true King of Naples, Louis to be a heretic, a Schismatic and a rebel, and granting indulgences for all who would take up arms against him. Urban then pronounced the war against Louis to be a crusade, and the army of Charles embarked on its task bearing the sign of the cross. Quite what the local population made of this corruption of the once noble chivalric ideal of warfare against the infidel is hard to say, but it is true that Charles had little difficulty raising a substantial army. Urban agreed to stay in Naples so that the two men might settle matters in southern Italy to everyone's satisfaction once the crusader returned victorious, as undoubtedly he would now that he had God on his side.

Nocera

The cardinals remained quietly confident that Urban would fail to keep his word to Charles, but only because they fully expected him to return to Rome. In this they had clearly underestimated their leader. The very same Pope who had publicly humiliated the cardinals, berating them for their lax living and low moral integrity, was quite prepared to put the wellbeing of his family ahead of the cure of souls and the Church at large. Urban was determined to sort out the issue of Francisco and his position in Naples with or without the help of Charles. As soon as the King and his armies had crossed the Apennines and were well out of reach, Urban did indeed announce his intention of leaving Naples. But to their horror, the cardinals were told that the papal party would repair to Nocera Castle in deepest

Campania for the immediate future. From Urban's perspective, the move was the only sensible one to make. His sole motive for coming to Naples was to establish his dynasty, and specifically to set up Francisco as a leading power in the kingdom of Naples. Locating the papal court in Nocera would ensure that Francesco would collect on at least one part of his promised legacy from Charles.

Nocera Castle was set in rich countryside south of Naples. The local farms grew crops of pomegranates, oranges and lemons,[iv] as indeed they still do, on farmland enriched on the outpourings of Vesuvius. Today Nocera is a thriving country town, but when Adam arrived there on June 16, 1384[v] it was a wretched little village of no more than 70 houses, equipped with precious little to sustain the usual dignity of a papal court. For Adam it must have been particularly grim, as much of his work revolved around books, either researching for them or writing them. In both Rome and Avignon he had access to the great libraries of the papal court and the Roman nobility. In a castle in southern Italy, set high above a dusty little town like Nocera, there was very little to work with. As Urban had removed many of the more learned cardinals from his court and had alienated most of those that remained, the possibility of carrying out serious academic work was considerably diminished. Although by now Adam had his own small library, the work he had started on the Office of the Visitation and the Canonisation of St Brigit were hardly things he could easily advance at the castle of Nocera. What had started off as an amusing diversion from the high heat of a Roman summer was fast turning into a farce. Nor was Adam the only cardinal with several reasons to be unhappy.

Luceria Christianorum

Shortly after arriving in Nocera, Urban announced that the town would be the capital of his papacy for the present and conferred upon the castle the title of "Luceria Christianorum".[vi] In the 12th Century the German Emperor Frederick II had brought a Saracen community to Lucera and the town had been popularly known as "Luceria Saracenorum". The Saracens were a useful tool for fighting the Pope as, not surprisingly, they had fewer religious scruples about attacking Italian Christians. Even fewer than the German mercenaries that Frederick had been accustomed to use to keep his Italian possessions under control. The renaming of Nocera was Urban's subtle tilt at Charles as the representative of secular power in southern Italy. Urban had set up his own Christian religious state as an example to the secular powers that surrounded him and he had done it in Charles's own kingdom. Albeit it was a kingdom granted to Charles by the grace of the Pope, so in a way he was just reserving his grace over this particular town.

With every turn of events it seemed increasingly likely that the stay in Nocera was not going to be a temporary one. The cardinals had not expected to be away from Rome for more than a few months, and it had not occurred to any of them that Urban, even at his most outrageous, might contemplate moving his capital. Mutterings among the curia began, some of the cardinals going as far as to suggest that they would rather the papacy had stayed in Avignon than come to reside in Nocera.

The power base of Luceria Christianorum was founded on the castle just outside the commune of Nocera. It still looms large above the town today, perched up on a rocky outcrop, the walls encircling the crest of the hill, with an upper and lower courtyard built into the contours. It was a substantial citadel with strong walls reinforced by square towers, but it did not offer a great deal of comfortable accommodation for a papal court. Urban and his secretaries had the fortified Torre Filangieri to themselves and the rest of the cardinals had to make do with rooms off the lower courtyard. Even in the inner sanctum of the courtyard the walls are thick and squarely built with windows in either oblong voids or plain Romanesque arches. The courtyard itself is a barren, dusty, open space devoid of trees or any other form of natural shade. There is a small gothic chapel off to the side of the courtyard, but with all the courtiers, the provisions for the castle and the bakers, butchers, coopers, smiths and all the other necessary hangers-on of the court, there would have been little space for quiet contemplation. Soon the castle was full of the stench of stale food rotting under the hot Neapolitan sun and the noise of the artisans at work on their daily tasks. To Adam the castle at Nocera must have seemed closer to hell than any of the rings in Dante's Inferno. To make matters worse, a brawl in the town resulted in the death of one of the few Englishman in the party, and despite Urban's personal intervention all the remaining English except Adam left Nocera shortly afterwards.[vii] The English Cardinal was well and truly on his own.

Louis of Anjou was not faring much better. The would-be King of Naples had not enjoyed life in his prospective kingdom. Plague had ravaged his army and Charles had refused to give battle, simply waiting for his rival's army to wilt and melt away under the hot Italian sun. Finally, in September the wretched and unlucky Frenchman died in the act of stopping his soldiers from looting a city belonging to his own allies. Without Louis, the Angevin cause looked hopeless. Charles caught the plague but, as it must have seemed to the populace at large, protected by the papal blessing and with God's support by implication, he recovered and returned to Naples. From there he wrote to Urban, a little perturbed that the Pope had not waited for him in the city as they had agreed, asking him to return for a conference. Urban had anticipated that Charles might react badly on his return and he had used the intervening weeks to get Francisco to repair and upgrade the formidable fortifications around the hilltop of Nocera. Urban felt safe at the castle, and he replied to Charles using the considerable reserves of arrogance at his disposal. In the view of the Pope, Kings were wont to come to the feet of Popes and not the other way round. When Charles indicated that the only way he would visit Nocera was at the head of an army, it became clear to the cardinals that they were in for a long stay. Even the most loyal of churchmen questioned the sanity of the man on the papal throne. He had stood for austerity whilst flagrantly and unapologetically indulging his own acts of nepotism. From a position of absolute authority in 1378 Urban had not only created the Schism but alienated most of his supporters in the six years thereafter. Now he found himself besieged in his own capital, a dusty village in southern Italy the extent of his authority, and all to keep alive his dynastic ambition.

Time for a Change

Something had to be done to curb Urban's authority before he brought the whole edifice of the Catholic Church crashing down. Adam certainly thought so, and together with the Cardinals of Venice and Genoa, Cardinal de Sangro, the Cardinal Archbishops of Corfu and Taranto, and the Bishop of Aquilea,[viii] he began to look for a way of tackling the problem head on. Perhaps they could overthrow Urban, or find a way of replacing the Pope's supreme authority with a committee of cardinals who would rule in his place.

The solution the plotters were working towards seems to have had a suspiciously English flavour. Whether or not any notion of election crossed the mind of Adam and his cohorts, the plotters do seem to have considered a representative committee ruling the Church by agreement and consensus. It smacks of the notion of "parliament", at least in the sense that Simon de Montfort used it as a curb on the authority of Henry III. The use of a parliament was, even by the 14th Century, an idea that had hardly developed beyond the shores of England. Nor was parliament meant to be a major restriction on the authority of the King, merely an implicit pact whereby money could only be raised from the people if they had a chance to air their grievances. This early, rather impotent, parliament of the sort that existed in England during Adam's life was exactly the type of model the cardinals appeared to have in mind for the Church. Although the full details of the plan were not recorded, the plotters clearly thought the Pope was going mad and that they needed to restrict his power in the best way that canon law could justify. It had never been tried before, but then neither had the idea of a parliament before the reign of Henry III. The cardinals sought out the services of a prominent canon lawyer to prepare a detailed case for their position.

As Charles and his army threatened to turn up in force and lay siege to Nocera, Adam used his skills to send coded letters from within the walls of Nocera to the King.[ix] They did not want to solve the problem of Pope Urban only to be attacked by Charles and his army. All the communication between the parties had to be made in secret with an army besieging the castle of Nocera. The cardinals were put in touch with the lawyer Bartolino da Piacenza[x] and he was engaged to make the case for removing Urban. Adam's expertise in theology and his studies at Oxford in canon law make him the most likely instigator of this move and he probably worked closely with da Piacenza in formulating the legal framework for Urban's removal.

Adam and his fellow plotters knew the risks they were taking. If Urban had been prepared to expel cardinals from the curia just because they did not wish to follow him on his Neapolitan expedition, there could be little hope of forgiveness if the plot was discovered. The fact that the cardinals knew how risky their venture was shows us how desperate they had become to get out of Nocera and to change the shape of a papacy that seemed to them to be characterised by madness. King Charles would also have been happy for a way out of the impasse with Urban VI. It did not look good to be fighting a war against the reigning Pope, and whether Charles felt it was bad for his soul or not, there were plenty of his subjects who might be minded to take that view.

For the time being, the politics of southern Italy were left in an awkward stalemate.

The Pope under Siege

To appreciate the predicament facing Urban VI in December 1384 we must view the scene around Nocera through the eyes of the Pope as he gazed down from the battlements of Nocera Castle. The castle has good views over the town and any unusual movements of men or supplies can be spotted immediately. To the south the high Lattari hills run in long lines of narrow ridges down to the coast at Sorrento. Dominating the landscape, they form an impenetrable mass hemming in the castle. In late afternoon, long before sunset, the elongated shadows thrown across the valley floor rapidly cloak first the town and then the castle in darkness. To the east another ridge of the Lattari range runs north-south along the route towards Salerno. The passes through these hills are narrow, through deep valleys cut into the hillsides and whoever controls the high ground commands the passes. Beyond the hills, the coastline at Castelmare and Salerno was plagued with pirates who were not averse to raiding inland and taking hostages.

Looking out to the north from the battlements, Vesuvius dominates the view, a blue outline shimmering on the horizon, a safe enough distance away across a reassuringly empty plain. From Nocera the plain offers few surprises, it is firm ground and easy territory for marching, but every movement can be seen easily from the castle. The open plain offers the perfect route into and out of the castle to the north, and the road to Rome. As Urban looked northwards from Nocera Castle this would have been his best hope of salvation, were it not for the fact that as he looked northwards across the plain he was staring straight at the capital city of his adversary, Charles Durazzo, King of Naples. By the end of December, Charles had marched his army to the gates of Nocera to confront the papal presence and try to force it out of the town.

Urban may have been surrounded, but he could at least take comfort from the strength of the castle in which he was trapped. Nocera Castle was no pre-Renaissance palace turned chateau. It was built in the 12th Century by the Norman Duke Ruggerio II and had more in common with the sturdy castles of Bodiam, Krak des Chevaliers and Chinon than it did with anything from the pre-Renaissance world of Italy or France. Thick curtain walls surrounded the castle, their foundations plunging deep into the rocky outcrops on the brow of the hill. The castle walls were lined at regular intervals with circular towers, each built to withstand a siege in isolation from the rest of the castle. Although the outer defences have now fallen into disrepair, the inner courtyard and one of the towers can still be seen to this day. Urban placed his hope in the strength of the castle walls and the intervention of the Lord. Even so, it seems rather odd that he should have allowed himself to be surrounded by Charles and cut off from friendly forces. Did he really believe that Charles would simply give up and go away?

By the end of December the town of Nocera had fallen into the hands of Charles. His men had surrounded the lower slopes of the hill on which the castle stood and started to set up camp. Urban stayed put in the castle, and Charles made little effort to climb the hill and attack. Besides, as long he corresponded with Adam and his colleagues in the castle, there was every possibility of a peaceful outcome. He could see little point in risking lives unnecessarily in a direct attack. On the other side of the castle walls, on December 17, Urban relieved the boredom by appointing another nine new cardinals, mostly Italian and from the kingdom of Naples. Perhaps he hoped to gain a little favour with the local populace in his dispute with their new King.

Urban's court celebrated Christmas and Epiphany in sombre mood. The castle had plenty of supplies brought in before the start of the siege, but they were not limitless and neither Pope nor King seemed in the mood to compromise. Adam alone had some reason to be of good cheer, although he didn't know it at the time. On December 26, 1384 John Wyclif suffered a seizure, was paralysed and two days later he died. The Westminster chronicler noted rather smugly that "he had sinfully spread a number of heretical and wrong headed doctrines in God's Church."[xi] Thus perish all heretics!

The Fall of Cardinal Adam

The morning of January 11, 1385 dawned with clear skies and a sharp chill in the air. Adam and the other cardinals were invited by Urban to a meeting[xii] to be held in the public forum in the lower courtyard of the castle. The whole papal court gathered, cardinals, bishops and their retinues together with the various artisans and labourers. The meeting seemed innocuous enough, no doubt Urban had called the gathering to rally his followers and invite them to look for the divine intervention that, to the Pope's mind, would surely come in due course. Perhaps he wanted to discuss the strategy for the siege and the tactics to outwit Charles, even perhaps how to make the castle's rations last longer.

His audience had no time to take in what was happening, for suddenly Urban was ranting and raving. He called down curses on his cardinals and then he shouted for his guards. Before they had the chance to move, Adam and his fellow conspirators were surrounded by soldiers and loaded with chains. Urban carried on upbraiding them, accusing them of treasons and crimes against God and more particularly against himself. The plot had been betrayed. The rest of the court looked on in stunned silence as the Pope denounced them for the letters they had written to Charles and told them in no uncertain terms that he had seen the letters himself.

Adam's coded letters to King Charles had fallen into the hands of Thomas Orsini, a fellow cardinal who had been on good terms with the plotters. Orsini, a Roman aristocrat, must have considered turning a blind eye to the plot; he was no great fan of the rather crude manners of the former Archbishop of Bari or of his increasingly erratic behaviour. But in the best tradition of the Orsini clan through the ages, he saw an eye for the main chance. Here was a perfect opportunity to gain favour. Orsini betrayed Adam and his colleagues for the favours of a Pope who was showing all the signs of dementia. Worse still, Adam and the six others were the most senior and learned of the clerics left at court. Urban was deeply shocked when he learned of the conspiracy. Moreover, as the conspirators were also men that he had promoted himself, it represented the worst form of betrayal.

The raging pontiff ordered that the cardinals be taken in their chains and thrown into a broken cistern among the outbuildings of the courtyard[xiii] until suitably uncomfortable and secure accommodation could be found for them. When Theoderic de Niem, one of Urban's personal secretaries, returned to the castle a few hours later he saw the wretched men locked in small cells set into the walls of one of the towers, open at the front to the cold winter winds. The unfortunate cardinals looked for all the world like gargoyles. Their cells were so small that the corpulent Cardinal di Sangro did not have room to sit down.

Torture!

Basilio de Genova took charge of the wretched conspirators. Basilio served Urban as his military commander at Nocera. A former pirate and renowned soldier, he had remained faithful to Urban's cause throughout the troublesome years that followed his coronation. Basilio made a deep impression on Theoderic de Niem, and it was not a good one! He described him as a malicious man who, in his pirate days, took pleasure in torturing Christians in general whilst retaining a particular loathing for clerics and other men of the cloth.[xiv] Urban tried to give Basilio an aura of respectability by making him a Knight of the Hospitalers of St John. If Urban was now reduced to relying on the services of a former pirate and notorious anti-cleric, at least he had a task in mind that would allow the man to use his talents. Basilio relished the opportunity of obtaining appropriate confessions from his charges, and Urban made it clear that he might use whatever means he found suitable.

Later the same day the Bishop of Aquilea, the oldest and weakest of the six conspirators, was the first to be interrogated. Under the painful ministrations of the conscientious Knight, the aged bishop repeatedly passed out and had to be revived in order to appreciate the full effects of Basilio's work. It was only the pride and pleasure that he took in his task that drove Basilio to carry on torturing the poor bishop long after he agreed to confess. Adam must have looked on in horror, knowing very well that each of the conspirators could expect the same treatment. Pinned into a cell in which he could barely move, he was exposed to the worst ravages of the freezing winds and driving rain. Even in southern Italy January can be severely cold. As he watched the courtiers gathering round to see the old bishop being tortured, he must have cursed himself for the foolishness of the enterprise and faced up to the certainty of the long and painful death awaiting him. For the time being, however, Urban satisfied himself with the confession that had been ground out of the bishop. He would let the cardinals endure the agony of anticipation.

Three days later, on January 14, 1385,[xv] their waiting was over. It was another bitter cold day, and in the open courtyard high above Nocera the wind felt particularly icy.[xvi] Urban invited Basilio to torture the remaining cardinals. In this gruesome task he was aided and abetted by Francisco Prignano, the Pope's loathsome nephew for whose benefit the whole Neapolitan expedition had been undertaken in the first place. A number of torments had been prepared for the benefit of each cardinal, and a rack and corda were set up in the lower courtyard. The latter was a rather ingenious device involving a high frame rigged with ropes and pulleys. The victim was roped up to a pulley and then a weight was attached to his feet. A counter-weight was put on the other side of the pulley, ripping the victim's limbs in opposite directions. If the arms were not ripped from their sockets, the unfortunate was eventually drawn, painfully, to the top of the frame. Then the counter weight was released causing him to plummet to the ground, smashing his legs against the stone paving of the courtyard .

Basilio organised the torture so that each man would take his turn at each instrument and their agony would be on full display to those who had to follow. The cardinals were ordered to remove their cloaks so they should be fully exposed to the cold. Urban's soldiers drew lots for possession of the rich clothes. Adam was the fourth to succumb to the venal pleasures of Francisco and Basilio. He watched the distress of first the Cardinal di Sangro, then the Cardinals of Venice and Corfu as each in turn suffered agonies under the close attentions of their torturers. Finally Adam had his turn, and when the poor man's body had been cruelly wrecked, he joined the others in an iron cage suspended from the ceiling of a damp vault on the edge of the lower courtyard. Whatever he thought as he watched the agonies of the others, he remained true to his religion throughout his ordeal. He may have indulged in excesses in his life as a monk, and he had certainly taken a pretty liberal view of the Rule of Benedict, but he did not lose his faith. Five years later he related how in the hours of despair in Nocera, he prayed to Brigit, the mystic he had met in Montefiascone and whose sainthood he had championed before his fall from grace. She was a natural source of comfort for Adam. A saintly woman would be, to the mind of a 14th Century cleric, ideally placed to intercede with God on his behalf. In a world where relics of the true cross and belief in the intervention of saints who had died centuries ago were a commonplace, it is logical that Adam should choose to follow his faith in such a direct way. He did not look to the Blessed Virgin or the patron of his old priory, St Leonard, but someone he actually knew. Someone who, at a practical level, would be able to intercede with God on his behalf, who might be in a position to understand his good points and his true worth. It was an odd mixture of pure faith and rationality but for the time being at any rate, Brigit kept him from death if not from the misery of captivity in Nocera.

Urban was accustomed to take a walk in a garden laid out in the upper courtyard, reading the holy offices of the day from his breviary, and he encouraged Basilio and Francisco to torture the cardinals with vigour so that he could take pleasure from hearing the full impact of their work as he read. Every now and then, as he heard one of his victims cry out, he stopped, smiled and then carried on walking and reading. De Niem says that his face glowed like a lamp as he let the full force of his fury fall on any of his courtiers who approached him. This might have been perfectly normal behaviour for the venal and viscous-minded petty princes ruling over the city states of Italy, but for a Pope it was scandalous. Adam and his fellows may have been poorly advised in their attempt to carry out the plot, but if anything could demonstrate that their intentions were good, it was the manner and attitude that Urban adopted throughout the spring of 1385. The Clementine supporters could not believe their luck. News did not generally travel fast in mediaeval times, but when it suited a purpose it could move pretty quickly. Catholic Europe was scandalised by the treatment of the cardinals. All of them were elder statesmen of the Church, three, including Adam, had outstanding reputations as men of learning. When, just days later, Charles's wife Margaret heard of the outrage she immediately locked up two of Urban's nieces in the dungeons of the Castello del Uvo in Naples. It did not take too long for the news to reach Clement in Avignon and by the start of the summer it had in turn filtered through to King Richard in England.

Urban VI Makes a Stand

Meanwhile, Urban had determined to put on a grand spectacle to show his holy and righteous anger at his betrayal. He set up a platform between the two square towers on either side of the main gateway into the castle. Today the approach to the gates is covered in woodland but then the slopes were cleared so the defenders could see precisely what the besieging army was up to. Mounted on a platform in clear view of his supporters and Charles's army, Urban and his remaining cardinals were dressed in their full regalia for the solemn spectacle. Each cardinal held a flaming torch in his right hand as Urban read out a long list of the crimes committed against his person. Finally he announced the ultimate betrayal, accusing King Charles and Queen Margaret of plotting against him and pronouncing their kingdom under interdict. The cardinals then threw their torches to the ground, pronouncing anathema and excommunication on the royal personages and offering indulgences to all who came to the walls of Nocera to hear the papal pronouncement. The very idea of offering indulgences to the faithful just to get them to come and listen to the Pope shows just how far Urban's authority had fallen. The ceremony on the platform was repeated daily over the following weeks.

On January 18 the Pope ordered that the cardinals should be brought once more before him. The bedraggled, broken-limbed men, dressed in torn and ragged clothes, were dragged into the papal presence. Under the influence of large doses of pain, the cardinals had produced a full written confession which had been signed by each in turn.[xvii] They should have sealed the document with their personal seals, but all but one had been lost when they were seized by Urban's soldiers, so they had to make do with the same seal applied against each of the six names. The confession was not unduly elaborate and it recorded simply the "facts" as extracted under torture.

According to the text of the confession Adam and his co-conspirators had plotted with King Charles, Queen Margaret of Naples, the Abbot of Monte Cassino and the Cardinal vulgarly known as Rieti. The latter was singled out for special abuse, described in the confession as a heretic, Schismatic and even as the antichrist.[xviii] The conspirators admitted that they had planned to take possession of the Pope's person and do away with him. He was then to be replaced by Cardinal Rieti. We can never know if that was the true nature of the plot, or whether it was made to seem more ruthless for effect. It does seem unlikely that the cardinals would have been prepared to kill Urban. The very idea of murdering the Pope would have been hard to sell to the Church at large, even as an antidote to the Schism. If Urban was merely to be replaced, or perhaps have his powers curbed by a committee of cardinals, it would hardly have justified the extreme treatment he had meted out. The confessions needed to justify the punishment! The cardinals implored Urban to have mercy upon them, but the man remained unmoved. They were herded back to their iron cage and left to endure the ravages of winter in Nocera. Throughout the coldest months of 1385 Adam and his fellow conspirators had to endure the freezing cold and the lice. To relieve his own personal boredom, Francisco threw reptiles into the cardinals' prison, taking pleasure in their discomfort. During the spring another group of cardinals, disgusted with Urban and his treatment of Adam, decided enough was enough and defected to Clement.

In the meantime more moderately minded individuals sent delegations to Urban imploring him to desist from dealing so harshly with such senior men of the Church. In February 1385 a delegation arrived from the University of Naples to try to broker a settlement between their King and their Pope. Urban was not interested in a reconciliation. Following the traditional line of argument that Adam had spelled out so neatly in the Defensorium, he suggested that as the Kingdom of Naples was in his gift and Charles had abused the position given to him, it was now up to the Pope, in fact it was the Pope's duty, to remove the wayward King and replace him with a more suitable steward of the kingdom. The only problem was that he had no other candidates suitable for the job.

Charles was not going to give him the option. He no longer had any motive for holding back, so he moved his troops up to the foot of the castle walls and the siege began in earnest. Furious at Charles's ingratitude, Urban pronounced anathema on the King and his soldiers each day from the battlements alongside the Torre di Filangieri. In response, Charles offered a 10,000 florin reward for anyone bringing him the body of the Pope dead or alive. The reputation of the papacy had fallen about as far as it could go.

Break Out!

Day after day King Charles used his siege engines to bombard the castle, and by early summer the walls were showing signs of wear. Urban had to try and break the siege, and to do that he would need help from the world outside Nocera. Messengers were sent out under cover of darkness to potential allies of the Pope in Italy, but when Urban tried to send word of his plight back to Rome his messenger was caught trying to sneak through the enemy lines. The unfortunate man was put in a catapult and hurled to his death against the walls of the castle. At last, in June, just as Urban's fortunes seemed to be at their lowest ebb, relief arrived from a most unlikely source. A party of French mercenaries broke through Charles's men and entered the castle, bringing supplies. The men were stragglers from the army of Louis of Anjou, the candidate for the Kingdom of Naples endorsed by Pope Clement, and had spent much of the past four years fighting against both Urban and Charles. Yet in common with many of the armed bands fighting in Italy at the time, their allegiance was based on need and hard cash rather than matters of scruple. Urban needed their help and as long as he could meet their price it hardly mattered to their leader, Raymond de Orsini, if Urban or Clement were the true Pope.

Despite the arrival of new men and supplies it was clear by now that the stocks of food within the castle at Nocera would not last much longer. The French helped Urban to plan an escape with his treasury and army of retainers.

Adam's life was now in the greatest danger. Urban might kill all the captives rather than take them with him. Even if they were left behind they might be slaughtered by Charles's men before they realised who the wretched prisoners were. Dressed in rags, broken, and bitten by lice, Adam and his fellow conspirators hardly had the appearance of princes of the Church. Whatever thoughts might have gone through his head, he could not have anticipated the actions of an increasingly eccentric and volatile pontiff. Urban had no intention of killing the cardinals and giving them the satisfaction of martyrdom. Not yet anyway. Nor would he leave them behind and risk the possibility that they might gain their freedom. He would take them with him and take them as captives, whether they slowed his progress or not, so that the world would see how grievously he had been betrayed.

Even now, at the nadir of his papacy, Urban was not without friends. The Doge of Genoa had heard of Urban's difficulties and offered to send ten galleys to his aid. It occurred to the Doge that to play host to the supreme pontiff and his court would enhance the prestige of his city. In early June he sent word to Urban that he would be sending his ships to help him and that Urban would be most welcome to take up permanent residence in Genoa. It was a good offer, but not without a few logistical problems. Urban still needed to get his troops and, most importantly, his treasury, from Nocera to the coast in order to rendezvous with the Genoese fleet. The Pope, desperate to escape, decided to attack the besieging army and try to break through their lines. On July 7 Urban and his troops charged out of Nocera Castle and down the hill into the startled Neapolitan army below. The Pope's men broke through the lines with surprising ease and rode as hard as they could down the valley to Salerno. The captive cardinals had to endure the indignity of being strapped to the underside of donkeys and pack mules during the sortie to ensure they did not hinder the escape.

Betrayal and Murder

When Urban's troops broke out of Nocera Castle, Charles was completely taken by surprise. He did not have a large force at his disposal and without stationing men at the top of the passes through the Lattari hills, he had no way of stopping the Pope heading down to the sea at Salerno. A few of his troops harassed the rearguard as the papal entourage fled to the coast, but he could not prevent the escape. The greatest threat to Urban's plan came from his own troops. Raymond had few principles, but a contract was a contract and he expected to do the job and receive due reward from his new employer. The Breton and Italian mercenaries in his troop had far fewer scruples. As the party travelled through the narrow valley towards Salerno the Bretons realised that if they seized Urban and sent him as a captive to Avignon, Clement would pay them a more substantial sum than they could ever expect from Urban. Cornered by men of their own army, Raymond (who, to his credit, acted as honourably as any mercenary throughout the episode) and Urban managed to buy the Bretons off for 11,000 florins. The troops took the cash rather than run the risk that Clement might not be as generous as they hoped, and leaving their captain and his employer behind, headed off to Salerno to spend their ill-gotten gains.

Battered by the experience Urban continued the journey with a much reduced but faithful retinue of 300 Germans and Italians.[xix] It is perhaps hard not to sympathise with Urban's plight, as once again he found himself betrayed and for the basest of motives. With the rebel Breton troops heading to Salerno, Urban decided it would be best to change direction; he did not wish to risk either another confrontation or the possibility of having to pay out even more money in ransom.

Progress was slow, mainly because the broken and tired Bishop of Aquilea was lagging behind. The poor man's mule had gone lame[xx] but the Pope could ill afford to risk any delays. Urban was still anxious that either the Bretons or the troops of King Charles, or indeed both, might be closing in on him. He berated the old bishop, whose incapacity was exclusively the handiwork of Urban's torturer, as if he suspected him of deliberately holding them back to increase the chances that they would be caught. When it was pointed out that the bishop was hardly in a position to either help or hinder, strapped as he was to the lame mule, Urban totally lost his temper. To the horror of the clerics in the party, he demanded that the wretched bishop should be killed immediately. Raymond took him at his word and the Bishop of Aquilea was stabbed to death by a common soldier and left at the side of the road for the ravens. No one dared raise a voice in protest.

In sombre mood the party headed east to Giffoni, where they found time to gather their strength and recover from the trauma of their escape from Nocera. They rested for three days, and once they had recouped their provisions the party made for the small fortified hill town of Flumeri in the middle of the Apennines. They set out across the Picentini Mountains and reached the town on July 9. Urban was now an enemy of the King of Naples, and whether or not he was Pope, he could not rely on a friendly reception in any town within the Kingdom of Naples. Fortunately the townsfolk opened the gates to the Pope and here the party rested in the castle for the next few days.

Looking for Lost Friends

Urban's desperate band of followers found some relief at Flumeri once it became clear that Charles was no longer pursuing them and that the treacherous Bretons had stayed in Salerno enjoying the fruits of Urban's largesse. Even so, the Pope was now in the middle of Italy and his only hope for salvation lay with Genoese galleys far out at sea, and he didn't as yet know if it was the Adriatic Sea or the Ligurian Sea. Urban needed to buy some time and arrange a rendezvous with the Genoese and sort out a plan of action. He had heard that he had supporters in the town of Benevento and decided that the party should head there in the hope of receiving the Doge's envoys and finding out more about the progress of the promised galleys. To that end he sent a young German clerk named Gobelinus to the town to meet Antonino Bulcano, a relative of Urban's who had stationed himself in the Rocca dei Rettori. The Rocca or castle of Benevento stood at the top of a steep hill overlooking the rest of the town, its solid walls making an ideal base for a Pope obliged to live as an enemy in the territory of the local king. Gobelinus was told to find out exactly what the state of play was, how much support there really was for Urban in the town, and then report back on the best course of action.

Throughout the long journey across Italy, Urban took the captive cardinals with him, a trophy of the treachery he faced and of the injustices he had suffered. At every stop they were imprisoned in chains, and during the day when the party was on the move, they were tied to their mules. Their clothes had been ripped and cut, hanging from them like rags, and the months of deprivation and torture had left their bodies thin and weak. Yet the sympathy that the sight of these once wealthy lords of the Church evoked wherever they went only fuelled Urban's anger. At Flumeri they were kept locked in the castle, quite unaware of what Urban was planning and by now they probably no longer cared. Urban was at last free to take care of more routine papal business. One of his first acts after breaking out of the siege at Nocera was to send word to Rome ordering the release of Nicholas of Hereford. With Adam now disgraced and an enemy of the Pope, it was inevitable that those who had suffered the wrong end of his judgement would now appear to be somewhat less guilty in Urban's eyes. Nicholas returned to England without making any further attempts to win approval from the papal authority, and in due course he simply changed sides, becoming a pillar of the established Church.

Back in Benevento, Gobelinus was finding out exactly what the state of play was, and rather more directly than he had planned. Unbeknownst to the young German and three of his friends who had been taken in by the monastery of St Sophia, Urban's supporters had been betrayed and driven out of town within a few hours of the papal clerk arriving. A mob surged through the town, attacking Urban's supporters wherever they found them. Gobelinus only heard the noise of the fighting at the last moment. He and his colleagues had just closed the doors of the monastery behind them when they realised they were in trouble. Sprinting up the hill to the castle, which was barely 150 yards from St Sophia, the four men only just got in and locked the gates in time. Poor Gobelinus had escaped from one siege only to find himself faced with another.

Urban's comfortable sojourn in Flumeri was broken when a desperate and tired messenger brought the news that his supporters had been thrown out of Benevento and Gobelinus was hanging on grimly in the Rocca with only a handful of men, surrounded by a hostile populace. Oddly, the dire news brought out the best in the Pope. Unperturbed by the apparent downturn in his fortunes and steady in the face of adversity (he was getting used to it) he decided on swift action. The demands of the occasion required a bit of subterfuge and Urban proved up to the task. First he sent messengers to the citizens of Benevento saying he had no intention of visiting their town but he would ask the young Cardinal of Naples, Petrinus Tomacellus, to visit them on his behalf. The citizens breathed a collective sigh of relief and on July 24 welcomed Petrinus, a young cardinal and fellow Calabrian who surely posed little threat to them, as representing the lesser of two evils.

They were caught completely by surprise as they greeted Petrinus at the east gate when Urban and his full entourage turned up and entered the town by the south gate. Surrounded by his guards, he went directly to the Church of St Bartholomew where he said mass with his captive cardinals chained together alongside him. Then he led his troops up the hill to the Rocca to join Gobelinus and Antonino.

With a force of armed soldiers camped in their town, the Beneventans found discretion to be the better part of valour. The papal troops took up positions around the castle from where they could do a lot of damage to the town, and eventually the citizens reluctantly accepted their guests and gave them a grudging welcome. Calm returned. Those citizens loyal to Urban who had been driven out drifted back into the town over the next few days. The Pope set up his court at the Rocca, but the accommodation had not been designed for comfort. The summer heat in 1385 was unusually unforgiving, and even the more fortunate papal courtiers with rooms to themselves found the conditions in Benevento oppressive. The heat of the day made them sweat and the living quarters were small and poorly ventilated. The captive cardinals were kept in the basement of the castle in a narrow chamber. The conditions must have seemed excruciating, and Adam can only have wondered how the ordeal would end. Perhaps as he prayed to Brigit and Mary it was not for help or salvation, but for a swift and painless end to his suffering.

Crossing the Apennines with Pope Urban

At last Urban received some good news. The long-awaited Genoese ambassadors arrived, having made the journey to Benevento with some considerable difficulty, not least as they needed Charles's permission to cross his territory. Although Charles could hardly hope to stop the Genoese doing anything they liked at sea, technically they needed his permission even to land on the coastline of the kingdom of Naples. Neither Charles nor the Doge were looking to start another war, so the delegation was given permission to visit the Pope in Benevento.

If the arrival of the Genoese was a relief, they brought bad news with them. Charles would not allow Urban to rendezvous with the Genoese fleet in the Bay of Naples or on the coast around Salerno. The King feared that a combination of the troops of Raymond and Urban, plus the galleys of the Genoese, might tempt the Pope to launch a direct attack on Naples. Charles was certainly anxious to be rid of Urban and to avoid any new confrontations with the irascible Pope, but did not want to take any unnecessary risk. Reluctantly, Urban agreed with the Genoese that he would take his party over the Apennines to the Adriatic coast, while the galleys would sail through the straits of Messina and meet the Pope near the town of Barletta. On Thursday August 3 Urban set out in full pomp, but only after awarding Benevento to Raymond together with the sum of 1,000 florins, which the Pope instructed should be collected from the citizens. Once more the Pope demonstrated the consummate ease with which he could dispose of something that did not belong to him. By Friday the papal party reached Flumeri once again, and they rested there before setting out the next day towards Lacedonia. At just over 2,500 feet above sea level Lacedonia sits at the heart of the Apennines. The road from Flumeri was a narrow winding track that took the travellers over the mountains.

The extreme heat makes August the very worst month for travelling across this part of Italy, and it was an uncomfortable journey. The hills stretched off into a barren dusty brown scrubland for miles in all directions. There was nothing to protect the traveller from the fierce heat of high summer and August was notorious for the strong winds washing the hills with hot, dry air and driving sandy dust clouds into the faces of anyone foolish enough to attempt to cross them. The only shelter was from a few scrubby and scattered trees hidden deep in the valleys next to the few streams that run all year round. Unfortunately the party had to move as fast as possible during the daylight hours to cross the hills in good time to meet the galleys. For Adam and the other captive cardinals, their clothes torn to rags and their bodies broken, the burning sun was even more oppressive. Despite the gruelling heat they managed to cover the 25 miles between Flumeri and Lacedonia in one day, arriving on August 5. That night they slept at the castle and, anxious to avoid any risk of being followed, they moved on again the next day, heading this time for the town of Minervino on the plain on the eastern side of the mountains.

The papal party had a torrid time crossing the hills. As they scanned the route ahead all they could see stretching to the horizon was the rough terrain of the high hills that form the backbone of southern Italy. Here the rivers regularly run dry in August, and this was made worse by the fact that for the second successive year the summer was unusually hot. With every slight breeze dust blew up from the barren land into their sweat-covered faces, there was very little water and no shelter from the sun. The only consolation for Urban was that, not surprisingly in such terrain, there were very few villages along the way, so there was less possibility of being attacked by the local population. As Urban urged his followers on to Minervino, the papal party must have looked more like bandits than the supreme pontiff and his entourage.

The route from Lacedonia to the coast took them to the banks of the River Ofranto, which even at the height of summer flows in waspish torrents and is a wide enough expanse of water to pose a problem to the traveller. Desperately the group rode along the bank, looking for the most suitable place to cross the river. The sun was beating down on an arid yellow and brown land, a dazzling and unbearable brightness filling the landscape. Plagued by flies and distracted by the heat, even when finally they found a place where the mules could cope with the water's flow it was only with great difficulty that they got everyone across. Here once again Adam found his life held by a thread as the mules were forced to swim across the river with the prisoners still tied to their backs. Gobelinus describes the desperate trek over the mountains in harrowing terms. In Urban he saw the wild desperation of the children of Israel in flight from Pharaoh, fleeing Egypt and captivity.[xxi] Yet there was also a magnificent determination within the pontiff who somehow drew immense inspiration from the severity of his plight. He drove his men on, keeping rations and supplies under tight control. He commanded with absolute authority and above all he ensured that the captive cardinals went with him everywhere, in chains, as a trophy to his betrayal.

Ships Ahoy!

It took three long days to reach the town of Minervino, a journey of just 40 miles. At least one day had been taken up getting across the River Ofranto. Yet Urban's troubles were not at an end even when the party finally arrived at the town on August 9. There was no word from the coast of the galleys, no sightings of any Genoese ships at all, and the party was now on the opposite side of Italy from Rome and potential safety. Was this to be the final betrayal of the Roman Pope? Had he been abandoned to rot in the plague-ridden heat of southern Italy just as Louis of Anjou had been the year before? Urban often saw himself as a martyr in the cause of the Church, fanatically leading the true faith against Schismatics and heretics. His determination in the end was magnificent. His cause by contrast looked hopeless. Deserted by some of his cardinals, conspired against by Adam and his fellows, abandoned by others, Urban had to endure successively his betrayal for cash by the Bretons, outright rejection from the citizens of

Benevento, and now this. The Pope had every justification for his paranoia.

Minervino was not the most verdant of communities either. The whole region had been afflicted by a severe drought. It had not rained for three months. The vines had failed and there was no wine to drink from the previous year's vintage, which had also been poor and drought affected. This was a far cry from the riches and comforts of Avignon. Pope and cardinals, courtiers and soldiers, had to survive on rations of wine vinegar diluted with a few precious drops of water, and inevitably the prisoners were given the least to drink to conserve rations.

For 12 long days they waited at Minervino until, with food scarce and nothing left to drink, at last there was some news of the galleys. Urban's remaining Italian allies had kept faith with him after all, the Genoese had been sighted off the coast near Bari. At sunrise on the August 19 Urban sounded a fanfare of trumpets and struck out for Barletta, a town a few miles to the north of Bari. Once more he was thwarted when the town held out for King Charles and refused to open the city gates to the papal entourage. Perhaps warnings had reached the commune from Benevento. It was another boiling hot day. The worst of it was that the papal party had to watch helplessly from a tower on the hills outside the town as they saw the white sails of the galleys billowing in the lethargic breezes far out at sea. The party headed along the coast road towards the town of Trani but not wanting to risk being rebuffed by Charles's supporters a second time, they picked their way through fields and vineyards around the edge of the town, trying to find a route down to the beach. On the lower ground away from the sea they lost sight of the sails once more, and blundering through the haphazard patterns of the fields, they could not even be certain they were heading for the shore. A despondent mood settled on Urban's followers. Finally, at two in the afternoon they saw the sails of the galleys once more, and after a few anxious moments waiting to see if the ships had spotted them, the fugitives breathed a collective sigh of relief as six of the ships headed in towards the shore.

Gobelinus was convinced that if it had not been for the juice of the grapes they drank in the vineyards outside Trani, they would have all perished of thirst.[xxii]

Chapter 11

The Wrong Sort of Salvation

What dear brothers is more delightful, than this voice of the Lord calling to us?

Rescue

Just outside Trani, on the afternoon of Saturday August 19, 1385, six Genoese galleys slipped close in to the shore to rescue the tattered remnants of Pope Urban VI's court. The Genoese welcomed the Pope on board with a fanfare of trumpets and pipes and a display of reverence to the supreme pontiff. It was a bedraggled, careworn group of churchmen that clambered aboard the galleys, receiving the pomp of their welcome with as much grace and enthusiasm as their desperate straits would allow. As they helped the fugitives up onto the deck, the Genoese sailors were shocked to see the six captives bound and ground down from their maltreatment, and they were even more astonished when they learnt who these unfortunate wretches were. If Popes in the past had found the need to take drastic measures, they had not made a habit of displaying the victims of their wrath for all to see.

Urban's rescue was not destined to be a triumphant affair. One of Adam's co-conspirators, Cardinal Bartholomew of the Friars Minor, was a citizen of Genoa. Bartholomew was a man of great learning, and being, like Adam, a professor of the sacred pages, he was deeply respected in the town of his birth. When he met the Genoese ambassadors in Benevento, Urban had been tactful enough to avoid discussing the fate of Bartholomew, or indeed that of the other captives. With that fate on public display and Bartholomew humiliated in front of the meanest Genoese sailor, an atmosphere of tension settled over the fleet.

The galleys sailed in to Bari, where the Genoese sailors managed to get involved in a massive street brawl with the locals. The fleet left in disgrace only to run into unfavourable winds. With the sails being of little help, the galleys had to depend on their oarsmen. In the end it took eight days to get from Bari to the entrance of the Straits of Messina. The galleys tacked slowly around the southern toe of the Italian mainland, passing Mount Etna before heading on up to Messina. On August 29 the Genoese and their guests rested at the monastery of St Salvatoris in Messina, staying there for three days to take on food and water whilst waiting for better winds. Finally they headed out to sea once more, back through the Straits between Sicily and mainland Italy and on up towards Naples.

Here a further humiliation awaited God's anointed ruler on earth. The fleet anchored outside the port of Corneto on 8 September in order to send messengers to King Charles's court in Naples. Urban still hoped to secure Francisco's release and to get Charles to return some papers and possessions he had been forced to leave behind in Nocera. The King was in no mood to negotiate with Urban, not least as it seemed to him that the Pope was not holding any good cards, but then he wanted to be rid of the man as well. He refused to hand over Francisco, but did release to the Pope's care a few of the books taken from Nocera and his two nieces. The poor girls were taken back without much gratitude, Urban making it quite clear that he was really only concerned with Francisco.

Adam and his fellow conspirators must have had mixed emotions about the rescue from Trani. Their best hope of safety might well have rested with King Charles and the hope that his army would corner Urban and force him to terms. Urban's salvation was the captive's damnation. Now they were firmly in the grip of the Pope and his allies, and as the galleys set sail, the six cardinals could take little comfort from the Pope's good fortune. Their fate was sealed. To date Urban had shown little inclination to mercy and the best they could hope for was a quick death. He had treated the cardinals harshly since their arrest, tortured them and even shown signs of enjoying their discomfort. The memory of the death of the Bishop of Aquilea must have haunted the captives. There was nothing Urban had said or done during the trek across Italy to suggest that he had softened his heart, nothing to suggest that they might be forgiven and released. As the galleys left Trani behind for the long voyage round Italy, the only thing Adam could do was to prepare himself for death, whether by public execution or by lonely, dark murder. What desolate thoughts went through his mind as he gazed out on Mount Etna and then watched the land close in on the galleys as they sailed through the Straits of Messina, legendary home to Scylla and Charybdis? Sites that in happier times would have thrilled him could scarcely numb the prospect of the fate his tormentor had in store for him. And if he retained any hopes of salvation, they were dashed at Corneto. During the talks with King Charles the issue of the captured cardinals was not even discussed. With no real prospect of further negotiation between the King and Pope, the last hope for Adam had vanished. He could only await the vengeance of Urban.

Onwards to Genoa

The Pope too was despondent. Urban had hoped to save his nephew, but had nothing he could use to persuade Charles to change his mind. He had excommunicated him, pronounced anathema on him and called all good Christians to resist him, but Charles remained resolutely on the throne of Naples. The Pope had run out of credible threats. Reluctantly he ordered the fleet to set sail for Genoa where, aided at last by a following breeze, they finally arrived on September 14, 1385.[i] Many travellers sailing into the harbour since Adam's day have been struck by the beauty of the city, cascading down the hillsides into the sea, whilst the bright sunlight plays on houses covered in rose- and ochre-tinted plaster. The city is built around a near circular harbour whose outer arms, like lobster claws, engulf each ship as it enters the harbour waters. As the ships drew in to their berths Adam would have been able to see the solid stone and timber of the warehouses down by the wharfside and the colonnaded walkways at the foot of the hill where traders sold (and still sell today) goods that Genoese ships had brought back from every corner of the known world. But Genoa is a city with a split personality, for inside the outer shell of light and colour is a dark centre. Close up, the city is full of dark alleys barely wide enough for a man to walk down, narrow streets that follow the contours of the hillside surrounded by buildings several stories high. In a city with so little land to build on, houses were tall rather than spacious. Even the streets leading up to the piazza and cathedral of San Lorenzo, the very heart of the city, are dark and dank. Hemmed in and starved of space, the mighty facades of grey and white marble seem artificially small by Italian standards.

Urban was welcomed by Doge Antoniotto Adorno and it was agreed that he would set up his court in the Commenda or Commandery of San Giovanni di Prè, the Genoese residence of the Hospitallers of St John. The Commandery lay at the west end of the city, outside the city walls and distinct from the main town and harbour area, and the papal administration would be able to function under the protection of the Genoese without actually getting under its feet. The Doge would continue to rule the

Genoese state from his palace within the city walls whilst affording the Pope every opportunity to run the affairs of the Church quite separately at the Commandery.

This arrangement also offered Urban the chance to bring his captives onshore quietly and unobserved by waiting until after sunset. Yet even as the Genoese welcomed the Pope to their city, Urban's natural arrogance and sense of righteous indignation got the better of him. Impatiently, he insisted on exhibiting his captive cardinals in broad daylight, dragging them from the port and parading them through the streets of Genoa in chains for everyone to see. The horrified Genoese, who as yet had not heard the full story of the plot, looked on aghast at the apparent cruelty of their lord Pope and inevitably once again the wretchedness of his condition failed to disguise the identity of Bartholomew of Genoa from his fellow citizens. The captive cardinals were ushered out through the West Gate of the city and then lodged in the Commandery with the rest of the party in a dungeon in the lower part of the church.

News spread rapidly among the Genoese that one of the captives was their very own Cardinal of the Friars Minor. The treatment of Bartholomew scandalised the educated classes in the city of his birth, and as word of his degradation spread, the warm welcome that the citizens had extended to the Pope turned to anger. For the moment the anger of the Genoese was expressed peaceably enough, but once again Urban had taken an unnecessary risk to prove a point. Over the next few weeks delegations of the great and the good of Genoa tried to plead with the Pope for the release of the captives. If the Genoese were proud at the idea of having the Pope in residence in their city, they were shocked and shamed at having to accommodate six ill-used and imprisoned elders of the Church.

Friends in High Places

Another of the captive cardinals had also inspired a great outpouring of support. Adam had not visited England for more than ten years, and at times his life, first in Avignon and later Italy, must have felt very remote from the country of his birth. Partly because of the length of time it took to travel around (it took 14 days to get from Bruges to Avignon, and often over a month from London to Rome) the extremities of Europe seemed very remote from each other. Letters could take two of three weeks to get from England to Rome[ii] and sometimes they failed to arrive at all. Not only was England physically remote, but the wealth and brilliance of courtly life in the curia was a very different world from the dark cloisters of Norwich. Adam had continued to exercise influence over the land of his birth but he inhabited a different world.

Despite the years of self-imposed exile Adam was still the most senior Englishman in the Church and the English had not forgotten him. They took his arrest and degradation as a personal affront. The slight on Adam was a slight on the whole nation. By the time the papal party had arrived in Genoa, over three months after breaking out of the siege at Nocera, news of Adam's plight had reached the land of his birth. Moreover, there had been sufficient time for a response to come back. Urban arrived in Genoa to find a full mailbag of protests from England. The Benedictines had written in his defence, not once but twice.[iii] The first letter was from the general chapter, the second from the Abbots of Malmesbury, Ramsey and Evesham. The Colleges of the University of Oxford, in a rare display of unity of purpose, wrote on behalf of their illustrious former student, asking the Pope to display mercy, imploring that he should take pity on the cardinal.[iv] They asked that Adam should not only be restored, but begged that Urban might be reconciled with him.

It is interesting to note that in all the letters from England, Adam's role in the conspiracy is played down as if he had been a bit player. If the belief that he had been in some way less guilty than the others was genuine, it was still hardly credible to anyone in the know. If he was using his skill in codes, to say nothing of taking a role as theologian and providing the intellectual grounds for the plot, he was almost certainly the leading figure behind it. Patriotism could, of course, excuse and reposition any excesses when appropriate. The level of support that Adam received from those who had followed his career from afar is a testament not just to the importance of his work but also to the sense of honour and pride with which his promotion to the cardinalate had been received.

There was more to come. The protests of his own University and fellow Benedictines might have been expected, if not the vigour of their pleas for his release. The personal intervention of King Richard II himself was a surprise. The young king was only 18 at the time, and it is hard to say how much his reaction was a personal response, and how much it was encouraged by his councillors as being important to the well-being of his realm. He wrote at least three letters, and quite probably more, in defence of his cardinal, whom he had never met. Richard berated the Pope, albeit within the terms of the courtly etiquette of the day, for treating Adam badly, and he too suggested that Adam's crimes were not great, although he could not have had the facts at his disposal. We can only guess at Urban's rage when he read that bit.

However, Urban had to tread carefully. One of the young King's letters was tinged with a sinister threat. If Adam was not released, Richard suggested, he might not have such great confidence in the pontificate of Urban and by implication might, reluctantly of course, feel obliged to transfer his allegiance to Clement.

The young King had barely asserted his authority over his own kingdom as he began to free himself from the attentions of the councils that had advised him in the early years of his reign. At last he was able to surround himself with his own favourites. He was flexing his muscles. During the summer of 1385 he led an expedition north against a combined army of Scots and French, and although there had been no major battles, the threat of invasion had been repulsed. Flush with a feeling of personal triumph, Richard was at his most assertive and arrogant, and in this instance with good reason. The King of England was without doubt the most powerful monarch left as an unambiguous supporter of Urban and he knew it. Whatever the Pope thought of Adam and his role in the conspiracy, he could barely afford to lose Richard's support. On October 10, 1385 a diplomatic mission arrived in Genoa headed by Nicholas Dagworth[v] and John Bacon (who died shortly after their arrival).[vi] The purpose of the mission was ostensibly to strengthen the links between England and the Urbanist cause, but the subtext was very clear: Urban could only expect help if he in turn would help the English Cardinal.

Another City, Another Prison

Meanwhile, life for Adam remained on a knife-edge. Unaware of the politics and powerbroking going on in the world beyond the San Giovanni, he and his fellow conspirators occupied a room in the basement. The Commandery is built into the hillside at Genoa, with entrances at three different levels and a Byzantine maze of passages linking each part to the other. The upper entrance, which today leads to the church of San Giovanni, was built after Adam's time, but the upper church into which it leads must be one of the darkest churches in Italy. Built of blackish stone with narrow windows and a low, squat ceiling suspended on rounded arches, it is utterly devoid of light. The middle church is even darker, with virtually no windows, and here in one of the old Romanesque vaults was the room that Urban turned into a temporary prison. Groping around this world of darkness, isolated from the politics of the Church going on a few feet above their heads, none of the cardinals could have a hope of even learning what their fate would be. Adam endured months of torment isolated from the outside, and sharing only the cries of his fellow prisoners for company. So it was very much to his own surprise that suddenly Adam was released from his prison.

The reaction of the English to his treatment and even the protests from the Genoese were up until then completely unknown to him. Only once he was released into a state of house arrest in the lower building of the Commandery did he begin to understand what had happened since he had arrived in Genoa. Urban was prepared to free his errant Cardinal to keep Richard's support, but he wanted to keep a close eye on Adam. When his ambassadors told him that although Adam had been released, he was still kept under close guard, Richard wrote again to Urban to make his point:

"Most blessed father, your humble little son commends to you the things we have discussed before. Several times letters have been sent to you concerning Adam, formerly the Cardinal of Norwich, beseeching that the same Adam be set free from the narrow prison where, with others, he is tortured, a position which we beg you to consider, for a person of his worth, formerly honoured as a cardinal, and equally as holy, he is worthy of your mercy.

After this in fact, we heard that our holy (Adam) himself was allowed only the freedom to walk in your holy palace and to eat in the same hall, but that nevertheless he was not free in turn to share his presence with his friends and others and we note that he told us he is excessively restrained.

Wherefore most blessed father, with this (news) we are struck with bitterness in our heart, it is most burdensome on our kingdom, we who are above all your principle liegemen, so much further will the distress in our heart stand out that we must be shown compassion.

By the instinct of our hearts, the magnates and the people are in sorrow, wailing continuously at the great blow against a person so of our nation, the one among the other captives whose testimony deserves your kindness as we heard his fault was little.

The same (kindness) in the knowledge of purity, trust and honest will has been known from ancient times, and happiness will multiply from our plea to you as we beseech you father, to follow in those footsteps, pouring wine and oil over the diseased wound if you set our penitent vicar free.

And the said Adam begs so greatly and entreats our royal power to look attentively at how he came to be dragged to this state and to take steps to restore him to his former dignity, out of kindness we appeal to your special grace and as your liege we solemnly call down compassion and piety that your example may resound and nourish those who would defend you against the attacks that have blazed up against you.

Farewell ever, and grow with God and upraise his apostolic church (under your) control".[vii]

It is of course the supreme irony that under the treatise that Adam had written so forcefully in 1381, King Richard should have had no right to interfere in such affairs. That was purely the prerogative of the Pope as the

THE LUTTERWORTH
PAINTING
Above: Richard II and Anne
of Bohemia.
Left: John of Gaunt.
Below: Adam Easton in
cardinal's regalia, with Bishop
Brinton.

NOCERA CASTLE, CAMPANIA
Top left: Looking out across the Lattari Hills.
Top right: The Torre di Filangieri, Urban's lodgings in the castle.
Centre: Ruins of the main courtyard buildings.
Bottom left: The view towards Naples and Vesuvius.
Bottom right: A broken cistern in the main courtyard.

THE FLIGHT FROM
NOCERA
Above left: Benevento city
walls.
Above right: St Sophia in
Benevento.
Right: The Rocca in
Benevento.
Bottom left: The River
Ofranto.
Bottom right: High
summer in the Appenines.

GENOA 1386

The Commandery was a base for the Pope, who set up his court there, and a prison for Adam.

Above left: The lower vaults of the Commandery, where the cardinals were held captive.

Above right: The airier quarters of the courtiers.

Left: The gate between the port and the old city.

Below left: Front view of the Commandery.

Below right: The narrow windows of the inner wall show what a perfect prison the Commandery made.

PERUGIA TO THE VATICAN

Perugia was Adam's home for most of 1387 and 1388, before he finally returned to Rome in 1389.

Above left: The Vescovado Palace, where Urban set up his base in Perugia.

Above right: The fountain Maggiore plays in front of the Vescovado Palace.

Left: The dark alleys were ideal for assassins.

Below: The Vatican as it appeared in the 14th Century.

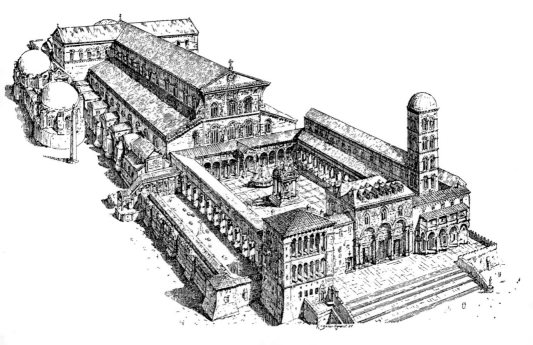

A SELECTION FROM
ADAM'S CHURCHES
Top left: Hitcham,
Suffolk.
Top right: Somersham,
Huntingdonshire.
Above left: St Agnes,
Ferrara.
Above right: St Severin,
Cologne.
Right: Beverley, Yorkshire.

ADAM IN ROME
Top left: The Merchant of
Prato's house.
Top right: Adam's house in
Trastavere?
Above left: The Via
Pelegrini, centre of the
English quarter east of the
Tiber.
Above right: Trastavere from
St Cecilia to St Peter's.
Right: St Cecilia's Church.

D · O · M
ADAM · ANGLO · TT · S · CÆCILIÆ · PRÆSBYTERO
CARDINALI · EPISCOPATVS · LONDINENSIS · PERGERAT
ADMINISTRATORI · INTEGRITATE · DOCTRINA
ET · RELIGIONE · PRÆSTANTI
OBIT · DIE · XV · AVGVSTI · MCCCXCVIII ·

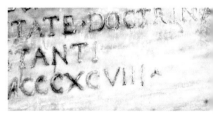

ADAM'S TOMB IN ST CECILIA
Top: The tomb in its setting today.
Above left: The full inscription on the tomb.
Above right: The mystery of the extra "I".
Right: The face of Adam.

Prince of the Church. The very idea that "the said Adam begs so greatly and entreats our royal power" to intervene on his behalf over a church matter beggars belief, which is not to say that Adam was not extremely grateful to the King for having done so. Nonetheless, Episcopus would have been horrified at Richard's intervention and Rex by contrast would have proclaimed the proof positive of Wyclif's view that the state had to intervene in Church affairs where the pontiff proved to be corrupted. The personality of Urban VI had successfully dismantled the force of Adam's argument more dramatically than he could ever have imagined when he presented the Defensorium just four years earlier.

As to the conditions in which Adam found himself, Richard had probably exaggerated his cardinal's plight quite a bit to make his point. It seems highly unlikely that Adam was ever tortured once he was released from his prison in the lower church. The upper floors of the Lower Commandery, the end nearest the harbour, is where Urban took his own rooms. In contrast with the dark grey stone of the upper and lower churches, this end of the Commandery is light and airy. Built in the Romanesque style, the interior of light red brick and wooden ceilings is really rather pleasant, and although redecorated in the 16th Century, it is clear the walls were previously plastered and the ceilings painted. The building had only three floors and it must have been quite hard for Urban to accommodate Adam and still keep him away from the proceedings of the court. Urban did not keep a substantial court with him at Genoa, but he still needed to attend to the matters of the Camera and the Apostolic Chamber as well as receiving delegations from foreign powers and the petitions of the local citizens.

A Freedom of a Kind

Initially Adam was effectively kept under house arrest, confined to the papal residence at the lower end of the Commandery under the care of a French priest who was tasked with keeping a close watch on him. He was not to leave the presence of the priest, and under no circumstances to leave the building. At least he had access to his precious books once more, and as both the upper floors had a colonnaded veranda facing onto the harbour and letting the light flood in, he was granted the most pleasant working conditions that he had seen for three years and the opportunity and materials to work as a theologian once more.

Adam had every reason to be grateful to his fellow countrymen and his King for intervening on his behalf. The fate of the other cardinal conspirators was settled before the end of November 1385. To the outside world they just vanished, and indeed the popular rumour was that Urban had them tortured and then thrown into the sea in sacks weighted down with rocks. In fact

Urban had them walled up alive inside the papal residence in Genoa, a parting gift for their hospitality that the Genoese did not discover until the 20th Century. The rumours of Urban's merciless treatment of the cardinals after he had publicly humiliated them by dragging them to the Commandery in chains in broad daylight was never likely to enhance the popularity of an already unpopular Pope. Only a man as angry, possibly as deranged, as Urban VI could have conceived of killing the Cardinal of Genoa, let alone doing the deed whilst a guest of the City of Genoa and then to add to the insult by leaving the victims' remains walled up in a building freely lent him by the City. To Urban it was of no great moment that he might commit this atrocity in the face of impassioned pleas from the populace to save the wretched cardinal's life.

Adam had escaped death, but his freedom of movement and routine remained severely curtailed throughout the stay in Genoa. He was confined to the Commandery, albeit now in the lighter end of the building, and if the information the English ambassadors reported back to Richard can be relied upon, he took his meals with the court, but was otherwise kept away from contact with other courtiers. The French priest followed Adam everywhere, and perhaps the only peace he could get was from immersing himself in work and trying not to notice the presence of his guardian.

Whilst Adam remained confined in the bowels of the Commandery, in February 1386 Urban received the joyous news that Charles Durazzo, his erstwhile liegeman and now sworn enemy, had been assassinated in Buda whilst trying to take over the crown of Hungary. Urban's joy was only muted by the fact that the Neapolitans had immediately elected his son Ladislao as their King. Not that Urban was in a position to offer an alternative. Having now alienated Joanna, Anjou and Durazzo and their followers, all decent candidates to the throne of Naples, he had seen each die in turn, at least in part a consequence of his own political machinations. In the event he found it easier to focus on getting rid of the Durazzo clan than worrying about who might succeed them. Perhaps the most alarming prospect for those still loyal to Urban was that the Pope might just be insane enough to propose Francisco as the new King.

The Peripatetic Papacy

In one of the few positive moments of his papacy, in October 1385, Urban granted a papal Bull to a delegation from the imperial city of Heidelberg granting them permission to found a University. Barely two months later, on December 15, 1386, Urban VI felt he had outlasted his welcome in Genoa.[viii] The questions about the fate of the cardinals were starting to be a little too persistent for the comfort of the papal entourage. Visitors to the papal court could see that Adam was very much alive and yet there was no word of the fate of the other cardinal conspirators, no word of the fate of the Genoese cardinal in particular. Urban feared that the situation might well turn ugly, Pope or no Pope. If Urban and his court had brought some prestige to the city, the citizens were beginning to wonder what exactly had been visited upon them.

The Pope gathered his court and, summoning as much dignity as he could, embarked everyone on three or four Genoese galleys and sailed down the coast of Tuscany. The Doge made no effort to persuade him to stay in the city or even to leave his court in place in the Commandery. Adorno seems to have been all too happy to lend Urban a few of his galleys just to be rid of him. Unperturbed, Urban and his court disembarked at the port of Motrone near Pietrasanta where they finally parted company from both the Genoese galleys and 80,000 florins. The latter was the price that the Doge now felt minded to extract from Urban for the use of the Genoese galleys and the accommodation he had received from the city over the past year. From Pietrasanta they travelled inland along some 20 miles of mountain roads and tracks of the Alpi Apuane before finally arriving at the city of Lucca,[ix] on Christmas Day. A special mass was sung in the Cathedral of San Martino in honour of the Pope's arrival and he was so overwhelmed by his reception that he declared his intention of staying for several months. For Adam it must have been a relief to have a change of scene and to be on the move again. Not surprisingly, the independent city states of central Italy were less enthusiastic about playing host to the papacy than the Doge of Genoa had been. The Doge may have found the visit of the Roman Pontiff prestigious, but then Urban had no pretext for taxing the Doge's subjects in the same way he might legitimately tax those citizens of the Papal States among whom he now travelled. To them, the papal presence was not an honour. The city states of central Italy looked at the expense of providing for the papal court and the presence of papal tax collectors and concluded that an extended stay would prove rather tiresome.

Urban spent the next three years wandering from city to city, still trying to drum up a crusade against the Kingdom of Naples, a vendetta that seems to have become more important in Urban's mind than either the cure of souls or healing the Schism. With few loyal followers left and even those opposed to Clement reluctant to support Urban's military schemes, it became obvious that the Pope would have to resort to the use of mercenaries. After the payment to Genoa, the papal treasury was in no state to fund Urban's grand schemes, and the Pope resorted to ever more exotic ways of raising money. His first move was to tax his hosts in the city of Lucca. Then not content with that he sent his envoys out to the other central Italian towns to see what he might extract from them. Orvieto and Spoleto however pointedly refused to receive Urban's emissaries or to entertain any thought of the Pope paying them a visit. Florence started secret negotiations with Clement in Avignon.

Urban also considered how he might use the income of the Church to extract more of a return. One of his more unusual schemes involved allowing Benedictine monks to become honorary officials of the papal court, or chaplains, in exchange for cash.[x] This bizarre arrangement suited both the monks and the Pope. The Pope was delighted to have found such a straightforward source of new revenue, while the monks could avoid the rigours of their order once they were nominally under the direct command of the Pope, but without the inconvenience of having to travel to Italy. This blatant abuse presented the abbots of the Benedictine monasteries with a dilemma. Should they allow brothers who had accepted a papal chaplaincy to remain in the monastery? After all, why should they have the expense of maintaining someone who was now, nominally at least, attached to the papal court? The whole scheme was a crude device in pursuit of cash and one that provoked further criticism not just of Urban VI but of the very institution of the papacy.

As Urban wandered through Italy, Adam was obliged to share in the peripatetic life if not the obsession with the defeat of the Durazzo clan. At least after the isolation and restrictions of Genoa it must have been rather a relief to enjoy the freedom of constantly changing locations as the party moved to Lucca. Even so Urban never allowed him sufficient latitude to establish a life beyond the watchful eyes of his French minder. He was certainly not to be permitted to leave the confines of the papal court. In these years of claustrophobic semi-captivity Adam kept his sanity by burying himself in his work. He kept alive the two major projects that Urban had entrusted him with in happier times, the review of Brigit of Sweden as a candidate for sainthood and the creation of a festival for the Office of the Visitation of the Blessed Virgin. The latter in particular contains plenty of references that suggest much of the work was done during the life of Urban VI. Whilst he was not able to complete either project, hampered as he was by a lack of books and facilities, at least he had a focus and purpose to his life in these barren years.

Musical Interlude

Eventually the long hours of enforced captivity inspired Adam to set to work writing other pieces to stave off boredom and idleness. During the years of his disgrace he worked on the only musical pieces that have been attributed to him. The title and words of these two works, both of which take depression and disaster as their theme, strongly hint that they were written during this period. The first of these, "De sua calamite", which the 16th Century antiquarian John Bale recognised as being Adam's work (Bale lists the motet amongst the writings attributed to Adam) is lost except for the

first two lines as "Dulcissime domine, expectans expectavi diucius".
However the second piece, the motet "Alma Pater", has for the most part
survived. The motet is part of a collection of manuscripts known as the
"Fountains Fragments" and was addressed to Urban VI and probably written
whilst Adam was in captivity after October 1385. Alma Pater was a choral
work written for four voices and it records for posterity the miserable state
of affairs in Nocera. It must have been written fairly close to the time of the
siege, as Nocera is pointedly referred to as Luceria Christianorum in the
motet, a name that would only make sense for those who had been with
Urban at Nocera during 1384 and 1385. Nocera is hardly ever referred to as
Luceria except in the writings of those who were in Urban's inner circle, all
of whom had been at the siege with the Pope, and this makes it much more
likely that the author of the motet had indeed been among them. The
surviving text of the motet reads as follows:

Alma Pater, pastor vere
Christicolarum omnium
Per te diu doluere
Mentes nostrorum omnium

Misera trucibus
Sustulisti tam perversa
Heu captivatus, minibus

Neepolitani nobiles
Quos diligebas tamen
Heu non fuerunt nobiles

Ulcisse tuum munere
Egena illorum atria
Repleverat innumere
Ingrata tua patria

Dudum profusis lacrimis
Nostre sunt uncte facies
Quod te dum malos comprimis
Atrox obcedit acies

Intra suos vidit muros
Omni cantanda feria
Casus diu pati duros
Te flebiles luceria.[xi]

213

The full text of the motet appears to be missing, the second and third verses are each short of a line. The tone is reflective. It recalls bad times and it is far from clear if the Neapolitan nobles complained of in the text are the Churchmen promoted by the Neapolitan Urban, or the henchmen of his secular rival, King Charles. The motet style is believed to be peculiarly English,[xii] which leaves Adam, the only candidate who knew of the events at Nocera intimately enough, as the writer. The pattern and rhythm in the motet is remarkably similar to the hymn "De Sacro Tabernaculo", written as the last hymn of his office for the Visitation of the Blessed Virgin. A similarity that, with the other circumstantial evidence, strongly suggests Adam as the author of the piece.

The music appears to have been set for four (presumably male) voices, at least one of which was a tenor part, two of which have survived with full notation. So Alma Pater then becomes especially interesting as the musical notation remains the only piece of music composed by Adam that has survived. Aside from the musical setting for the Office of the Visitation, if he also wrote the motets De Sua Calamite and Alma Pater, it is quite possible that he had written a number of other musical settings that have not survived. In Alma Pater there is an opportunity to glimpse the musical work of a man whose canon has been lost to us.

By any standards Adam had been through the mill in 1385 and the year that followed. After a year of imprisonment, torture and the likelihood of death, Adam the scholar was back amongst his books. Whether writing motets or the larger works that he would complete after Urban's death, he found solace in his work. Alma Pater is a verse penned by a man who knew just how awful the deprivations of Nocera had been, a lucky man who had survived by the skin of his teeth and was happy just to be alive. Adam kept his head low and lived a quiet and unobtrusive life for the remainder of Urban's pontificate.

He may still have had a French priest watching his every move, but he would not have been completely devoid of friendly company. By the time Urban had left for Lucca, a number of English mercenaries, knights who were under-employed during the lull in the fighting with France, had taken up service with the Pope.

Several companies of these men, most notoriously Sir John Hawkswood, had travelled the length and breadth of Italy, hiring themselves out to the highest bidder and destroying everything in their path. In his desperation to raise an avenging army Urban was having to be ever more devious in finding ways of paying his men. Eventually he realised that he could pay mercenaries by awarding them titles to church incomes. He simply appointed the relevant mercenary to receive a portion of Church income and allowed them to collect money just as if they were clerics.[xiii] If it had been seen as corrupt for Churchmen to take more than one vicarage to increase their wealth, this further abuse was pushing the reputation of the papacy beyond the pale. Urban, in his usual arrogant fashion, thought nothing of the criticism. To him it offered a cheap way of running an army and one English captain, John de Beltoft,[xiv] a man who had served with Hawkswood, found the arrangement very much to his liking. He served Urban on and off from 1386 to 1388 and probably had a large number of other Englishmen in his troop.[xv] The company of his countrymen, however rough and ready, must have been a comfort to the English Cardinal so many months where he had been isolated and alienated from the court and his fellow countrymen alike.

Miracles at Perugia

The city of Lucca had not been especially welcoming, but there were still some Italian cities that had not learned a lesson from Genoa's experience. In January 1387 the city of Perugia sent 20 ambassadors to the Pope to ask if he might honour the city by establishing his court there. Urban was genuinely pleased, possibly even surprised. Perugia had not been well treated by the papacy during its sojourn in Avignon and Urban had not gained a reputation for being an ideal houseguest during his meanderings across Italy. The offer was nonetheless welcome.

By high summer 1387 Urban had made his preparations to leave Lucca, arriving before the gates of Perugia on August 1[xvi] with an entourage of soldiers, bishops, nobles and 11 cardinals not including the now disgraced but free Adam Easton. Ten of the Perugian ambassadors who had greeted Urban at Lucca went down to the town gates with a crowd of commoners to welcome the Pope and escort him into the town. As Urban walked through the gatehouse a white dove flew onto his hat. For several minutes concerned courtiers and citizens tried to remove the dove but it refused to budge, until Urban, Christ-like, picked the bird up gently in his hand and passed it to his capellanus. The awestruck crowd spread news of the miracle. This was surely a good omen, and six days of feasting were proclaimed.

The stay in Perugia proved to be one of the highlights of Urban's pontificate. Not only did he strike up a genuine rapport with both the local dignitaries and the populace at large, he seems to have found the city much to his taste. Perugia is built on a rocky citadel that rises from the plains above Lake Trasimeno, source of the eels that were a local delicacy and had accounted for the death of more than one Pope in the centuries before Urban's arrival.

If Genoa is a city of light with a heart of darkness, then Perugia is its antithesis. A maze of dark alleys tumble down the hillside from the Piazza

Danti towards the city walls, where houses are built up several storeys high on both sides squeezing the last of the light out of the alleyways. High above, walkways and arches give perfect cover for the city's most notorious professionals, its assassins. Blind alleys with secret ginnels and dead ends bemuse the hapless visitor, it is a city where it pays to know where you are going.

And yet in the midst of the darkness is a heart of light in the form of a wide central corso that splits the city in two. As the sun floods down this thoroughfare it lights up the terracotta and pinkish sheen of the local marble on the merchant houses, guildhalls and palaces that line it. Here in the centre is one of Italy's finest fountains, the Fontana Maggiore, embellished with allegories of the months, the seasons, the ancient gods and the liberal arts. Created just a century before Urban and Adam arrived the fountain is the centrepiece of the city and around it are the Palazzo dei Priori (the town hall), the Cathedral and the Palazzo Vescovado, the Bishop's Palace. The latter was where Urban set up his court.

The area around the fountain looks today much as it did when Adam arrived there. From the first floor windows of the palazzo Urban could gaze down on the glorious fountain and, if he chose, address the faithful in the square below, whether excommunicating cities or preaching crusades. The ochre stones of the Palazzo Vescovado get the best of the morning light and as the rest of the Piazza soaks up the afternoon heat cool shade starts to envelope the building. The back of the Palazzo however faces into the dark side of Perugia, and the lower levels are utterly devoid of light. Hemmed in by the shadows with narrow windows and solid stone walls this side of the Palazzo Vescovado belongs to a different world more akin to a dungeon than a palace. Whilst Urban was enjoying the hospitality of the Perugians, Adam inhabited the dark world in the quiet rooms at the back of the Palazzo. His only escape was the enclosed cloisters, which allowed the papal party to enter the cathedral undisturbed for their daily worship.

The citizens of Perugia proved to be convivial hosts to Urban and his court, and the city became his base until August 1388. However, some matters kept coming back to annoy and distract him. Shortly after his arrival in Perugia he was greeted by yet another missive from England complaining of Adam's treatment, this time from the English chapter of Benedictine monks. By 1387 the Benedictines had become so concerned that they sent John Welles to Italy as their ambassador, sending with him a letter written by the General Chapter on July 9, 1387 pleading with Urban for Adam's release (they also wrote directly to Adam to tell him what they were doing and that he should not give up hope; however they could not be sure that he would ever receive their letter and it was probably never delivered).

Welles was tasked with finding out what exactly had happened to Adam and to drum up support for their campaign to have him fully reinstated.[xvii] He caught up with the papal entourage in Perugia and immediately started to apply pressure and petition the Pope for Adam's release. Adam, with the dubious benefit of years of dealing with Urban, would have known that this was exactly the wrong way to approach dealings with the supreme pontiff. The unfortunate Welles had never been much of an advocate. John Wyclif had famously run rings around him at the Blackfriars debates, and he fared no better when he came up against Urban. The Pope would not budge. He had freed Easton already and spared his life. Bearing in mind the treasonous behaviour of a man he had rewarded and elevated, that was as far as Urban VI was prepared to go. John Welles had only been in the city for a few frustrating days when, worn out by the journey and the trials of a diplomatic mission he was ill equipped to handle, the poor man died.

Urban had more pressing concerns than the fate of the English Cardinal, and for once he was among friends. To the citizens of Perugia the Pope could do no wrong, even in his favourite occupation of pronouncing excommunications and preaching crusades. In October Urban held a grand ceremony to place under interdict three of the central Italian cities who had rebelled against his authority by refusing to receive his ambassadors or to play host to his court. In the midst of the ceremony he appeared with a flaming torch at a window overlooking the piazza. Even though the strong winds were blowing across the square, the flame could not be extinguished. Once again the crowd were convinced they had witnessed a holy miracle.[xviii]

Perugia provided a pleasant diversion for Urban but nothing could disguise the fact that outside the city walls his authority was collapsing. Rinaldo Orsini, Count of Tagliacozza, was rampaging across the countryside, plundering whatever he could for his own coffers whilst acting under the guise of supporting Clement. Orvieto and Spoleto had already declared for Clement and Urban was now in great danger of being cut off from Rome. The Pope would need to deal with the troublesome Orsini if he was to have any hope of furthering his ambitions against the Durazzi. And for that he would need an army.

Urban's Third Crusade

Urban VI was not destined to be a fortunate man or a successful Pope. Even on the rare occasions that he courted popularity, his obsession with the problem of Naples got in the way. Whilst staying in Lucca he had received embassies from Naples entreating that Urban might be reconciled with Charles Durazzo's son, Ladislao. The Neapolitans wanted a papal blessing for his coronation as King of Naples, but as far as Urban was concerned, he was tainted with the sins of his father. The negotiations came to nothing.

217

This was a poisonous and ungrateful family who had spurned Urban's munificence, a family that should be removed from power altogether. The only problem was that Urban hardly had the means to achieve it. The obvious answer for Urban was to proclaim a crusade against the ingrates and wait for the good Catholic princes of Europe to send men and money for the cause.

During his extended and happy stay in Perugia he spent most of his time raising funds and troops for the great expedition against Naples. Unfortunately the secular rulers of Europe were not flocking to the papal banner. There was no prospect of financial reward, and therefore they found this latest crusade less than enticing. You might perhaps hope to pull off one suspect crusade in any one papacy. Urban VI was now on his third, and as yet he had failed to show an appetite for attacking the more traditional enemies of the Church, such as the Saracens. Unable to raise troops under his own standard, utterly dependent on mercenaries, Urban even had to pay for an escort to keep his person and his treasury secure. In Perugia he hired John Beltoft again, who with 300 knights of his company formed a papal guard.[xix] Mercenaries were easy enough to hire as long as you had the cash, or as we have seen, the capacity to award them a benefice or two. They tended not to have great scruples about the purpose of their mission as long as they were paid.

Pope Urban was faced with the grim choice of either abandoning his pet project or paying for even more mercenaries to help him achieve his goal. Inevitably, Urban opted to use the papal treasury to pay the mercenaries. Anything rather than give up. He left the city of Perugia on August 8, 1388 with 1,000 lances, the sum total of his crusading army, and by the 17th he had reached Narni.[xx] From there the small army bypassed Rome and headed south to the castle of Ferentino on the road to Naples.

The final humiliation was not far off, and it came just a week after the Pope left Perugia. Marching south towards the Kingdom of Naples at the head of his crusading army of mercenary Englishmen, Lord Urban VI, supreme pontiff and God's Lieutenant on Earth, was thrown to the ground from the back of the mule he was riding.[xxi] The Pope was badly injured in the fall and they took him to Ferentino to nurse his wounds. He was barely 75 kilometres from Rome.

Whilst they rested, Beltoft started enquiring after the pay for his men. The Pope had little money with him on the march, a fact he had chosen not to share with the English mercenary, but now it came to light that Urban's own officials had prevented sufficient funds from reaching Beltoft to pay his men for back pay owed to them from their time in Perugia. Beltoft had been expecting the Pope to make good the difference. As soon as the real position became clear the soldier of fortune deserted with his men.

The Demise of Urban VI

Battered and humiliated, once again he retired to Rome, the scene of his great triumph 11 years before. The unfortunate Urban was fading fast. He never fully recovered from the injuries he sustained falling from his awkward steed, and the disappointment at his failure to destroy the Durazzo clan weighed heavily over him.

As the end drew near and Urban cast around his few remaining followers, an odd thought occurred to him. He realised rather late in the day that Adam had, in his own way, been more loyal to him than many of the men he had rewarded during his papacy. That loyalty had survived extreme adversty, torture, disgrace and yet still Adam had stayed at his court and held to his position that Urban was the legitimate Pope. At any time since they had left Genoa, Adam could have easily left Urban's entourage unnoticed; he would have been welcomed with open arms by Clement in Avignon and could well have taken the English King with him. Yet he had stayed with Urban to the bitter end. He had shown astonishing loyalty to a Pope who had treated him harshly. He had demonstrated far more loyalty than the many others who had benefited from Urban's largesse and then deserted him. The Pope expressed regret over the rough justice he had handed out to his English Cardinal. Both Auberius and Cardella reported in their respective histories of the cardinals that Urban had privately talked of his remorse to his few remaining followers.[xxii] In fact even after his death, Adam continued to insist that Prignano had been the true Pope and denounced the Avignonese as anti-Popes. For his part Urban must have always known that the confessions extracted in 1385 were exaggerated, that Adam and his fellow conspirators had only sought a more democratic style of papacy with the pontiff's authority curbed rather than crushed.

Given the treatment handed out to him, Adam had been given every justification to recant his good opinion of Urban and his right to be Pope. Of course fear might have been the justification for his loyalty to the Pope before Urban's death, but it does not explain his continued support afterwards. In the end, as Urban started to dwell on his own mortality, perhaps the treatment he had given Adam may have suddenly seemed rather harsh. Did he perhaps repent altogether? How far Urban might have gone to restore Adam is unclear, but it is interesting that in a collection of miracles taken down in 1389, Adam is referred to as the Cardinal of England. The manuscript refers to Urban as the ruling Pope, and so may well have been written before his death, or at the very least before the coronation of the new Pope. Given that Boniface was crowned just two weeks after Urban died, the latter seems unlikely.

And what of Adam? Did he change his mind about Urban? After all in

1385 he had been prepared to overthrow him at the very least, even if it was unlikely that the plotters would have put the Pope to death. The actions of Urban since 1385 had been eccentric in the extreme, enough to question the man's sanity. Crucially though, not enough in the eyes of a sincere advocate of Adam's standing, to question his legitimacy. A legitimacy and reputation that Adam continued to defend right up until the pontiff's death, even while making reference to the suffering he had experienced at the Pope's hand. It appears, on the face of it, to be a complete about-turn from the views he had held in Nocera when he plotted against Urban.

Perhaps Adam saw the hand of divine intervention in the discovery of the plot and in the fact that Urban survived time and again when the odds seemed stacked against him. Did he see his captivity and torture as just suffering for having doubted the truth of God's anointed head of the Church? It would not have been an unusual point of view for the time. I think in the end Adam was more pragmatic in his approach, even to matters religious. He seems to have distinguished between Urban's legitimacy as God's elected Pope, a position he defended vociferously against the Avignonese, and the very human actions of the Pope after his election. These actions, which could be separated from the divinely inspired election, justified Adam and his colleagues in taking the steps that they did. Although Adam does not go into great detail in the Defensorium, it is clear by implication that the key to removing a Pope was that it should be the action of the religious authority not the secular. By contrast Wyclif had argued that an unjust cleric should be removed by the secular authority without recourse to the religious. Unfortunately, in writing the Defensorium Adam did not really consider the circumstances where the unjust authority is the Pope himself!

Urban held no formal consistories for promoting new cardinals in the later years of his reign as Pope, but it does raise the question as to whether Urban had restored Adam, at least unofficially, to the rank he had deprived him of in 1385. Whether or not he had been officially restored, Adam was finally released from his tribulations when Bartholomew Prignano, Pope Urban VI, breathed his last on October 15, 1389.

Chapter 12

Restoration

I do not wish the death of a sinner
but that he turn back to me and live

Boniface IX

Urban VI was not greatly mourned. However, the cardinals who had stayed loyal to the Roman Pope showed no inclination to reconcile themselves with the French in Avignon. Clement VII and his entourage of French cardinals remained for ever damned in Italian eyes. Even leaving aside his central role in the massacre of Cesena, not only was Clement a Frenchman, he had split the Church in two and taken the papacy back to Avignon. Added to which the French had behaved badly at Anagni and whether or not Urban had been exasperating, it was hard to forgive the cynical way Clement and the French King had manipulated the events of the summer of 1378 to their own advantage.

If they were not prepared to accept Clement, the supporters of the Roman papacy needed to move quickly in choosing a new pope from among their number. They desperately needed a credible leader to whom those secular rulers still opposed to Clement might pledge their support. A long interregnum would be disastrous. And above all else they had to avoid the calamitous circumstances that had surrounded the election of Urban VI. The decision was made rapidly, in barely a fortnight, and without controversy.

The unanimous choice of the Roman curia was Cardinal Petrinus Tomacellus, a native of Naples who had been presented with his cardinal's hat on the same day as Adam at the tender age of just 27. And if Adam had received his to appease the English supporters of Rome, Petrinus had benefited from Urban's need for political support from Naples. Urban had wanted more Italians in the curia, and for preference, those from his own region of Italy who might be more sympathetic to his whims. Petrinus was a pragmatist, he accepted his elevation with good grace and managed not to cause offence to Urban during his pontificate. He had been quite happy to go along with his benefactor, staying at his court to the bitter end but without ever showing any great enthusiasm for Urban's extremes of behaviour.

Petrinus was crowned Pope in St Peter's on November 2, 1389, and once again the Romans could celebrate the fact that an Italian had been elected, in their eyes at least, as the one true Pope. Furthermore, as a young man of just 34 he had every prospect of outlasting the anti-pope Clement, which to the Roman mind, increased the possibility of a reconciliation with the Avignonese Church and a triumphal reunification of the Church in Rome.

However, the new Pope was conscious that whilst he had to try to win over the supporters of Avignon, he also had to keep his backers on side. Against that background his choice of pontifical title is interesting. Petrinus took the papal throne as Boniface IX, taking the name of the man who was then one of England's most renowned saints. St Boniface, was an 8th Century Englishman, probably from the Kingdom of Wessex. He was also a Benedictine monk whose great mission in life had been the conversion of the Germans to Christianity. However well known and revered the saint was in English and Benedictine circles, Boniface had not been a popular choice of name for new Popes; the last to choose it had done so nearly a hundred years earlier. The naming was therefore more than just a nod to the English King, and certainly a sign to the former English cardinal that things were about to change. And change they did.

At the first consistory of his papacy, held on December 13, just six weeks after his election, Boniface IX restored Adam Easton to the rank of cardinal.[i] the new Pope went out of his way to bring the English Cardinal back into favour and into the mainstream of Church life. He also gave him the honorary title of Cardinal Priest of St Cecilia. It was not unusual for cardinals to be given an honorary title, most often an honorary bishopric or priesthood associated with one of the ancient pilgrimage churches of Rome, but this was a first for Adam.

Cardinal of England or St Cecilia?

Antiquarians and historians frequently referred to Adam as the Cardinal Priest of St Cecilia from the time of his elevation in 1381, but this is an error that has crept in to historical records as a result of a misunderstanding. In 1381 there already was a Cardinal Priest of St Cecilia, a certain Bonaventura of Padua, one of the cardinals created by Urban in 1378 after the start of the Schism. Bonaventura stayed loyal to Urban, and not only was he never stripped of his title, but he was in due course canonised by the Church. There could hardly have been two cardinals of St Cecilia at the same time.

Prior to his downfall in 1385 Adam had been known either as the Cardinal of Norwich or the Cardinal of England,[ii] in much the same way that Simon Langham had been referred to as the Cardinal of Canterbury before an honorary title fell vacant (Simon then became known as the Cardinal Priest of St Sixtus and later the Cardinal Bishop of Palestrina). There are no contemporary records from the period 1381 to 1388 that refer to Adam as the cardinal of St Cecilia. So how could biographers and religious historians of previous generations get confused over his title?

The facts are straightforward enough. In 1389, just as Adam was about to be reinstated by Boniface, Bonaventura rather conveniently died and the St Cecilia title fell vacant. When the new Pope restored Adam it was only natural that he should award him the honorary title that had most recently become available. Those 14th Century writers such as De Niem or Gobelinus who gave Adam the title of Cardinal of St Cecilia in their writings, knew him both in the period before and after his restoration in 1389. Likewise writers of letter books in the early 15th Century knew Adam by the titles he held at his death as well as his reputation as a renowned Benedictine and churchman.

None of the letters or chronicles in which Adam is referred to as the Cardinal of St Cecilia were actually committed to parchment before 1389. Whenever Adam is referred to by this title in the written record he is being described in work written after 1389. As a result they had an unfortunate, but perfectly natural, tendency to write his story using the title the writers knew him by at the time they were writing, even when they are describing events from before 1389.

Faint Praise Indeed

Nor was his restoration and the acquisition of his new title of Cardinal Priest of St Cecilia only noticed by the chroniclers. The news of Adam's restoration was greeted in England with a real sense of vindication. The imprisonment of the English Cardinal had been an affront to the nation, and his restoration was by the same token a redress of that grievance. Adam's stature, not just as cardinal, but as a leading writer and theologian, made him one of the best known English intellectuals of his time. He remained the only English cardinal in the curia and not surprisingly his elevation by Boniface was mentioned with pride by most of the contemporary English chroniclers.

By contrast, Geoffrey Chaucer had never been much of a fan of Adam and his sort. However, he owed his financial security to the patronage of Richard II and his court. He had a long record of loyal service to the crown, starting with his work as a diplomat for Edward III in the 1360s and 1370s. Inevitably, in this capacity he could not have failed to have come across the work of Simon and Adam. When in 1373 Chaucer returned to England from a trip to northern Italy on the King's business he may well have met them both whilst they were camped outside Calais waiting for Edward's ambassadors. As Adam was working for the Pope, they would not have been exactly on the same side, but perhaps they shared a common interest in working for a truce to end the war. Although in 1373 Chaucer had yet to write his most significant works, Adam was renowned throughout Europe for his learning, and his knowledge of Hebrew in particular. Chaucer would surely have been intrigued to meet him.

Chaucer remained very much his King's man. Without the income from government sinecures, he could scarcely have afforded to devote time to his writing, and the favour of the King and the support of the royal court gave him an audience for his works. To this extent Chaucer was not so very different from the clergy he had been prone to mock. He had his sinecure in the government in the same way as Adam had his collection of benefices. For both men it was a means to an end. Adam had made a career as a theologian and advocate supported by the income of the Church; Chaucer supported his career as a secular writer on income similarly provided by the secular power.

The King's man had always held a jaundiced view of the church and he admired the work of Wyclif during the 1370s. The anti-clerical sentiment so prevalent in Wyclif's work shows through on many occasions in Chaucer's tales, but by the late 1380s the political agenda had swung heavily away from Wyclif and his ideals. The radical views expressed during the Peasants' Revolt had illustrated the danger of spreading the word of God too freely, particularly when given to the common man to interpret as he might. By 1385 the stance, almost nationalist in tone, which Richard had taken in defence of Adam, was very unambiguous. Chaucer may have had his prejudices against the monks and friars, but in 1389 at the court of Richard II he was hardly in a position to express his derision for a man of Adam's standing who clearly had the full support of his sovereign.

When he came to assemble The Canterbury Tales, Chaucer chose for the Second Nun's Tale the life of St Cecilia. The idea that he had written this Tale as some sort of tribute to the Cardinal of St Cecilia is not new: it has been suggested for over 50 years. Yet the dates of the specific tales within The Canterbury Tales are hard to pin down precisely, and Chaucer claimed that he had already written a story about St Cecilia by the time he wrote the Legend of Good Women in 1386/87.[iii] This fact has been conveniently overlooked in the past when Adam Easton's name was first linked to this Tale.[iv] Unfortunately, as we have seen, Easton was not the Cardinal of St Cecilia in 1386, which at first seems to present a problem.

However, Chaucer often wrote several versions of his tales, and the version that appeared in The Canterbury Tales and more specifically the prologue to the tale does look as if it might well have been written at a later date than the Legend of Good Women. Certainly there is little evidence to suggest that the prologue was written before 1389, and it is the prologue that is critically important in linking Adam to the Second Nun's Tale.

The 17 verses that comprise the prologue are split between an introduction, a prayer to the Virgin Mary and an explanation of the meaning of the name Cecilia. In each section there are hints that although the tale can be seen at one level as a straight narration of the life and virtue of St Cecilia, it works just as well as an allegory for the life of the newly reinstated Cardinal Priest of St Cecilia.

In the introduction Chaucer makes much of the virtues of his nominal heroine and in particular draws attention to living the chaste life. Whilst chastity can be used at one level to conform to a model of Roman virtue, equally it applies as a fundamental practice for a Benedictine monk. Of course Adam was less than perfect in his observance of other aspects of the Rule, he owned (quite a lot of) property, drank and ate in excess of the prescribed amounts. However, the one Benedictine virtue he did hold true to was chaste living, so perhaps Chaucer was being ironic by deliberately singling out chastity in the prologue to this tale.

The narrator of the prologue uses the next verses to form a prayer to the Virgin Mary in which he, and it clearly is a he, imagines himself in prison and suffering torment from which the Virgin gives him comfort. It is interesting that the narrator is speaking as a male at this point and the reference to being in prison and suffering (to say nothing of experiencing redemption) makes an interesting and very direct parallel with Adam's own story. What is particularly noteworthy is that these lines would be irrelevant to Adam's story if the prologue had been written before 1385. Later in this section there is even the use of the word "whelps", a strange echo of the words of Wyclif's sermon against Adam that Chaucer was undoubtedly familiar with.

Finally, as Chaucer explains the meaning of the word Cecilia he brings out the importance of sapience or knowledge and good teaching. And so the prologue closes with a subject that was as true to the life of Adam as it had been to the life of Cecilia herself.

The body text of the Second Nun's Tale is a fairly straight narration of the story of St Cecilia, but the substance of the material in the prologue skews the presentation of the tale. The whole story of St Cecilia, a virtuous woman laid low by the vices of men and then redeemed, is a story that echoes the patterns of Adam's own life. With his upbringing among the virtuous cloisters of the Benedictines, his degradation by a vicious enemy and finally restoration by a compassionate Pope on behalf of a forgiving God, Adam's tale runs parallel to that of St Cecilia. And just as Cecilia was raised to sainthood, so Adam was restored to the dignity of cardinal.

The use of the prologue places a very direct context for the Tale of St Cecilia. It gives the reader the opportunity to consider the life of the saint as an analogy for the life of the cardinal. In a contemporary context, the restoration of Adam was clearly topical at court in a period when Chaucer was working on The Canterbury Tales, and perhaps it was that relevance that prompted Chaucer to write the prologue in a way that seems to turn the tale into an allegory. Whether the mood in which Chaucer wrote the prologue for the tale was genuine or deeply ironic is a matter of conjecture!

Real Praise

Aged around 60, Adam was by now one of the most senior cardinals in the Church and quite clearly had the Pope's ear. Boniface, by contrast, was rather young for a Pope and had spent much of his time as a cardinal in somewhat unusual circumstances, following in the wake of Urban's mad rush from end to end of the Italian peninsula. Boniface needed support, and by 1389 Adam had served the curia for 21 years. He was one of the most experienced cardinals left in the service of the Roman pontiff. He was also well versed in the etiquette and procedure of the various papal chanceries. Adam could be of great help to the new Pope, and before long Boniface grew accustomed to leaving matters that came to the papal ear from England in the tender care of his English cardinal.

Nor was the significance of Adam's new position lost on the clergy in England. The writer of the Westminster Chronicle noted that at the same consistory that restored Adam to the role of cardinal, Boniface named him as his chief advisor[v] and second in command. The restored English Cardinal was brought back to the heart of the papal court, with even greater authority than before. He was effectively the second most senior member of the Catholic Church and the most likely successor to Boniface in the event that any accident should befall the young Pope.

John Fraunceys, an English clerk who worked at the Papal Court on behalf of the Bishop of Winchester, quickly found out how influential Adam could be on English affairs. When he asked Adam's advice on how best to ensure that the Bishop's petition received papal favour, he was told that it would be quite normal for Adam to be consulted on all matters relating to English affairs but Boniface used him in particular where there was an issue on which he was unsure of the details or where he wanted a second opinion. In a humorous mood the Cardinal explained to Fraunceys that this was a helpful device by which the Pope might defer or delay a petition that had the potential to prove controversial.[vi] Adam would then go through the process of informing himself fully on the matter before the petition could be considered again.

The English Cardinal was now in a position where he effectively had a veto over all Church matters relating to England. No small matter when you consider that with the kingdoms of France, Castile and Aragon all supporting the Avignon Papacy, England was, together with the Holy Roman Empire the most powerful of the Roman Pontiff's supporters. And any issue on which he considered he had not been able to "inform himself" to his satisfaction would never make a return journey to Boniface's desk for approval and implementation.

Adam suddenly found himself wielding considerable power at the papal court.

Insignia

His release may have provided some good news for patriotic chroniclers and inspiration for Chaucer, but it would be quite wrong to suggest that there was rejoicing in the streets at the news of his restoration. The impact of such weighty matters on the ordinary people, even among those he had left behind in the village of Easton, would have been minimal. Among the great and the good it was a different story. The intellectuals, the clergy and even perhaps the royal court, all saw some significant cause for celebration. The English had won their point. Furthermore they could look forward to significant influence at the papal court and good prospects for advancing the interests of the English clergy.

Restored to power and given a fine honorary title, Adam started to use some of the more visual trappings associated with his position for the first time. It was almost as if he felt the need of a psychological boost to legitimise his restoration, to establish through the insignia of power an image of potency and position, which was very important to the mediaeval psyche. And perhaps with that he hoped to project a sense of permanence onto his role at the papal court that he had not felt since his elevation in 1381.

In common with the practice of the time he adopted his own coat of arms: an eagle set on the red cross of St George. His choice of arms is interesting. The eagle bears a striking resemblance to the blue eagle used by Urban VI for his own arms. Had he borrowed the device as a sign of respect for the man who had first raised him to the rank of cardinal? If that was what he did, then once again it serves to demonstrate a remarkable degree of loyalty given the harsh treatment he had received at the hands of the pontiff and his henchmen. Similarly the red cross of St George on a white background is ambiguous. It has always been taken to be a reflection of Adam's title as the Cardinal of England and his English origins. However, the same cross of St George also happens to form the arms of the City of Genoa. As the city of his redemption from certain death and the place where he was released from captivity, Adam had good reason to regard Genoa as a significant turning point in his life. The theme of redemption was important to Adam and it seems to me more likely that Genoa, not England, was the source of the cross of St George that he incorporated into his own personal standard.

Adam also started to use his own monogram from this period, something we certainly do not see in his earlier letters, even from his time at the papal curia. The monogram comprised the word "cardinalis" written over the top of the word "anglie" repeated four times in each corner of an imaginary square. In the centre of the square is the word "Adam" with four diagonal lines joining it to each corner of the square. Many scholars and prelates of the day created their own personal monograms as an alternative to a personal seal. Simon Langham for instance had used a diagram of a castle that he placed over his name, a device that appears on a number of his personal letters.

From this period of his life he also appears to have adopted a personal motto. Not surprisingly the text of the motto was taken from verses of the Bible, and the Venetian writer Palazzi, in his "Fasti Cardinalum Omnium" of 1703, recalled that Adam chose the words from Job Chapter 30 verse 9 "and now I am their song, yea I am their byword." As a motto it sounds a little hollow, it does not seem to carry a message, or moral or even a statement. The words do not make a lot of sense because they are out of context. but now look at the extract below, taken from the Book of Job:

Job Chapter 29[vii]
Moreover Job continued his parable and said, Oh that I were as in months past, as in the days when God preserved me. When his candle shined upon my head, and when by his light I walked through darkness. As I was in the days of my youth, when the secret of God was upon my tabernacle when the Almighty was yet with me, when my children were about me; when I washed my steps with butter, and the rock poured me out rivers of oil; when I went out to the gate through the city, when I prepared my seat in the street! The young men saw me, and hid themselves: and the aged arose, and stood up. The princes refrained talking, and laid their hand on their mouth. The nobles held their peace, and their tongue cleaved to the roof of their mouth. When

the ear heard me, then it blessed me; and when the eye saw me, it gave witness to me. Because I delivered the poor that cried, and the fatherless, and him that had none to help him. The blessing of him that was ready to perish came upon me: and I caused the widow's heart to sing for joy. I put on righteousness, and it clothed me: my judgment was as a robe and a diadem. I was eyes to the blind, and feet was I to the lame. I was a father to the poor and the cause which I knew not I searched out. And I brake the jaws of the wicked, and plucked the spoil out of his teeth. Then I said, I shall die in my nest, and I shall multiply my days as the sand. My root was spread out by the waters, and the dew lay all night upon my branch. My glory was fresh in me, and my bow was renewed in my hand. Unto me men gave ear, and waited, and kept silence at my counsel. After my words they spake not again; and my speech dropped upon them. And they waited for me as for the rain; and they opened their mouth wide as for the latter rain. If I laughed on them, they believed it not; and the light of my countenance they cast not down. I chose out their way, and sat chief, and dwelt as a king in the army, as one that comforteth the mourners.

Chapter 30

But now they that are younger than I have me in derision, whose fathers I would have disdained to have set with the dogs of my flock. Yea, whereto might the strength of their hands profit me, in whom old age was perished? For want and famine they were solitary; fleeing into the wilderness in former time desolate and waste. Who cut up mallows by the bushes, and juniper roots for their meat. They were driven forth from among men, (they cried after them as after a thief;), to dwell in the cliffs of the valleys, in caves of the earth, and in the rocks. Among the bushes they brayed; under the nettles they were gathered together. They were children of fools, yea, children of base men: they were viler than the earth.

And now am I their song, yea, I am their byword.

Shown in context it all makes sense. This is Adam's story. Through this simple motto he acknowledged his rise and downfall, implicitly noting the sin of pride and the process of justice and once again the theme of redemption. Then by drawing a parallel between his life and the story of Job (just as Chaucer does in the Second Nun's Tale), he showed a refreshing degree of humility, at least for a wealthy and highly regarded cleric. By choosing this verse from Job, Adam appears to acknowledge the frailty of the line between good and bad fortune and that, in his own mind at least, the easy living of his days in Avignon and Rome had brought his misfortune on him as the wages of his sin.

1389 had proved to be a turning point for Adam. The dying Urban had finally made his peace with his English Cardinal and his death had marked the end of the semi imprisonment in which he had spent the last four years. By the end of the year he had made a triumphant return to the papal court, and been acknowledged as the Pope's most senior cardinal and chief advisor. Confident in his new elevated position he adopted some of the stately trappings of his role in the Church. All he needed now was to seal his reputation as a scholar and establish a learned court in the eternal city.

Chapter 13

Saints and Sinners

Clothed then with faith and the performance of good works,
let us set out on the way, with the Gospel for our guide

Work to be Done

Adam had not spent the years of his degradation indulging in idle thoughts, nor did he allow himself to become paranoid. He patiently endured the nagging efficiency of his French minder, who was permanently checking up on his every move. It had been a great relief to escape from the tension of an existence where every swing in Urban's mood might have meant an immediate and unpleasant death. Sealed off from the outside world in a claustrophobic confinement, Adam's life had hung by a thread. Adam needed something to occupy his mind and keep his darkest thoughts at bay. Throughout these years of tribulation, his work offered an escape route to a different world where he could immerse himself in matters that were of great moment to the Church at large. A small and enclosed world perhaps, but one in which he could exert his authority and express through the written word the knowledge and learning accumulated across a lifetime.

By the time Urban VI died, Adam had made significant headway on the two major projects that had been stalled at Nocera in 1385: the new order of service for the festival to celebrate the Visitation of the Virgin Mary and the canonisation of Brigit of Sweden. Just as Boniface restored him to the rank of cardinal at the end of 1389, both projects were nearing completion and he devoted much of the years 1389 to 1391 to finishing them off.

The Office of the Visitation

The first of the projects to be completed was the Office of the Visitation. By the time that Urban and his court had returned to Rome at the start of 1389, Adam had virtually finished the Office, and he was starting to lobby for support among the papal courtiers to have it officially recognised. As Adam finalised the text of his work he expressed openly the sentiment that Pope Urban might promulgate the new service to heal the wounds of the Schism. The lessons included in the mass clearly show that Adam hoped the Office of the Visitation might be an inspiration to good Catholics everywhere, regardless of which Pope they supported.

Getting the service adopted as an official part of the Catholic liturgy would prove to be anything but straightforward. At this late stage in the process and still not exactly Urban VI's favourite prelate, Adam suddenly found himself opposed at the Roman court by a familiar face. Edmund Bromfield, the would-be Abbot of Bury St Edmunds who had lost out in the bitter dispute over the abbacy as a direct result of Adam's intervention, had been working in Rome since the start of 1389 as Master of the Sacred Palace. Edmund was still looking vainly for a good opportunity in England. Initially he seems to have taken a formal role examining the case against promulgating the feast[i] and Adam, still disgraced and insecure in his own position in Urban's court, can only have suspected that there was some professional jealousy at play. It was to be a frustrating few weeks. No doubt Bromfield was getting his own back. Yet Bromfield was clearly not a man to bear a grudge for ever, for by April he was preaching before an ailing Pope Urban on the virtues of Adam's Visitation and arguing in favour of it being proclaimed. Somehow Adam, the master advocate, had talked him around. Perhaps Bromfield had seen which way the wind was blowing and second guessed how events would turn out after Urban's death.

If so it was a prescient move. By December of the same year Urban had died and Adam had been restored to power in Rome. Bromfield's support did not go unnoticed, and he was rewarded with the bishopric (that of Llandaff) that he craved. With that the man was packed off to Wales and he left the Roman court never to return. This time the royal power in England accepted the decision of the Pope and Edmund got to enjoy the fruits of his appointment.

Back in Rome, the death of Urban VI was less fortuitous for Adam's plans and it dashed the high hopes he held for his Visitation Office just at the point when it seemed that he had established a bedrock of support. Now he would have to start all over again with the new Pope, Boniface.

The manner in which Adam completed his Office shows us once more the straightforward integrity of his character. As the Office of the Visitation was virtually completed at the time of Urban's death, it would have been easy for Adam to delete the references to Urban in his text after the old Pope died, and substitute them with praise for Boniface. It would have been quite normal to use the opportunity to praise the virtues of a new Pope so soon after his coronation. Moreover, Adam could quite justifiably have concluded that, as Urban was dead, he was irrelevant to the Schism, and that the only parties to whom the issue should be addressed were Boniface and Clement. Yet once again Adam was strangely faithful to his former master and constant in his conviction as to the correct order of things. He chose not to rewrite whole passages of the Office to praise Boniface but stood by the legitimacy of the man who had imprisoned and tortured him, retaining in his work all the remarks complimentary to Urban. It was said by all of the old Pope's biographers that Adam asserted the legitimacy of Urban right to his own dying day. By the standards of the 14th Century this was a most unusual trait, even for a monk!

Honesty and integrity might enhance his reputation as a clergyman, but they would not be enough to guarantee that Adam's version of the Office would be accepted into the Liturgy. Although he had been working on the Office for five years, it was by no means inevitable that Adam's final draft would be approved. There was now yet another hurdle to be overcome, in the form of a rival version.

John of Jenstein, a Czech bishop, had also taken an interest in the Office for the Visitation, and although prior to 1385 Adam's work was the officially blessed and sanctioned exercise, Jenstein continued work on his own version. As Adam was languishing in the dungeons of Nocera, John had been applying the finishing touches to his efforts. With the officially blessed author locked up with his life under threat and his titles stripped from him, John took advantage of the situation. His office was promulgated throughout Bohemia from 1386[ii] and it was widely used. During the latter years of Urban's pontificate John petitioned the Pope to consider his mass to be officially adopted by the Church. Given that the Office had proved popular in Bohemia and that, in Urban's view, Adam remained a disgraced prelate, it is surprising that Jenstein's work should not have been adopted and Adam ignored. Here, however, luck was on the Englishman's side. As Urban moved from one unwelcome reception to another, semi-exiled and intent only of revenge on the Kingdom of Naples, somehow the new Office of the Visitation was never quite important enough to merit considering.

As soon as Boniface restored Adam to favour the tables were turned on John of Jenstein. Adam, at the heart of the papal court in Rome, had ample opportunity to advance the cause of his version of the Visitation and at last he seemed to be succeeding.

Approved by a Higher Authority

An important part of collecting together the documentation to make the case for any new addition to the Catholic liturgy was the attribution of miracles. The process was not unlike the way we might get a product endorsement from a celebrity to launch a new brand today. Adam collected at least 15 miracles associated with his version of the Visitation service even before it had been officially recognised and publicly used. The miracles are recorded in detail in the Vatican archive, including incidents where the narrative seems to fly in the face of the facts. One miracle from 1389 tells of a certain clerk Hugh, who may have been an associate of Adam, who was travelling to Rome in the heat of summer at a time when a great pestilence was raging.[iii] The unfortunate Hugh contracted the disease and in the agony of fever he prayed to "Our Lady". As he all but despaired of life under stress from the fever and suffocating heat he called to mind the festival of the Visitation of the Blessed Mary (even though it had yet to be officially published or sanctioned). The notary tells us that the said Hugh knew of the festival, which is why it seems likely that he must have been an associate of Adam. When at last it seemed that he must be on the verge of death the fever suddenly left him. Later he recalled that it was only when he had considered in his mind the Visitation of the Blessed Virgin that the fever abated! No doubt Hugh was encouraged by Adam to provide suitable evidence in support of his new festival.

The flimsy credulity with which these miracles are recounted may seem strange to us now, but they were the substance of belief in the 14th Century, when the magical and miraculous properties of religion were an important ingredient of religious belief. A new Office of the Church needed to make a powerful impact to ensure that true believers would adopt it as part of their faith. With a series of miracles attesting to the quality of the Office, the believer could take it into their ritual with confidence.

However, Adam was not the only person looking for testimonials. John of Jenstein was also busy scouring Bohemia and collecting similar instances for his own portfolio of miracles to support his version of the Office of the Visitation. Now it was a race to see who could get enough support and crucially win the approval of the Pope. Perhaps Adam had the upper hand, an unfair advantage by virtue of being at the centre of the Roman court and close to the man who would ultimately make the decision.

The Safe Choice

In the end inevitably, Adam won the day, but the decision to choose his version of the Office owed much to Boniface's election. Boniface was almost bound to prefer Adam's work, and the very fact that he reinstated

Adam as a cardinal just a few weeks after his own election shows just how much favour Adam could expect. Boniface had known the English Cardinal since 1381, he had spent time at the papal court with him, they had worked together and coped with the strain of dealing with Urban together. They had both suffered the deprivations of Nocera and even though Boniface had stayed loyal to Urban and not taken sides with Adam and his fellow plotters, he clearly had great sympathy for the pitiful state to which the Pope had reduced Adam and his allies.

Boniface knew Adam's views; he was familiar with his writing and understood his reputation as a meticulous theologian with a disposition towards the orthodox. Choosing Adam's Office carried relatively few risks. John of Jenstein may well have had very similar credentials, but to Boniface, he was an unknown quantity. His work might well be orthodox but it would need to be checked carefully, and in any case the new Pope saw an opportunity in Adam's text. By publishing a new Office almost as soon as his papacy began, Boniface would be able to stamp his authority on the Church with a grand gesture, perhaps one that might impress the Schismatic Anti Pope Clement's supporters around Europe. This was a device through which the new Pope could show his spiritual leadership and enhance his credibility in the eyes of those cardinals who had remained loyal to the Avignon papacy.

Adam's Office of the Visitation was ready, orthodox, and only needed to be agreed and then promulgated by a papal Bull. All the new Pope had to do was draft the papal Bull and authorise it. This he did on November 9, 1389, just one week after he had been crowned as Boniface IX in St Peter's.[iv]

Across Europe the breviaries of the faithful would now need to be updated with the new Festival of the Visitation, which was to be celebrated on July 2.

A Masterpiece of Devotion

Whatever the soundness of the theology, Adam's Office was an outstanding piece of spiritual writing. He had used his years in captivity to good effect, preparing an Office of nine lessons, three hymns and a series of antiphons. In the process he produced what was arguably his finest work. The Office of the Visitation was not meant to provide material at the cutting edge of philosophical debate, it was unequivocally orthodox and offered no new possibilities to Christian thought. Left with a blank canvas, Adam produced the one work of genuine beauty from his long career as an intellectual and theologian. Freed from the need to make a point, writing creatively and for effect rather than for advocacy, Adam demonstrated his flair. The rhythms are simple but the language is evocative, using the mediaeval Latin of the day to its full potential. The scansion and phraseology give colour not just to the story of the Visitation of Mary to her cousin Elizabeth but also shed light on the reason for her visit. To mediaeval Christians this involved sincere belief in the most unlikely story of their religion, the impregnation of the Virgin by the Holy Spirit. It was a sensitive subject to handle, with temptations to digress from the spiritual to the sexual and the potential to merge pagan superstition with a central belief of Christian theology. Adam played it straight and tackled the subject matter in detail, using a degree of mysticism to create a deeply spiritual feeling around some difficult subject matter. Unfortunately all traces of the original musical settings of the Office have been lost. Perhaps we can catch glimpses of it by scanning the style and musical notation for Alma Pater, but once again we are left with just enough to tantalise and too little to know. One thing is certain, Alma Pater and the Office of the Visitation were written within a year or two of each other, at some point between November 1385 and October 1389.

The ethereal beauty of the Office of the Visitation hides one of Adam's word games in the opening antiphon, so carefully crafted that it was not until the 19th century that it was noticed. It is a brief glimpse of Adam the codebreaker, the writer of secret letters, the papal diplomat. I like to think it is equally the mark of a monk who always maintained a sense of fun alongside the slightly po-faced rigour of monastic life. A man who once took a subject based on his own name for an Oxford debate, who hid the letters of his name among the opening words of the Defensorium. Here he used a similar device to give us a clue to the authorship of the Office of the Visitation.

The office opens with the following antiphon:

Accedunt laudes virginis
Admirande indaginis
Noviter promulgate
En, visitat Elizabeth
Maria mater ipsamet
Celica probitate

Divo repletur munere
Maria, sine murmure
Cum filium concepit,
Surrexit ab oraculo
Statim in montis calculo
Abiit et profecit

Accendit ardor spiritus
Mariam tangens celitus
De Nazareth migrando,
Mox ad montana transtulit,
Ubi tumulti caruit
Superna degustando.

Monstrans culmen dulcedinis
Maria sui sanguinis
Elizabeth salutat
Stantem in domo proximi
Propinqua templo Domini
Devote subministrat.

Carisima sancti spritus
Diffudit se divinitus
In puerum, cum sensit
Conceptum salutiferum
Marie sibi ovium
Elizabeth consensit.[v]

The first letter of the first word of each verse is arranged to form the name of the author: ADAM C (the "C" being for Cardinalis), signalling his authorship in a work that would not normally have an author's attribution. The Church took a strict view of the sin of pride and it was uncommon to attribute authorship of a devotional work to the world at large. In fact it was only in Adam's lifetime that painters started to become known by their names and famed for their work. Many were still known only by reference to their town of origin or to a particular painting, and the identity and lives of most of these early artists are unknown to the modern world. So the author of a devotional work and specifically a holy office, could expect anonymity. Even in the bull issued by Boniface to promulgate the Office of the Visitation there is no mention of Adam and his role. By this simple and clever device Adam ensured that a clue to his authorship would be preserved for generations to come.

Adam's new Office proved popular in England, and by 1392 was already being used at St Albans, which as a Benedictine House was always going to be kindly disposed towards Adam and his work. The Charterhouse of Axholme in Lincolnshire went even further and was actually dedicated to the Visitation when it was founded in 1396.[vi] If the new service was popular, Adam's profound hope that the promulgation of the service might in some way heal the wounds of the Schism was a little too optimistic. When the wounds of the Schism were finally healed by the Council of Basle in 1441 the event was marked by the commissioning of a brand new version of the Office of the Visitation. It may seem ironic that this was written to replace Adam's version in the breviary, but one must remember that Adam had clearly been a partisan on the Roman side of the Schism, as indeed had John of Jenstein and it would be insensitive to the French to allow either man's work to be retained.

Despite this setback, Adam's work remained popular and in use. Adam's Office was being celebrated throughout much of northern and western England many years after it was supposed to have been replaced. Hereford Cathedral[vii] has a copy of Adam's version of the Visitation Office in an early printed breviary. It dates from 1505 and although some of the lessons have been altered it is clear from the text that it is the same Office and shows that it remained in use right up to the time of the Reformation.

Several copies of the Visitation have survived in breviaries scattered around Europe: in Germany, Utrecht and Rome for instance. If the mass has now fallen from favour, its extensive use during the 15th Century at least ensured that the text that Adam created has survived intact.

An Old Debt to Repay

Adam did not allow the undoubted success of his new Office to distract him from his other major project: the canonisation of Brigit of Sweden. The original commission called by Urban VI to investigate Brigit's worth consisted of three cardinals, and Adam had played a central role in their work. However, the Cardinal of Nucerinus had died in January 1389 and the Cardinal of Corfu, one of Adam's fellow conspirators at Nocera, had been killed by Urban in Genoa. The travels of the papal court under Urban and the trauma of the events of his reign had inevitably caused the investigation into Brigit's life and works to lose momentum, and by the end of Urban's pontificate they had ground to a halt. Without Adam to help the process, the job had become virtually impossible.

Brigit's commanding presence and her powers of prophesy had made a great impression on Adam, and he still felt a strong attachment to her cause some 20 years after they met at Montefiascone. Now, at the moment of his triumphant return as the senior cardinal of the Catholic Church, he did not forget the women he had prayed to in his darkest days in Nocera. His prayers had been answered in that grim dungeon in sourthen Italy and he had a debt of gratitude to repay. The task would not be straightforward. Even though he was determined to breathe life back in to the project of her canonisation, it would take time to gather together the material to support her case. In this he was fortunate to have a helping hand. During the period of Adam's imprisonment and disgrace Alfonso of Jaen had recorded Brigit's prophesies and published them in a book of her "Revelations". The book had proved very popular across Europe, raising Brigit's profile and drawing attention to other women mystics of her era who shared a similar lifestyle and held similar views, women such as Catherine of Siena and Julian of Norwich.

However, not everyone shared Adam's enthusiasm.

Brigit was a controversial figure whose directness had not always won friends within the hierarchy of the Church. Whilst many Catholics found her works inspiring, some doctors of theology took exception to them. Most controversially, she had prepared her own "Rule" for an order of nuns that she claimed to have composed following instructions received directly from a vision of Christ.

To a 14th Century cleric there was something rather distasteful about the idea of God choosing to commune with the world at large through a woman. Brigit had caused offence to some churchmen simply by drawing attention to herself. Women were not just second class citizens, they were mostly uneducated and, worse still, Brigit heralded from the uncouth north European Kingdom of Sweden. Ignoring the importance of various women in the Bible, Mary Magdelene, Mary the Virgin and all the others, 14th Century man was discomforted by women who meddled in religion. It was bad enough that Brigit had claimed to be blessed with communication directly from God, but writing down the words of God in a sacred Rule seemed to some to be preposterous.

In her homeland it was a very different matter, and the respect and esteem in which Brigit was held enabled her to achieve one of her most cherished ambitions. She persuaded the Swedish ruler, Queen Margaret, to allow her to use the buildings of the old castle of Vadstena, which she converted into the first convent to adopt her Rule. A number of religious houses around Europe followed Vadstena's lead in adopting Brigit's Rule, and although he never formally sanctified the Rule, Urban VI had been content to allow the spread of Brigit's order.

For his part Adam was a conservative in matters of religious dogma, as his dispute with Wyclif over secular power had shown. He was not an obvious feminist either, as his remark to Egidius de Velinse that women had a natural tendency to change their minds seems to demonstrate. Yet if he veered towards a traditional view of theology, Adam was certainly not a bigot. A man who was still working hard on an Office in praise of the Blessed Virgin Mary had good reason to recall that God had been known to reveal his presence and purpose through women in the past.

The Defence of a Reputation

During the years that Adam had lingered in captivity, the cause of Brigit's canonisation had suffered a bitter blow. A Perugian scholar (his name is unknown) produced a vitriolic attack on Brigit that was intended to quash any possibility of the movement for her canonisation being revived. Adam heard about the attack whilst still under house arrest and although his freedom of movement was severely curtailed, the debt of gratitude he felt towards Brigit put him under an obligation to defend her reputation and memory. He asked his French minder to obtain a copy of the Perugian's text so that he might study it in detail. It did not take long for Adam to convince himself of the need to publish a riposte to the Perugian. He was almost certainly engaged in this exercise when Urban moved the papal court to Perugia during 1388/89, and he may well have known and met his adversary during that year.

Although the Perugian's text has not survived, the approach Adam took to his response was to set out his arguments as a straightforward piece of advocacy. In other words, he started each section by outlining the Perugian's objections before going on to demonstrate why they did not hold water. He refuted each point, apparently in the order they were presented, so that one can virtually reconstruct the Perugian's document from Adam's own work. There were 41 objections in all, aimed at both Brigit and her Rule. However, the main thrust of the Perugian's argument was set out in the first 15. Adam's "Defence of Brigit" is part of the Bodleian collection in Oxford.[viii] It consists of a manuscript of 20 folios of handwritten script in a hand sufficiently close to that of Adam's letter to the Abbot of Westminster to suggest it is his own (certainly after allowing for the fact that Adam was at least 15 years older and suffering the effects of torture).

Adam introduced his Defence with a petition to the Pope in which he states categorically that nothing in the life and works of Brigit could be seen as heretical. Although the Pope is not named, and the research into the Perugian's accusations was undoubtedly carried out during Urban VI's reign, the petition is almost certainly addressed to Boniface. It is signed with what is the only surviving example of Adam's personal monogram.

The main body of the Defence of Brigit starts by noting that the Perugian had raised four main objections to Brigit's work. First he alleged that the content of the prologue to Brigit's Rule was of doubtful orthodoxy, second that the style of her Rule is too simple and poorly composed to be acceptable, third that it was heretical in that it states that God the Father was born of the Virgin Mary and finally (and one suspects, from the Perugian's point of view, most importantly) that Christ would not have dictated the Rule or any other religious matter to a woman. In fact it is hard to escape the conclusion that most of the Perugian's objections really stem from this last point. Brigit's real crime was to be female.

However, the third point is also worth noting. To us it may seem a little pedantic to argue over whether God the Father, rather than God the Son (i.e. Christ) was born of the Virgin Mary. To an educated person in the 14th Century this was the difference between orthodoxy and heresy, and a man could be executed for heresy. For much of the first millennium of the history of the Church, scholars had heated debates over the nature of the Trinity and whether God was in fact three separate beings or one being in three representations. It mattered a great deal at a time when Christianity separated itself from paganism by the fact that there was just one Christian God. Adam, as a student who had been immersed in the scholastic debates at Oxford, was the ideal person to provide a detailed riposte to the Perugian.

The Perugian was in fact being mischievous. Brigit had never said that God the Father was born of the Virgin Mary, and the Perugian knew that. What she did say was that Christ (God the Son) assumed the body of God the Father and was then born of the Virgin Mary. This was absolutely orthodox belief and a point that Adam laboured. As he threw down the gauntlet to his adversary he declared that "this is clear to any one". The Perugian had deliberately but subtly misinterpreted Brigit's words in order to make it appear that she was guilty of heresy, to show that if anything she should be damned by the Church and certainly not canonised. It is confusing, but the correct interpretation was of great importance, a minor change of words could make the difference between heresy and orthodoxy.

Adam set out across this dangerous theological territory and dismantled each of the Perugian's principle arguments in turn. There was never any doubt in his mind that the main task was to write a document that would pave the way for Brigit's canonisation and there could be no question of the process starting if the Perugian's diatribe went unanswered.

The Defensorium of Brigit is a structured piece of argument and it tells us much about the criticisms raised by the Perugian. It does also give us a number of interesting insights into Adam's own views. These are interesting as, by the standards of the time, they were, to say the least, unusual. They were certainly not what we might expect from a senior churchman who had spent much of his life taking a conservative and orthodox stance in defence of his church.

Women's Lib? A 14th Century View

The first surprise is the vigour with which we find Adam writing in support of the role of women in religion. Some of his writing is very pedantic, taking issue with specifics, but he also draws sweeping comparisons from across religious history to defend Brigit and her role as a servant of God and his Church. He is at his most radical when he attacks the Perugian for suggesting that Brigit could not have received instructions to found her order of nuns or the wording of her Rule directly from Christ simply because she was a woman

Adam attacked in two stages. First he dealt with the idea of a Holy Rule per se being dictated by Christ and identified two specific examples where this had happened as a result of divine intervention. The Rule of St Pachomius had been dictated to the good man by Christ himself, and the Blessed Doctor Basil[ix] had also formulated a Rule that was dictated to him by an angel. Adam concludes from this that in the past it has been perfectly natural for Christ to assist in dictating a holy "Rule" directly and if it had happened in the past, it could happen again.

Then he goes much further and states that the significant issue is the circumstances under which Christ will intervene to dictate a "Rule". He reminded his audience of the Book of Daniel,[x] where man is told that by mourning, fasting and prayer he may make himself fit to receive holy visions and revelations. Adam developed his argument further. A woman who is devout and fulfils these requirements is surely just as likely to receive holy inspiration as a man. Brigit had not only herself employed these self same devotions of fasting, mourning and prayer but had inspired several others of her time to do the same. In Adam's view, if she regularly sought divine help ("ergo cum ipso Dominum Ihesu Christum devotissime de pluribus et presertim de regula monialium supplicavit") she would surely have received Christ's instruction just as would a man who had done the same.

To suggest that it was possible for a woman to receive revelations direct from Christ, if not God himself, was reasonably radical, certainly to men of the Perugian's persuasion. But if we look at what he says, Adam has gone further and is saying that women who follow the instructions of God, who mourn and fast and pray are equally likely to receive divine inspiration as any man who acts in the same way. In a 14th Century context this is not just astonishingly radical, it all but amounts to women's lib.

For a senior cleric given to such views it is no surprise to share the frustration that Adam clearly felt at the baseness of the Perugian's assault on Brigit's character. Even so, just as in his attack on Wyclif, Adam remained the consummate advocate, calm and lethally effective in constructing his case. In his fifteenth point, the Perugian starts by belittling women in general and their role in religion in particular, and then he calls into question "the unsurpassed excellence of the Blessed Virgin Mary". Adam's response is initially the usual neat and detailed riposte. He offered four arguments to refute the Perugian's view. Suddenly, and just once, Adam explodes: "if the adversary (the Perugian) doesn't even understand the unsurpassed excellence of the Blessed Mary, I remit him to the Street of Straw in Paris (remitto eum ad Vicum Straminum Parisius) to learn the answer!" In his fury at the ignorance of the man, Adam accused the Perugian of being so lacking of understanding that he needed to go back to school. The Street of Straw was the centre of the old university where the great 13th Century doctor Thomas Aquinas lectured to his students who sat on straw bales, which gave the street its name.[xi] The place can still be found in Paris (now known as the Rue de Fouarre) on the left bank of the Seine just to the south of Notre Dame cathedral.

This uncharacteristic outburst over, Adam returns to disciplined and unemotional criticism an his support for the importance of women and their rightful place within the Church. It was nonetheless a rare and revealing moment.

In Defence of the Jews

Women were not the only victims of mediaeval society that Adam spoke up for in his Defence of Brigit. In the midst of his diatribe against Brigit, the Perugian expresses the view that it was shaming for Christ that he should have been crucified under the inscription "King of the Jews". The 14th Century was one of the regular low points in the treatments of the Jews, who, as ever, were seen as a problem throughout Europe. In states and cities across the continent they were repeatedly persecuted and then perversely welcomed back. The stigma of being responsible for the death of Christ might be a convenient point of attack for clerics without intellectual integrity, but the real problem was money. At a time when both the Catholic Church and the Muslim faith banned the loaning of money for interest, the Jews were the only major group in Europe able to offer structured financing. To kings who wanted to fight wars and to cities that needed to finance trade, this was the foundation of a love-hate relationship. The Jews were widespread and ingrained into the fabric of mediaeval society. In the counties of Cambridgeshire and Huntingdonshire at the end of the 13th Century they were not just found in the towns of Cambridge and Huntingdon, which we might expect, but they were also present in smaller communities such as Bottisham and Holme.[xii] The need for a source of finance gave the Jews opportunities to become embedded as personal finance houses across the countryside as well as in the towns. And inevitably, making money from the needs of others and becoming wealthy in the process (though actually, as often as not, most could barely make a passable living) was not going to be popular.

Adam had a different experience of the Jews from that of most of his contemporaries. To him they were not just bankers and financiers who you borrowed from first and then expelled to avoid repaying the loans. He had spent much of his life studying Hebrew and had undoubtedly formed a close attachment to the learned Jews of Avignon, who over several years had worked with him on his re-translation of the Old Testament. He, more than most scholars of his generation, was aware of the debt that Christians owed to the Jews for the very existence of the Old Testament. After all, they had written it and now it was supposed to be the undeniable fount of all scholastic knowledge.

He got stuck into the Perugian on the subject straight away.

His strident defence of the Jews started with the assertion that there was no inherent shame in being the King of the Jews. If there was shame to be attached to any Jews at all, it was on those specific Jews whose error of judgement led to the crucifixion. Unlike many contemporary scholars, Adam knew the Bible as much from the Hebrew as he did from the Vulgate. He was prepared to use quotes from the Old Testament to remind his audience of the fact that the Jews were indeed, initially at least, God's chosen people. Adam then went further, stating (perhaps with more than a nod to his old friends in Avignon), that it was not good enough to blame an entire race for the actions of one or two men who may have been complicit in the death of Christ.

By the standards of his time this was pretty liberal stuff. If there were others like Adam who had a more tolerant view of the world, very few had ever felt inclined to promote that view in writing and certainly not from Adam's lofty position as a senior cardinal.

Conclusion

Adam's passionate Defence of Brigit and her reputation is a remarkable piece of work, but it is very different in style to the Office of the Visitation. There is no beauty to be found here, except perhaps the elegant geometry with which the arguments and counter-arguments are constructed. Here the symmetry and the rhythm of his work are hauntingly reminiscent of the structured debates of his time at Oxford. These are not words to convey a sincere act of devotion, or to bring the faithful back into harmony with one another, it is a structured piece of logic and rhetoric in the classical tradition.

As the Brigit Defensorium draws to its close, there is little doubt that Adam considers the Perugian to be guilty not only of attacking the memory of Brigit, but of considerable religious error. Although it remains unsaid, it is hard not to read the full text of the Defence without emerging with a strong sense that Adam considered his adversary to be both intellectually challenged and guilty of heresy as well.

Yet it reveals as much about Adam as it does his adversary. There was no conflict in his mind between religious orthodoxy and tolerance and respect for the position in society of both women and Jews. To put those views into the context of mediaeval thinking, it is worth reading the detail of the Magna Carta. A document that is so often quoted as a defining charter of liberty and freedom for ordinary people is scathing in its treatment of both Jews, who are not to be treated as other debtors, and women, whose word cannot be accepted in serious court cases. Adam may have been a conservative when he cast his mind over the weighty subjects of power and lordship, but in other areas his views were somewhat uncharacteristic of the time in which he lived.

Commended to Papal Care

Though he had finished his Defensorium, Adam needed to be sure that Boniface would accept his work as a satisfactory rebuttal of the Perugian. Without that acceptance the work of the commission looking into the canonisation of Brigit was unlikely to come to a successful conclusion. A summary of Adam's judgement was delivered to Boniface in the petition referred to above:

> Most holy father, with reverence as ever and for the enlightenment of your great knowledge and teaching. According to (my) sufficient, diligent and vigilant judgement, all of the preceding articles I consider to be admissible, publishable and readable in the Holy Church of God, just as they are. For just as they are, they are true Catholic (i.e. orthodox) propositions of faith either following from faith or from the truth of Holy Scripture, consistent and in agreement with good mores and (based on) the teaching of philosophers, saints, learned men and doctors. Nor do the said articles speak ineptly as the adversary (Perugian) has construed and asserted, but they speaking the same way of speaking as Holy Scripture, the saints and doctors of great antiquity. Thus it is evident that they were special revelation of God. And so these articles are not heretical material, but material of faith and devotion and an inducement to good mores and works and are given for the glorification of Holy Mother Church who always conserves in prosperity and protects in adversity, the knowledge of God the Father. Amen.[xiii]

This was not a time to be found sitting on the fence. In this manuscript we see a rather sensitive devotion to the cause of a woman who had clearly touched the cardinal's emotions, albeit in a very chaste and monkish fashion. Adam was prepared to defend Brigit against her detractors in the strongest terms and before the highest authority. Yet even that was not enough.

With Personal Commendation

Not content with submitting the Defensorium for papal approval he went on to make some strong claims of his own for Brigit's worthiness. At the end of the manuscript containing the Defensorium there is a copy of a letter written by Adam to the Abbess of Vadstena in which he writes of his personal experience of Brigit, revealing how important she had been for him and giving his own striking affirmation of her miraculous powers:

> To the Religious lady Abbess at the conventual monastery of the blessed Virgin and blessed Brigit at Vadstena, ordained our sacred saviour in the Kingdom of Sweden, diocese of Linkoping, we pray to her in devotion.

> Dearest Mistress and Sisters
> I encourage your devotion of your most consecrated mistress Brigit. When I was placed under great tribulations, without cause, in the time of Urban VI formerly pope; because of his fury and a feeling of great peril, I had not expected to escape death without some sacred miracle being enacted. I looked to the blessed Brigit and she interceded for me with the blessed Mary and her son Christ; she freed me from my peril and because of this, I placed all my care and attention to her canonisation and committed to continue at it (ie the canonisation) since that time. In as much as she was my assistant, I state that she deserves singular sanctity for the freedom I had from the aforesaid tyrannical raving.
> I had suffered various tribulations and always when I beseeched her to help me, I was given relief from these torments so that even those tyrannies were by no means a punishment. On account of my vow aforesaid to you all, I am greatly roused to work with you, her sisters and friends, in bringing about her canonisation. Before you all I am moved to charity in my heart, as are all your entreaties worthy of stretching up to God and to the blessed virgin Mary, because she herself inspires and helps our deliberation in this act. Someone truly following her shining saintliness will turn aside from the hindrance and confusion that you have lately had. For I have seen the written accusation that the Perugian put together to speak against her rule of sanctity. And I saw that the accusation had been very difficult to refute but Lady Brigit herself continuously entreated with me to go on in the name of the Blessed Virgin, in return for that clear declaration of scriptural truth that had freed me from my peril and from the actions taken against me. And immediately I read through the accusations put together against

her, I saw that I had a solution, and knew the truth that would remove all doubt about her, for I had collected so much material and ideas that I had total clarity; and I put together a rebuttal based on the testimony of the sacred scriptures and drew on the approval of other doctors of the law; and she took in hand my book and the words of my response. And I despatched the Lord Alfonso in January this year to consecrate my declaration against that accusation. Hence I count myself free of cares, as if you had all been working with me, repaying the debt I owe to God himself that you have set before me. Never would I have done less for the debt that I owe to her (Brigit). Recommend my oration to her possession just as she herself interceded with God to preserve my life and dignity from danger and greet her, the holy Brigit, from me, praying to all powerful God who clothes us in prosperity and preserves us.

Adam Cardinal of England[xiv]

Adam was clearly moved to recall his experiences in Nocera and obviously felt that Brigit had in some way saved him from certain death. Yet was it really possible that an educated, intellectual scholar, a man of Adam Easton's stature, could believe in such a miraculous intervention? After all, Adam had always been pragmatic in his approach to some of the more eclectic ideas espoused by his religion. He had certainly not followed the letter of the Rule of Benedict to which he had sworn obedience. Surely this was just another testimony of the sort that Adam had put together to support his work on the Visitation?

Not so. It is too easy for us to dismiss a sincere religious belief as trivial or superstitious when such things have, frankly, very little impact on 21st Century life. The world that Adam inhabited was very different. It was a world of deep superstition with a natural inclination towards devout belief in the mysteries of religion. There is no reason to doubt that, in the depths of despair at Nocera, Adam might very well have prayed to Brigit for salvation. He can have had little hope of survival without some form of miraculous intervention and then it had happened. So Adam had witnessed at first hand two apparently remarkable events: events that in any terms could be considered miraculous and that he clearly believed had been directly inspired by the Swedish mystic.

First of all there had been her prophesy of the death of Urban V if he dared return the papacy to Avignon. A prophesy that had come true in such dramatic fashion precisely as she had said it would, within less than three months of Urban's return to the city. Secondly Adam had prayed to her in the depths of his despair in the dungeons of Nocera Castle. What had followed? He had been miraculously saved from death, avoided the fate of the unfortunate Bishop of Aquilea and then, against the odds, he had survived the trek across the Apennines with the remaining cardinals. More importantly, when the party reached the city of Genoa he had been released from captivity when it seemed inevitable that he would be put to death (as indeed all his remaining colleagues were). If that was not miraculous then what was?

It is not difficult to see why Adam would have believed passionately in the righteousness of her case for canonisation. To his mind these things could not possibly be explained away as mere coincidences.

Decision Time

There were other voices being raised in favour of Brigit's canonisation. Shortly after Boniface IX had been elected as Pope, a delegation from the Swedish Diocese of Linkoping (the Diocese which contained Brigit's convent of Vadstena) arrived in Rome to press for Brigit's case to be reopened. The delegation led by a certain Brother Magnus,[xv] brought the necessary scripts and, more importantly, funds, to ensure that the cause of Brigit could be advanced before the Pope.

Nudged by his senior cardinal, Boniface set up a new commission to re-examine the Revelations of Brigit, her prophesies and her Rule. Three cardinals were appointed to carry out the review and, not surprisingly given his experience and his relationship with Brigit, Adam Easton was invited to take a leading role. He was almost certainly the only member of the Roman Curia left who had actually met Brigit, added to which he was also the only cardinal who had sat on the earlier commission organised by Urban VI. He was joined by the Cardinal of Bari and Cardinal Philippe of Alencon "of France". The cardinals started by asking Brother Magnus to prepare a book for each of them consisting of testimonies to Brigit's virtue and the texts that the cardinals would be obliged to examine. Magnus duly obliged, presenting each cardinal with a book in ornamental binding that he noted, without any trace of bitterness, had cost him the sum of 20 ducats (or florins) each, an enormous sum of money equivalent to a clerk's salary for a year.

The commission of cardinals worked throughout 1390 and into 1391 before submitting its findings to the Pope. The unanimous conclusion was that Brigit should be canonised. A petition to this effect was presented to Boniface on behalf of Brigit's monarch, Margaret, Queen of Sweden and Norway, signed by each cardinal on the commission, showing their support.[xvi]

The Pope had several good reasons to accept the findings of his commission. Sweden had remained loyal to Rome during the Schism and canonising Brigit would help to keep them onside. Brigit herself had been vocal in her assertion that the only true place for the papacy was in the Eternal City. This was a powerful message at a time when the Schismatic Pope was based in Avignon. Perhaps even more compelling, this rather young Pope had already given his flock a new Office within a matter of days of his coronation and now, just two years into his reign, he had the chance to offer them a new saint as well. Putting on a display of such spiritual vigour would do no harm to the kudos of the branch of the Catholic Church being run from Rome.

Boniface made his pronouncement and agreed that a three-day official ceremony to canonise Brigit would be held starting on Friday October 6, 1391. The ceremony would climax on Sunday October 8, at which point Brigit would be recognised as a saint of the Catholic Church.

A New Saint is Born

The canonisation of a new saint was not an everyday occurrence, and Rome would be alive with spiritual fervour, with thanksgiving and rites and a series of ceremonies spread across the whole weekend. The Swedish contingent under Brother Magnus set to work to make sure that it would be a celebration to remember. They prepared a plan to decorate the Vatican and the area around St Peter's on a vast scale. On the Thursday before the ceremony, the papal palace, St Peter's and all the surrounding streets were turned green with olive branches and grasses. Ten heavily laden asses were hired to carry the greenery into the Holy City. The whole area from the Tiber to St Peter's was filled with light, using over 15,000 oil lamps, 500 candles and 100 torches, with more than eight pounds of candle wax in each torch.[xvii] With all the streets surrounding St Peter's decked in green and lit with white candles the effect must have been spectacular. For the finishing touch, the Swedes paid for green wicker baskets full of white turtle doves to line the streets of the Vatican.[xviii]

On Friday evening, on the stroke of seven, the festivities began with all the church bells of Rome chiming out together. Rome, with its scores of churches, could throw a vast wall of sound across the countryside, and as we are told that the ringing went on through the evening until midnight, it must have been deafening as well as spectacular. The next morning the ringing started again, this time the churches in Rome being joined by those outside the city walls. The bells rang out all the way through the weekend and into the early hours of Monday morning.

The Pope announced an indulgence for anyone who travelled to Rome during the weekend of the canonisation ceremony, and the streets around St Peter's were filled with crowds of the faithful from early on Saturday morning. Imagine an early morning in October, the intense heat from the high Roman summer a fading memory. The streets were cool as the crowds started to make their way to St Peter's. As the night receded it was slowly replaced with a vision of green, the pre-dawn sky illuminated by the flickering lights from thousands of lamps and candles. The effect must have been spectacular. The Pope and the three cardinals who had led the examination of Brigit led a procession of the senior prelates of the Church into the chapel of the papal palace. Each had dressed in white vestments and carried a large candle in front of him,[xix] while four attendants held a golden canopy over the head of the Pope. The walls of the chapel had been decorated with olive branches and washed with incense. The Pope then preached a sermon in which he emphasised how difficult it was for the life of a person to be considered saintly. Yet the life of Brigit had been so meritorious, and the miracles she had performed so substantial, that made it impossible to deny her justice. It was quite clear that she should be made a saint. Ending his sermon by dramatically calling on the Holy Spirit, the Blessed Virgin and God himself as witness, Pope Boniface concluded his approval of the act of canonisation. Mass was said, and finally the Pope led the congregation in the antiphon "Come Holy Spirit" as they processed three times around the papal palace, singing in plain song.

The highlight of the weekend was a meal hosted by the Swedish party for the Pope and the cardinals who had worked on the canonisation. A grand feast was prepared on Saturday evening. Brother Magnus had bought a year-old calf, 24 roosters, 24 hens, 24 pigeons, together with a variety of sweets and all to be washed down with over 300 litres of wine.[xx] This was not going to be a day for observing the Benedictine Rule in its strictest sense! Whilst at the table enjoying the meal, a large pie was set down in front of Adam. The cardinal, expecting some kind of game or chicken pie, cut into it and, so legend has it, several small birds hopped up out of the dish and flew off to freedom.[xxi] The assembled crowds took this as a sign of a miracle, perhaps Adam had been favoured because of the work he had done defending the new saint.

In the evening a motley collection of extremely well-fed clergy said Vespers in St Peter's whilst flares and lamps were lit around the cathedral to add to the candles that were burning around the city. Finally, at daybreak on Sunday, the last stage in the process began. The Pope was led by 100 of his servants into the sanctuarium, where all the senior clergy of Rome had assembled. A gold cross and large candle were placed in front of the Pope and he started by saying a mass for the soul of Brigit. At the mid-point in the service each of the cardinals from the canonisation commission came forward with offerings for the soul of their new saint. Adam presented half a barrel of wine, Philippe of Alencon, the Cardinal of France, a giant loaf of bread decorated in gold, and finally the Cardinal of Bari came forward, although the nature of his gift was not recorded. A monk dressed in white delivered a sermon on the life of Brigit and the great grace that God had placed upon her. The Pope was then presented with the Golden Book containing the names of the saints of the Catholic Church, and with great ceremony he added Brigit's name to the list.[xxii] The book was then carried from its stand and turned so that the congregation could see that the name had been written there by the Pope. That concluded the papal ceremony of canonisation.

In a quiet and moving climax to the weekend's events, on the evening of Sunday October 8, the mortal remains of Saint Brigit were carried in solemn procession by Adam and his colleagues from St Peter's to the church of St Laurence in Panisperna, which had been Brigit's home during the years she lived in Rome. A silent parade, the bells of Rome had fallen still for the moment, moved at a sombre pace from the Vatican down towards the banks of the Tiber. Slowly they processed through the narrow streets around the Piazza Navona and on up the side of the Quirinale hill.

Eventually they reached the gates of St Laurence, a stern, plain church set on the top of the Quirinale from where the new saint would be blessed with the view looking back down over Rome towards St Peter's, home of a papacy that she had laboured for so many years to bring back to the Eternal City. Here she was laid to rest, sanctified and at peace.

But only after a couple of pieces of bone had been hacked off to be broken up and distributed as holy relics to other churches around Europe. This rather gruesome finale helped to feed a commercial reality born of one of the more macabre practices of the Catholic Church. The Church encouraged a popular belief that the bones and organs of holy people could, if properly venerated, arrange for holy works, miracles and other gifts to be bestowed by God. There was a ready trade in these holy relics across Christian Europe and the bones of a newly created saint were as likely to be in popular demand as those of one of the disciples of Jesus, and Brigit, the Church's newest saint, would have a substantial following, not least in her native Sweden. In due course, such popularity might well encourage more liberally minded people to help the laws of supply and demand along a bit by passing off animal and less saintly human bones to the gullible. By hacking off a couple of bones from the corpse of the unfortunate Brigit, at least the trade in her relics would be started off with the genuine article.

An official Saint's Day had to be set for the new saint, and this was settled as October 8, commemorating the day on which Brigit had been canonised (in more recent years this was changed to July 23). And with that final official confirmation Adam had at last repaid his personal debt to St Brigit of Sweden.

Chapter 14

The Court of
Cardinal Adam

Whoever hears these words of mine and does them is like a
wise man who built his house on rock;
the floods came and the winds blewbut it did not fall,
it was founded on rock

Trastavere

Slowly Adam got used to his new-found freedom. He started to take pleasure in his life in Rome, a city that was going through its own renaissance. The return of the papacy under Gregory XI had kick-started a new boom for the capital city of the Catholic Church, and despite the eccentricity of Urban VI's rule and the upset of the Schism it was clear that Rome was to be an important city once more. More to the point, with the papal administration reinstated, money started to flow into the city again. From the 1370s all across the city new houses and palaces were being commissioned for the cardinals and the papal administrators, and old buildings that had fallen into decay during the Avignon years were brought back to their former glory.

The newly reinstated Cardinal of St Cecilia now had both the time and the method to bring together his own court in the Holy City for the first time since his elevation in 1382. By tradition, when a cardinal was granted an honorary association with one of the ancient Roman churches, he set up his court in the neighbourhood of that church.[i] Adam's new title tied him, nominally at least, to St Cecilia's, an ancient church in a labyrinth of narrow streets at the heart of the district of Trastavere. There is no reason to believe that Adam did not follow the tradition and set up his household here. Trastavere (literally "across the Tiber") was conveniently close to the ancient commercial centre of Rome, just across the River Tiber from the Coliseum and the Circus Maximus. It was a busy area with small-scale artisan firms of tanners and cobblers, smiths and iron workers spilling out into the narrow streets of the quarter. The smells of the tannery and noise of the smiths made for a colourful if cramped atmosphere. It also boasted a small but growing contingent of Adam's fellow countrymen.

Throughout the 14th Century there had been a small community of Englishmen in Rome, a collection of merchants, clerks and pilgrims who had habitually stuck together in their own "ghetto" around the Via de Monserrato. They were not alone. Several groups of foreigners tended to cluster together in this area of Rome half way between the commercial centre of the Piazza Navona and the religious capital of the Vatican. There were quite a number of merchants, and by the middle of the century there was an active English guild of merchants in Rome, mostly trading in English wool. Woollen cloth from the home counties of England was so renowned in the markets of the city that trade laws of the time distinguished between local cloth and English cloth.

On the Via de Monserrato an English rosary bead seller, John Shepherd, donated a house to establish the Hospice of St Thomas, a resting place for pilgrims and poorer travellers who had business in the Eternal City. Before long it became the focal point not only for travellers from England but also for Englishmen who lived and worked in Rome.

Adam's base in Trastavere also, not surprisingly, became a magnet for the English. It was only a matter of a few hundred yards from the via de Monserrato on the east bank of the Tiber to St Cecilia's in the heart of Trastavere on the west bank. Within a couple of years of Adam's elevation, a rundown hostel that had been occasionally used by English pilgrims was taken over by John White.[ii] White was an English merchant who, in 1396, re-founded the hostel dedicated to St Chrysogonus half way between the churches of St Cecilia and Santa Maria. The two-storey hostel had a similar role to that of St Thomas's, being a home away from home frequented by pilgrims and poor travellers coming to Rome on business. Adam's base just down the street near to St Cecilia's established a presence and focus for English clerics seeking to advance their claims for preferment. A large number of English clerics were drawn into the area. Many of the founders of the new hostel of St Chrysogonus in Trastavere were churchmen and papal administrators, in contrast to St Thomas's, where most of the founders were merchants and traders. Adam seems to have been on good terms with the St Chrysogonus hostel and the English community there, and the two seem to have provided mutual encouragement to each other.

As well as being neighbours, White[iii] and Adam both used Lombard bankers with offices in London, Angelus Christofori[iv] and Nicholas Lukes respectively, to deal with money transfers between England and Rome. It would not be surprising if White had advised Adam on his banking arrangements. By the end of the 1390s Trastavere could boast of a significant English contingent and St Chrysogonus's was flourishing, having acquired most of the block of houses nearby between the Via de Genovesi and the Via Monte de Fiori and at least one other house in Trastavere right next to Adam's church of St Cecilia.[v]

From his new home in Trastavere, at the heart of a community of compatriots, Adam could make his way to the papal court on foot, walking along the Via della Lungara to the Borgo Leonine, passing through open countryside and the formal garden of the occasional villa thrown up in the narrow strip of land between the long ridge of the Gianicolo Hill and the River Tiber. The whole of this area was enclosed by the old city wall, so a cardinal might find his way from his church in safety and reach the Vatican in a mood of quiet contemplation and reflection. Paulo Cortesi, in his 15th Century work "De Cardinalatu", suggested that the ideal cardinal's palace should be located close to the Vatican so that the cardinal wasted no time getting to the papal quarters and to ensure he would be present for the feast days, consistories, conclaves and councils of war! Trastavere certainly met Cortesi's criteria, but I wonder if they met Adam's. As he walked in peaceful contemplation between Trastavere and the Vatican, his thoughts must have returned to the intellectual challenges of the scholarly life and the simple pleasures he had enjoyed as a Benedictine monk before he made his life-changing journey to Avignon with Simon Langham.

In Search of an Income

If Adam was to have any hope of assembling a substantial court of his own to promote intellectual debate and the study of doctrine and Church law, his first priority was to gather together the income needed to support his ambitions. A cardinal might be able to attract followers to his court by providing them with livings and benefices so that they were not a drain on his own purse, but even so he would need substantial funds to be able to feed his retinue and servants, to say nothing of entertaining his fellow cardinals and the proctors of the Benedictine order. Adam was not completely without income on his restoration for he already had the rights to the proceeds of two benefices dating back to the time of Gregory XI and Urban VI.

At the time of his downfall Adam held the parish church of Somersham, which was worth 95 marks (about £60) per annum,[vi] and the Deanery of

York, with a value of approximately £250 per annum[vii].Whilst neither would provide enough income to support a substantial court, it was still a decent sum. When John Shepherd bought the building for the English Hostel of St Thomas it had cost him 40 gold sovereigns, less than Adam's annual income from Somersham. However, Adam now discovered he would have a problem in getting his hands on the income from his old benefices.

In his anxiety to secure this income, he ran headlong into a conflict with his sovereign. King Richard II, the boy king, was now a young man of 24, in the prime of his life. He was getting used to governing in his own name and was increasingly less reliant on regents, councils and favourites. As he started to assert his royal authority, Adam presented him with an easy target. In 1385 and 1386 the King had been happy to intervene on behalf of the English cardinal. It was, after all, a matter of national honour, and it flattered the young King's sense of authority and power. The intercession had been done willingly, but at a price. As far as Richard was concerned, whether Adam had been languishing in prison or wandering around Urban's court under house arrest, his benefices were effectively vacant. That meant, in Richard's view, that it was the job of the Sovereign, not the Pope, to find candidates to fill them. Richard had taken the initiative without troubling to refer to the Church or its officials in Rome and awarded Adam's benefice of Somersham to John Boore, a member of his court, and the Archdeaconry of York to Edmund Stafford, a relative of Richard. Stafford had graduated as a doctor at Oxford during the 1350s[viii] and was already a rising star in Richard's administration. He was the keeper of the privy seal, and as such exercised great influence with the King. Nonetheless, he had chosen the Church as a career and he had probably met Adam during his time at university. He clearly respected England's most senior churchman, and throughout their correspondence over the next few years he always addressed Adam as "confidentissime"[ix] at the very least. Given that much of the correspondence related to issues where Adam was being obstructive to Stafford's ambitions, this was optimism in the extreme. Richard, on the other hand, did not feel overly constrained with such niceties. When Adam pointed out that the two benefices were rightfully his, Richard was piqued; he thought the attitude of the cardinal whose life he had saved to be strangely ungrateful. When it came to matters of philosophy and the natural hierarchy of power, Richard had the same refreshingly straightforward view as his Plantagenet predecessors. There was never any possibility that he could be persuaded by Adam's defence of the Church's view of the correct hierarchy of power. He was adamant that both Somersham and York were within his gift; they were after all within his kingdom and he had the absolute right to dispose of them as he saw fit.

In the short term Adam carried on collecting the income from these benefices as if nothing had happened. He used his network of bankers and proctors, and the parishioners and tenants continued to pay him as they had in the past, but his sovereign was not happy. On March 6, 1389 Richard wrote to Robert Mansfeld,[x] one of the proctors collecting money from Adam's benefices in England for onwards transmission to Rome, instructing that none of the money from the Archdeaconry of York should be paid to Rome. Instead it was to be frozen whilst the King decided who had the best claim to the position of Archdeacon. The King did not refuse Adam outright, but he had hit the cardinal hard. York provided nearly three-quarters of Adam's annual income. Richard started by treading carefully. In 1389 he simply set down his marker and then deferred judgement to get a better feel for the reaction that might come back from Rome. Nonetheless, it was already clear that the King was minded to face down the Church's position over the appointment of clergy to benefices in England.

King Richard Regrets...

As the year 1390 drew to a close and rolled into 1391, the situation deteriorated rapidly. Adam refused to accept Richard's right to reallocate his hard-won benefices and continued to collect the fruits from both as if nothing were amiss. This put Robert Mansfield in an increasingly difficult position, caught as he was between his duty as Adam's proctor and the demands of his sovereign. If he failed to collect for Adam, he could have been charged with fraud in a papal court and deprived of his livelihood; Richard on the other hand, could imprison him simply for flouting the royal will. For the time being, money continued to arrive in Rome, suggesting that Mansfield hoped that Richard would not notice so small a matter. Neither of the men whom Richard had appointed to Adam's benefices wanted to risk the outright enmity of the Pope or his English cardinal. They had, after all, chosen careers in the Church, and alienating the powers in Rome was unlikely to be a propitious career move. Considered from Adam's point of view, the whole issue was a straight-forward case of religious administration, a matter for the Pope and nothing to do with the King. However, Adam was in Rome and Richard was in England, and not only feudal overlord, but also a distant relative of the men he had appointed to Somersham and York.

Even as the cardinal and his sovereign were embroiled in the argument over Adam's two long-standing benefices, Boniface proffered his cardinal another three, all in England, that would have provided sufficient funds to double Adam's personal wealth. The provostship of St John's Beverley carried with it a healthy income of some 400 marks a year, though the church of Monks Wearmouth in Durham was worth a more meagre £23 (in 1290, the nearest date for which we have information), and the Deaconry of Yetminster Secunda worth still less, something in the order of £10 per annum. The relatively low value of Monks Wearmouth and Yetminster suggests that the dispute with Richard meant that Boniface was scraping the barrel to find benefices that might not attract royal attention. If that was the hope, it was a vain one, as Richard had already placed his own nominees in each of these two benefices. If Boniface was trying to help, he had shown a remarkable lack of tact by selecting benefices for Adam that the King believed were in his gift.

Of the three awards, the most valuable by far was that of St John's Beverley, and this was the one that, in the end, proved to be disastrous for Adam's relations with his homeland. Richard claimed that Beverley was within his gift, staring down Boniface's assertion that the provostship was a papal provision, which under the legal niceties of the time was almost certainly true. Unfortunately, from a practical point of view Beverley was a lot closer to the King of England's court. Even so, the dispute could have meandered on for months if Richard had not exercised his manipulative genius through the simple expedient of granting the provostship to Robert Mansfeld. Robert now had a real dilemma on his hands. Richard had offered him a temptingly rich benefice, one which would set him up for life, and he could only accept it by refusing Adam access to it.

Much as Adam needed to increase his income, he had been completely out-manoeuvred and had ended up in conflict with both his sovereign and his own proctor. Beverley was slipping from his grasp. As proctor to Adam, Robert was responsible for collecting money from his English benefices but he was hardly likely to enforce collection from Beverley, even if he did not actually take possession of the benefice for himself. Worse still, the dispute jeopardised Adam's ability to collect from his other English benefices where Robert represented him, and he needed the income to fund the lifestyle he was leading in Rome. Adam could appeal to the Pope, but this would put proctor and cardinal in opposition to each other in a Roman court without making any practical difference back in England. Meanwhile, the King was holding forth to anyone that would listen that the whole issue was a matter for him to decide and no-one else. The inevitable and protracted lawsuits started to make their way through the papal court, but in the meantime Adam could not enjoy the financial support of these benefices. Adam fought for Beverley unsuccessfully throughout the rest of his life, but the relationship with Robert Mansfeld appears to have been broken permanently by the dispute, and after 1393 Robert is never again recorded as Adam's proctor.

In the short term Adam did carry on trying to get access to the funds from

Monks Wearmouth, at least until the end of 1393, apparently unsuccessfully and at the close of the same year he had given up completely on Yetminster Secunda.

Another Troublesome Priest

If King Richard had outmanoeuvred Adam he still had to tread carefully. Adam had already proved his worth as a pair of eyes at the papal court during the Schism. The diplomatic way in which he had stepped in to resolve the difficult dispute over the election of the Abbot at Bury St Edmunds could not be forgotten. Now as the highest ranking churchman from England, his court in Trastavere was a magnet for English clerics seeking to advance their careers. This simple fact was obviously of great value, even to Richard, as those Englishmen who sought to advance their careers in Rome did so at a cost to the papal treasury rather than the King's! Adam, as we have seen, quite clearly had the Pope's ear, he was now the most senior of the cardinals adhering to the Roman papacy, so not unnaturally Boniface was accustomed to leaving English affairs to the English cardinal. Adam could, at the very least, get in the way of the King's wishes.

Initially Richard decided to sort out his troublesome cardinal with a bit of old-fashioned Plantagenet coercion. A series of three carefully worded letters left England for Rome as Richard tried to explain why Adam was wrong and why it was his duty to obey his sovereign. The letters track the deterioration in the relationship between the two men. In the first letter Adam is described as "most reverend" and "our dear friend"[xi] and the tone was one of supplication, asking if Adam would use his influence to solve such a delicate problem. The letter conveniently ignores the fact that it was actually Adam's problem, not someone else's! Time and again he pleaded with Adam not to obstruct the royal will and allow Boore and Stafford to gain the incomes he, the King and Adam's sovereign, had awarded them.

Here however was the nub of the problem. In the best tradition of Pope Urban VI, Richard was embarrassed because he had awarded two of his courtiers something which he did not own. In his second letter he tried to cause Adam the maximum discomfort: "We remember that we have often written to your reverence asking that you cause no trouble for but leave in peace our two beloved clerics, master Edmund de Stafford, our relative and guardian of our private seal concerning the deaconate of York and John Boore, deacon of our hospice chapel concerning your church at Somersham. There are many reasons for this as we have explained to you elsewhere. These were a great test of your reverend wisdom, particularly when you were deprived by Pope Urban through his papal bulls. The significance of these is apparent not so much to us and to our uncles the Dukes of Lancaster, York and Gloucester as to others of whom we have interrogated many".[xii] By implication the barons and populace were right behind the King in this dispute.

By the time the third letter was winging its way to Rome, the frustration of Richard at the lack of progress in this matter was evident. The formalities were cold and dismissive, the cardinal had been relegated to merely "reverend" and the tone of the letter was blunt and threatening. Richard pronounced starkly that he considered that Adam had pretended (i.e. intruded) on the rights of John Boore[xiii] and was being obstructive by refusing to withdraw. The King did have a case for claiming the right to appoint a cleric to the benefice but only if it could be established that it was vacant. Inevitably that in turn hinged on whether or not Urban had deprived Adam of his benefices and possessions when he imprisoned him. At the time Urban may well have seen little point going to the trouble of depriving individuals who were about to die anyway. A fact that had been an irritating matter of detail to a Pope who was more intent on putting to death or torturing his opponents in the court of cardinals now assumed a new importance. There seems to be good reason to suppose that Adam was never formally deprived, and there was no documentation that Richard could point to supporting his view.

The King might have been advised to read the Defensorium Ecclesiastice Potestatis before he put pen to paper! Stalemate ensued, with Adam clinging on to York and Somersham but being wilfully excluded from Dorset, Beverley and Monks Wearmouth. In desperation, Boniface tried to break the stalemate, wading in with all guns blazing. He meant well! On March 15 he wrote to the Great Council of England[xiv] asking them to intervene and persuade those who were depriving Adam (i.e. the King) to do the decent thing. The very fact that he wrote to the Council and not the King was bad enough, without also suggesting that the King might be wrong.

The Most Ungrateful of Subjects

This was way too much for Richard, whose Plantagenet temper and obstinacy would have given Urban VI a run for his money. On May 3, 1391 he resorted to a variation of that old favourite of the Plantagenets, the device of praemunire, the statute by which Edward III had asserted that no-one was entitled to bring into his kingdom any form of order or instruction from a foreign power. The decree was clearly aimed at Adam and any of his followers still in Rome in an attempt to increase the sense of legitimacy behind Richard's gift of Adam's benefices to his courtiers. Richard considered that Adam was interfering in the affairs of his realm at the behest of a foreign power (i.e. the Pope) "to the prejudice and the hurt of the realm and people." The King tried to assert his authority absolutely. He ordered all of his liegemen residing in Rome to return to England forthwith, telling them that if they did not arrive by the feast of St Martin (November 11) they would be deprived of their benefices.[xv] If they did come back and the King had not confirmed their right to those benefices by Michaelmas 1392, then the proceeds would be forfeit to the King anyway.[xvi]

By using praemunire Richard was essentially asserting royal control over all religious property in England. If Adam was foolish enough to return, so much the better, he would be at the mercy of his sovereign. The cardinal was now in a dangerous position. He could only continue to defy Richard by staying in the relatively secure environment of Rome and relying on papal support. If he did not return, he ran the risk of losing his income as all his benefices were in England. If he did return, however, he might be imprisoned and quite possibly worse. Adam had made his point about the right of the Church to appoint clerics to benefices, but the King had drawn a line in the sand. The representatives of Church and State in England were on the verge of the most destructive confrontation since the time of Thomas a Becket and Henry II.

Over the summer of 1391 the situation deteriorated still further following a dispute over the appointment of a minor cleric, Nicholas Slake. Slake was trying to obtain an archdeaconry in the see of Bath and Wells. Adam believed that he had a prior claim on the archdeaconry based on the fact that by now Boniface was putting him forward for each and every vacancy in England as they came free. Initially Adam prosecuted his case against Nicholas Slake in the papal court of Rome. Unfortunately the Bishop of Bath and Wells got involved and persuaded Slake to take up the archdeaconry regardless of the court case. Slake took his advice and he started to draw on the income from the benefice. A furious and intemperate cardinal now started a prosecution against the Bishop as well as Slake. Before long Edmund Stafford found himself drawn into the dispute, writing as Keeper of the Privy Seal to ask Adam to help him (and by implication his sovereign) by allowing Slake to take up the office that Richard had awarded him. Although Adam was not collecting revenue from the benefice, he was in no mood to lose yet another potential source of income in England.

In November Stafford asked Adam "in all humility"[xvii] to consider his request, and rather self-righteously urged the cardinal not to annoy his sovereign. Adam was piqued, not just at the loss of income, but by the fact that Slake, Richard's "commensalis", was yet another courtier being pushed by his King into a position where he could collect funds from Church property. Richard would have seen it from the opposite point of view. Every time he awarded a benefice to a member of his own court, the wretched cardinal appeared and attempted to thwart him. Court cases in Rome could come and go, but that was never likely to stop a true Plantagenet from trying to get his own way. Richard started to provoke the cardinal in particular, and the Church in general, into a showdown.

The King wrote two further letters, this time to Boniface himself, raging against his cardinal "inter omnes Anglicos Angligena plus ingrates" (the most ungrateful of all the Englishmen[xviii]). Richard defended the action of the Bishop of Bath and Wells, claiming he had not wanted to appoint Slake out of respect for Adam, but had done so out of fear of the wrath of his sovereign. Richard chose to make matters worse by asserting that Adam was encroaching on the rights of the crown, something that neither Boniface nor Adam were ever likely to accept when the subject matter was an archdeaconry.

As the dispute over Nicholas Slake raged, Adam had to consider what to do about returning to England. Should he comply with Richard's demands and trust in his sovereign's good will? At the start of the summer Adam may well have thought about obeying Richard's decree and returning to England before the November deadline. Yet to return would be very dangerous. Adam no doubt thought long and hard about the fate of Becket, particularly in the light of his own close encounter with death in the city of Genoa.

He had never met Richard and he had no way of getting the measure of the man, no easy way of deciding whether his sovereign lord could be trusted. Then again, as a cardinal of nearly ten years' standing Adam had finally and only recently established a position at Rome and had at least started to maintain a small court of his own for the first time since in 1382. If he stayed put, Richard could rant and rave as much as he liked but he could not touch him. As the dispute over Nicholas Slake dragged on, relations between sovereign and cardinal worsened, and Adam must have feared for his safety if he returned to his homeland. Of course if Adam stayed on in Rome, Richard might try to deprive his cardinal of the money from Somersham and York, but would he dare risk an open rift with the Pope?

In the end Adam decided there was too much to lose by returning and he stayed in Rome, but he had certainly agonised over the pros and cons before coming to his decision. It is easy to forget as we follow his career path through the vagaries of life that the boy from Norfolk had lived the last 23 years of his life abroad, and with his decision to stay in Rome he was effectively giving up any prospect of ever returning home. However, some of Adam's possessions were packed up and sent back to England. A number of his books were sent to Norwich;[xix] the Norwich Priory Rolls for 1391 record payments made by the Prior of Lynn, the Norwich Communer, Cellerer and Almoner totalling 90 shillings and seven pence towards the cost of shipping Adam's library back to England. Meanwhile the drinking cup bequeathed to him by Simon Langham was, by 1393 in the possession of Thomas de Walton, a monk of Norwich Priory.[xx] Why would he send some of his goods on to England, particularly his beloved books, if he had no intention of following?

The reason may well have been tied to the dispute over Somersham church. At the height of this dispute the church was re-roofed, and whilst this would not have been a cheap exercise, if a new house in Rome could be had for 40 gold florins, a church roof in Somersham could clearly be remade for somewhat less. It would make sense for Adam to keep the local people in the village on Adam's side in his dispute with the King. When he sent his revenue collectors to the village to harvest the money and produce that were due to him as tithes or for rent of Church lands, he could expect competition. He did not want to risk the possibility that the villagers would excuse themselves on the grounds that they had already paid what was due to the collectors acting for John Boore.

If he sent back a few personal possessions and had them sold to raise the money to re-roof the church, at least he would have given the villagers good reason to remember him when his tax collectors turned up. Perhaps enough good reason to buy the loyalty of a community from whom he might, under normal circumstances, expect to collect 60 pounds (equivalent to 60 florins) every year.

Climax and Anti-climax

Adam's bold stance seems to have paid off. Richard could have forced the issue with his cardinal overseas, but in the end he made little attempt to deprive Adam of the funds from either Somersham or York after 1391 (although Edmund Stafford may well have taken the funds from York from 1392, the records are unclear). Deciding that he had enough political conflicts in England to deal with, without inviting one with the Roman Church or his cardinal, Richard let things drift. Adam certainly held on to Somersham and continued to collect revenue from the benefice until his death.

Nor did the English Cardinal find himself isolated in Rome after the deadline of the November 11, 1391. Whilst a number of English clergy did return to England, by no means all of them did. What had promised to be a dangerous stand-off and a potentially damaging rift between the forces of the State and the Church gradually fizzled out. No harm seems to have come to either the families or the property back in England belonging to those clerks who stayed loyal to Adam and remained in Rome.

Adam may have made the right decision by staying in Rome, but he was still faced with a financial problem. The stand-off left him without much hope of building up the funds he needed to support a more substantial court. He now persuaded Boniface to find him livings in other parts of Europe beyond the reach of King Richard. From 1392 onwards most of his income would come from outside England, but he had to be patient. It was harder to find vacancies outside England that could be allocated to Adam without offending either the local clergy or the local king. Other monarchs liked to find sinecures for their own courtiers just as much as Richard did.

Unfortunately Adam's position was not unique. In these exceptional times, the self-same issue had already landed on Boniface's desk and it involved the case of Cardinal Philippe of Alencon. Since 1379 Philippe had been known as the Cardinal of France for exactly the same reason that Adam was known as the Cardinal of England. Following the mass defections of the French to the other Pope, Clement VII in Avignon, Philippe was the one and only French cardinal who had remained loyal to the Roman papacy, first to Urban and later Boniface. Philippe, however, had a distinct advantage over Adam. The English were broadly loyal to the Roman papacy anyway, whereas the French were not. Looking after Philippe was a priority. as he might yet play a significant role in bringing the French Kingdom (and just as important the French cardinals) back to the Roman papacy. In theory Philippe was in the same boat as Adam. France and the French King supported the French Pope Clement VII and that meant Philippe could not get hold of French benefices to add to his wealth. This only served to make matters worse for Adam. Whilst Adam was languishing in captivity and later in disgrace, Urban had gone some way to making Philippe happy by offering him appointments in England.[xxi] So even when Adam was released, the possibilities for the English cardinal had already been substantially reduced. Now he would have to wait for any new benefices to fall vacant, knowing that Philippe would be given first choice!

Boniface Tries to Help

Luckily for Adam, Pope Boniface continued to work hard to advance the interests of his senior cardinal. In November 1390 he awarded him the canonry of Lisburn in Ireland and another of Aylesby in Lincolnshire which taken together should have increased his annual income by 200 marks,[xxii] or more than a third, but both were in the realm of Richard II. It was a generous offer, but in practice it was virtually impossible for Adam to collect the funds due to him whilst the dispute with the King ran its course. And if Boniface appeared generous, it was at least in part to compensate for other difficulties that Adam was starting to experience in getting his hands on the cash that his benefices were supposed to provide.

During Urban's reign Adam had been awarded a foreign benefice, the Archdeaconry of Shetland, but such remote islands had always proved to be beyond the reach of his proctors. The remoteness of both the islands and their ruler only partly explains the difficulty Adam had in enforcing the papal will. In the 14th Century, Scotland was a foreign country and Shetland was not even Scottish, belonging instead to the Kingdom of Norway, run on behalf of King Hakan VI by a close-knit group of local families led by William StClair, the Earl of Orkney. The Earl allowed one of his associates, William de Buchan, to take over the Archdeaconry, and he in turn passed it on to his son, Sir Walter de Buchan. These local men had no trouble in persuading the islanders to deliver their tithes and rents into their coffers. Walter, a secular, was not recognised as legitimate Archdeacon by the Church in Rome, but the repeated attempts of the Church authorities to enforce their will through the courts proved utterly futile. By 1390 the ruler of Norway was the same Queen Margaret of Sweden (widow of King Hakan) whose suit Adam had supported over the canonisation of Brigit. Adam and Boniface clearly felt this would strengthen their hand, and Boniface sent letters to Buchan ordering him to hand over the Archdeaconry. Confident in his local power base, Sir Walter ignored the letter from Rome and the Bishop of Orkney tactfully absented himself. It is hard not to sympathise with the Bishop, who was being put in the unenviable position of having to choose between Boniface in faraway Rome and the cosy relationship between the local Church and The Earl of Orkney and his followers. Seeing that his instructions to Buchan had been ignored, Boniface supported Adam in taking another lengthy case through the papal court. It ran on until 1393. The stark reality was that even the long arms of the papacy could not enforce a decision in distant Shetland without the direct intervention of the Queen (who had other rather more pressing matters to deal with). Even the redoubtable Margaret, who by now ruled not only Sweden but Norway and Denmark as well, could not keep her eye on all of her far-flung territories. Buchan defiantly held onto the Archdeaconry and the money that went with it until the end of his life.

The luckless Adam had to scrape by on his income from Somersham and use it as best he might to run his Roman court. His first priority was to meet the basic household expenses for the upkeep of his court, however generously he might have wished to provide for his familiars and the English community in Rome. In straightened circumstances, Adam could only run a small court, probably containing barely half a dozen followers and no more than a couple of servants. If that was a disappointment, it was partly compensated for by the fact that Adam was still able to attract young hopefuls looking for a career in the Church. A number of English clerics became associated with his household and patronage in the first years after his restoration. Those who remained with him in Rome in 1391 had bet on the prospects for their advancement against their prospects in England. By refusing to return to England when ordered by King Richard, those English clergyman had effectively exiled themselves from the land of their birth, a compliment to Adam perhaps, but he would now have to provide for these men.

Two of them, Richard Benet and Richard Possewick, catalysed the start of Adam's "court". Benet,[xxiii] a Norfolk man who may well have been introduced to Adam through Norwich Priory, had joined Adam during 1390, became a member of his household later that year and stayed with him during the crisis with the King.

Richard Possewick, a young Englishman who had been brought up in Rome by his merchant family, joined him in 1391. Richard's parents had been involved in the foundation of the English Hospice in Rome, and Richard stayed there for a while in 1391[xxiv] when he first entered Adam's court, possibly because Adam did not have enough room to accommodate him at Trastavere. As a young man of just 16[xxv] he had little to lose in seeking a career in Rome; he had been brought up in the Eternal City and knew it rather better than England. These young churchmen looked to Adam to support them in their quest for benefices of their own, something that suited Adam well, as otherwise he would be bound to feed them at his expense. Yet even this was a double-edged sword. He could of course exploit the patronage system to provide livings for anyone who wanted to join his court, but only by depriving himself of the same opportunities to increase his wealth. Adam seems to have been pragmatic about the situation he was in. He clearly wanted to establish himself in Rome and was prepared to work within his means to do so, expanding his influence without hurting his own finances. Nonetheless, in the period between his restoration and the end of 1393, Adam's establishment in Rome was necessarily modest.

At the Centre of Power

Initially Adam was in a strong position to help English clerics in other ways. As Boniface was inclined to take his advice on matters relating to England, he could use his influence to help advance the interests of those who felt it impolitic to join his court but still wanted to make their mark in Rome, at least until King Richard's deadline of November 11, 1391. During 1391 he successfully supported petitions from Thomas de Walkington and William de Chesterton for preferment to new benefices. Only after Richard attempted to recall the clergy from Rome and reinforce the statute of praemunire in November 1391 did it become dangerous for English-based clerics to appeal to Adam lest he be construed as a foreign authority. The King would insist that all appeals for favours in England or for Englishmen should be made through himself.

Despite the King's assertions of power in England, Adam was still able to help a new generation of clergymen at the start of their careers in Rome. By the end of 1391 there was a network of English clergy working around Adam who could use his patronage to extend their influence. If it was no longer a good idea for Adam to show his patronage directly to a young cleric, he could do it indirectly instead. Thomas Walkington went on to become an auditor of papal causes at Boniface's court,[xxvi] a position he undoubtedly owed to Adam's sponsorship. John Trevor, another clerk who had been appointed papal auditor in addition to his role as auditor at Adam's own court, did rather better for himself. In 1394 he was promoted to the Bishopric of St Asaph's and eventually (changing sides to the Avignon "anti-popes") translated to the even wealthier Scottish Bishopric of St Andrews.[xxvii]

This small clique of English clerics working at the curia built a network of mutual support. So just as Adam was seen to petition Boniface in favour of benefices for both Walkington and Trevor, when the Pope appointed a commission to look into the difficulties his cardinal was experiencing in getting access to his position at Monks Wearmouth, it was Walkington and Trevor who were asked to look into the matter.[xxviii] In the same way, when John Trevor was promoted to his bishopric, many of the benefices he held at the time went to Richard Possewick. The English clerics in Adam's circle became adept at looking after each other.

The influence of Adam and his high favour with Boniface would prove helpful to the young clerics who attached themselves to him, and even those who were not destined to hold the highest office had good cause to be grateful for his patronage. Richard Possewick is a good example. Having joined the cardinal in 1391 at the tender age of 16, he stayed with him until Adam's death, and he was rewarded with a string of benefices. In 1397 Adam passed him the church of Hitcham, worth £66 per annum, to add to a canonry of Tassegard and prebend of St Davids, worth £50 a year between them, both granted at Adam's behest in 1394 (by which time the tension between Richard and Adam had abated a little). After Adam died, Richard Possewick was recommended to Cosmatus, the Cardinal Priest of St Cross in Jerusalem, whom he served for the rest of his life. By 1398 he had appointed his own proctor, Peter de Esculo, to look after the wealth from his many benefices. Through the good offices of Cosmatus he studied law in Perugia,[xxix] following which he was rewarded with no less than three new benefices in Orvieto and one in Maastricht. Richard spent his days in the sunshine of Italy, in the bosom of the Church, and enjoyed a life of considerable ease.

Meanwhile, Adam was still able to exert some influence in England in less controversial areas of ecclesiastical administration. From Rome on March 14, 1391 he arranged for his old priory of St Leonard's to be granted a special dispensation. Any penitent who visited the chapel of St Leonard's "in bosco" outside the walls of Norwich on the Feast of St Leonard and gave alms for the chapel's conservation would be granted a reduction in the period of penance for their sins of four years.[xxx] Penitents were confessed sinners who had been given a set of tasks to perform by their confessor, in order to atone for the sin committed. Once that had been achieved, the sinner would then be eligible for Heaven once more. It sounds a little like a reduction in a prison sentence and, in a way, to the mediaeval mind, that is pretty much how it was perceived. However, there were always short-cuts and other possibilities that were available to lighten the load, and the award made to St Leonard's fulfilled that very role. The conscientious penitent would of course make a substantial payment of alms to St Leonard to underwrite his worthiness for a lighter sentence. In earthly, practical terms it not only gave penitents a reason to go to St Leonard's, it enhanced the possibility of the Priory raising funds to help maintain its buildings.

An International Angle

Adam, a respected scholar and a cardinal who had spent several years at the centre of the papal court, was bound to attract a following greater than that of his fellow countrymen. The Flemish and German princes, Bohemians and Swedes who had all remained loyal to Urban had failed to secure a significant presence at the highest levels within the curia. This left churchmen from those regions with something of a dilemma. Those who sought preferment had no natural point of contact at the papal court, and several of them graduated towards Adam's sphere of influence. A fellow north European learned in the ways of the Church who had earned the respect of the academic community somehow seemed more relevant and easier to identify with than the mass of southern Italian cardinals with whom Urban had filled his court. And Adam willingly provided them with the same service and support with which he helped his English followers. Men such as the German clerk Hildebrande Lobeke, who in 1391 was described as a "familiar" of the cardinal[xxxi] and a member of his household. In return Adam provided him with a benefice in his home town of Merseberg to give him financial support and relieve the strain on his fragile finances. In June of the same year he supported a Flemish cleric, Goswinus Koc, in a successful petition to win a canonry and prebend of St Peters Church at Middleburg in Zeeland (modern day Holland).[xxxii]

Adam already had good personal reasons to be on the lookout for vacancies in benefices across Europe that might fill his own financial needs. That in itself ensured that he would know in advance of opportunities that, should they prove unsuitable to his own needs, could be proffered to those in his circle. He had built up his own network of English clergy to present petitions to the Pope, many of which he would back covertly if not openly, a system that could be useful to a foreign cleric in those politically charged times. A petitioner could use this network to secure Adam's covert support and with it a high chance of success when the petition came before Boniface. A German or Flemish cleric did not necessarily want his secular lord to know that his advancement was being secured through the offices of an English cardinal. There were several instances where men of Adam's circle supported a petition in this fashion, and Thomas Walkington and John Trevor in particular seem to have worked together on a number of cases, presumably under Adam's sponsorship. In November 1393 they successfully petitioned Boniface on behalf of Rupert Wetter,[xxxiii] and again in September 1394 on behalf of Reynard Cougnol.[xxxiv] Both Rupert and Reynard were Flemish citizens looking for a benefice in the Low Countries, a region split in its loyalties between support of Avignon and support of Rome. Under the circumstances the grant of a petition presented by relatively junior officials with positions in the papal court would be less provocative. At the same time, Adam could give his backing to their petitions tacitly through the use of those very papal functionaries John Trevor, who was in any event a member of his own household, and Thomas Walkington, who had benefited directly from his patronage.

Nonetheless, this must have been a frustrating time for Adam. At the pinnacle of his career, respected across Europe, he still could not rely on the support of his own King. The fallout from the dispute with Richard II restricted his ability to increase his income, and without a substantial source of income he could not hope to grow his court or his prestige in Rome during the early 1390s.

Success and Wealth

In the end the years of patient restraint paid off. Having rather handsomely sated the monetary needs of Philippe of Alencon, Boniface was at last able to reward his English Cardinal. The year 1394 was to be a watershed for Adam's finances, and at long last he started to acquire substantial new benefices outside England. Boniface rewarded his cardinal with preferment to accessible titles in friendly territories that had remained loyal to the Roman papacy. This time he would not only be awarded the benefice, he would actually be able to collect the revenues as well!

His first reward was the grant of the ancient Romanesque church of St Severin in Imperial Cologne,[xxxv] which served a large parish by the southern gate of the city and brought in an annual revenue of 35 silver marks. Matters were clearly improving. At the same time Boniface provided Adam with the town church of Hasselt near Liege[xxxvi] in Flanders (modern day Belgium), which was also worth 35 silver marks each year, and later in September of the same year Adam was granted a canonry worth around £150 at St John de Rabhia in the Lamego diocese of Portugal[xxxvii]. The cash was flowing into the cardinal's coffers, and up until the year of his death Adam's personal wealth increased substantially each year. In 1396 Adam traded Hasselt in exchange for a canonry at St Albans Church in another parish in Cologne.[xxxviii] In September of the same year he was granted the priory of St Agnes in Ferrara at an annual value of 200 gold florins[xxxix] followed in 1397 by the revenues from the Canonry of St Martin Cedoseyta in the Diocese of Oporto, which served to swell the Cardinal's fortune by a more modest £20 each year.[xl]

In the short term though, if he was to increase the size of the court substantially, there was still a piece of the jigsaw missing. In September 1394 he obtained a petition from Boniface that allowed members of his court to be absent from their benefices.[xli] This was an important document for a cardinal, as without it his courtiers and familiars were technically obliged to work in the churches that Adam had awarded to them. So if he had successfully obtained the vicarage of Walpole in Norfolk for Richard Benet, then Richard should have headed off there to attend to his flock, rather than stay on in Adam's court in Rome. Officially Adam should have had the permission in place from 1389 to protect the positions of Richard Possewick and Richard Benet, but with such a small following in those early days he probably did not feel it was worth troubling Boniface with the petition. From 1394, however, Adam's courtiers had permission from the Pope to hold offices without the inconvenience of having to actually be present in the benefice they had been granted. From this point onwards the clerks who joined Adam could officially be attached to his court and still earn revenues from benefices around Europe. At last, after 12 long and often painful years since he was first made a cardinal, he had everything in place to build a substantial and powerful court.

Then just as things were starting to come together for the Cardinal, the news came through from England that Thomas Brantingham, Bishop of Exeter, had died. His death created a vacancy in one of the wealthier dioceses in England, and King Richard had plans to fill the vacancy. Edmund Stafford was still hoping to advance his career in the Church, and although still smarting from his rebuff over the Deanery of York, King Richard lost no time in putting him forward as the royal candidate as

Bishop of Exeter. No doubt expecting trouble, if not outright opposition from Rome, Richard tried to get his candidate installed before his truculent cardinal had a chance to do anything about it. Adam, he naturally assumed, would be having a word in the papal ear with a view to making sure that Boniface refused him.

Richard's manoeuvring was interesting, not least as it suggested that the King had completely misunderstood Adam's disagreement with the royal position over Somersham and York. Richard appears to have assumed that Adam in his arrogance had intended nothing less than a personal sleight to his King. Perhaps having glanced through the Defensorium, Richard decided that Adam was not much given to respect the power of secular lords, particularly the power of those lords that asserted rights over the assets of the Church. Yet this was far too simplistic an assessment of the dispute. All Adam had ever sought was to retain those benefices that he had been awarded before his downfall, that in his view had never been Richard's to offer. In many ways we could look on his action as purely selfish and more to do with the grubby business of money than any higher principle. Adam had no quarrel with Boore or Stafford per se, only in that they had been granted something that Adam believed was his in the first place and Richard had no right to dispose of.

The death of Thomas Brantingham gave Adam just the excuse he needed to mend fences with the English court. Far from opposing Stafford's appointment, Adam actively promoted it, and even as Richard was preparing for a fight, news came through from Rome that Boniface had confirmed the appointment. A delighted and clearly astonished Stafford wrote to Adam on April 21 in effusive terms: "I have often received bitter words through your letters and it was with fear that I waited for a final bitter blow; then I learn of your great sweet kindness... now I discern your paternity and the great dignity you have expended on me I am forever obliged to you..."[xlii]

The help and support that Adam gave to Stafford not only secured his gratitude, it seems to have finally assuaged Richard's anger towards him. Richard's reaction is unrecorded, but he must have been as pleasantly surprised as Stafford, and it is clear that, from mid 1395, attitudes towards Adam in England improved markedly. Suddenly the political stand-off, the anger of 1391, were all a long time ago. Of course it may well be true that by the end of his reign Richard's attentions were focused on keeping his realm together, but that would have been of little concern to Adam. At a stroke the impasse over the funds from his benefices in England was resolved without further acrimony. All the difficulties he had experienced over the previous four years, the humiliation of having to make do with Philippe of Alencon's leftovers, all evaporated overnight, and without royal opposition the cardinal's coffers were now full of English gold as well. In 1396 he was successful in gaining the revenues from the church of Hitcham in Suffolk, valued at £66 per annum, and by the time of his death he was in possession of the archdeaconry of Dorset, worth another £100 (150 marks) per annum.xliii

We do not have enough information to be precise about Adam's wealth, but on a simple view of the benefices that we know he controlled it is reasonable to assume he could rely on an annual income of around £1,000. To this would be added whatever proportion of the revenues of the papal court he could extract from Boniface. This would have made Adam a very wealthy man by the standards of the time. If we bear in mind that a clerk in a village church might be given an annual income of £5 to £15 to live on, and that a decent house in Rome could be bought for 40 florins, a yearly income in excess of £1,000 would clearly have provided for a very handsome lifestyle.

Reflecting on the Benedictine Rule

So now that Adam had all the wealth and power he had ever striven for in his long career in the Church, what should he do with it? He had the resources to live the cardinal's life he had dreamt of since the heady days he had spent at Avignon in the court of Simon Langham. He could build up a lavish presence in Trastavere, run a grand palace, employ servants and create a powerbase for the English clergy in Rome. All the possibilities that the Church could offer lay at his feet.

And yet, ironically, even as funds flowed into his coffers from around Europe and as Boniface held him up as his most senior cardinal and embraced his liturgical contribution to the Church, something checked him. Brought up as a Benedictine monk and now living in close proximity to the Benedictine house attached to his titular church of St Cecilia, perhaps Adam felt misgivings at the life he had led. Not that we should suppose that Adam had lived an unduly loose or immoral life. There is nothing in his story to suggest wild orgies, drunkenness or loose living in the sense we might consider immoral. Nonetheless the Rule of Benedict was very strict, and as we have seen, Adam had certainly not followed it to the letter, and had often openly flouted its provisions. To his, indeed to any 14th Century mind, that would have counted as loose living, and certainly contributed to a sense of guilt. He had not been forced to join the Benedictine Order. Everything about the process of becoming a Black Monk was designed to dissuade all but the most determined from pursuing such a stern life.

Back in Rome with his titles restored and ruling over a court in which he could encourage learning and study, Adam seems to have returned to a stricter adherence to the Benedictine Rule. There are hints from this period in the autumn of his life that he felt a sense of remorse at the looser living of his earlier days. His choice of motto from that passage in Job, for instance, suggests a man who felt a sense of punishment for his failure to adhere to his vocation. There are similar hints of his sense of being "saved" in his letter to the monastery of Vadstena (see p246), a suggestion that Adam had reflected upon his life's work and found it wanting. By 1395 Adam was in his late sixties, feeling a real sense of his own mortality and increasingly reflecting back on what, by the standards of the time, had been a long and highly eventful life. For much of that life he had been a scholar and a leading theologian who had spent much of his time working on texts that were important in themselves but that had also served to advance his own brilliant academic career. So it is particularly interesting that from his restoration in 1389 until 1391 his work was focused solely on completing the two projects that he had started before his fall from favour. After 1392 Adam produced no further substantial written works, and that too suggests that he had returned to a more rigid observance of the monk's life. This is not to say that he retired from public life.

His duties as a cardinal and his functions within the papal administration did not have to be incompatible with the observances of the Benedictine life. As a senior churchman, he should have felt an obligation to ensure that all members of his household followed his own strict observance of the Benedictine life, even if that had hardly been common practice either in Avignon or in Rome. It is also notable that having finally established a court of his own, it remained relatively small, despite his considerable wealth. Adam seems to have lost the ambition to recreate the grandiose court of the Avignon cardinals. He no longer aspired to build up a palatial household and fill it with 50 courtiers or more at his beck and call, overflowing with servants, kitchens, stables and the trappings of luxurious living. Indeed, there is some suggestion that although Adam clearly did build up his presence and influence in Rome, he intended his court to be of a very different character.

The success and flamboyance of Philippe of Alencon provides an interesting contrast to the style and manners of Adam's court. The French Cardinal appears to have attracted a following around three times the size of Adam's, and yet a comparison of the two men's tombs (Philippe and Adam died within a month of each other) in Rome begs the question that if Adam could afford a tomb of such opulence when Philippe's last resting place, whilst ornate, is of a wallmounted tomb of somewhat lesser quality, surely Adam could have afforded to run a far greater court during his lifetime. Why would Adam have maintained a much lower-key presence in Rome than his colleague? Given the evidence for his wealth in the period after 1394, when he certainly had an annual income to rival that of Philippe, there is little doubt that Adam had the opportunity to enrich his court and expand it to the sort of size and prestige of that which Simon Langham had run in Avignon; certainly to one that dwarfed the size of the following that he kept with him in Trastavere.

In the end, when he had the chance, he chose not to.

I think we should consider Adam's household in the latter years of his life as a place of quiet contemplation, not full of the noisy and frivolous palatial life that the Livrees of Avignon had encouraged. The house would have been well ordered and disciplined. Based in Trastavere, in close proximity to the Benedictine monastery and Church of St Cecilia, there was every opportunity to observe the routine services and prayers of the Benedictine ritual; just as in his work at the Vatican he could allow time for the usual observances prescribed by the Rule. Even amongst a household of 25 people, the cardinal would have been able to instil a sense of quiet Benedictine discipline in his followers. To belong to a cardinal's household still offered security and prestige for servants and a great opportunity for those with careers to advance. Adam would have been able to impose his will on the house and set the standards that he asked his courtiers to follow. No courtier would risk annoying the cardinal and losing his support and, with it, the right to eat at his table and the possibility of being granted a benefice or living in the future.

A Cardinal's Court

The court that Adam kept in the later years of his life may not have been ostentatious, but the structure was similar to that of Simon Langham's. The head of the household was known as the camerarius, and he took charge of all the other personnel and the overall running of the house. There would also be an auditor who would provide intellectual (or at least legal) support to the cardinal, but whose work was kept separate from the running of the household. Two Englishmen who stayed on in Rome during the crisis of 1391 took the senior posts at Adam's court. John Trevor held the post of auditor and Roger White functioned as camerarius as well as apparently acting as Adam's confessor. Roger was a similar age to Adam, he had certainly been a cleric since 1362[xliv] and as one of the older men at the court, the roles of head of household and personal confessor would have sat easily with him. Two German clerics, John Gammen and Peter Rembold,[xlv] held the job of cubicularios or chamberlain, at least from 1396. They reported to Roger White (not as far as we know a relative of the trader John White), the camerarius, and were responsible for looking after the household provisions, the food, other victuals and wine cellars that a good household was expected to maintain.

Apart from those with official positions in the household, there were courtiers who worked with the cardinal and looked to him to advance their careers as a sponsor. These men were known as familiars. By 1394, in addition to Richard Benet and Hildebrande Lobeke, who had by then been members of his court for more than three years, two Englishmen had lived in the court long enough to be considered familiars of Adam: John Skenderby and John Inglewood. By 1396 they had been joined by the German cleric John Iselhorst. Those who were more established members of the household, longer serving familiars, were usually referred to as continuo commensalis, the name indicating that their seniority was gained from their length of service with the cardinal. The papal records show at least four men had served Adam in his household long enough to be considered continuo commensalis, the Germans Robert de Hokelheim and Theoderic Bukelken (who died in 1394),[xlvi] Richard Possewick and the Flemish Gerardo Everard.[xlvii]

Inevitably, the only members of court whose names we know are those who Adam was successful in supporting and promoting to benefices. There would no doubt have been a number of others, including those who, he helped indirectly through the English network at the papal court. Although he ran a very different style of court to that of Simon Langham, he still needed to pay a salary to, or at least provide food and lodgings for, his servants, scribes and other junior officials with more routine jobs to do. In a typical cardinal's court there would be a Master of the Hall, a Buticulario or butler, a buyer or emptore, a cook, a food manager and cellar master, and a master of the stables. These positions would be common to any major household and the roles of each were sufficiently fixed in practice to be written out in "La Maison Cardinalice"[xlviii] that sought to define the proper order and organisation of a cardinal's house.

All in all Adam would have had a household of around 20 to 25 followers during the period from 1394 until his death. It was a cosmopolitan affair, with Burgundians, Germans and Englishmen rubbing shoulders at his table, although at least in Latin they shared a common language. Although no Italians appear to have served at his court, many of the servants, the stable boys and cooks would have been locals from the district of Trastavere.

Only the lack of Castillians, Aragonese and French amongst the gathering stood out. That sadly reflected the political reality of the Schism and the fact that, for the most part, as these nations had supported Clement VII, their clerics really had no good reason to pursue their business in Rome.

And a Palace of his Own

Adam may not have sought palatial quarters in the style of Simon Langham's Avignon apartments, but with a household of some 25 people, he still needed a substantial building to accommodate everyone. The exact whereabouts of Adam's house in Trastavere is unknown, but there are a number of buildings from his time that survive and they give us an idea as to how the court might have looked. Some clues as to the sort of living quarters that a cardinal might take in Rome are offered by Cortesi's De Cardinalatu".[xlix] Cortesi was extremely precise in his prescriptive view of a good cardinal's house. He recommended that it should be north-facing to avoid the heat of the day and, in Rome in particular, to avoid the blast of the "pestilentially" cursed south winds. The building itself should be approached through an entrance hall or vestibule with stabling for the horses of visitors and the groom's quarters, leading in to a palace designed around a square central courtyard or atrium with each side having a covered loggia (rather like a cloister in pattern and inspiration). Around the atrium, guests and familiars of the cardinal would be housed in rooms that opened out onto the loggia. The library, with a music room next door, should also lead into the atrium, allowing the members of the household to read in the strong light of the south-facing loggia. The north loggia would have a staircase in the corner leading to the upper levels of the house. Cortesi recommended putting the rooms of the steward or cubiculum by the staircase so they could see everything that was going on in the household. Also in the northern part of the palace the rooms of the court scribes and auditors should be kept, as their work too required good light. Climbing the staircase to the upper floor should bring the visitor face to face with the sala grande with a side chapel. The upper floor must also contain an audience chamber, the cardinal's bedroom and the dining room. The latter, Cortesi rather thoughtfully suggested, should overlook the loggias and a garden set in the centre of the courtyard to make the ambience more suitable.

Most importantly for Adam, his court would have had a separate library to keep his collection of books secure. As the main resource for an academic, advocate and theologian, such a substantial library would have been one of the great attractions for young clerics joining his court. Adam's library was sufficiently large that some seven years after his death (by which time no doubt a large number of books had found their way into other collections in Rome) it was still sufficient to fill six large barrels. To put that in context, when Simon Langham's library was sent back to Westminster after his death in 1376 it contained 116 works and they filled seven barrels.[l]

Adam would have employed a librarian to look after his collection and supervise access by scholars as well as arranging for copies to be made. The role of copying books was very important, as in Adam's time, several decades before the printing press arrived in Europe, it was the only way of disseminating a text. Most often the task was carried out by monks, and the master of the library would be responsible for ensuring a tab was kept on which books had been sent for copying and making sure they were all returned to the household in due course.

But Where?

Although cardinals in Cortesi's day were building grand palaces and using the great artists of the early Renaissance to decorate them, Cortesi was writing 50 years after Adam's death. Half a century of banking and merchanting later, Italy was richer and the Church and her princes more ambitious. However, he was also describing qualities that had evolved over time from general principles of a perfect cardinal's house that would have been just as relevant in Adam's time.

So what would Adam's own court have been like? There is a notable (and rather rare) survivor from the 14th Century[li] directly opposite the church of St Cecilia, a building that is a plausible candidate for having housed Adam's court, and if it did not, at the very least it gives us an excellent example of the sort of building that he would have used. The house is north-facing exactly as prescribed by Cortesi and gazes out over the elegant 17th Century portico of St Cecilia. Unusually for Trastavere, the house is surrounded by open space and light, rather than hemmed in by the narrow streets and dark alleys that characterise this part of Rome.

The house has a layout that suggests it was originally built around a central courtyard with an arcade on each side and a covered portico facing onto the street. The portico has now been filled in, but the marble columns are still clearly visible. On the upper storey a crenallated veranda looks out over Trastavere, and this is attached to a main room designed for the master of the house. The main difference between this building and the ideal described by Cortesi seems to be that in the older houses of Trastavere the staircase connecting the upper and lower floors was on the outside of the building rather than being enclosed within the loggias around the courtyard.[lii] Regrettably neither the staircase nor the loggias have survived and we are left glimpsing the marble columns still set into the side of the house and guessing at the grand facade that once adorned this house.

What has survived is a substantial 14th Century Roman brick house, three storeys high, that looks from its shape to have had an interior courtyard, a portico on the south and west side, and an upper room with a portico and veranda. It was an imposing building and in stature quite in keeping with the church of St Cecilia opposite, particularly bearing in mind that much of St Cecilia was built in brick before the Baroque era façade was added.

The house opposite St Cecilia is not on the sort of grandiose scale that Cortesi desribed, but that is not surprising in itself. The courts of the Roman cardinals at the end of the 14th Century would simply have been a little more modest in scale. Of course the Avignon cardinals had not lacked wealth, but the scale of 14th Century domestic building, even in Avignon, was not of the same order as that achieved by the middle of the 15th Century. The context of the 14th Century domestic palace is illustrated by another rare survivor in the Tuscan town of Prato. The palace was built for the merchant Francesco Datini. It is a substantial building and certainly larger than the one opposite St Cecilia, but not a great deal larger and not at all on the scale described by Cortesi. Indeed, unlike the Trastavere house it was surrounded by narrow streets and although heavily frescoed, presents an austere exterior to the outside world. Yet Francisco Datini, the notorious "Merchant of Prato", was generally considered by his contemporaries to be the wealthiest person in the (European) world, and if a palace built for such a notable and wealthy man was constructed on such a relatively modest scale, then we should expect similar qualities in the palaces and courts built for the princes of the Church.

Another possible candidate for the site of Adam's court is the formal courtyard buildings at the front of the church of St Cecilia. This would not be unusual. In the 1430s Pope Eugenius IV established his palace at Santa Maria in Trastavere, another titular church just a few hundred yards from St Cecilia's. Once again we can see similar features to the layout described by Cortesi, although the buildings were redeveloped in the 17th Century and in this case a pleasant formal garden in the centre of the court forms a pleasing centrepiece to the arrangement.

Whichever building served as his court, here at last in the heart of Trastavere Adam seems to have found his place and inner peace at the heart of the Catholic world. A man who was by now in his late sixties, a senior cardinal experienced in the ways of the Roman court, he established a model court in Rome. He did not in the end encourage those excesses of Avignon that had provoked so much criticism of the Church. In a gentle and scholarly atmosphere, his court in Trastavere promoted the Benedictine values that had been instilled in Adam in his youth and to which he now returned. The scholar whose life had been turned upside down by the politics of the day, who had done so much to add to the Catholic liturgy and who had helped secure the future of orthodoxy could now concentrate on encouraging and nurturing a new generation of churchmen. Men like John Trevor and Richard Possewick would also be a part of the legacy that Adam Easton left behind.

Adam has had a lot of bad press from modern historians. When he is referred to at all it is usually to make the comment that he was a notorious pluralist (having the rights to benefices across Europe). Yet as we have seen for most of his life, certainly to 1391, he had just one benefice, very occasionally two. In fact it might be fairer to describe Adam as an unsuccessful pluralist, as many of the benefices he was assigned failed to produce revenue for him and were occupied instead by a local man. Only in the last seven years of his life did he have anything like a substantial income from several benefices held concurrently, and he was neither as ostentatious nor as wealthy as the cardinals of the Avignon years.

More to the point, even in this late period of his life he did not carve out the life of a great prince of the Church but instead established a court of learning and contemplation that was, in a very quiet way, something of a personal triumph. In the end it reflected those values of the Benedictine life that he had been brought up with and perhaps, in the end, those that he felt most at ease with.

Chapter 15

Death and Legacy

By God's grace I am what I am

Richard II Back in Charge

It had been nearly 30 years since Adam left England, and during that time life in the kingdom of his birth had been far from happy. Edward III, the great warrior king, had declined into senility and his place had been taken by the haughty but ineffectual boy king Richard II. Plagued with internal divisions and frequent fighting between the King and his senior nobles, the country had been through periods of anarchy and unrest. Finally, in 1388, Richard's pride had been severely dented when the Earls of Arundel, Gloucester and Warwick joined together with John of Gaunt's son, Henry Bolinbroke, to seize power. Even though these so-called Lords Appellant, took their action in Richard's name and shied away from taking the ultimate step of deposing him, they used every opportunity to destroy the power of his personal favourites. It was an ugly period of recrimination, of exile and execution, that not only cost the lives of those who had used their friendship with the young King to enrich themselves, but also affected a number of honourable and learned men. Pope Urban VI remained aloof from the changes in England in 1387 and 1388 which enabled the promotion of men sympathetic to the new order, men such as Thomas Arundel, younger brother of the Earl. Arundel was made Archbishop of Canterbury and his appointment received papal approval. Urban had no great reason to oblige Richard in his hour of difficulty any more than he felt inclined to show undue favour to the Lords Appellant. The Kingdom of England would, in Urban's view, remain loyal as long as he served those who wielded effective power. In this respect Urban was proved right and Richard would, in due course, show loyalty to the Roman papacy. In the meantime Richard was left isolated. The new regime had arrived with high ideals and meek declarations of loyalty, but it did not take many months to demonstrate a penchant for greed, corruption and incompetence no better than that of the old court favourites of the King. The mood amongst many of the senior nobles began to shift, and Richard started to think thoughts of the revenge he would have if the tables were ever turned on those Lords Appellant.

And turn they did. Richard's authority increased throughout the 1390s until finally, by the end of 1397, at the age of 30, he moved to consolidate and assert his grip on the throne of England once more. He called a parliament at Westminster and demanded that Gloucester, Arundel and Warwick appear before it. He had them charged with treason, and within a matter of months Gloucester had been murdered, Arundel executed and Warwick deprived of his lands and other possessions.

On September 28, 1397 the King moved to exile Thomas Arundel, his Archbishop of Canterbury. Arundel, a man who owed his advancement in the Church to his family connections during the period when the rebel lords had seized power, had been a harsh critic of Richard. He could expect few favours. With the Lords Appellant crushed, the King had the perfect opportunity to exact his revenge on Thomas. There was little the unfortunate cleric could do except be grateful that he had escaped with his life. There was certainly little to be gained by appealing his case to Rome when the King was wreaking a bloody revenge on anyone who crossed him.

Only Bolinbroke appeared to be secure, and Richard professed himself comfortable with Henry's protestations of loyalty to the crown: he was after all a close relative of the King. The stable relationship between the two was not destined to last. In 1398 Bolinbroke's father, the aged John of Gaunt, finally died, and Henry Bolinbroke was first in line to inherit his father's property. In 1398 the Duchy of Lancaster was the most wealthy in England, and Richard quickly realised that he only needed the excuse of Bolinbroke's former treachery to the crown to seize the Lancastrian lands for his own private gain. A little inconsistency should never be presumed to get in the way of a higher purpose! Such a temptation placed in the path of a newly assertive King proved too much. The old wounds were opened up and Bolinbroke duly followed Arundel into exile and all of the lands of the Duchy of Lancaster were seized by the King.

And yet the exercise did not serve to strengthen the power of Richard per se, in fact quite the reverse. Within just two years it had backfired on the King, who had demonstrated to his nobles that even the most powerful of them could not escape from his venality and greed. And if even those closest to him could not be safe from Richard's ambition, then equally it became obvious that no-one had much to lose by opposing the King's will.

Exile of an Archbishop

Initially the Archbishop's exile proved to be a bizarre travesty, as Richard refused to give him a safe conduct to leave the country. Not that Arundel was in any hurry to leave the land of his birth. His career had always been focused on England. A member of one of the most senior noble houses in the land, his rank had assured him of a long and successful career in the Church. A bishopric or two had passed his way and ultimately the greater prize of the Archbishopric of Canterbury. Arundel was a churchman whose views were rather more conservative than Adam's. He proved to be a harsh critic of Wyclif and his followers and an ardent burner of heretics. His opinions on Church power in general, however, were closely allied to those that Adam had set down in the Defensorium. He was also a staunch supporter of Henry Bolinbroke; after all it was their former political alliance that had brought both men their exile. Only when the King relented and arranged a safe passage for the Archbishop on October 19[i] could Arundel and his entourage made their way to France. The former Archbishop's instinct on reaching the relative safety of French territory was to head to Rome to seek redress for his grievances from the head of the Church, and to enlist the support of the Cardinal of England in the dispute with his sovereign. In the short term Arundel was merely looking to get support for his own reinstatement, but he probably had a bigger plan in mind.

Arundel's trip to Rome would be a first tentative step towards paving the way for Henry's campaign to claim the English throne. Adam, as the senior English cleric, would be a valuable supporter if he could be enlisted to help to legitimise the overthrow of Richard.

The English Cardinal was now in his early seventies, a good age for the time in which he lived, especially considering the circumstances of his life. He had survived the Oxford riots, the Plague, the ravages of the Hundred Years' War, torture and imprisonment, and now he ranked as the most senior cardinal after the Pope himself. He had authored an Office of the Catholic Church and instituted the festival to go with it and had been instrumental in the creation of a new saint. Reinstated with his own court in Rome, he commanded respect and authority in the Church (even if that authority remained more limited in the land of his birth). Cardinal Easton was a survivor.

Arundel had good reason to hope that Adam would side with him and Bolinbroke. He recalled the bitter dispute between Adam and Richard in 1391 and guessed that Adam could be persuaded on a matter of principle to lend his support to the overthrow of a "corrupted" king. Adam had set down in writing the principle that it was an essential duty of the papal power to deal with corrupted kings. This had been one of the central planks of the Defensorium, and Arundel must have hoped that Adam could be flattered into supporting the principle of a change in the monarchy, and then use his influence with Boniface. It was well known that Boniface always deferred to Adam on English affairs. Papal support and blessing for a new dynasty of kings would depend on winning over Adam first. Popes had been known to declare a crusade for less weighty matters in the past, so why not to overthrow the English King?

Arundel came to Rome to prepare the ground, and Adam's support was an important part of the plan. There is a tradition dating back at least as far as 18th Century historians that Adam met Arundel in Rome (some have ventured to suggest that he met Henry as well[ii]). Indeed there was little obvious point to Arundel visiting Rome at the end of 1397 for any other purpose. Just two years after Arundel had set off for Rome, Bolinbroke successfully took control of the country from Richard. In the autumn of 1399 there was considerable debate as to whether to use the principles of canon law on the basis that the Pope could intervene to depose a corrupted king and relieve the suffering of his people. Adam was the ideal person to provide the intellectual basis for the Lancastrian coup d'etat.

The Curious Conflict of Dates

In the end the two men were not destined to meet, for as Arundel set off for the Holy City, Adam breathed his last. His death was formally entered in the records of the Vatican Archive on September 20, 1397.[iii] He died peacefully in his sleep.

Or did he? Whilst it is certainly possible that Adam did die peacefully in September 1397, in death the crucial facts surrounding Adam are shrouded in uncertainty. At first glance the carved lettering on the base of his tomb states unambiguously that he died in September 1398. A whole year later than the record in the Archive. However, as the bystander looks more closely at the carved inscription at the base of the tomb, one notices that the last Roman numeral "1" is not carved as neatly as the other letters and it is a slightly different length. It seems to have been carved at a different time, almost as if it has been added as an afterthought! So now we have the question in front of us, 1397 or 1398? Matters get more confusing when we consider that Eubel, that precise German historian of the papacy, claimed that Adam died in August 15, 1398,[iv] but we do not know the source of his information. The existence of a manuscript drawing in the Vatican[v] that depicts the detail of Adam's tomb as it was before it was moved at the end of the 16th Century only makes matters worse. The drawing clearly shows that the original text written on the base of the tomb included the date carved as MCCCLXXXXVII. Of course there could be an error in the drawing in the Vatican manuscript, but the 1397 date does tie in with the entry in Obligationes and Solutiones in the Vatican Archive. Does this mean that an extra "I" was carved to alter the date of his death, perhaps after the tomb had been moved? If it does, it simply begs the question "why?" What could have motivated the masons renovating the tomb 200 years later to alter the date of Adam's death? It surely cannot be that some new information had come to light that suggested the records of his death were wrong.

The change of date has great significance, because if Adam did not die until September 1398 a meeting with Arundel would not have been merely a possibility, it would have been unavoidable. Once more we are forced to admit that the waters are muddy. 1398 is undoubtedly a more enticing date, with overtures of high diplomacy and plots to remove Richard.

Perhaps someone wanted to go to some lengths to suggest that Adam and Arundel had met and the cardinal had blessed the Lancastrian adventure? Was this an attempt to add legitimacy to the Lancastrian cause? Today this appears to have little credence, but that is because we have forgotten who Adam was. In the centuries following his death his name was respected and his achievements and importance remembered, and that may have given the Lancastrians a good motive for suggesting that Adam had given his blessing to their cause.

If Adam did die in 1397, the news would not have reached England until after Arundel had set off for Rome. Letters moved notoriously slowly between London and Rome, and it is unlikely that Arundel would have heard of Adam's demise much before he reached Rome. Whether they met or not is perhaps not the point. The incident serves to illustrate the fact that Adam, as a cardinal of the Church, had grown so much in stature and reputation that it was worth the former Archbishop of Canterbury seeking him out in Rome to bless a change in the royal line in England. It was by no means certain that Adam would have given his blessing to the enterprise. He may have had little reason to support Richard II, but then much the same could have been said of his support for Urban VI after he had had Adam imprisoned and tortured at Nocera. We know that Adam remained intensely loyal to Urban VI, a man whose inadequacies had caused many others to waver. Surely Adam would have shown the same loyalty to his sovereign, who, since 1394, had shown some signs of having forgiven his obstreperous cardinal. On the other hand, support for Henry would have given him a final chance to return to the land of his birth, something that might have had a strong appeal for an elderly man who had lived abroad for so much of his life. The fact is,whether he died in 1397 or 1398 he did not live to see Henry IV installed as King of England and the establishment of the House of Lancaster. Adam's death before the invasion of 1399 and the demise of Richard meant that any impact his blessing might have had on Henry Bolinbroke's campaign would have been marginalised.

If there was ever any doubt as to the true purpose behind Arundel's trip to Rome, the surprisingly short time he spent there made his reasons transparent. If he had intended to get redress in the papal courts or to involve Boniface in his deliberations over Richard, he would surely have stayed at the papal court for several months. To get advocates to process his case through the papal court in the face of opposition from his King would have taken years. To make his case to Adam and Boniface, to let them consult other English clerics and then ponder on the consequences, would certainly take months. Yet Arundel was only in Rome for a few short weeks. He could not have arrived in Rome much before the middle of November but on January 8 1398, the exiled Archbishop was writing back to his former brothers in the monastery at Canterbury from the banks of the Arno in Florence.vi He can have stayed in Rome no more than seven weeks.

If we assume that Adam did indeed die in 1397, then his death had removed Arundel's reason for being in the Eternal City. And if Adam's death removed his main reason for being in Rome, there were plenty of good ones for moving on to Florence. The city was a major centre for finance, and by the mid 14th Century it already had more than 80 banks and 600 lawyers. Florence was a place of particular interest for someone who might have been looking to raise money to finance an army for his friend.

Arundel passed on very little to his brothers at Canterbury as he told them of his progress abroad. The fact that Arundel did not mention a meeting with Adam in his letter is not surprising, even if it took place. He would hardly have referred to the meeting and its purpose in a letter to an England that was still very much in Richard II's grip, particularly if the outcome had not been favourable. Arundel was far too astute a politician to risk revealing his hand to the monks of Canterbury.

Death of Adam

Whether in 1397 or 1398, Adam was buried in accordance with tradition in his titular church of St Cecilia in Trastavere. His tomb provides ample evidence of his status, importance and prestige within the Church. It was not uncommon for tombs in Rome to be marked by nothing more than a marble plaque above the side aisle under which the deceased was interred. Wall-mounted monuments were also commonplace, with carvings in relief of the deceased, possibly featuring an allegorical carving hinting at their life's work. Philippe of Alencon has just such a tomb in the nearby church of Santa Maria in Trastavere.

Adam's tomb was very different. It was a remarkable work, stylistically unique in Rome and one of the grandest and most lavish of the period. Originally a fine, free standing tomb with a marble canopy supported at each corner by an ornamental pillar, it was the first of its kind to appear in the Eternal City. The tomb was placed at the centre of a chapel to the right of the apsidal end of the church[vii] near to the tomb of St Cecilia. Each of the supporting pillars was twisted extravagantly and had ornamental stripes running down the side. Running around the base of the canopy were the words "Artibus iste pater famosis in omnibus Adam Theologus summus cardiquenalis erat Anglia cui patria titulum dedit ista Beatae Caeciliaeque morsq. Suprema polum anno mccclxxxxvii mens sett." (In essence, the inscription suggests, "Father Adam was renowned in all famous arts. He was a consummate theologian and cardinal whose homeland was England and title St Cecilia. He died and ascended to heaven in 1397 month of September.") On top of the marble sarcophagus, an effigy exquisitely carved from a single block of marble gives us a real sense of what Adam looked like. This in itself is unusual: there are barely a handful of characters from 14th Century England whose image we can discern as clearly as that of Adam Easton. The carving is certainly that of a master craftsman, as is shown from the fine detail of the folds of his robes and the damask pillow on which his head is laid to rest, and the smooth features of his face and hands. As a sculpture this early in the Renaissance era, it is most unusual and it is all the more frustrating that the name of the sculptor has escaped detection!

Adam was five foot four inches tall, of average build, and the outline of his cardinal's robes tells of a life of moderation, if perhaps not the abstemiousness that Benedict's Rule would have preferred. His face was dignified, marked by strong features that are emphasised by a slightly hooked Roman nose, his hands, slender and refined, are definitely those of scholar: there is little evidence of manual work to be found here! With a furrowed brow and eyebrows seemingly slightly raised, there is something imperious, almost patrician about this peasant's son from Norfolk. He lies in state in fine robes, his feet in decorated slippers and his head resting on a pillow of the richest cloth, ornamented with tassels and damask work. There can be no doubt that this was a rich man's tomb.

The tomb itself is adorned with emblems of England that may well record his title as Cardinal of England, but just perhaps a little homesickness as well. The three lions passant and the fleurs de lys (bearing in mind that since the time of Edward III the Plantagenets claimed to be the rightful Kings of France) are mounted on a shield in the centre of the tomb with on each side Adam's own arms, a single headed eagle set on a cross of St George. On the base there is a further inscription that contains the second intriguing mystery of Adam's tomb. The inscription is not, as we have seen, necessarily the original[viii] but it reads as follows:

Adam Anglo Tit. S. Caeciliae Presbytero Card. Episcopatus Londinensis Perpetuo Administrat. Integritate Doctrina et Religione Praestanti. Anno MCCCLXXXXVIII.

Roughly translated the text reads, "To Adam the Englishman, by title Cardinal priest of St Cecilia, perpetual administrator of the Bishopric of London and outstanding in pure learning and devotion. The year 1398."

The Riddle of the Tomb

The inscription holds two mysteries. The first, as we have already seen, is in the contradictions that surround the date of Adam's death.

The second arises from the reference to Adam being connected to the Bishopric of London. Adam is often described by Church historians as having been the Bishop of London, and the source of this error is almost certainly the inscription on his tomb. One of the few things that is absolutely clear from the written record of Adam Easton's life is that he was never appointed as Bishop of London, or for that matter to a role connected to the Bishopric of London. For much of the time that Adam was a cardinal, the post of bishop was occupied by the patrician William Courtney, who was offered (and rejected) a cardinal's hat before Adam.

There is no documentary evidence to link Adam to any post within the Diocese of London. Even if he had been granted an office associated with London by the Pope, Courtney and his King did not acknowledge or record the fact and, importantly, there is no record of the appointment in England. Yet if he had been granted the appointment in Rome and it was not recognised in England then Adam, a trained canon lawyer, would have brought a claim, coming before the papal court to enforce the appointment, particularly if he had genuinely been appointed to a role in London, one that was important enough to be mentioned on his tomb. He had certainly put a great deal of effort into protecting the other posts he had been granted which had been occupied by rival claimants.

It is possible that Boniface IX offered him an honorary post, not so much Bishop of London, but as the tomb describes "Perpetual Administrator of the Bishopric of London". Perhaps an honorary title such as this, with no revenues involved, was offered as an easy compromise. One that would not have given offence to the Bishop and might have avoided any form of dispute and yet bestowed a certain status on the English cardinal at the same time. But surely some record of the appointment would have been made in either the papal archive or in English Church records.

There is another possibility. Perhaps it is a joke. We have seen numerous examples from Adam's life of a love of puns, codes and word games appropriate to a man of learning. I wonder if Adam was rather amused by the fact that Courtney, a bishop who owed his progression to his wealthy background, had been offered the cardinal's hat by Urban VI, that great ascetic and self-proclaimed reformer. Did this grate just a little with Adam, with his humble birth and considerable acheivements? Perhaps Adam looked on his own life of hard work and monastic piety and poured scorn on the life of ease and privilege that had attended the patrician bishop all his days. We might look at the words on the side of Adam's tomb as an ironic statement, one in which Adam offers himself Courtney's title in mocking revenge for the title that Adam coveted and Courtney was offered before him. At the same time it also pokes fun by implication at his old adversary Urban VI. If it was a joke, it was certainly missed by most of the Church historians writing in the centuries following his death! In fact most of them took the words rather too literally. Joseph Eggs, in his history of the cardinals of 1714, called Adam the Archbishop of London, Palatio simply the Bishop of London and then both Ziegelbauer and Cardella followed suit.

Adam's will has not survived, but aside from spending lavishly on his tomb he gifted his library to the Benedictine Priory at Norwich. Other than that we can only guess at the beneficiaries of his will. Most likely they would have been the prominent cardinals and theologians at Boniface's court. The process of winding up his affairs clearly took several years, for the books were not on their way to England until 1407. On October 3 of that year the Collectors of the Port of London were ordered not to charge taxes on six barrels of books being sent on from Bruges that had been bequeathed by Adam, late Cardinal, to the prior and convent of the Holy Trinity, Norwich.[ix] The ever trustful officials stipulated that only the books could come through the port tax free and anything else enclosed with them should be taxed in the normal fashion. Each barrel must have been opened and checked to ensure no contraband had been included amongst the folios. In the same year a contribution of twelve shillings was paid out of the Norwich priory Communar's account for carriage of the Lord Cardinal's books, presumably from London to Norwich.[x] Inevitably the dissolution resulted in the dispersal of much of the fine library of Norwich Priory, and those books that were transferred to the care of the newly Protestant cathedral suffered later in a severe fire. As the collection was broken up over the years many of Adam's books vanished into the mists of time, and of the six boxes of books that arrived from Rome, only four books have survived that are certainly his. It is telling that two of them are in the Parker Library of Corpus Christi Cambridge, a library started shortly after the dissolution to preserve just such works.

Adam in History

If his library suffered during the Reformation, his reputation survived beyond it. For the next 300 years Adam was generally regarded as one of the leading clerics of his era. Nor was he noted merely for his importance as a churchman. John Bale, in his work on English writers,[xi] gives Adam a lengthy eulogy and lists some 24 works reputed to be created by him. Adam was reasonably prolific by the standards of the day, but unfortunately Bale seems to have muddled those books from Adam's own library with works that he had written himself. Even so, it is interesting to see that Bale regarded him to be significant as a writer as well as a senior cleric.

In the late 16th Century Adam's legend grew. A restoration and renovation of the whole Church of St Cecilia was undertaken by Cardinal Paul Sfondrato, the then Cardinal of St Cecilia, in 1599. As part of the rebuilding programme, all the major tombs of the Church were relocated. It was during the renovation that Adam's tomb was moved from its location in the centre of one of the side chapels to its current position by the entrance to the church. During the rebuilding, many of the tombs were opened, including that of Adam. His body was found to be whole and uncorrupted.[xii] Whether this is a testimony to the extravagant embalming process that Adam would certainly have been able to afford, or to the belief of the faithful in the preservation of the righteous, is perhaps best left as a matter for personal interpretation. To the Catholic faithful of Counter-Reformation Italy, it was a sure sign of a godly life led by a blessed servant of the Church. Adam's body was carried in full ceremony and re-interred in the tomb in its new resting place to the right hand side as one enters the Church of St Cecilia. The fact that Cardella, writing in 1793, saw fit to record the incident some 200 years after it occurred shows that the legend of the Cardinal and his example lived on in Italy, even if memories in England were becoming rather more hazy.

Yet in the first half of the Stewart era, long after the Reformation appeared to have become a permanent fixture, Adam continued to be regarded as worthy of attention in his country of birth. In his classic work tracing the history of the English clergy,[xiii] Bishop Godwin accorded Adam a glowing and lengthy tribute in an appendix devoted to the lives of that small band of English cardinals. It is amusing to compare Adam's entry with that of Wolsey (who eventually succeeded to Adam's own title of Cardinal Priest of St Cecilia), who merited no more than a couple of lines. In fact Adam was accorded the longest eulogy of any English cardinal other than Nicholas Brakespeare who, as Hadrian IV, remains the only English Pope in history.

The Cardinal Vanishes

As time passed, Adam's fame receded. Accidents of written history allow some figures from our past to become pre-eminent whilst others fade from view. As a leading prelate from the Catholic era, it was inevitable that less interest would be shown in him in post-Reformation Britain. The same fate befell most of the English cardinals of the mediaeval catholic era. Even Nicholas Brakespeare remains a relatively unknown figure who has attracted little interest from English historians.

Adam's written legacy also faded from view, falling from favour with the collapse in the authority of the Catholic Church. The Reformation killed off interest in his finest work, the Office of the Visitation. It had no place in English worship after the death of Queen Mary I. The service had survived in England up until the early 16th Century, but a work in Latin and one that venerated the Virgin Mary, was out of keeping with the worship and practices of the reformers and puritans. The Defence of St Brigit had resonance in Sweden, where the saint continued to be revered even after the Swedes had lined up alongside Protestant Europe, but a woman who was a Catholic and a foreigner had no special place in the affections of the English.

In the same way, the Defensorium de Ecclesiastice Potestatis became irrelevant and irreverent to Protestants, who placed no value on a book that defended the rights of the Pope and the Church over secular authority. The copies that remained gathered dust in libraries to the point where history had forgotten who had written the book in the first place. Yet it is ironic that by the mid 17th Century, several of Adam's ideas re-emerged in a very different context, forming a foundation for the ideas of the new Protestant religious faithful. As the Puritans sought first to overthrow the royal authority in the shape of Charles I, then move to execute their King, it is impossible not to draw parallels with the Defensorium de Ecclesiastice Potestate. Were the more learned reformers familiar with Adam's lengthy and detailed justifications for the overthrow of the secular power by the righteous power of God and the religious authority of the day? There is an undeniable thread that links the thought process of these most unlikely of bedfellows. Is it not ironic that John Wyclif, the stooge of John of Gaunt and the Plantagenet royal authority, should be recognised as the forerunner of the Protestant rebellion when it was the same ideals and philosophy that the ultra orthodox Adam Easton had expressed that in the end evolved into the intellectual cornerstone for the final triumph of the Puritan revolution in 1649?

To Adam, the idea that a secular power that had failed to rule in accordance with God's will should be replaced, was if anything more natural and instinctive than it was for the embarrassed Parliamentarians of the

English Civil War. After all, many of Cromwell's adherents struggled hard with their consciences before bringing themselves reluctantly to the point of removing Charles from power.

Nor was the Defensorium the only work that Adam had produced that would have been of lasting interest to the reformers. The fact that Adam drew heavily in his work on the Bible for the substance of his argument would have appealed greatly to the Reformers. His reworking of the Old Testament from the original sources was an approach that went to the heart of the principles of the new religion, and would have been admired by Calvin, Luther and Cranmer. Regrettably, Adam's work appears to have vanished in the mid 16th Century. Robert Wakefield, its last known owner, said that it had been stolen.

Gradually Adam the man has also faded from view. By the end of the 18th Century he had been forgotten and his work lost in the archives of the great libraries of the Catholic Church, mostly overseas. Worse still, when Adam's name was mentioned at all by historians it was disparagingly linked to those words "notorious pluralist", a slur on his character still repeated today by those who have not taken the trouble to look in detail at the facts behind his career. It is an injustice that belittles his contribution to the Church and the fact that when he eventually, late in life, acquired wealth, he put it to use in a relatively ascetic court, promoting learning and the virtues of the Benedictine life.

Modern historians have, on the whole, been a little kinder to his memory. It is only thanks to the painstaking research of a few dedicated 20th Century historians, Messrs. Pantin, Macfarlane and Harvey in particular, that Adam has not vanished from our view completely.

Cardinal Adam and Cardinal Thomas

Adam was the last English cardinal for a century to play an active role in the life of the Roman Church and the last but one before the Reformation made the English interest in the papal court and Catholic hierarchy marginal at best. That last pre-Reformation cardinal, Thomas Wolsey, is the only cardinal to have attracted significant attention from English historians. In Thomas and Adam we have two extremes, historical obsession and historical obsolescence, and that is what makes a comparison between the two men so enticing. It is by comparing Wolsey and Easton that we can best appreciate and understand Adam's legacy to English history. Both men were from humble backgrounds in East Anglia, Wolsey from a family of Ipswich butchers and Easton a Norfolk peasant's son; both used the Church to gain an education (Wolsey was also educated at Oxford, at Magdalene College) and then used it as a vehicle for their careers. There the paths diverge.

Adam, the great theologian, used the central power of the papal court to advance his own position and provide an intellectual platform for a papacy working on an international stage. Wolsey, the politician and deal-maker, remained in England making himself indispensable to his sovereign. Here he built a relationship between Church and State that he felt he could manipulate for the benefit of his master. But although Wolsey was a good Catholic, his master was clearly the King. For Adam it was the religious authority of the Pope that ruled supreme.

Wolsey saw himself as a Renaissance churchman. He had the palace, the art and the prestige, but beyond acquiring the wealth and trappings of culture, he contributed little or nothing to the ethos of the Renaissance. Adam was the opposite. Living somewhat before the period we generally associate with the Renaissance, he introduced through his work a spirit of enquiry and investigation, producing a complete reworking of the Old Testament solely to test the basis of scholarly presumption. He was responsible for a rather beautifully constructed service for the Office of the Visitation and for at least two motets. He remained a widely respected intellectual throughout his life, actively promoted Jewish learning and practised tolerance towards Jewish scholars in Europe. Although his outspoken defence of St Brigit may have been rather laboured, the text hardly an example of shining rhetoric or prose, the central espousal of the possibility of women having the same capacity as men to receive inspiration and divine intuition was quite extraordinary for his time. Adam was a man who not only offered intellectual challenges to the society he lived in, but had the force of personality to carry them to fruition. He may have enjoyed fewer of the trappings of a Renaissance princeling than Wolsey, but he contributed much more to the principles that were fundamental to the Renaissance itself.

For all the coincidences, similarities and contrasts, the central issue that dominated the lives of both men turned out to be theological, and to this extent, not surprisingly, the theologian proved to be the better equipped. Adam understood the threat that men like John Wyclif posed to the established power of the Catholic Church, and he knew how to deal with it. At the centre of papal power in Avignon and Rome he used his connections to have Wyclif condemned and his ideas suppressed. He was later able to use his authority as a cardinal to impress upon the English clergy the importance and urgency of following the lead of Rome in stamping out Wyclif and his followers. If his triumph was at least in part due to the Peasants' Revolt, he knew how to use the authority of the Church within the context of the political life of the time.

When faced with his own political crisis, the divorce of Katherine of Aragon, wrapped up as it was in the trappings of religion, Wolsey by contrast did not know how to play the political game with Rome. He could not cajole other cardinals or indeed the Pope into a pragmatic solution because in the end he was not the internationalist he thought he was. His ideas amounted to a parochial stand to serve a parochial interest.

That his crisis proved insoluble was of course because an alternative religion offered an alternative solution, and in that Wolsey can only blame himself. This was not his territory, he was not a theologian and he did not have the intellectual muscle or the philosophical base from which to fight back when the crisis engulfed him. He could not deal with the religious issue because, unlike Adam, he had not seen the significance of the threat that it posed. He did not see the crisis coming. He failed to understand the impact that the reformed religion might have on England and he also failed to combine political and religious expediency in the 1520s to remove the threat when it might still have been removed.

If Adam had failed in the same way, and perhaps if Edward III had not been senile, Wolsey might well have grown up in a Protestant England, not a Catholic one. Wolsey's failure to deal with the growth of the reformed religion, to some extent, has served to diminish our understanding of the significance of Adam's success in dealing with the same issue a century and a half earlier. It has helped to hide Adam's own importance. The problem inherent in Adam's greatest achievement was that nothing happened where something might have done. That is always a tough challenge for historians to assess.

Our modern obsession with the Tudors and the Reformation has raised Wolsey's stock and Adam, for all his achievements, was a European cleric and a Catholic dignitary first and foremost. His impact on English history has been forgotten not least because having achieved the highest rank and influence he chose to stay in Rome at the centre of the international affairs of his time rather than return to spend any time in the country of his birth. That does not make the lack of interest in his life and work any more excusable.

The supreme irony is that whereas Adam's role in the international Church brought him into conflict with both Edward III and Richard II, he ended up in debt for his life to King Richard. Wolsey, on the other hand, the faithful servant of Henry VIII, died on his way to a sentence of death pronounced by his master. Cardinal Thomas passed away at Leicester Abbey, half way through the journey from Sheffield, where he had been arrested, to the Tower of London, where Henry had planned for his demise. And it is in death that the contrast between the two men is most poignant. Wolsey, in character, had designed a grand tomb for himself with a black marble sarcophagus and fine bronze statuary. The failure of his policy and the defeat of his political designs ensured that he was destined to use neither.

The Cardinal's fall from power was absolute. He was buried in Leicester Abbey without any monument or great ceremony. The bronzes that had been kept at Windsor were melted down and sold during the time of the Commonwealth and the sarcophagus was used for a different kind of hero from a very different era, providing the finishing touch on Admiral Lord Nelson's tomb in St Paul's.

Adam died in Rome at the height of his power and success. He received a burial on a grand scale in one of the finest Roman monumental tombs of his age. Safely beyond the long reach of the English reformers, it can still be found in a dark corner of St Cecilia in Trastavere. The canopy and supports have long since been removed, but this was done in the name of the Italian sense of form and architectural innovation, rather than out of any sense of revisionist malevolence. Yet even amongst the murky shadows on the inside of the portico, the tomb is still a striking monument. We can imagine the finery of the original design with its canopy and posts, painted no doubt in the fashion of the age.

I often visit the tomb when I am lucky enough to be in Rome. There is something strangely reassuring in the expression of the marble effigy, but it also has the ambiguity of the Mona Lisa. After all the trials and tribulations of life, here is Adam, long forgotten but at peace. An Englishman buried at the heart of the Catholic Church in Rome, an English monk who lived a full life, defying us to ask why he is here. We see a jowly gaze over slightly pursed lips. His furrowed brow contrasts with serenely closed eyes, contradictory to the end. I am sure he is suppressing a grin.

Appendix I
DATING ADAM

The early part of Adam's life is difficult to piece together, and his date of birth is particularly hard to place. The first point of certainty that we have is the date when he incepted as a Doctor at Oxford, 1365. We also know that for seven years between 1356 and 1363 he was back in Norwich working for the suppression of the Friars. Added to this we know the following:

- Novice monks did not usually join a monastery until they were in their early teens.
- Monks were supposed to take between six and 10 years' education in their monastery before going on to Oxford.
- A degree in the Arts was expected to take eight years and a further degree in Theology seven years.
- To gain a Doctorate at the end of that process was meant to take a final two years.

If we assume that Adam had the minimum six years of education before going on to Oxford, he should have spent 23 years on his education, on top of which we know he was in Norwich taking a break from his university course for seven years. If that education started as soon as he entered St Leonard's then he would have joined the monastery in 1335.

As, by Adam's own admission, he was "40 years or more" by 1379, he must have been born somewhere between 1339 and 1329. There are only three possibilities that we can use to explain the time elapsed in the different stages of Adam's early life:

- Adam did not have a good grasp on his true age.
- He joined the monastery as a child.
- He was a bright pupil who went through the monastic system much faster than his contemporaries.

The more one looks at the logic, the more likely it seems that at least two of these conclusions are correct. If Adam did not correctly remember his birth date and he was indeed born in 1325, he would still have been very young when he entered the monastery. We have already assumed that he had the minimal number of years of education in his monastery before going on to Oxford; even so it would have been unusual to admit him to a monastery before he was in his teens, and that suggests that he would have gone to St Leonard's around 1340 and to Oxford in 1346. If he then graduated in 1365 after a seven-year break, he would still have undertaken his studies at Oxford three years under the norm.

The other possibility is that Adam entered the monastery as a child, possibly as an orphan. If we take Adam at his word and suggest he was born in 1330 or later, he could have been taken into St Leonard's by, say, 1332 but could hardly have started his education until he was five or six, and allowing for a further six years of teaching, he could have gone to Oxford as a 12-year-old in, say, 1342. However, the prospect of a boy so young at Oxford in the early days of the University is unlikely. It would certainly have excited comment from contempories. In these circumstances it seems more likely that Adam would have received a longer education at St Leonard's and Norwich, perhaps entering Oxford in his later teens. Even so, given a birth date of 1330, this still places Adam as a new student in Oxford between 1346 and 1348.

Appendix II
TOPONYMS

If you pick up a copy of your local telephone directory and thumb through the pages looking at the list of surnames, you can be reasonably confident that two types of name will predominate: the names of jobs and the names of places. Surnames were not commonplace in the early mediaeval period and it was only by the 14th Century that they started to be used more frequently. The tendency to develop and use second names was a natural consequence of the growth in size of communities. The more people there were in a village, the more Alans and Adams rubbed shoulders with each other, so the need to distinguish between them became more important. If for no other reason, it helped when collecting taxes and in identifying one complainant from another at the manor court. By the 14th Century it had become normal for villagers to have a surname in regular use, and this is clear from both the manorial court records and the frequent tax rolls of the period.

For the majority of people in mediaeval England, travel of any kind was not an option. Three hundred years after the Norman Conquest it was still common for people to live and die in the same village in which they had been born. Holidays, pensions and leisure time are relatively modern ideas; they were as irrelevant to the struggle to survive as the need to grow a decent crop in land the farmer knew and understood was essential.

If you did venture beyond your own community, it was unusual enough to attract attention. So whilst the local blacksmith might be known as Adam the Smith, if he came from a neighbouring village he was more likely to be known as Adam from Somersham. This was even more likely if the local village was large enough to support two smithies. However, as travel was unusual, it was more common in village communities to identify a person by their trade. Hence the large numbers of smiths, millers, coopers and the like that we find in the phone directory.

The importance of place names is sometime hidden by the waxing and waning of the communities themselves. Whereas you might know a Mr Scarborough or a Mrs Wigan, many names derived from places are less obvious simply because the villages that gave rise to the name have withered away and are now relatively small and obscure. For instance, people with as diverse a background as Alan Titchmarsh, John Prescott and Paul Scholes all have names that have been derived from places.

In a large economic community such as a monastery the problem of identifying one brother from another was exacerbated by the fact that it was hard to distinguish the monks by the tasks they did. Many of these tasks were clerical rather than artisanal. To make matters worse, the tasks of the monks would vary from year to year, and there was therefore little point in giving a monk a name that referred to a specific task in the monastery. It might be easy to distinguish in the village community between the miller, the smith and the baker, but harder to find a specific title for a monk. In his work at the monastery he might be engaged, quite possibly at the same time, in copying documents, working for the cellarer or the almoner or acting as an estate manager.

Nonetheless as many monasteries boasted a population as large and often much larger than that of an average village, there was a need to identify one brother from another. The monks also had something in common with each other that was still rare in the villages. They had all travelled from somewhere else in order to join the monastic community. It is unsurprising then that it became commonplace to name a monk by reference to his village or town of origin. By the time of Adam Easton the use of place names had become common in English monastic houses. These names that are derived from places we call toponyms.

Appendix III
TRANSCRIPTIONS FROM SOURCE DOCUMENTS

1. The Office of the Visitation of the Blessed Virgin

Transcribed from Ottobone Lat 676 ff 355-359 in the Vatican Library
Ottobone Lat 676 ff 355-359
Folio 355 r

Incipit officium visitationis beate Marie Virginis ad Helysabet.
Approbatus per dominum Bonifacium papam nonum, et cantatus iuxta
cantum beati Francisci.

In primus Vesperis

Antiphona

A ccedunt laudes virginis
Admirande indaginis
Noviter promulgate
En, visitat Elizabeth
Maria mater ipsamet
Celica probitate

D ivo repletur munere
Maria, sine murmure
Cum filium concepit,
Surrexit ab oraculo
Statim in montis calculo
Abiit et profecit

A ccendit ardor spiritus
Mariam tangens celitus
De Nazareth migrando,
Mox ad montana transtulit,
Ubi tumulti caruit
Superna degustando.

M onstrans culmen dulcedinis
Maria sui sanguinis
Elizabeth salutat
Stantem in domo proximi
Propinqua templo Domini
Devote subministrat.

C arisima sancti spiritus
Diffudit se divinitus
In puerum, cum sensit
Conceptum salutiferum
Marie sibi ovium
Elizabeth consensit.

Capitulum
Ego mater pulcre dilectonis et timoris et magnitudinis et sancte spiritu. In me omnis gratia vie et veritatis. In me omnis spes vite et virtutis. (Ecclesiasticus XXIV)

Hymnus
1 In Mariam
Vite viam
Matrem veram viventium
(folio 355v)
Pie venit
Qui redemit
Peccata delinquentium.

2 Gressum cepit
Cum concepit
Maria multum properans
Visitavit
Comfortavit
Elizabeth compatiens.

3. Salutatur
Inflammatur
Elizabeth et filius
Inaudita
Fiunt ita
De dono sancti spiritus.

4. Impregnata
Gravidata
Fit mater olim sterilis;
Infans datus
Nondum natus
Exultat Christo iubilis.

5. Servit maior
Gaudet minor
Maria fert solatium
Visitatis
Preparatis
Ad spiritum propheticum.

6. Precursorem
Et doctorem
Maria plebi indicat
Qui rectorem
Purgatorem
Digito mundo nuntiat.

7. Leva gregem
Duc ad regem
Maria cunctos visitans,
Ut salvetur
Et letetur
Cum tu sis mater medians
Amen.

Responsario
V speciosa tua et pulchre tua
R Intentionem prospere

Ad Magnificat
Antiphone
Acceleratur ratio
In puero non dum nato
Instinctu sacri neumatis
Divinitas sibi dato
Novit presentem Dominum
In virgine clam latentem
Adoravit servulum venientem.

Oratio
Omnipotens sempiterne Deus qui ex habundantia caritatis beatam Mariam tuo filio ad salutationem Elizabeth inspirasti, presta quesimus, ut per eius visitationem donis celestibus repleamur, et ab omnibus adversitatibus eruamur id eundem.

Ad Matutinum
Invitatorium
Reginam celi Mariam concorditer adoremus

299

Que visitans Elizabeth spem
contulit ut laudemus.
Pro venit

O Christi mater celica
Fons vivus fluens gratia
Lux pellens cuncta scismata
Maria, Deo proxima.

Ex motu veri luminis
Transivit in monticulis
Virgo iuvare vetulam
De precursore gravidam.

Mater venit de Nazareth
Ut salutet Elizabeth (folio 356r)
Replentur dono spiritus
Anus et eius filius.

Elizabeth complacuit
Quod mater Dei affluit
Infans gaudet in utero
Presente Christo Domino.

Marie visitatio
Exemplum dat, pro bravio
Quod sit parata omnibus
Ipsam pie querentibus

Trinitatis clementia
Cuncta lavet facinora
Per matris Christi merita
Nos ducat ad celestia.

Amen.

In Primo Nocturno

Antiphona
De celo velud radius
Descendens sacer spiritus
Elizabeth intravit,
Mox benedictam virginem
Sanctitatis propaginem
Prophetice clamavit.

Psalmus de sancta Maria

Antiphona
Inter turmas femineas
Et sanctarum ex cubias
Maria collaudatur
Propter fructum, qui queritur.
Quo iure mundus emitur
Et plene visitatur.

Antiphona
Vocat hanc matrem nomine
Domini primo famine
Elizabeth in superna
Quod fuit clausum aliis
In velatis misteriis
Notitia interna.

Lectio Prima
Beatissima virgo Dei mater a suis primordiis modo consacrata. Propter beneficia eius in audita exhibita populo invocanti omnes in necessitate constituti adeam confugiunt tam quod ad singulare remedium. Ubi humanum subsidium non sufficiens requisitum. Disponit namquis omnia inferiora sua sapientia

providentia industria et gratia pro pulsata virgine gubernatrix seculi et terrene potentie. Maria virgo mater miserie et in(m)petrarix venie io maria virgo mater militantis ecclesie in maria virgo advocata seculi io maria.

Responsoria
R: Surgens Maria gravida
Migravit per cacumina
In civitatem Iude
Intravit domum propere
Zacharie cum opere
Salutis consobrine

V: Ut audivit Elizabeth
Salutes mox de Nazareth
Exclamat mirative.

Lectio II

Huius rei consideratione (folio 356r) Urbanus romanus pontifex sextus dure ferens materiam scismatis occurrentem perpendensque animo perspicaci, quod beata Virgo sit pertissima discrepantium animorum, et visitatrix diligentissima errantium singulorum, pro gratia extinctionis scismatis impetranda pie statuit, quia licet festum visitationis Marie de Elizabeth illo tempore post annuntiationem dominicam debuerit celebrari, quo ipsam sanctam Elizabeth visitavit propter maximas virtutes in ibi operatas.

Responsoria
R: dixit verba prophetica
Elizabeth celicola
De Virgine Maria
Beata est, que credidit
In hac fient, que didicit
A deo mente pia.

V: Venit ex te sanctissimus
Vocatus Dei filius
Sicut predixit angelus
Sue matri in via.

Lectio III
Quia tamen illo tempore ecclesie circa officium quadragesimale ante passionem Christi specialiter occupatur, ne tanti officii pretermitatur ad laudem et gloriam visitationis virginis gloriose, idem Urbanus pie statuit institutionis prefati festi memoriam in crastinum octavum Iohannis Baptiste cum octavis sequentibus de festo visitationis Marie a cunctis fidelibus celebrari.

Responsoria
R: Elizabeth congratulans
Profunde se humilans
In adventu Messie.
Unde ait, condeceat,
Quod mater Dei veniat
Ad me cum plausu vie?

V: En, felix salutatio
Duplata exultatio
Dabantur in sophia.

In Secundo Nocturna
Antiphone
Non fuit Christus oneri

Nec gravis moles pueri
Visceribus matris digne,
Sed ignara de pondere
Cum corporali robore
Transiliit benigne.

Antiphona
Transivit in itinere
Mariam multum propere
Monticulos scandendo
Evitavit lasciviam
Propter morum constantiam
Colloquia spernendo.

Antiphona
Longam viam pertransiit
Maria montes circuit
Hilaris laborando
Honores mundi respuit
(folio 357r)
Devotionem tenuit
Celica meditando

Lectio IV
Ut autem omnis fidelium
multitudo ad memoriam profate
visitationis marie de helisabet
artibus et devotibus excitetur. Voluit
idem romanus pontifex urbanus
sextus ut omnibus vero confessis et
contritis idem festum visitationis
marie celebrantibus cum octavis.
Loco distributionum materialium in
ecclesiis sicius consuetis de thesauro
spirituale ecclesie nunc indulgentia
sicut in festo corporis christi futuris
temporibus ibi effectualiter
largirentur.

Responsoria
R: Maria parens filio
Plangens querit deperditos

In scalere mortali
Clamans clamat, ut relevet
Manum ponit, ut sublevet
Ne pena ruant mali.
 V: Elizabeth quesierat
Iohannem doctum noverat
De vita supernaturali.

Lectio V
Cum Gabriel angelus Marie
nunciavit quod in venit gratiam
apud deum et quod de ea
conciperetur filius de ad salutem
omnium populorum quoddam cito
ipsa credidit statim concepitur in
utero filium dei. Et per gracias
exhibitas de tanto beneficio sibi
sancto ex magna caritate et pietate.
Studuit suam cognatam helizabet
iam sex mensibus gravidam in
Hierosolyma salutare et sibi compati
et servire. Unam deorum de eadem.
Exurgens maria abiit in montana
cum festinacione in civitatem Iudee
et intravit domus Zacharie et
salutavit helizabeth.

Responsoria
R: rosa de spinis prodiit
Virga de Iesse floruit
Maria visitavit
Vis odoris diffunditur
Domus tota perfunditur
Gratia cum intravit

V: Miranda salutatio
Fit plebi gratulatio
Que fructum expectavit.

Lectio VI
Abiit enim in montana Maria cum

festinacione que ab angelo in itinere feliciter ducta fuit spiritus sancti in flammatione. Is abruta montium ducebat (folio 357v) que eiusdem spiritus motione suaviter fuerat agitata. Beatam graciam mariam confidens ylariter migravit super cacumina sic passer in asperitate itineris congaudebat.

Responsoria
R: Stella sub nube tegitur
Maria mundo premitur
Rutilans in splendore,
Elizabeth perducitur
Ad solamen, lux spargitur
Roborans in vigore.

V: Luna soli coniungitur
Elizabeth devolvitur
Estuans in amore.

In Tercio Nocturna

Antiphona
Tunc ad sermonem virginis
Dabatur donum flamminis
Matri simul et proli
Hic gaudebat in utero
Hec prophetat de puero
Et de regina poli.

Antiphona
Adest mira credulitas
Ac virginis fecunditas
Per exemplum monstratum
Concepit prius sterilis
Que vox est impossibilis
Nisi per verbum datum.

Antiphona
Fit nature propinquus

Quod sterili fit filius
Quam virgo fiat pregnans,
Sed nichil impossibile
Deo nec intractabile
Per verbum suum dictans.

Secundam Lucam I 39-40
In illo tempore exsurgens Maria abiit in montana cum festinatione in civitatem Iuda. Et intravit domum Zacharie et salutavit Elizabeth. Et reliqua.

Lectio VII
Morale est omnibus ut que fidem exigunt fidem astruant. Et ideo angelus cum abscondita nunciaret ut fides astrueretur. Exemplo senioris feminae sterilis quam virginis mariae conceptum nunciavit ut possibile deo esse quod enim placuerit assereret.

Responsoria
R: Occasum virgo nesciit
Velut lux mundi profluit
De summo fundens lumen
Elizabeth applicauit
Devotas sibi attrahit
De celo pandens numen.

V Spiritus capit symbola
Celestibus conformia
Tanquam aquarum flumen

Lectio VIII
Ubi audivit hoc Maria non quia incredula de (folio 358r) oraculo nec qui in certa denuntio. Nec qui dubitans de exemplum sed quia lecta pro noto religiosas officio. Festina pro gaudio in montana perexit

(prorexit). Duo enim inde plena deo. Nisi ad superiora virgo cum festinatione conscendere nescit tarda molimina. Spiritus sancti gratiam.

Responsoria
R: Thronum lucis prospexerat
Que ut aurora fulxerat
Sole mane splendente
Elizabeth ubi vidit
Verba que palam protulit
Speculo suadente

V: In Marie presentia
Plura patent latentia
Elizabeth dicente.

Lectio IX
Discite et vos mulieres sancte sedulitatem quam pregnantibus de beatis exhibere cognatis mariam
que anus sola in intimissa
penetralibus versabatur non
a publico pudor virginitatis.
Non studio asperitas montium. Non ab officio prolixitas itineris retardavit.
In montana virgo cum festitione officii memor iniurie immemor.
Affectu vigente non sexu relicta perrexit in domo.

Responsoria
Elizabeth ex opere
Signorum dat pro pignore
Mariam invocare,
Quam gratia contraxerat
Et pietas commoverat
Vetulum visitare.

V: Nullus diffidat hodie
Ad Mariam confluere
Sibique supplicare.

Quam.
Ad Laudes et per Horas

Antiphona
Sacra dedit eloquia
Maria responsoria
Elizabeth laudanti,
Clamavit Deo canticum
Magnificando Dominum
De sursum bona danti.

Psalmus
Dominus regnavit, (psalmus 92, 99, 62)

Antiphona
Tunc exultavit animus
Cum ipsius fit filius
Angelo nuntiante
Ancilla Dei credidit
Confestim verbum genuit
Maria supplicante.

Responsario
Vera humiliatio
Fuit Christi conceptio
Deo respiciente
Ex hoc laudabunt singuli
Mariam matrem seculi
Ipsamet (folio 238v) sic dicente.

Antiphona
Magna perfecit Dominus
In Marie virtutibus
Deum concipiendo,
Fit mater plena gratie
Et impetrarix venie
Omnibus miserando.

Antiphona
Maria tribus mensibus
Quasi stetit laboribus
Elizabeth subdendo

304

Conferebat de angelo
Et verborum mysterio
Que protulit salutando

Mutum audivit eloqui
Et prophetias Domini
De Christo declarando.
Plura vidit de puero
Mirabili ab utero
Precursorem vocando.

Facta post reverentia
Reversa est ad propria
Maria contemplando.

Capitulum
Ego mater pulchre

Hymnus
De sacro tabernaculo
Virtutum flos egreditur
In montis diverticulo
Odor Marie spargitur.

Ex caritatis germine
Elizabeth adpropriat
Et pietatis culmine
Ipsam devote visitat

Salutat servam domina
Hec matrem Christi nominat
Confertur ingens gratia
Matrem et prolem satiat

En, Christi incarnatio
Per nondum natum panditur
Hunc adorat cum gaudio
Qui ventre matris clauditur

Clamat senex in iubilo
Videns Marie gloriam
Beata credens angelo

Fuisti rem veridicam.

Hic stupet rerum regula
Nature mutans ordinem
Ubi fiunt miracula
Per solum celi principem.

Presta virgo piisima
Sufficiens auxilium
Cum sis mater largissima
Nos visites in seculum
Amen

V: Diffusa est gratia
R: Proptea

Ad Benedictus

Antiphona

Adiutrix visitatio
Et frequens ministratio
Elizabeth oblata
Mariam dat propitiam
Ad impetrandum gratiam
Cum fuerit vocata.

Nam mater est ecclesie
Fluctuantis navicule
Subditos gubernando
Promptos suo regimini
Dirigentis sue flamini
Deinde visitando.

Oratio ut supra

Ad iii Capitulum
Ego mater pulcre

Ad iv Capitulum
Surge, propera, amica mea,
columba mea, et veni. Iam enim
yems transiit, ymber abiit, et

recessit. Flores apparuerunt in terra nostra, tempus putationis advenit.

Ad ix Capitulum

Surge, propera amica mea, speciosa mea, et veni. Columba mea in foraminibus petre, in caverna macerie, ostende mihi faciem tuam. Sonet vox tua in auribus meis. Vox enim tua dulcis, et facies tua decora.

In Secundis Vespris

Antiphona

Sacra dedit eloquia
Maria responsoria
Elizabeth laudanti
Clamavit Deo canticum
Magnificando Dominum
De sursum bona danti (cum reliquis psalmis de sancta Maria)

Capitulum
Ego mater pulchre
In Primis vespris

Ad Magnificat

Antiphone
Jesu, redemptor optime
Ad Mariam nos imprime
Ut mundi advocatam
Pari forma nos visitet
Sicut fecit Elizabeth
Per summam pietatem
Mores et actus dirigat
Et ad celos alliciat
Per gratiam collatam.

Oratio ut supra.

2. One of Adam Easton's debates at Oxford

Questione Estone et Responsio Redeclif.
Worcester Cathedral MS F65 folio 20v

Utrum Adam ex lege status innocencie visionem immediatam Dei essencie habuerunt sicut natura angelica optinebat.

Quod sic arguitur tripliciter, et sic primo:

Adam in statu innocenie perfectus erat omni cognicione naturaliter sicut natura angelica, ergo in sua propria cognicione naturali non discurrebat a noto ad ignotum, et per consequens cum Adam pro eodem statu divinam essenciam naturaliter cognovit, sicut natura angelica, sequiter quod ipsam non cognovit per discersum, nec per speciem aliquam creature, ergo per visionem immediatem.

Confirmatur per magistrum Sentenciarum, IV, dist.I, capitulo V, dicentam quod homo qui ante peccatum sine medio Deum videbat, per peccatum adeo debuit ut nequeat divina capere nisi sensibilibus excitatus.

Secundo sic: Adam in statu innocencie tantum erat dispositus ad videndam divinam essenciam sicut anima eiusdem si fuisset separata, et ratione peccati nullatenus impedita.

Sed si anima eiusdem fuisset separata et ratione peccati nullatenus impedita habuisset visionem immediatem divine essencie sicut natura angelica optinebat, ergo questio.

Patet consequencia et maior, quia per materiam non erat intellectiva eius impedita plusquam fuisset si a materia esset separata.

Minor eciam videtur patere quia tunc fuisset approximatio sufficiens potentie naturalis ad suum obiectum nullatenus impedite, ergo veritas minoris.

Tercio sic ad idem: Cognicio Adam in statu innocencie quoad Deum fuisset eque perfecta sicut dileccio eiusdem, sed dileccio eiusdem erat ita perfecta quod terminabatur immediate ad divinam essenciam ergo et cognicio.

Ad oppositum arguitur sic:

Per nullam visionem quam habuit Adam in statu innocencie ponebatur extra statum vie, sed visio immediata divine essencie ponit hominem extra statum vie, ergo oppositum questionis, patet eciam per Augustinum Primo "De Trinitate" versus finem, ubi ponit quod visio Dei per essenciam est tota merces sanctorum; ex quibus videtur oppositum .

Respondendo ad istam questionem difficilem et subtilem suppono quod totum hoc

"visionem immediatam divine essencie" supponat in proposita questione "pro eiusdem essencia est intuitu faciali", quo supposito sit hec conclusio prima:

Adam ex lege status innocencie divine essencie immediatam visionem non habuit, sicut nec ante suum casum natura angelica optinebat.

Hec conclusio suadetur sic:

Omnis visio immediata divine essencie est eiusdem intuitus facialis qui solis iustis promittitur premium habendum in patria subiectivum. Sed nec natura angelica ante casum, nec natura humana ex lege status innocencie, fuit in patria beatifice premiata ergo conclusio.

Ista consequencia est bona et maior quoad primam eius partem patet ex prius supposito; et quoad secundum eius partem patet per idem dictum Augustini Primo "De Trinitate" ; et minor principalis patet per Hugonem "De Sacrimentis" libro primo, parte Sexta, capitulo XXV.

Secunda conclosio est hec: Adam ex lege status innocencie vidit intuitive essenciam creatoris.

Suadetur hec conclusio sic: Adam ex lege status innocencie vidit divinam essenciam et non solum abstractive, ergo intuitive.

Ista consequencia est bona, et totum antecedens patet ex processu Hugonis "De Sacrimentis", libro primo, parte Sexta capitulo XIV.

Tercia conclusio est hec: Tam natura angelica quam humana ante peccatum vidit intuitive divinam essenciam euis specie propria mediante.

Hec conclusion suadetur sic: Tam natura angelica quam humana ante peccatum vidit intuitive divinam essenciam et non per clarum intuitum facialem, ergo conclusio.

Ista consequencia est bona et minor quoad natura angelicam patet ex processu biblia Augustini questio super "Genesim ad litteram" capitulo XXXI, usque ad finem libri; et quoad naturam humanam patet ex probacione conclusionis.

Secunde, et minor principalis patet ex conclusione prima.

Quarta conclusio est hec: Anima intellectiva a corpore separata, et in statu innocencie constituta intuitive videret divinam essenciam mediante sibi specie concreata.

Hec conclusio suadetur sic: Anima intellectiva a corpore separata, et in statu innocencie constituta, haberet tam perfectam intuitionem divine essencie, quam de facto habuit primus parens ex lege status innocencie, et non haberet perfecciorem divine essencie intuitionem, quam habuit natura angelica ante casum, ergo conclusio.

Consequencia patet et totum antecedens.

Quinta conclusio est hec et ultima: Illius actus, quo Adam ex lege status innocencie Deum dilexit, erat species aliqua terminans suum obiectum.

Hec conclusio suadetur sic: Illius actus, quo Adam ex lege status innocencie vidit Deum, erat species aliqua terminans suum obiectum, ergo conclusio.

Consequencia patet quia omnis dileccio et ab ea presupposita intelleccio ad idem obiectum terminantur; et obiectam antecedens patet et tercia conclusione, et ex prima istarum conclusionum patet oppositum questionis et per alias quattor conclusiones.

Ad omnia argumenta difficilia et eorum materias licet exiliter respondetur preter quam ad auctoritatem Magistri Sentenciae allegatam, cuius intellectus talis est quod homo ante peccatum sine discursu mediante Deum videbat, qui intellectus nequaquam obviat dictis meis, hec sit racio etc.

3. The testimony of Cardinal Agrifolio to the delegation of the Kingdom of Aragon

(Armarium LIV volume 16)

Ad primum interrogatorium respondit dictus Cardinalis de Agrifolio se habere notum dictum Franciscum Petri qui erat familiaris suus, non tamen commensalis, sed non recordatur dictus dominis cardinalis predicta verba unquam dixisse. Ymmo tenet firmiter non dixisse nec etiam ipse consuevit nec alii domini cardinales consueverant aliqua verba detractiva ali cui domini cardinali publicare seu dicere esto quod essent vera.

Ad secundum interrogatorium respondit quod contenta in dicto interrogatorio sunt totaliter falsa et mendosa nec de tota illa die qua dominis cardinales exiverunt conclave ipse dom cardinalis vidit dictum Franciscum Petrum.

Ad tertium interrogatorium respondit se non recordari predicta dixisse nec credere ea dixisse nec etiam dictus Franciscus Petri qui ut predicitur non erat familiaris commensalis suus, positus fuerat in rotulo suo quod scriverit dictus ipse cardinalis nec dictus rotulus fuit oblatus usquequo dictus dominis cardinalis fuit in Anagnia nec postea vidit ipse dominum dictum Franciscum nec dictum rotulum.

Ad quartum interrogatorium respondit in sua conscientia quod ante ingressum conclavis non dixit nec dici fecit verbum aliquid de eligendo predictum dominus Barensis vel aliquem alium dicto dominus sct. Petri nec alicui alii nisi prout in depositione per eum tradita superius continetur nec etiam ipse unquam fuit in domo dominus sct. Petri.

Ad quintum interrogatorium respondit quod nunquam ipse procuravit quod dictus scutifer sororius suus qui vocabatur Bertrandus de Veyraco mitteretur ad imperatorem pro nunciando sibi electionem dicti dominus Verum est tamen quod tempore felicis recordationis dominus Gregorii nuncii imperatoris pro sequebantur in curia Romana confirmationem fieri de electione in regem Romanorum facta de filio imperatoris qui erat rex

Bohemie et causa ista commissa fuerat per dominus Gregorium ipsi dominus de Agrifolio et quia tempore mortis dicti dominus Gregorii dicta confirmation nundum facta erat licet causa esset conclusa et dictus dominus Gregorius iam se disponeret ad ipsam confirmationem fiendem et ut ipse dominus de Agrifolio audiverat suggestum fuerat imperatori quod ipse dominus de Agrifolio fuerat in culpa de nimia tarda dicte confirmationis ipse dominus procuravit sociare dictum Bertrandum tanquam sibi fidum cuidam milita Neapolitano qui mandato Bertrandus portabat nova dicte electionis ad dictum imperatorem et scripsit ipse dominus unam litteram imperatori informando eum de diligentia et directione quas ipse dominus adhibuerat circa expeditionem confirmationis predicte committendo credentiam circa informationem predictam dicto Bertrando de Veyraco et mandavit ipsi Bertrando quod si absque dicto milite Neapolitano loqui posset secrete cum imperatore informaret eum de impressione quo dominis cardinalibus facta fuerat in electione dicti Barensis. Sed ex relatu dicti Bertrandi quam postea habuit dictus miles Neapolitanus scrivit tantum facere quod ipse Bertrandus dicto imperatori non potuit loqui ad partem nec eum informare de impressione predicta.

Ad sextum interrogatorium respondit dictus dominis cardinalis quod ipse bene cognoscenat dictum Christoforum Gallina sed quod predicta verba nunquam dixit.

Ad septimum interrogatorium respondit quod ipse bene cognoscebat dictum magistrum Adam qui erat satis sibi familiaris sed quod nunquam dixit dicta verba nec recordatur etiam ipsum introduxisse ad dominus Barensiensis pro faciendo sibi reverentiam tamen si fecit fecit ad eiusdem magistri instantiam et ut dixit non est verum quod ipse retinuerit dictum magistrum ad dormiendum in domo sua quia sibi nunquam fuerit consuetum ad dormiendum in domo sua aliquos retinere.

Ad octavum interrogatorium respondit se nunquam dixisse verba predicta dicto magistro Adam nec alicui alii addens eciam quod falsissimum est quod ordinatum fuerit illo tempore in Anglia Cardinales Gallicos non recipere ibi sua beneficia nam ipse dominus recipiebat in Anglia tunc pacifice et quiete de beneficiis que ibi habebat tria milia florenorum annuatim vel circa et dominus Pictavensis circa duo milia et dominus Albanensis circa quinque milia et dominus Ursinis circa duo milia et dominus sct. Eustachii magnam pecunie quantitatem et quam plures alii cardinalis Gallici.

Ad nonum interrogatorium respondit quo ad ambaxiatam dicti Bertrandi de Veyraco ut superam in quinto interrogario quo ad litteras de quibus fit mentio respondit se in conscientia sua nunquam de Anagnia nec de Roma scripsisse ratione predicta episcopis Alamanie nec ut dixit habebat in totam Alamaniam notum aliquem prelatum nisi dominis Maguntinensem qui tunc erat remotus ab imperatore bene per xx dietas.

Ad decimum interrogatorium respondit quod in fide et conscientia sua ipse nunquam dixit episcopo Viterbiensi verba predicta ymmo sunt falsissima et mendosa.

4. Boniface IX grants a petition whereby Adam will be given the post of canon and prebend of St John in Rabhia in the Portuguese diocese of Lamego

Motu proprio providemus dilecto filo Ade tit sancta Cecilie presbytero cardinalis de parochiali ecclesia sancti Johannis de Rabhia Lamencensis dioceses ac canonicatu et prebenda secularis et collegiate ecclesie sancti Martini de Cedoseta Portugalensis diocesis vacantibus ex eo et pro eo quod Nunius Martini qui dicta benefice obtinebat ordinem Cisterciensem et professus etiam si per promationem de eo per non factam ad monasterium sancti Johannis de Tarauca dicti ordinis vacant non obstante quod dicta parrochialis ecclesia sit de iure ptronatus Iaicorum, quorum omnium fructus centum quinquaginta librarium Turonensium parvorem communi extimatione valorem annum non excedunt. Cum non obstantis et clausulis oportunis. Fiat motu proprio et dispensamus. Sine alia lectione.

Datum Rome apud Sanctum Petrum tertio decimo Kalendas Octobris anno quinto.

Archivo Segreto Vaticano, Reg Suppl 104A, folio 77v

5. Boniface IX grants a petition on behalf of one of Adam's familiars, Gerard Everard

Gerardo Everardi, consideratione Ade, tituli sancti Cecilie presbyteri cardinalis, pro familiari, continuo commensali suo supplicantis, conferi altare sine curia s.s. cruccis et Katherine situm in ecclesia de Foren, Leodiensis dioc. vi marca argen. Vacans per obitum apud sedem Danielis Thome de Ruttis. Cum clausula anteferri. Vite ac morum. Datum Rome apud Sanctum Petrum nones februarii anno quinto.

Archivo Segreto Vaticano, Reg Lat 31 folio 232v

6. Boniface IX grants Adam a benefice on the death of one of his familiars

Dignetur sanctitas vestra devote creature vestre Ade, tituli sancta Cecilie presbytero cardinali motu proprio de canonicatu et prebenda ecclesia sancti Severini Coloniensis nec non parrochiali ecclesie in Hasselt Leodiensis diocese quorum fructus trigintaquinque marcarum argenti valorem annum non execdunt vacantibus per mortem Theoderic Bukelken familiaris sui continuis commensalis in romana curia defuncti etiam si alias quovismodo aut ex alterius cuiuscumque persona vaet , eidem dignemini misericordia providere. Cum clausulis et non obstantibus ut in forma ac dispensatione cum eodem de gratia speciali. Fiat per datum Rome apud Sanctum Petrum nonas Octobris vicesima prima hora anno quinto.

Archivo Segreto Vaticano, Reg Suppl 104A folio 174v

7. Adam is granted the right for his familiars to be absent from their benefices, thereby allowing them to serve at his court

Dignetur sanctitas vestra quod concedere devote creature videre Adam titulo sancta Cecilie presbytero cardinali privilegium consuetum dar cardinalibus videlicet quod familiares sui possunt praecipere fructus beneficiorum suorum et gaudere eisdem in absentia eorundem cum ac aliis non obstantis et clausulis oportunis ut informa. Fiat per sine alia lectione. Fiat per datum apud Rome apud Sancti Petrum Tertio decimo kalendas Octobris anno quinto.

Archivo Segreto Vaticano, Reg Suppl 104A, folio 77v

8. A bill in favour of Simon Langham, drawn on the banker Frauncis de Kyto, which allows him to draw in Avignon on money collected in England

Mons. le cardinal de Canterbury le iiij jour de mai prochaine, un mille ccc lxxv sousdite. Florenis viii mille d'or de chambre les queux sont per vue arest dmz acompt fait oneses lui ceste mesme de mes livres a moi de mesme et de mes compaignons de brugges et dantregent resten per lui en plusores precelles. Et de tout nous avons paie forspris dite viii mille florenis ensescriptes. Les queux permettonis de bailer a lui paier a lui totew sa volimite et comandement et per contentement de lui nous lui sateonis cest escript du manu de moi ffraunceys de kyto facto de la dite compaignie de mettonie notre seal de signe de la dite compaingnie.

Westminster Abbey Muniments collection, WAM9227

9. An extract from the Defensorius Ecclesiastice Potestatis dealing with the role of cardinals (fo 110v)

Rex
Admiror quod statum cardinalum et collocas ita alte cum secundum testimonia diversorum opinionum hactenus obtentarum nominorum episcopus huis mundi habet maiorem auctoritatem in ecclesia et iurisdiccione quam cardinalibus superior in hac vita et super hoc clamitant omnis libri. Item de episcoporum institutionibus evangelium Christi clamat. Sed de cardinalibus non loquitur unum verbum. Item vide episcopales antiquorum et invenies quod in scribendi archiepiscopi et episcopi cardinalibus se proponunt. Item tempore sancti petri legitime quod episcopos instituiit et alii ampliam ad fecerunt sed de cardinalibus ubi tunc fuerant non est memoria nec scriptura.

Episcopus
Lego ecclesiam dei per spiritum sanctum regi et per ecclesiam in statibus antiquiis ordinata non possum leviter capere nec de eis nisi cum bono scrutinio iudicare quoniam secundum beatum Augustinium "De Confessi" evangelio starum non crederem evangelio nisi crederem ecclesie quoniam a christo multa de descendarent in ecclseia ordinata magis per testimentio ecclesia approbanda quam per scripturam sacram poterit inveniri et quia inferiorum omnis ierarchia debet ad superiorum similitudiem exemplari congrue videtur status in ecclesiam ponere sacrosancta secundum inventam similitudinariem in angelica ierarchia et quia status cardinalum in predictis quatuor decim condicionibus tribus superioribus angelorum ordinibus maxime simulatur. Videtur rationabilis quod in ecclesia instinctus spiritus sanctus ad eorum similitudinem inprimis fundebantur et horum similitudinem tempore Christi amplium quodammo quod tenuerunt primo prae quod beato petro universalis omnium jurisdiccio fundata ampliam tunc exeuntes nullam iurisdiccionem extrinsecam habueret sed ad Christum et ad se invicem et (111r) ad alios habuerunt similitudines trius superiorum ordinum angelorum et ad modum hodie inventum dominorum cardinalium statum et ordines tenuerunt postea a petro in eos iurisdiccione fuat

313

dispertita et ut inter omnes terram exeunt fons eorum et in fines orbis terre verba eorum. Per diversas mundi plagas fuerunt amplius divisi pariter et transmissi alii tamen loco primi status eorum assumpti suerat et admissi. Qui status cardinalium et primi Christi discipulatus cum petro continue remanenserunt. De quibus et propter necessitatem ecclesie quandoque apostoli erant sancti istud verisimile debet esse cuiuslibet ratione et quod petrus numquam solus relictus fuerat in ad tempores persecutio et locum dabat quousque alios potuit ordinare et Paolus cum dicit amplius ad romanos xiii c. prepositorum vestrorum qui nobis locutur sunt verbum dei.

10. Prologue to the Second Nun's Tale – Geoffrey Chaucer

The ministre and the norice unto vices,
Which that men clepe in Englissh ydelnesse,
That porter of the gate is of delices,
To eschue, and by hir contrarie hir oppresse
That is to seyn by leveful bisynesse
Wel oghten we to doon al oure entente,
Lest that the feend thurgh ydelnesse us hente.
For he, that with his thousand cordes slye
Continuelly us waiteth to biclappe,
Whan he may man in ydelnesse espye,
He kan so lightly cache hym in his trappe,
Til that a man be hent right by the lappe,
He nys nat war the feend hath hym in honde.
Wel oghte us werche, and ydelnesse withstonde.
And though men dradden nevere for to dye,
Yet seen men wel by resoun, doutelees,
That ydelnesse is roten slogardye,
Of which ther nevere comth no good n'encrees;
And syn that slouthe hir holdeth in a lees,
Oonly to slepe, and for to ete and drynke,
And to devouren al that othere swynke.
And for to putte us fro swich ydelnesse,
That cause is of so greet confusioun,
I have heer doon my feithful bisynesse,
After the legende in translacioun
Right of thy glorious lyf and passioun,
Thou with thy gerland wroght with rose and lilie,
Thee meene I, mayde and martir, Seint Cecilie.

Invocacio ad Mariam
And thow that flour of virgines art alle
Of whom that Bernard list so wel to write,
To thee at my bigynnyng first I calle,
Thou confort of us wrecches, do me endite
Thy maydens deeth, that wan thurgh hir merite
The eterneel lyf, and of the feend victorie,
As man may after reden in hir storie
Thow Mayde and Mooder, doghter of thy Sone,
Thow welle of mercy, synful soules cure
In whom that God for bountee chees to wone,
Thow humble and heigh, over every creature
Thow nobledest so ferforth oure nature,
That no desdeyn the Makere hadde of kynde
His Sone in blood and flessh to clothe and wynde,
Withinne the cloistre blisful of thy sydis
Took mannes shape the eterneel love and pees
That of the tryne compas lord and gyde is,
Whom erthe and see and hevene out of relees
Ay heryen; and thou, Virgine wemmelees,
Baar of thy body – and dweltest mayden pure –
The Creatour of every creature.
Assembled is in thee magnificence
With mercy, goodnesse, and with swich pitee
That thou, that art the sonne of excellence,
Nat oonly helpest hem that preyen thee,
But often tyme, of thy benygnytee,
Ful frely, er that men thyn help biseche,
Thou goost biforn, and art hir lyves leche.
Now help, thow meeke and blisful faire mayde,
Me, flemed wrecche in this desert of galle
Thynk on the womman Cananee, that sayde
That whelpes eten somme of the crommes alle,
That from hir lordes table been yfalle,
And though that I, unworthy sone of Eve,
By synful, yet accepte my bileve.
And for that feith is deed withouten werkis,
So for to werken yif me wit and space,
That I be quit fro thennes that moost derk is.
O thou, that art so fair and ful of grace,
Be myn advocat in that heighe place
Theras withouten ende is songe 'Osanne,'
Thow Cristes mooder, doghter deere of Anne!
And of thy light my soule in prison lighte,

315

That troubled is by the contagioun
Of my body, and also by the wighte
Of erthely lust and fals affeccioun,
O havene of refut, O salvacioun
Of hem that been in sorwe and in distresse,
Now help, for to my werk I wol me dresse.
Yet preye I yow that reden that I write,
Foryeve me, that I do no diligence
This ilke storie subtilly to endite,
For bothe have I the wordes and sentence
Of hym that at the seintes reverence
The storie wroot, and folwen hir legende,
And pray yow, that ye wole my werk amende.

Interpretacio nominis Cecile quam ponit
Frater Jacobus Januensis in Legenda
First wolde I yow the name of seinte Cecilie
Expowne, as men may in hir storie see.
It is to seye in Englissh, 'hevenes lilie'
For pure chaastnesse of virginitee,
Or for she whitnesse hadde of honestee
And grene of conscience, and of good fame
The soote savour, 'lilie' was hir name.
Or Cecilie is to seye, 'the wey to blynde,'
For she ensample was by good techynge;
Or elles Cecile, as I writen fynde
Is joyned by a manere conjoynynge
Of 'hevene' and 'Lia,' and heere in figurynge
The 'hevene' is set for thoght of hoolynesse,
And 'Lia' for hir lastynge bisynesse
Cecile may eek be seyd, in this manere
'Wantynge of blyndnesse,' for hir grete light
Of sapience, and for hire thewes cleere
Or elles, loo, this maydens name bright
Of 'heven' and 'leos' comth, for which by right
Men myghte hire wel 'the hevene of peple' calle,
Ensample of goode and wise werkes alle.
For 'leos' 'peple' in Englissh is to seye,
And right as men may in the hevene see
The sonne and moone and sterres every weye,
Right so men goostly, in this mayden free,
Seyen of feith the magnanymytee,
And eek the cleernesse hool of sapience,
And sondry werkes, brighte of excellence.

And right so as thise philosophres write
That hevene is swift and round and eek brennynge,
Right so was faire Cecilie the white
Ful swift and bisy evere in good werkynge,
And round and hool in good perseverynge
And brennynge evere in charite ful brighte.
Now have I yow declared what she highte.

11. Edmund Stafford's letter to Adam Easton

Transcript from the Royal Letter Book
MS183 – Edinburgh University special collections
Folio 45v

Reverendissime in christo, pater et domine mi confidentissime postquam innotuit michi tam per literas amicorum quam ex relatu dilecti licenti/licitum mei Magistri Johannis Park quod vestra reverendissima paternitas summis desideriis expectabat horam in qua posset feliciter mei status exaltatonem in conspectu sedis apostolice praemonere et qualiter auditis de obitui bone memorie domini Exoniensis episcopus titulis rumoribus non quievit eadem vestram paternitas donec de prefata ecclesia apud sanctam sedem gracam obtinui satis bene praecipere poteram quod licet frequenter amara verba per litteras affate dominacionis acceperam que michi timorem incuterent finaliter tum amaritudinem illam re(p)peri in magne suavitatis dulcedine esse commisam sicut facti experiencia manifestat. De quo sinceritatis vestre constantiae regracior ex intimo cordis mei cernens me iam dicte paternitati pro tante dignationis impendis perpetuis temporibus obligatum.   Nec miretur queso vestra benignitas quod non scribe vobis hac vice de negotiis vestris quoniam omni die responsum expecto michi de Romana curia transmittens quid clericus domini mei Cantuarien. domino Johannes Montagu fecerit in negotio sibi commisso cuius effectus ut teneo vobis afferre poterit comodum et quietam et michi omnia statum meum tangentia posui in suspenso semper eo positus illa perficere que sub posse meo dependeant et vestre paternitatis reverencie conservet fuit accepta suam altissimus ad regimen ecclesie sue sancte.
Scriptus Londoniensis xxi die Aprilis

Domino Cardinali Anglie
Reverendissimo in Christo Adam dei gratie titulo Sancte Ceciliae sacro sancta Romane Ecclesie Cardinali

Orator vestre Edmund de Stafford, electus Exoniensis

Appendix IV
KNOWN MEMBERS OF ADAM'S COURT IN ROME AFTER 1389

English

Richard Benet (familiar)
Richard Possewick, brought up in Rome (familiar)
John Trevor (auditor to the court)
Roger White (camerarius and confessor)
John Inglewood (familiar)
John Skendelby (familiar)

German

Robert de Hokelheim (familiar)
John Islehoerst (familiar)
John Gammen (cubicularum)
Peter Remboldi (familiar)
Hildebrand Lobeke (familiar)
Theoderic Bukelken (continuis commensalis)

Flemish

Gerard Everard (continuis commensalis)

Appendix V
THE LUTTERWORTH
PAINTING

In 1375, Lutterworth Church, just to the south of the city of Leicester, was granted to John Wyclif under the patronage of the Crown.

Nearly 500 years later, a mediaeval wall painting was discovered on the north wall of the church that has provoked some controversy. Originally discovered when a wooden gallery was dismantled, the painting had been concealed under whitewash since the Puritan era. It depicts what are clearly three large figures in brightly coloured mediaeval costume. It was assumed that they represented King Richard II, his wife Anne of Bohemia and John of Gaunt. The man to the left of the painting is clearly very young, from which we might assume that it was painted in the early 1380s when Richard was newly married to Anne.

As more restoration work was carried out it became apparent that to the right of the painting were, barely discernable, the image of three skeletons. The immediate aftermath of that discovery changed the prevailing view of the painting. Now it was asserted to be an example (a fine one to be sure) of a mediaeval church motif of "Les trois morts at les trois vifs". The pattern to these paintings is quite standard and there are a number that survive in churches in England. Generally they show three kings in the prime of their lives meeting up with three skeletons to remind them that even those who have everything in life must face up to their own mortality.

Yet the strange thing is that these two possible explanations have always been seen as mutually exclusive. What we seem to have at Lutterworth is a painting that satisfies both suggestions. The three main figures that survive do have all the right characteristics to represent Richard, Anne and John of Gaunt. The King holds a diadem in his hand and is looking towards his young bride who returns his gaze. The man on the right, the John of Gaunt figure, is considerably older and bears a striking resemblance to other contemporary images of Gaunt.

So what Lutterworth seems to offer is three real nobles of the day, real people, confronting their own mortality. In many ways this makes the message of the painting far more powerful because it is not just another allegory. Furthermore it is virtually unknown for the standard production of three kings and three skeletons to feature a woman. In fact, as far as I am aware, Lutterworth is unique in England in this respect. If the painting was nothing more than a whimsical allegory, it would hardly have occurred to the artist to include a woman in the painting. Why stray from the approved formula? It is her presence that lends some credence to the idea that this was a very specific painting where the artist has consciously decided to portray the message of "Les trois morts at les trois vifs" using real characters.

Yet the Lutterworth painting has still more to offer. In the later period of restoration in the 1980s two new figures were discovered in the middle of the painting. By general agreement they have been added to the original painting at a later date. The two figures are clearly churchmen and they are much smaller than the main figures of the original painting. They are also placed out of context, half-way down the figure of John of Gaunt. Yet what is most interesting for our story is that one of them is very clearly a cardinal. The other, clearly tonsured to indicate a monk, appears to be wearing fine vestments and carries a staff in his left hand. Just to the right of his hand is what seems to be a hat, most likely a bishop's mitre, although the remnants of the painting make this unclear.

It is hard to avoid the conclusion that the two men depicted here are Cardinal Easton and Thomas Brinton, Bishop of Rochester. After all there was only one English cardinal during Wyclif's time at Lutterworth, and if Adam had a co-conspirator in the persecution of Wyclif, it was most certainly the Bishop of Rochester. If this is, as it is believed to be, a later addition to the original (added just before or just after Wyclif's death in 1384) then the depiction fits the status of the men, as Easton was only made a cardinal in 1382 and Brinton a bishop in 1373.

The context of the two figures within the original painting is most interesting. They appear looking up towards the right hand side of the painting, where the three skeletons are respresented. The bishop in particular is staring up, his head bent back, contemplating the towering figures of the three skeletons, threatening the judgement that awaits him. It is as if Wyclif has had them added to the original to make his point, defying them to contemplate their own mortality. Here he turns the religious allegory on its head. Never mind the wealthy seculars confronting death, what about the fate of the wealthy and self-assured clergy? Particularly those who, in Wyclif's mind at least, had been theologically in error and yet had caused him so much misfortune.

It is a compelling case, featuring the two men Wyclif feared most, the men who had done most to confound his career and oppose the dissemination of his views. And if this is the case, it is the most direct example that has survived into our times linking Adam Easton to the persecution of John

Wyclif. It is also one of only three images of Adam to have survived into the modern era (the other two being his tomb and in the lower panel of a manuscript illustration of St Brigit). It is of note that the face of the cardinal is rather young, perhaps recalling that the last time the two had met was some 30 years earlier. For by 1384 Wyclif was one of the few Englishmen who knew what Adam looked like, and the likeness of the picture is not implausible when compared with that on his tomb. This in turn adds substance to the suggestion that the painting, added later to the original images of "Les trois morts at les trois vifs", was executed on the specific instruction of the dying incumbent of Lutterworth, on or around 1384.

This painting is a remarkable discovery and one that finally brings some substance and form to the circumstantial evidence surrounding the struggle for supremacy between John Wyclif and Adam Easton.

BIBLIOGRAPHY

Maunscript Primary Sources – Rome
Vatican Library Manuscripts
Lat. 4116 – Defensorium Ecclesiastice Potestatis
Ottobone Lat 676 ff 355/359 – Visitation of the Blessed Virgin
Lat. 1122 Miraculum XII – miracles associated with the Feast of the Visitation
Vatican Segreto Archivo
Armarium LIV volume 17 – Testimony of Adam Easton on the election of Urban VI
Armarium LIV volume 16 – Testimony of Adam Easton on the election of Urban VI
Collectoriae 464 fo 193 – Gift to Simon Langham on the coronation of Gregory XI
Reg. Suppliche 104A fo15v, 77v, 174v, 232v, – various appointments of Adam's courtiers
Reg. Aven. 200 fo75 – Adam is granted Somersham
Reg. Aven. 200 fo197r – Adam is granted the right to have his own confessor
Reg. Aven. 201 fo485v – Adam is granted the right to carry and use a portable altar
Reg. Lat 30 fo 147, Reg Lat 31 fo 232, Reg Lat 41 fo 4 – Adam's familiars petition for benefices

Manuscript Primary Sources England
All Souls Oxford
MS182fo 82v
British Library
Additional Manuscript 48179 folio 10 – Letter from Oxford University to Urban VI
Harley 612 – Letters and petitions in support of the canonisation of Brigit
Cambridge University
Library Additional MS 2957
Corpus Christi Cambridge,

Parker Library MS 74
Parker Library MS 180
Durham Cathedral
Muniments Misc MS 5378
Edinburgh University
Special Collections MS183 – Various letters from a royal letter book
Ely Diocesan Records
Register of Prior Walsingham folio 7 (not 5 as given by Pantin)
Lambeth Palace Records
Whittlesey Register fo 48/49 – Letters from the papal embassy to the Archbishop of Canterbury
Sudbury Register folio 46 – Wyclif's condemned dicta
Lincoln Record Office
Bishop Buckingham's Register fo301 – Exchange by Simon Langham of Wearmouth for Somersham
Norwich Diocesan Records
DCN 1/1/33 Roger de Eston at Norwich
DCN 1/1/65 and 1/6/23 Payments in 1390 for Adams books
DCN 1/4/35, 1/1/49 and 1/8/43 Contributions to Adam's inception feast
DCN 1/12/23 Costs of Norwich Scholars for carting their books to Oxford
DCN 1/12/29 Payments in 1355 for Adam's preaching
DCN 1/12/30 Payments towards Adams costs of going back to Oxford in 1364
DCN 1/12/41 Payments in 1407 for Adams books
Westminster Abbey Muniments
WAM 9223* Langham leases his English benefices to William Palmer
WAM 9224* – Bill of Exchange between the Stozze bank and Simon Langham
WAM 9225 – Will of Simon Langham
WAM 9227 – Bill of exchange drawn on Frances Kyto in favour of Simon Langham
WAM 9229* Letter from Adam Easton to Nicholas Lytlington
WAM 9232 – Letter from Avignon by Richard Merton
WAM 9238 – William Daventry tells Simon Langham of the offers of money from various Heads of State in return for favours
Worcester Cathedral Library
MS 65 ff13, 20, 21 – Three disputations of Adam Easton whilst at Oxford

Printed Primary Sources
Archivo Storico Italiano, Volume XVI, parte Prima, Cronaca della citta di Perugia

T. Arnold (ed) – Memorials of St Edmunds Abbey

J. Bale – Index Britannae Scriptorum

A.S. Bernado (ed) – Petrarch letters of old age

J.G. Black (ed) – Calendar of the Patent Rolls

G. de Blassis (ed) – Cronicon Siculum

G. Boccaccio – The Decameron (translated J M Rigg)

Calendar of Papal Letters to England

Caroli Cocquelines – Bullarum privilegirorum ac diplomatum

A. Chacon – Vitae et Gestae summorum pontificum

I. Collijn – Acta et processus (British Library)

Communar Rolls of Norwich Priory – Norfolk Record Society Vol XLI

F. Conelori – Elenchus eminentissima et reverendissima SRE cardinalium

Sister M.A. Devlin – The Sermons of Thomas Brinton

T. De Niem – De Schismata (British Library)

Frere and Brown – Henry Bradshaw Society Volume XL Printed Breviary of 1505 containing Adam Easton's Mass for the Visitation of the Blessed Virgin Mary (Hereford Cathedral Library)

V. Galbraith – The Anomille Chronicle 1333-1381

L. Gayet – Le Grand Schism d'Occident (British Library)

C. Gejrot – Diarum Vadstenense (British Library)

B. Harvey and L. Hector (ed) – The Westminster Chronicle

F.S. Haydon (ed) – Eulogium Historiarum

S. Himsworth – Winchester College Muniments

A.F. Leach (ed) – Memorials of Beverley Minster

Libri Cancellarii et Procuratorum

J. Loserth (ed) – Wyclif Sermones

J.R. Lumby (ed) – Chronicon Henrici Knighton

K. Krofta (ed) – Monumenta Bohemiae Vaticana, Tom V

J.G. Nichols (ed) – Chronicle of the Grey Friars of London (Camden Society)

D. Owen – John Lydford's Book – Devon and Cornwall Record Society Vol XX

W. Pantin – Canterbury College Oxford (Oxford History Society New Series)

W. Pantin – Documents Illustrating the Activities of the Black Monks 1215-1540 (3 Vols) (British Library)

E. Perroy, The Diplomatic Correspondence of Richard II

Gobelinus Persona, Cosidromius

R.L Poole (ed) – Wyclif's De Dominio Divino and FitzRalph's De Pauperie Salvatoris

P.E. Probst – Register of William Bateman

J. Raine (ed) – Letters from the Northern Registers

Repertorium Germanicum Vol II (Vatican Library)

H.T. Riley (ed) Annales of Johannes de Trokelowe

H.T. Riley (ed) Gesta Abbatum Monasterii Sancti Albani

Lars Romares – Samlingar Utgifna, Wadstena Kloster Reglor (Vatican Library)

R. Selfe – Selections from the first nine books of the croniche fiorentine of G. Villani

J.B. Sheppard (ed) – Literae Cantuariensis

W.W. Shirley (ed) – Fasciculi Zizaniorum – Magistri Johannis Wyclif Cum Tritico

J.A. Smidtke – Adam Easton's Defense of St Birgitta – Bodleian MS Hamilton 7

Georgius Stella – Annales Genuenses col 1127

W.H. Stevenson, AB Hinds, WHB Bird (eds) – Calendar of the Close Rolls

G.B. Stow (ed) – Historia Vitae et Regni Richardi II

The Venerabile – 1962 sexcentenary edition

Victoria County History of Norfolk

R. Wakefield – Syntagma De Hebreorum

T. Walsingham – Historiae Anglicana

Weil Garris/D'Amico – Cortesi's De Cardinalatu

Wyclif's Latin Works – Opera Minor

Wyclif's Latin Works – Polemic Works

Secondary Sources

M. Aston – Thomas Arundel: a study of church life in the reign of Richard II

D. Aers and L. Staley – The Powers of the Holy

I. Atherton and others – Norwich Cathedral, Church City and Diocese

C. Auberius – Histoire Generale des Cardinaux

W.S. Baddeley – Charles III of Naples and Urban VI

H. Beeching – The Library of the Cathedral Church of Norwich

Bellenger and Fletcher – Princes of the Church

M. Bennett – Richard II and the Revolution of 1399

W. Bensley – St Leonard's Priory Norwich

M. Bent – The Fountains Fragments

L. Bisgaard/C. Jensen/K. Jensen/J. Lind (eds) – Medieval Spirituality in Scandinavia and Europe

F. Blomefield – Essays Towards a Topographical History of the County of Norfolk

R. Bowers – Fixed points in the chronology of English 14th century polyphony

Edward Brayley – The History and Antiquities of the Abbey Church of St Peter, Westminster

L. Cardella – Memorie de Cardinali Vol II (Vatican Library)

C. Cheney – Bishop Batemans Injunctions, John Rylands Library

C. Cheney – Norwich Cathedral priory in the 14th Century

W.P. Cumming(ed) – Revelations of St Birgitta (Early English Text Society 1929)

G. Dahan – Les Intellectuels Chretiens

C.H. Daniel and W.R. Barker – Worcester College

G.M. Dreves – Analecta Hynica Medii Aevi

M. Dykmans – Le Ceremonial Papal Vol III and IV

M. Dykmans – Les Palais Cardinalices d'Avignon

G.J. Eggs – SRE Cardinalium (Vatican Library)

C. Eubel – Hierarchia Catholica Medii Aevi (British Library)

E.R. Fairweather – A Scholastic Miscellany: Anselm to Ockham

S. Fodale – La Politica Napoletana di Urbano VI

T. Fry – The Rule of St Benedict

M. Gail – The Three Popes

J. Gardiner – The Tomb and The Tiara

F.A. Gasquet – The Venerable English College in Rome

S. Gibson – Statuta Antiqua Universitatis Oxoniensis

M. Glasscoe – The Mediaeval Mystical Tradition

Bishop Francis Godwin – De Præsulibus Angliæ Commentarius

M. Grabmann – Das Defensorium ecclesiae das magister Adam

J. Greatrix – Biographical register of the English cathedral priories of the province of Canterbury, c.1066-1540

J. Greatrix – Monk Students from Norwich (English Historical review, July 1991)

M. Griffen – Studies in Chaucer

C de Hamel – The Book, a history of the bible

M. Harvey – The Adherence of England to Urban VI

M. Harvey – The Condemnation of John Wyclif

M. Harvey – The English in Rome

M. Harvey – The Household of Simon Langham

M. Heale – Veneration and renovation at a small Norfolk Priory (Historical Research Vol 76 2003)

J.B. Holloway – Saint Bride and her book

A. Jonsson – Alfonso of Jaen

N.R. Ker – Books Collectors and Libraries

E. Kershaw – The Fountains Fragments

D. Knowles – The Religious Orders in England Vol II

P. Lefferts – The Motet in England in the 14th Century

L. Macfarlane – An English Account of the Election of Urban VI

L. Macfarlane – Dictionnaire de Spiritualite

P. Melli – La Citta Ritrovata – archeologia urbana a Genova
T. Magnuson – Studies in Roman Quattrocento Architecture
G. Mollat – The Popes at Avignon
B. Morris – St Birgitta of Sweden
J. Nicholls – The Black Monks Workshop
N. Orme – English Schools of the Middle Ages
G. Palazzi – Fasti Cardinalum Omnium (British Library)
W. Pantin – The Defensorium of Adam Easton
W. Pantin – The English Church in the 14th century
L. Pastor – History of the Popes
E.H. Pearce – The Monks of Westminster
E. Perroy – L'Angleterre et le grand schisme
E. Perroy – The Anglo French Negotiations at Bruges
R.W. Pfaff – New liturgical feasts in later Mediaeval England
O. Prerovsky – L'Elezione di Urbano VI
Y. Renouard – The Avignon Papacy 1305-1403
R. Rex – The Lollards
Robinson and James – The Manuscripts of Westminster Abbey
J. Robinson – Simon Langham (Church Quarterly Review 1908)
M. Rothbarth, Urban VI und Neapal
C.L. Sahlin – Birgitta of Sweden and the voice of prophecy
R. Sharp (ed) – English Benedictine Libraries
M.W. Sheehan – History of Oxford
M. Souchon – Die Papstwahlen
R.W. Southern – Scholastic Humanism and the Unification of Europe
E. Spearing (ed) – Medieval Writings on Female Spirituality
P. Spufford – Handbook of Mediaeval Exchange
R. Strohm – The Rise of European Music 1380-1500
L. Tachella – Il Pontificato de Urbano VI a Genova
J.B. Tolhurst – The Customary of the cathedral priory Church of Norwich
P. Tomei – L'Architettura a Roma nel Quattrocento
K. Walsh – Richard FitzRalph in Oxford, Avignon and Armagh
S. Wenzel – Latin Sermon Collections
R. Widmore – An history of the church of St. Peter, Westminster, commonly called Westminster Abbey, chiefly from manuscript authorities
F. Williams – Lives of the English cardinals
A. Wood – History of the University of Oxford
N. Zacour – Papal Regulation of Cardinal's Households
M. Ziegelbauer – Historia Rei Literariae Ordinis Sancti Benedicti (British Library)
P. Zutshi – The Papal Court (Cambridge Mediaeval History Vol VI)

NOTES TO THE TEXT

PROLOGUE
i Papal Letters to England Volume IV 1362-1404
page 79

CHAPTER 1
i The opening lines taken from the prologue to the
Rule of Benedict
ii Leslie Macfarlane, "An English Account of the
Election of Urban VI"
iii F. Blomefield, Essays towards the topographical
history of the County of Norfolk, Vol II
iv Annales, Johannes de Trokelowe (ed H.T. Riley)
v Thomas Walsingham, Historia Anglicana
vi Ibid
vii Annales, Johannes de Trokelowe (ed H.T. Riley)
viii F S Haydon (ed), Eulogium Historiarum
ix Survey of Somersham Manor 1221 (from Cotton
Tiberius)
x Register of William Bateman Volume I, edited
Phyllis Probst
xi Norwich Record Office DCN 1/1/33
xii N. Orme - The English Schools of the Middle
Ages
xiii F. Blomefield, Essays towards the topographical
history of the County of Norfolk, Vol II
xiv F. Blomefield, Essays towards the topographical
history of the County of Norfolk
xv Communars roll for 1326/27, Norfolk Record
Society, Volume LXI
xvi C.R. Cheney, Norwich Cathedral priory in the
14th century
xvii The Rule of Benedict, Chapter 40
xviii J.B.L. Tolhurst, The Customary of the
Cathedral Priory Church of Norwich
xix J.B.L. Tolhurst, The Customary of the Cathedral
Priory Church of Norwich
xx Thomas Walsingham, Historia Anglicana (ed
E.M. Thompson)
xxi Norwich Record Office DCN 1/2/1,8,10,14,15
xxii C.R. Cheney, Bishop Bateman's Injunctions,
John Rylands Library p23
xxiii Ibid page 17
xxiv Ibid page 20
xxv W.T. Bensly, St Leonard's Priory Norwich
xxvi J. Nicholls, The Black Monks Workshop
xxvii Beeching and James, The Library of the
Cathedral Church of Norwich

CHAPTER 2
i C.H. Daniel and W.R. Barker, Worcester College
ii W.A. Pantin, Documents Illustrating the Activities
of the Black Monks 1215-1540, Statutes of 1343
p78
iii Manorial records quoted in Victoria County

History of Huntingdonshire.
iv Henrici Knighton, Leycestrensis Chronicon (ed
J.R. Lumby)
v F. Blomefield, Essays towards the topographical
history of the County of Norfolk
vi Joan Greatrix, Monk Students from Norwich in
English Historical Review July 1991
vii Henrici Knighton, Leycestrensis Chronicon (ed
J.R. Lumby)
viii Boccaccio, The Decameron - day one
introduction (translation J. M. Rigg 1921)
ix John Lydford's Book edited Dorothy Owen in
Devon and Cornwall Record Society, Volume 20
x R.W. Southern, Scholasticism, Humanism and the
Unification of Europe - Volume 1
xi Petrus Lombardus, Sententiarum Quatuor Libri,
Liber Primus, Distinctio IV, Cap I
xii Petrus Lombardus, Sententiarum Quatuor Libri,
Liber IV, Distinctio I, Cap I
xiii Close Rolls 1354-60 p200
xiv Close Rolls 1354-60 p146-148
xv R. W. Southern, Western Society and the Church
in the Middle Ages
xvi T. Tanner, Notitia Monastica, or a short history
of the Religious Houses in England and Wales
xvii W. Dugdale, Monasticum Anglicanum Vol IV
xviii Norwich Record Office DCN 1/12/29
xix W.A. Pantin, Documents Illustrating the
Activities of the Black Monks 1215-1540, Volume
III
xx Oxford, Libri Cancellari et Procuratorum, Rolls
Series p142
xxi Oxford, Libri Cancellari et Procuratorum, Rolls
Series p205
xxii Oxford, Libri Cancellari et Procuratorum, Rolls
Series p207
xxiii Norwich Record Office DCN 1/12/30
xxiv Note also the fact that the cost of routine trips
back to Oxford with their books cost other
students around 5 or 6 shillings, there are
numerous examples from the Norwich records.
xxv Worcester Cathedral Library MS F65 ff 20
xxvi Book IV, Chapter V, Distinction 1
xxvii Oxford, Libri Cancellari et Procuratorum,
Rolls Series p224
xxviii Worcester Cathedral Library MS F65 ff 13
xxix Worcester Cathedral Library MS F65 ff 21
xxx S. Gibson, Statuta Antiqua Universitatis
Oxoniensis
xxxi Norwich Record Office DCN 1/4/35
xxxii Norwich Record Office DCN 1/8/43
xxxiii Norwich Record Office DCN 1/1/49

CHAPTER 3

i See Pantin, Documents Illustrating the Activities of the Black Monks 1215-1540, Volume III

ii Norwich Record Office DCN 1/12/23

iii Corpus Christi MS180

iv Corpus Christi MS180 folio 2v he notes the omission of "exercere" from the text

v Corpus Christi MS74

vi Corpus Christi MS74 especially fo xxxix r where the device appears three times

vii Oxford MS Bodley 151

viii N.R. Ker - Book Collectors and Libraries

ix Pantin, Black Monks, Statutes of 1343

x Pantin, Documents Illustrating the Activities of the Black Monks 1215-1540, Volume III pp30-32

xi Pantin, Documents Illustrating the Activities of the Black Monks 1215-1540, Volume III p60

xii Pantin, Documents Illustrating the Activities of the Black Monks 1215-1540, Volume III p69

CHAPTER 4

i Widmore - An history of the church of St. Peter, Westminster, commonly called Westminster Abbey, chiefly from manuscript authorities

ii Reg Aven 200 fo 75/75 in 1376. Adam wrote that he had been working faithfully for the Roman Church for more than eight years - otto annos ultra

iii Pantin, Documents Illustrating the Activities of the Black Monks 1215-1540, Volume III 219

iv Calendar of Papal Letters to England Vol V 25

v Papal Letters to England Volume IV 1362-1404

vi Marc Dykmans, Le Ceremonial Papal, Tome III

vii CUL add MS 2957

viii Collectoriae of 1371, Langham's Will of 1376 and Easton's testimony in Armarium LIV vol 17

ix Vatican Archives Reg. Lat. 13 fo 128r/v

x The Anonimalle Chronicle (V.H. Galbraith ed.) pp57-58

xi The Anonimalle Chronicle (V.H. Galbraith ed.) pp57-58

xii E Spearing (ed) - Medieval Writings on female Spirituality

xiii Conrad Eubel "Hierarchia Catholica Medii Aevi" Vol I

xiv Westminster Abbey Muniments WAM 9238

xv Canterbury College Oxford by W.A.Pantin

xvi Ibid

xvii A. Jonsson, Alfonso of Jaen

xviii Ibid

xix J.B. Holloway, St Bride

xx A. Jonsson, Alfonso of Jaen

xxi Papal Letters to England Volume IV 1362-1404 page 92

xxii Sudbury Register fo 49v Lambeth Palace

xxiii Collectoriae 464 fo 193

xxiv Whittlesey Register fo 48 second item

xxv Whittlesey Register fo 49

xxvi Ziegelbauer Historia Rei Literariae Ordinis Sancti Benedicti Volume II p563

xxvii Simon Langham by J.A. Robinson in the Church Quarterly Review 1908

xxviii E. Perroy, The Anglo French Negotiations at Bruges

xxix Close rolls for 1372

xxx Sudbury Register fo49r/50v Lambeth Palace

xxxi Sudbury Register fo50v Lambeth Palace

xxxii CUL additional MS 2957 (Bentham)

xxxiii John de Dormans, Simon Langham, Adam and Roger were all parties to a deed which places their movements in the region, Durham Cathedral Archives Misc MS 5378

xxxiv E. Perroy, The Anglo French Negotiations at Bruges

xxxv Papal Letters to England Volume IV 1362-1404 page 114

CHAPTER 5

i G. Moffat, The Popes at Avignon

ii Margaret Harvey, The Household of Simon Langham

iii Lincoln Archive Bishop Buckingham's Register X folio 301

iv Westminster Abbey Muniments WAM 9223*

v Westminster Abbey Muniments WAM 9227

vi Vatican Segreto Archivo Collectorae 464 folio 193

vii In England matters could be slightly more confusing for whilst the Pound was the unit of currency linked to the Florin, the Mark was also commonly used for expressing monetary amounts. The Pound was made up of 240 silver pennies and the Mark, which was two thirds of a Pound, was 160 pence.

viii WAM 9224* a bill of exchange from Michael and John Strozze dated 14 December 1372

ix N. Zacour, Papal Regulation of Cardinals' Households

x Charles Latham, A translation of Dante's Eleven Letters, letter VIII

xi Sermons of Thomas Brinton, (Sermon 4, page 2) Sister Mary Devlin 1954

xii G. Boccaccio, The Decameron Day 1 Novel II

xiii Second Testimony of Adam Easton - Macfarlane - an English Account

xiv Simon Langham by J. Robinson in the Church Quarterly Review 1908 p360

xv Sed ut dicam solidam veritatem apparet quod fides Christianorem quo ad opera sit peius condicionata quam Iudeorum, nam Iudei in diebus festiuis opera secularia non faciunt, Christiani vero in diebus dominicis et festiuis communiter tenent nundinas et mercata et ubi illis diebus soli deo et sanctis esset vacandum dies illos multi dedicant carni diabolo atque mundo. Iudei pauperes suos ne mendicent refocount per collectas, Christiani vero pauperes suos fame perire permittunt et si fiant collecte diuites euadunt et pauperes totum soluuent. Sermon 35,

(The Sermons of Thomas Brinton, Sister Mary Aquinas Devlin)

xvi St John's Cambridge MS 218

xvii Folio 2r Defensorius Ecclesiastice Potestatis in Vatican lat. MS 4116

xviii Vatican lat. MS 4116 fo 15v Adam refers to his user of Kimhi. The book with a Norwich pressmark is preserved at St John's College Cambridge as MS218

xix Folio 2r Defensorius Ecclesiastice Potestatis in Vatican lat. MS 4116

xx Godwin, De Prœsulibus

xxi Palazzi, Fasti Cardinalum Omnia, 1703

xxii Auberius, Histoire Generale des Cardinaux

xxiii Lorenzo Cardella, Memorie de Cardinali, Vol II 1793

xxiv Ziegelbauer, Historia Rei Literariae Ordinis Sancti Benedicti

xxv Chronicon Angliae, T. Walsingham - Cardinalis Angliae dum sedit in collatione sua post prandium, subito paralysi percussus loquelam omnio amisit.

xxvi Westminster Abbey Muniments WAM 9225 Item lego domino Ade de Estone monacho Norwiciensi, sacre pagine professori, ii c florenos camerae, et meliorum lectum cum cooperculo de variis pictis et unum ciphum deauratum de opere Calicis.

CHAPTER 6

i Westminster Abbey Muniments WAM 9223*

ii Vatican Segreto Archivo - Armarium LIV vol 16 133v

iii Leslie Macfarlane "An English Account of the Election of Urban VI" p83

iv Vatican Segreto Archivo - Registra Avinoniensis 200 folio 74-75

v Papal Letters to England Volume IV 1362-1404 page 79

vi Westminster Abbey Muniments WAM 9232 letter from Avignon written by Richard Merton

vii Ibid

viii E.H. Pearce, Monks of Westminster

ix Pantin, Documents Illustrating the Activities of the Black Monks 1215-1540, Volume III

x Lambeth Palace, Archbishop Sudbury's Register - folio 46

xi See Margaret Harvey "Adam Easton and the Condemnation of John Wyclif"

xii Vatican lat. MS 4116 see folios 302,330,331, 356 and 357 for the Wyclif quotes

xiii Westminster Chronicle (ed. B. Harvey and L. Hector)

xiv Wyclif's Latin Works, Opera Minora

xv Wyclif Sermones - J. Loserth

xvi Defensorius Ecclesiastice Potestatis in Vatican lat. MS 4116

xvii Wyclif Sermones - J. Loserth

xviii Thomas Walsingham, Historia Anglicana

xix Eulogium Historiarum, edited F. S. Haydon

xx Sermons of Thomas Brinton, (numbers 99 and 101) Sister Mary Devlin 1954

xxi W.W. Shirley (ed) - Fasciculi Zizaniorum - Magistri Johannis Wyclif Cum Tritico

xxii Eulogium Historiarum, edited F. S. Haydon vol III

xxiii J. Foxe - A history of the lives, sufferings and triumphant deaths of the early Christian and the Protestant martyrs

xxiv Thomas Walsingham, Historia Anglicana

CHAPTER 7

i P.N.R. Zutshi, The Papal Court, Cambridge Mediaeval History Volume IV

ii Vatican Segreto Archivo - Registra Avinoniensis 201 folio 584v

iii Defensorius Ecclesiastice Potestatis in Vatican lat. MS 4116 fo 3

iv W A Pantin The Defensorium of Adam Easton (English History Review 1936)

v Vatican lat. MS 4116, folios 293 and 328

vi Ibid see ff353r

E. "Sicut predixi oportet distinguere tempora atque loca. Aliter enim agere et vivere congruebat Christo et suis apostolis nove doctrine nec mansionem certam habentibus, nec alias possessiones immobiles habere volentibus, et aliter eorum successoribus habentibus bona immobilia et possessiones huiusmodi congruentes. Illis enim predicta reservare nolentibus quevis litigia, repeticiones, vindicans iuris prosecuciones fugere congruebat, ne offendiculum preberent, super quos nullam cohercionem habuerunt, ne predicacioni evangelice nocuissent. Sed modernis temporibus et ubi veritas evangalia est firmata, potest Christi vicarius vicia cohercere quod non potuit facere ipse Christus, iurisdicciones civilis dominii exercere, tamen cum moderamine ne fiat offendiculum evangelio Ihesu Christi; propter quod est sepe a licitis abstinendum, secundum doctrinam prima ad Corinthios viii c. Et sic eciam potest ecclesia et prelati tenere ex causa legitima dominia civilia in communi et esse divites, sicut fuissent in statu innocencie nostri patres, dum tamen in animo sint parati ad communicandum cum aliis pauperibus loco et tempore et circumstanciis oportunis. Nec ex hoc sunt in eorum ordine imperfecti, quoniam nec paupertas nec dicacio sicut nec in angelis, ita nec in hominibus sunt condiciones essenciales perfeccionis aut imperfeccionis, liect utraque suo modo instrumentum fuerit ad virtutes; dicacio quidem per se et paupertas solum per accidens efficit ad virtutem; ex quibus patet responsio ad quesitum."

vii From a letter by Petrarch on life at Avignon in the Papal Court c1350

viii Defensorius Ecclesiastice Potestatis in Vatican lat. MS 4116 ff 110v-111v ix L. Macfarlane "The Writings of Adam Easton"

x John Bale, Index Britanniae Scriptorum

xi English Benedictine Libraries quoting BL MS Arundel 34

xii Vatican lat. MS 4116, folio 364 "Explicit liber primum defensio ecclesiastice potestatis qui fuit in cohatis ad stabendum per me faciem Nardellum de Napoli. Anno domini mccccxxxi pontificus dominus Martinus pape V. Et sicut finnis per me supra dictum fratem Nardellum Anno domini mccccxxxii de mense January x Ind. In die conversionis sancti Pauli tempore pontificati domini pape Eugenus divina prudential pape iiii nacione Veneti.Amen"

CHAPTER 8

i Second Testimony of Adam Easton "An English Account of the Election of Urban VI" L. Macfarlane

ii Ibid

iii Gayet "Le Grand Schism D'Occident"

iv Second Testimony of Adam Easton "An English Account of the Election of Urban VI" L. Macfarlane

v Ibid

vi Ibid

vii Theoderic de Niem "De schismata"

viii Second Testimony of Adam Easton "An English Account of the Election of Urban VI" L. Macfarlane

ix Eulogium Historiarum, ed F.S. Haydon

x Vatican Archive, Armarium LIV vol 16, Testimony of the Cardinal Agrifolio

xi Second Testimony of Adam Easton "An English Account of the Election of Urban VI" L. Macfarlane

xii Gayet "Le Grand Schism D'Occident" Vol I

xiii Gayet "Le Grand Schism D'Occident" Vol II page 60

xiv Vatican Archive Armarium LIV vol 16 fo133

xv Vatican Archive, Armarium LIV vol 16, Testimony of the Cardinal of Florence dated August 27, 1386

xvi Conrad Eubel "Hierarchia Catholica Medii Aevi" Vol I

CHAPTER 9

i Westminster Chronicle (ed. B. Harvey and L. Hector)

ii Eulogium Historium sive Temporis vol III

iii Conrad Eubel "Hierarchia Catholica Medii Aevi" Vol I

iv Ibid

v Felice Contelorio, Elenchus eminentissima et reverendissima cardinalum

vi Calendar of Close Rolls, Richard II year 6 to year 17

vii Rymer Foedera, Volume VII p369

viii Rymer Foedera - Syllabus to the Record Office Edition

ix Ely Diocesan Records, Register of Prior Walsingham, fo 7 (not 5v as noted by Pantin)

x The letter refers to Adam as Cardinal of Norwich and St Cecilia in which respect it is unique as the only time Adam is referred to by both titles. Although the original letter was contemporary, the surviving text is in fact a 15th Century copy made in the Prior of Ely's records. This almost certainly accounts for the reference to St Cecilia, a title Adam was given later in his life, but that he certainly did not have prior to 1389. It seems most likely that the monk copying the letter, simply added Adam's honorary title out of respect.

xi Acta et Processus, Isak Collijn, Upsala 1924

xii Rolls Series - Memorials of St Edmunds Abbey

xiii Gesta Abbatum Monasterii Sancti Albani, Vol II

xiv K. Krofta (ed) - Monumentae Bohemiae Vaticana

xv J. Foxe - A history of the lives, sufferings and triumphant deaths of the early Christian and the protestant martyrs

xvi J.R. Lumby (ed) - Chronicon Henrici Knighton

CHAPTER 10

i The Westminster Chronicle (ed. B. Harvey and L. Hector)

ii Dr Margarete Rothbarth "Urban VI und Neapal"

iii Theoderic de Niem "De schismata" is particularly scathing about Francisco

iv Theoderic de Niem "De schismata"

v Dr Margarete Rothbarth "Urban VI und Neapal"

vi Thereby causing confusion for anyone reading De Niem who refers regularly to Luceria, a town on the other side of Italy, when he actually means Nocera!

vii T. Walsingham, Historia Anglicana

viii Ibid

ix Ziegelbauer "Historia Rei Literariae Ordinis Sancti Benedicti" Volume I p563

x Theoderic de Niem "De schismata"

xi Barbara Harvey, The Westminster Chronicle 1381-1394

xii Theoderic de Niem "De schismata" LIII

xiii Ibid chapter LIII

xiv Ibid chapter LII

xv Ibid chapters LII/LIII

xvi Ibid chapter LI

xvii H Simonsfeld "Konoglich Bayerische"

xviii Lorenzo Tachella, Il Pontificato di Urbano VI a Genoa (quoting Simonsfeld)

xix Gobelinus Persona "Cosmidromius" Chapter 80

xx Theoderic de Niem "De schismata" LVI

xxi Gobelinus Persona "Cosmidromius" Chapter 80

xxii Ibid

CHAPTER 11

i Georgius Stella "Annales Genuenses" col. 1127

ii All Souls Oxford, MS182

iii British Library Add MS 48179 folio 10r and v

iv British Library Add MS 48179 folio 9v

v E. Peroy, The Diplomatic Correspondence of Richard II p203

vi L. Tachella, Il Pontificato de Urbano VI a Genoa

vii E. Peroy, The Diplomatic Correspondence of Richard II

viii Georgius Stella "Annales Genuenses" col. 1127

ix Chronicon Siculum p66 (ed. G. de Blassis)

x Gesta Abbatum Monasterii Sancti Albani, Vol II

xi This follows the transcription of Roger Bowers in English Church Polyphony

xii Lefferts, The Motet in England in the 14th Century

xiii In November 1387 Urban awarded John Beltoft 300 marks a year for life from the camera of the English Chruch - Papal Letters to England Volume IV 1362-1404 page 265-269

xiv Papal Letters to England Volume IV 1362-1404 page 265-269

xv We know the name of at least one other, John de Liverpool

xvi Chronicon Siculum (ed. G. de Blassis)

xvii Letters from the Northern Registers

xviii Archivo Storico Italiano, Vol XVI Parte prima - Cronaca della citta di Perugia

xix Chronicon Siculum (ed. G. de Blassis)

xx Ibid

xxi Archivo Storico Italiano, Vol XVI Parte prima - Cronaca della citta di Perugia

xxii Lorenzo Cardella, Memorie de Cardinali, Vol II (1793), Auberius, Histoire Generale des Cardinaux

CHAPTER 12

i Conrad Eubel "Hierarchia Catholica Medii Aevi" Vol I

ii Gobelinus, de Niem and others who were near contemporaries and do give the title of St Cecilia did not actually write their histories until after Adam had been given the title officially in 1389. They were simply referring to Adam by the honorary title he had acquired as a matter of respect.

iii See Aers and Staley, The Powers of the Holy

iv See Mary Griffen, Studies on Chaucer and his Audience

v The Westminster Chronicle 1381-1394 p410-11 (ed. B. Harvey and L. Hector)

vi Chitty and Jacobs, Some Winchester College Muniments, HER 1934

vii Wording taken from the King James version of the Bible

CHAPTER 13

i Margaret Harvey, The English in Rome 1362-1420 p164

ii G. Dreves, Analecta Hymnica Medii Aevi (vol 24)

iii Vatican Archives, Vat Lat 1122 Miraculum XII

iv Coquellines, Bullarum privilegiorum ac diplomatum Vol III pars secunda

v Ottobone Lat. 676 ff355-359 (Vatican Library)

vi Pfaff, New Liturgical Feasts in Later Mediaeval England

vii Hereford Cathedral Library: Henry Bradshaw society Volume XL, edited Frere and Brown, Volume II of III

viii Bodelian MS Hamilton 7 folios 229-248

ix Presumably referring to St Basil the Great 329-379 A.D.

x Book of Daniel Chapter 10 verses 1-7

xi The University of Paris traces its origins to the Street of Straw and the area immediately around it.

xii From Selden Society 1902, Exchequer of the Jews 1272

xiii Based on the transcription of the letter in Bodleian MS Hamilton 7 by James Schmidtke

xiv Ibid

xv Samlingar Utgifna, Wadstena Kloster Reglor, Lars Romares

xvi Harley 612, fo 287 British Library

xvii Samlingar Utgifna, Wadstena Kloster Reglor, Lars Romares

xviii Vatican Archives Vat. Lat. 5747 in Dykmans, Le Ceremonial Papal Vol IV

xix Diarum Vadstenense, ed. Claes Gejrot

xx Samlingar Utgifna, Wadstena Kloster Reglor, Lars Romares

xxi Vatican Archives Vat. Lat. 5747 in Dykmans, Le Ceremonial Papal Vol IV

xxii Samlingar Utgifna, Wadstena Kloster Reglor, Lars Romares

CHAPTER 14

i Dykmans, Les Palais Cardinalices D'Avignon

ii Margaret Harvey, The English in Rome

iii Calendar of Close Rolls Year 6-17 Richard II p535

iv Close Rolls 6-17 Richard II p535

v Gasquet, The Venerable English College in Rome

vi Papal Letters to England Volume IV 1362-1404 page 79

vii This is not an exact figure but a crude extrapolating backwards from the time of the Valor Ecclesiasticus when the Deanery was valued at £307.

viii Oxford, Libri Cancellari et Procuratorum, Rolls Series p189

ix Edinburgh University MS183 see fo45v and 156v

x Close Rolls 1389

xi Perroy, The Diplomatic Correspondence of Richard II, 211-216

xii Ibid pages 211-216

xiii Ibid pages 211-216

xiv Papal Letters to England Volume IV 1362-1404 page 279

xv Calendar of Close Rolls 1391

xvi Barbara Harvey, The Westminster Chronicle 1381 -1394

xvii Edinburgh University MS 183 fo156v

xviii E. Perroy, The Diplomatic correspondence of Richard II page 156

xix DCN1/6/23 pro carag. Librorum domino cardinalis x s.

xx DCN 1/8/48

xxi Ibid page 203

xxii Papal Letters to England Volume IV 1362-1404 page 335

xxiii Calendar of Papal Letters to England Vol V p439

xxiv Membranae of the English College, Rome quoted in The Venerabile of 1962

xxv Calendar of Papal Letters to England Vol V p80 notes he was 21 in 1397

xxvi Calendar of Papal Letters to England p468

xxvii Calendar of papal Letters to England Vol VI

xxviii Calendar of Papal Letters to England p468

xxix Calendar of Papal Letters to England Vol V

xxx Papal Letters to England, Volume IV

xxxi Repertorium Germanicum, Vol II, Column 527

xxxii Repertorium Germanicum Volume II column 345

xxxiii Vatican Archives Reg Lat 30 fo147

xxxiv Vatican Archives Reg Suppl 104A folio 15v

xxxv Repertorium Germanicum Volume II column 37

xxxvi Reg Suppl. 104A fo 174v

xxxvii Reg Suppl. 104A fo 177v

xxxviii Calendar of Papal Letters to England Vol V p536

xxxix Ibid

xl Ibid

xli Vatican Archives Reg Suppl 104A folio 77v

xlii Edinburgh University MS183 f45v

xliii Calendar of Papal Letters to England Vol V

xliv Calendar of Papal Petitions to England

xlv Registra Lateranensi Vol 41 fo 4

xlvi Vatican Archives Reg. Suppl 104A fo 174v

xlvii Vatican Archives Reg. Lat. 31 fo 232v

xlviii Dykmans, Le Ceremonial Papal, vol III refers to Vat. Lat. 122285

xlix The Renaissance Cardinal's Ideal Palace: a Chapter from Cortesi's "De Cardinalatu", Weil Garris/D'Amico

l Robinson and James - The Manuscripts of Westminster Abbey

li Magnuson, Roman Quattrocento Architecture

lii P. Tomei, L'Architettura a Roma nel Quattrocento

CHAPTER 15

i Thomas Arundel, Margaret Aston 1967

ii J. Eggs, SRE Cardinalium 1714

iii Vatican Archives, Obligationes et Solutiones Vol 52 folio 92

iv Conrad Eubel "Hierarchia Catholica Medii Aevi" Vol I

v J. Gardiner, The Tomb and the Tiara

vi Literae Cantuarienses ed J.B. Shappard 1889

vii J. Gardiner, The Tomb and the Tiara

viii Ibid

ix Close Rolls 1407 (9 Henry IV)

x DCN 1/12/41 Communar Roll 1407/08

xi J.Bale, Index Britanniae Scriptorum

xii Lorenzo Cardella, Memorie de Cardinali, Vol II (1793)

xiii Bishop Francis Godwin - De Præsulibus Angliæ Commentarius

INDEX OF NAMES

334